e

Green Onions

ngerine Butter Sauce

w/ Herbed Butter
Macadamia.

shroom Zinfandel &

rb Marmalade

lor Mushroom Hollandaise

Ratatouille w/ Pesto

w/ Roast Peppers &
ette

w/ Ginger,
r Sauce

w/ Grilled
e over Pinot Noir
Red Butter Sauce

Noire Caviar Bouillon
Lettuces

Peppers &

w/ Alabama Fried
rb Butter Sauce

over Pungent Tomato Sauce

rlic Brouille

n w/ Chutney Hollandaise

Veal w/ Essensia, Orange
n. Andre Cream

Soft Shell Crabs w/
lime & jalapeño pan butter

P Pan-cooked Young Chicken stuffed w/
cornbread, cashews & chorizo w/
Fruited Port Glaze.

Roast Leg of Lamb w/ Mint, Roast
Garlic, Pine Nuts & Port-soaked Sultanas

Country Bacon studded Venison Roast
w/ Zinfandel & Wild Mushrooms

Mediterranean Swordfish w/ Ligurian
Olives, Skordalia & Lemon Butter

Cajun Rib Steak w/ Sweet Peppers &
Hot Chilies

Grilled N.Y. Strip w/ Pumate'd
Olive Bearnaise

Pan-cooked Grouper w/ Tropical
Fruit Salsa

~~Braised~~ Braised Rabbit w/ Glazed Pearl
Onions, slab bacon & Vinegar Brown Sauce

Pan-cooked Ginger-studded Blackfin
Tuna w/ Essensia & Soy Butter Sauce

Pan-cooked Grouper over Ancho Butter
Sauce w/ Avocado & Tomato Bearnaise

Pan-cooked Yellowtail w/ Roast Peppers &
Fried Plantains, Lime Pan Butter

Braised Halibut w/ Julienne Vegetables
& Martha's Vineyard Oysters in a
Curried cream

Herb-crusted chargrilled Tuna
w/ Ginger, Soy & Macadamia Butter

Pan-cooked Breast of Capon w/
Spicy Fig Sauce

Grilled Stuffed Breast of
Chicken w/ Chorizo,
Green Olives & Hard-cooked Eggs
Black Bean Sauce

Co
Ne
C.
Gr
Cor

So
you wil

To read these quotes in their entirety and catch up on the latest *No Experience Necessary* news, visit www.NoExperienceNecessaryBook.com and www.rowman.com.

"Not only is Norman Van Aken's culinary career astonishing, but his personal journey is perhaps even more amazing. He is completely self-taught as a chef, and he is perhaps the most literary-focused culinarian in America. This wonderful book brilliantly documents his extraordinary odyssey." **—Charlie Trotter, James Beard Award–winning chef and author**

"For Norman Van Aken, being a chef is a passion that has taken him on an incredible journey that he's artfully poured into *No Experience Necessary*. His brilliant, witty storytelling will leave you inspired and hungry for more. It's a must-read for aspiring chefs across the globe." **—Emeril Lagasse**

"Norman Van Aken is the Jimmy Page of his profession—a man who was THERE at almost every important moment in its history. The OG of South Florida, New World cuisine, and a guy who knows where every body is buried . . . many of them to be found in *No Experience Necessary*." **—Anthony Bourdain**

"Fasten your seat belts—*No Experience Necessary* is here. Anyone wondering what it's like to live as a chef, and anyone who is wondering if they should, must read this book. Best stories since *Kitchen Confidential*: everything from an 'Orgasmic. Lethal. Righteous' steaming rice raised to Charlie Trotter's lips to the hilarious story of local gadfly and bartender ('a notorious flamer even by Key West standards') failing to kill himself in two feet of Caribbean sea water. I adore this book." **—Jeremiah Tower, chef, author, architect, adrenalist**

"No career path is straightforward, but some are fated. Norman Van Aken took a circuitous route to the kitchen, but it is where he was meant to be. The American culinary landscape would not be the same without his vision, his authenticity, and his highly personal and remarkably provocative food—and his food would not be as delicious if not for his story and the recipes in this essential tome." **—Mario Batali, chef, author, entrepreneur**

"Norman Van Aken was a true pioneer of the American food movement in the 1980s, when chefs began to combine regional inspirations with modern cooking techniques. He was the first to blend Florida and Caribbean flavors with a classically trained approach to fine cuisine, and the first meals I ever ate in his restaurant were revelations and are still memorable today. One of the best things about dining experiences with Norman is his warm, kind-hearted, good-humored personality. It comes through in this book, just as it does in his cooking to this day." **—Wolfgang Puck**

"Norman Van Aken's memoir is as byzantine as a Russian novel but lots more fun. It's bawdy, bizarre, and often brilliant, with an abundance of marquee names. Appearances by Tennessee Williams, Jimmy Buffet, Julia Child, and, behaving badly, Burt Reynolds and Prince Stefano of Monaco. (Queen Victoria gets a mention, but posthumously.) One of the most delightful menu-writers of his generation, Van Aken has crafted an exhilarating groaning board of uninhibited culinary writing. It spans the length of the American food revolution, historically and geographically, and could have been titled *Continental Confidential*." **—Alan Richman, GQ *Magazine***

"One of the most compelling and page-turning memoirs I've read. *No Experience Necessary* is pure Norman as I have come to know him as a friend—revealing, funny, and brutally honest." **—Thomas Keller, The French Laundry**

"Anyone contemplating becoming a chef has got to read Norman Van Aken's new book. . . . [He] offers a personal odyssey of hard work, low pay, high anxiety, and comic relief before he achieved the recognition as one of America's most innovative chefs who became an inspiration for many to follow." **—John Mariani, food and travel columnist for *Esquire* magazine**

"A sort of nonfiction picaresque novel as full of color and spice and wit as his celebrated cooking." **—Colman Andrews, editorial director, TheDailyMeal.com**

"A memoir as wild, lovely, and free as the winds off the Florida Straits. . . . A marvelous piece of culinary history. . . . A rich, vital image of America as seen through the kitchen door." **—Diana Abu-Jaber, author of *The Language of Baklava* and *Birds of Paradise***

"Part *Kitchen Confidential*, part *On the Road*, and completely Norman Van Aken." **—Jessica Harris, food historian, professor, lecturer, and author of *High on the Hog: A Culinary Journey from Africa to America***

"A rollicking tale of a kid with heart who dives headfirst into cooking, and into life." **—Nathan Myhrvold, James Beard Award–winning coauthor of *Modernist Cuisine* and *Modernist Cuisine at Home*, and author of *The Photography of Modernist Cuisine***

"Norman's life with food transcends that of a chef. . . . How wonderful to finally have this amazing journey documented for everyone to enjoy." **—Steve McPherson, president, ABC Television Network, and owner of PROMISE Wines**

"An energetic and entertaining read. . . . It's a tale of naughtiness, niceness, and deliciousness as he invites the reader to experience his travels as a teenager responding to a 'no experience necessary' ad to becoming a James Beard Award–winning chef. His life story is both romantic and tantalizing. He left me hungry for even more recipes and stories!" **—Susan Ungaro, president, James Beard Foundation**

"[Van Aken's] story and drive to make a name for himself as the Father of New World cuisine not only put the rich flavors of the Florida region on the map, it provided insight and universal attention to our craft." **—Marcus Samuelsson, James Beard Award–winning chef, author, and owner of Red Rooster Harlem**

"[Van Aken is] a riveting and wonderful writer. His passion for food is artfully woven with his remarkable career and rich experiences. . . . I, for one, cannot wait to see the widescreen version of this book!" **—Ken Hom, OBE, BBC-TV presenter; and author of *100 Easy Chinese Suppers* and many other titles**

"Norman's been blessed—he was given a talent and a gift and has shared them, letting others 'enjoy the ride.' What can one say but mmm, mmm, good. No, great!!!" **—Richie Furay, founding member of Buffalo Springfield, Poco, and the Souther Hillman Furay Band, Rock and Roll Hall of Fame inductee, and pastor of Calvary Chapel**

"With sturdy charm and addictive aplomb, Norman Van Aken traces his remarkable, wholly unconventional culinary education. 'I was hungry for a lot of things,' Van Aken admits early in his picaresque primer, and instantly you believe him, and start rooting for his younger self—a long-haired, hitchhiking kid from Illinois." **—Monique Truong, author of *The Book of Salt* and *Bitter in the Mouth***

"Norman has a great story and tells it so well—it's smart, funny, soulful, engaging. Let this be an inspiration to anyone who wants to become a top chef without going into insane hock for cooking school." **—Regina Schrambling, gastropeda.com**

"Norman tells a great story . . . lives a great story . . . IS a great story." **—Dickie Brennan, New Orleans chef/restaurateur**

"Norman Van Aken has had an incredible journey in the world of food. . . . Anyone interested in how great American chefs do it, this memoir is for them." **—Paula Wolfert, James Beard Award–winning cookbook author**

"*No Experience Necessary* is . . . a must-read for anyone who's ever worked in the restaurant industry!" **—Eric Ripert, chef/co-owner of Le Bernardin, New York**

"*No Experience Necessary* . . . shares the heartbreaking, heartwarming, and occasionally hilarious struggles of one of the country's leading New American chefs." **—Karen Page and Andrew Dornenburg, two-time James Beard Award–winning authors of *The Flavor Bible*, *What to Drink with What You Eat*, *Culinary Artistry*, and *Becoming a Chef***

"An honest and compelling life story interspersed with a lifetime of great recipes. . . . I enjoyed every minute!" **—Barbara Fairchild, writer, educator, and former editor-in-chief of *Bon Appetit***

"This is one of those equally sacred and profane (well OK, lots more profane) memoirs of life in the kitchen told by one of America's greatest chefs." **—John DeMers, journalist, author, and host of radio's Delicious Mischief**

"*No Experience Necessary* is packed with so many unexpected twists and turns . . . that it reads more like a thriller than a chef's autobiography. Cooks and noncooks alike will have a hard time putting this book down." **—Sara Moulton, host of *Sara's Weeknight Meals***

"One of the best memoirs you will ever read. . . . This book will forever hold an elevated spot in my library." **—David Myers, chef/founder of Hinoki & the Bird, Comme Ça, and Pizzeria Ortica**

"An enticing odyssey indeed, rich with success and failure, collegiality, loyalty, and most of all, dedication." **—Mimi Sheraton, food journalist and former restaurant critic for the *New York Times*, *Time*, and *Condé Nast Traveler***

"Norman Van Aken, in this brilliant and witty biography, tells us to stick to our gut instinct—to do what we want to do, and to work hard and unceasingly to reach our goals." **—Hiroko Shimbo, award-winning cookbook author and consulting chef**

"Norman's adventure from prep cook to rock-star chef, with all its hair-raising pit stops is hilarious. Fasten your apron strings—it's a thrilling ride!" **—Mary Sue Milliken, chef-owner of Border Grill restaurant and truck**

"Norman's story is captivating—you'll keep reading and forget to eat." **—Tom Corcoran, author of *The Quick Adios (Times Six)***

"Reading Van Aken is like being a fly on the wall during the American food revolution of the last thirty years." **—Dorothy Cann Hamilton, founder and CEO, The International Culinary Center**

"This is a must-read for all aspiring cooks." **—Bradley Ogden, James Beard Award–winning chef and president of Bradley Ogden Hospitality**

"This is the vivid, true story of what restaurant life used to be." **—Clark Wolf, restaurant consultant, TV/radio personality, columnist, and avid blogger**

"A well-written and engaging life story." **—Alain Sailhac, Master Chef of France, dean emeritus at the Culinary Center in New York City**

"Van Aken invites us to ride shotgun along the back roads of America's steamiest food region. . . . Buckle up!" **—Liz Balmaseda, Pulitzer Prize–winning columnist and food and dining editor, *Palm Beach Post***

"In his exquisitely penned memoir, we travel with Norman Van Aken through years of personal reminiscing that never ceases to delight. . . . His words are witty, irreverent, riveting, and poignant." **—Sandra A. Gutierrez, author of *The New Southern-Latino Table***

"No-holds-barred here: *No Experience Necessary* is a truly amazing and well-written book. It is a real glimpse into our culinary world, complete with profanities." **—Alan Wong, James Beard Award–winning author and restaurateur**

"Norman Van Aken looks at sunsets differently than most. . . . His story is straight ahead (with detours)." **—Jim Poris, *Food Arts* magazine**

"As this humorous and insightful memoir makes clear, Norman's has been the life of an artist. . . . Rethinking a planet of sensations, Norman has made the world taste great." **—Ricardo Pau-Llosa, poet and art critic**

"Follow these pages to live Van Aken style—with brilliance, generosity, and without a dull moment." **—Suvir Saran, author of *Masala Farm* and *Indian Home Cooking* and owner of Sacred Monkey**

"An amazing story from one of the true culinary heroes of America. This book will keep you up all night!" **—Vinny Dotolo, chef, cofounder of Animal, Son of a Gun, and Trois Mec**

"This book is a captivating record of a turning point in American history when young chefs were discovering their talents and passion for food. Norman's part in that movement is fascinating." **—Daniel Boulud, chef/owner, The Dinex Group**

"*No Experience Necessary* is a classic chef memoir in the *Kitchen Confidential*, no-holds-barred style. . . . I am truly grateful for this excellent, bawdy record of America's restaurant kitchens in the late twentieth century." **—Michael Ruhlman, author of *The Soul of a Chef* and many other books**

"Food worth eating and a story well worth reading." **—Peter Greenburg, travel editor, *CBS News***

"Van Aken recounts scores of hilarious escapades from his mad, mad career. . . . *No Experience Necessary* is a must-read for soul searchers, whether in the kitchen or out of it." **—Juliette Rossant, editor and publisher, *Super Chef***

"Norman's story is a full-throttle roller-coaster ride . . . strap yourself in and witness how an unbridled journey can lead to culinary greatness. His food, like his journey, is bold, brazen, delicious, and totally uncompromising; an American original." **—Sanford (Sandy) D'Amato, chef and author of *Good Stock: Life on a Low Simmer***

"*No Experience Necessary* embodies the journey one takes when they become enamored by the restaurant business." **—Tony Abou-Ganim, founder and proprietor, The Modern Mixologist, and author of *The Modern Mixologist* and *Vodka Distilled***

"By far the most emotionally accurate read of what it means to live a life as a chef—told by the Huckleberry Finn of the food world." **—Mark Miller, chef, writer, culinary adventurer**

No Experience Necessary

The Culinary Odyssey of Chef Norman Van Aken

NORMAN VAN AKEN

TAYLOR TRADE PUBLISHING

LANHAM · BOULDER · NEW YORK · LONDON

Front endsheet: My dream sheet for MIRA, circa 1988; back endsheet: my dream sheet for *Feast of Sunlight*, circa 1986.

Published by Taylor Trade Publishing
An imprint of The Rowman & Littlefield Publishing Group, Inc.
4501 Forbes Boulevard, Suite 200, Lanham, Maryland 20706
www.rowman.com

Unit A, Whitacre Mews, 26-34 Stannary Street, London SE11 4AB

Distributed by National Book Network

First paperback edition 2015

British Library Cataloguing in Publication Information Available

Library of Congress Cataloging-in-Publication Data

The hardback edition of this book was previously cataloged by the Library of Congress as follows:

Van Aken, Norman, 1951–
No experience necessary : the culinary odyssey of Chef Norman Van Aken / Norman Van Aken.
pages cm
1. Van Aken, Norman, 1951– 2. Cooks—United States—Biography.
3. Cooks—Florida—Key West—Biography. 4. Cooking, American. I. Title.
TX649.V36A3 2014
641.5092—dc23
[B]

2013030865

ISBN: 978-1-58979-914-1 (cloth : alk. paper)
ISBN: 978-1-63076-088-5 (pbk. : alk. paper)
ISBN: 978-1-58979-915-8 (electronic)

∞™ The paper used in this publication meets the minimum requirements of American National Standard for Information Sciences—Permanence of Paper for Printed Library Materials, ANSI/NISO Z39.48-1992.

Printed in the United States of America

This book is dedicated to the girl I met in the first kitchen: my Janet.

I also dedicate it to our son, Justin, and to the amazing love we were taught by your "Grand" and will always share in this Circle of Life; grandchild Audrey Quinn and her mother, Lourdes, are testaments.

Contents

Acknowledgments

THIS BOOK HAS BEEN shepherded by a few—some without knowing it. The person without whom it would still be a dream is Dennis Hayes, for whom I am very grateful. Dennis and I have the best contract I've ever cosigned. It's on a coconut. Really. He brought in heavy metal thunder (in the most angelic form) when he asked Veronica Randall to do the editing. She picked up the track from another one of Dennis's trusted tribe, Tom Wanamaker. Photography kudos to Donna Ruhlman and Richard Watherwax.

And now a grateful shout-out to my newest partners in publishing, Taylor Trade Publishing, who roared out of some Colorado dream town of my past called Boulder to lift me up and get this work out to all the world! Many thanks to Rick Rinehart, Karie Simpson, and Kalen Landow.

I also need to harken back to Kim Witherspoon of Inkwell as well as Panio Gianopoulous who were there encouraging me in the early days of this memoir. And before (some with us still, some beyond us now . . .) Risa Kessler, Jason Epstein, Dan Halpern, Lisa Ekus, Phil Wood, John Harrisson, Gordon Sinclair, Michael and Ariane Batterberry, Tony Bourdain, Emeril Lagasse, and a roll call of chefs too long to list, especially knowing I'd surely forget one or more of the most deserving. But one must be singled out here: Charlie. The day will come, my brother, when we do open up that no-name bar with the killer jukebox in a sunny place, and we will know we finally wised up.

This book would not, nor my entire vision of cuisine, have been possible had it not been for the love affair I've had with the island of Key West.

I also want to thank the good people of Diamond Lake and Mundelein, Illinois, who shared a land to which I still return and where I always feel the best and closest embrace. I will meet you all at Bill's Pub for a party soon.

My family and our friends are my rock. On both sides of this forty-year marriage I am beyond blessed (some with us still, some beyond us now . . .). I love you all.

Prologue
The Triangle

JULIA CHILD WAS WAITING. Along with 350 other well-dressed, well-heeled folks in an opulent hotel ballroom in Aventura, Florida, she sat in her gold-and-black dress and waited beneath glittering chandeliers. She was waiting for her birthday cake, which would come much later. She was waiting for the first course of a seven-course celebration dinner in her honor at the exclusive and hyperexpensive Turnberry Resort. She was waiting for a dish that I had coproduced with my relatively new friend Emeril Lagasse, as well as another dish coproduced by my great friend/brother, Charlie Trotter.

Emeril and I were teamed up to do the first course of the gala. That is not the way things are typically done. Usually each chef does his or her own dish from start to finish. But "Em" and I were still getting to know each other and this was not only a very prestigious event in honor of the woman widely viewed as the grand dame of American cuisine, but it was also fun to plan, refine, and then execute a dish partnered up like this. Emeril was a party to cook with. He was, in fact, a one-man Mardi Gras!

Julia was waiting, but not because of us. She was sitting through a long dissertation on the wines being served that evening. This is one of the most challenging parts of doing the first course for one of these dinners. You don't make the food and simply hold it in a hot box. We didn't cook that way and never would. This had to be as à la minute as humanly possible. Emeril and I had been prepping all day on our collaborations: Grilled Key West Shrimp and Chorizo Sausage (my recipe) and Delta Crayfish with Red Beans and Rice Cake (Emeril's recipe).

We couldn't put the shrimp on the three grill stations we'd created around the huge kitchen until a minute or two before we began the plating operation. We kept running from station to station to be sure the support teams were keeping it honest and *not* grilling any of the shrimp and holding them (you had to watch some of these hotel dogs) until we gave the green light.

A dark-haired, very pale young man in a shiny black tux, evidently in charge of managing the waitstaff, had them lined up and waiting, too. He would provide our official eyes on the dining room. When he ordered, "Fire first plate!" we'd be off and there'd be no turning back.

Charlie Trotter's course followed ours and he was watching the clock and trying to gauge the precise moment he would be ready to begin laying out his Chilled Skate Wing Terrine with Blood Orange Emulsion and Toasted Pistachio Oil.

We waited, we worried, and we cursed under our breaths—still waiting—for this dandy maître d' with the "Werewolves of London" hairdo to give us the word. Emeril prowled around with his arms crossed tightly across his chest, his chin nearly lying on top of his arms. His eyebrows twitched back and forth like heavy telegraph wires conveying an imminent Cajun storm front. He came up to me, got very close to my face, and said, "Fuckin' hate waitin', Noam." That's how he pronounced my name. I hated waiting, too. I hadn't had this much fun hating something in a long time.

Charlie came over with three espressos on a tray, one for each of us. Great. More energy to worry and hate with! It was a ritual, like slapping each other's faces to psyche ourselves up. Sometimes we'd drink like six of these babies, knowing we'd find plenty to wind down with after the dinner. The three of us had begun to hang out in the past year or so. It was Charlie who somehow orchestrated our getting close. I had known Charlie ever since he asked me for his first cooking job. He was a slim, impossibly intense busboy working in our dining room back in Lake Forest, Illinois, where I was chef. I had just returned to Illinois after almost ten years of cooking in Key West. I told him, "No. We don't need anyone." And I thought, *Poor kid. So scrawny, someone should feed him.* But our sous chef nagged me for a few days, "We could use him making salads." So it began. Years passed and Charlie showed first Chicago and then America what he could do. My scrawny "little brother" was tearing up the rule book. Charlie had gotten to know Emeril a year or two before I did. Em was the chef at Commander's Palace in New Orleans and Charlie had gone down to do an event with him.

I remember Charlie calling me on the phone in Miami Beach where I was chef of a Mano at the old Betsy Ross Hotel on Ocean Drive and telling me that we all needed to get together. He told me that I would "fall in love with Emeril." "So will Janet" (my wife). "You two are gonna be like brothers. This guy's great! He got this psycho-killer red Porsche straight out of a Hunter Thompson collection and he took me all around the Big Easy. He owns that town. He's gonna open up his own place like any minute."

And so that began, too. We got nicknamed "The Triangle" for our geographical locations on the grid of the American map. We were also connected by the same sense of passion that athletes and musicians feel. And now in this kitchen—with 350 folks, plus Julia Child, waiting for our food—was the part when it's still quiet and your adrenaline is flowing and you are ready to rock and roll!

And it was then that the well-dressed maître d' gave us the signal: "Fire first plates!"

We jumped into the river of no return. Over seven hundred shrimp that we had peeled that morning and marinated that afternoon hit three blazing hot grills. Emeril made some last-minute adjustments to his huge cauldron of rice. He raced over to Charlie and me and lifted up two tasting spoons brimming and steaming to our lips. Orgasmic. Lethal. Righteous. When he saw our faces he broke into a huge grin. He looked like the kid who hit the winning home run at the Little League World Series and was now rounding the bases, waving his cap to the crowd.

Thirty chefs were lined up at two long plating tables. Emeril and I made one sample dish for each group to show the other chefs the way we wanted our food plated. The assembly line went into gear, steadily gaining momentum until we were ready to hand the servers two plates each—no fucking *trays*—to take to the grand dining room past the ice machines down a long hall with gathering speed and hell-bent-for-leather determination. The Delta Crayfish with Red Beans and Rice Cake was at the perfect temperature now. The shrimp with chorizo perched just so on top sent out its hot and smoky perfume. The plates were given a last-second swipe with a hot cloth by our wives at the far end of each line. Either they or we personally inspected the assembled chefs' efforts and then and only then allowed the plates to go out. We had about thirty dishes ready and moving out to the hall when the tuxedoed dandy came running from the dining room and screeched, "Stop! Stop! *Stop!* They are not ready! Another speech has begun!"

Emeril was on him first. "What are you saying? You said to *fire* the *food* and it is *fired*, man!"

Thirty chefs froze in horror. Everyone understood the gravity of the situation. Our shrimp would be overcooked. Our rice cakes would be cold. And Julia Child was out there in that dining room! Fucking Julia fucking Child, man!

The feeling was nauseating and I almost couldn't take it. The espresso churned in my guts and sloshed around my heart. Charlie dashed over to us and we huddled quickly. We were agreed.

Emeril and I marched back to the top of the plating lines. You could have heard a sprig of parsley fall.

Charlie bellowed, "SEND THE GODDAMN FUCKING FOOD NOW!"

Jim Morrison in his "Whisky a Go Go" prime couldn't have screamed any louder or looked any more possessed than Charlie did at that moment. The maître d' was nearly knocked down by the servers rushing the hot plates past him, into the banquet hall, and on to Ms. Child's table first.

Over the next two and half hours we sent out the remaining six courses. Three hundred and fifty guests. That is a lot of china. The kitchen is often described as being a place that takes on a balletic grace, a place where a disparate group of human beings become a fluid dynamic of precision and perfect accord, and if the chef chooses to change a garnish at the last second each *chef-de-partie* would see that and immediately conform to the new way of doing things. That can be true of small kitchens catering to guests arriving over the course of ten half-hour intervals: we fill the tickets and fill the orders table by table. But an event where hundreds of people all sit down at once is *not* a ballet. It is a military exercise that is run with no room for mistakes or sudden gusts of whimsy. Stand at your position. Do what I ask of you. Keep the line moving. Clear. Reset. Next course!

Finally the desserts were sent out and the executive chef of the hotel invited Emeril, Charlie, and me into the Verandah Bar for whatever beverages we desired.

These were the halcyon days of grand events, and the after-hours carte blanche we enjoyed back then was truly remarkable. Emeril came over with two bottles of Jim Clendenen's luscious Au Bon Climat Chardonnay and we collapsed, stained and sweaty in our chef's whites, into chairs normally reserved for club members only.

The long day and night of work had ended and it was our time now. As usual the only thing we'd consumed that day since a pastry and a coffee that morning was more coffee. No lunch. No food of any sort was in our bellies. But you are fooled as a chef. Your sense is that you have eaten because you've tasted so many little spoonfuls of things and been around all the aromas of cooking. But you haven't eaten. And the wine can hit you. In fact, it does. And when it does, we get wacky. And things can happen. We start to tell tall tales, tease each other, flirt, drink more—and that is when things can get even wackier. We'd been drinking for a while now. The Verandah Bar was in a full uproar. All the chefs had managed to get in plus a few of the guests who wanted something stronger than dessert. Everyone was having the time of their lives. But then I saw something very, very strange. The maître d' was standing at the bar next to my wife and it looked like he had his arm around her shoulder. They were facing the bar and Emeril and I were sitting on a long banquette facing their backs. I turned to Em and said, "Hey, brother. Do you see what I see?"

Em scanned the room and then he saw it. His eyes locked in place like a bird dog's. Was this worm trying to paw my wife? She'd have none of it, of course, but she was just as dazed from the long day and night as we were and maybe she didn't realize the depraved nature of men. That's when the maître d' slid his arm from her shoulder (harmless) to her bottom (not).

The next moments were a blur. I stood up and Emeril must have, too. A Louis XIV–style chair was in my hands. I had it by two legs and there was an empty space just to the left of the maître d' leaning against the bar, his head close to Janet's ear, his face smiling an oily smile, his hand not moving, his eyes not seeing. Smitten, he was slipping that hand around the curves of my girl. I could see her face in the barroom mirror and saw that she was just realizing it was his hand on her and not the pressure of Emeril's wife's purse as she had thought. Too late. I smashed the chair next to him. Janet jumped six feet in the opposite direction. A space now opened up to the maître d's right. Emeril smashed another Louis XIV chair exactly there. Then he charged the guy, grabbed him by the back of his tux, got right up in his face, and said, "Do you want to die right now in this bar, fuckhead?"

Three guys grabbed me from behind, three guys grabbed Emeril, and Charlie grabbed Janet, pulling us out of the bar and out by the pool. We struggled but the battle was over. What had happened in the bar might not even have been what it looked like, but the certainty was that there were two very expensive and very splintered chairs lying on the oak floor of the Verandah Bar at Turnberry Resort.

The enormity of what had just transpired began to dawn on our wine-damaged minds and we hightailed it up to our rooms. We now needed more drinks and we called room service for several bottles of red.

When I woke up Emeril was sleeping next to me. I couldn't comprehend the image but it was irrefutably the case. Emeril's wife and mine probably retreated to the adjoining room to get away from our snoring and heaved our passed-out bodies there. Charlie appeared and hovered over the bed with a crazy-as-a-loon smile. I knew he'd been right about this guy Emeril, and I knew Charlie was going to enjoy retelling this saga for decades to come, adding a wrinkle or two each time, as he loves to do. He had brought toothbrushes, toothpaste, aspirin, bagels, cream cheese, and coffee. Emeril woke. The Triangle came to life.

CHAPTER 1

Pre-Chef

BY 1972 I HAD WRAPPED UP my version of college that included a great deal of, shall we say, "personal study." Vietnam finally had me out of its crosshairs. My childhood days ended. I was at that milestone age of twenty-one and it was time to find a way in the world. But I wasn't quite ready.

In fact, I hadn't a clue.

So I lay there, in my own world, waiting for some signal from the outside; some sign or direction that would lead me out into a life I had dreamed about since just a little boy—the life of an artist. Yes! Of course! How obvious! But what form would be mine? I didn't know and was not prepared or schooled in anything distinct. I was, like Henderson the Rain King, just wanting.

Before the titles, before the kitchens, and before the positions of much-craved rank and status of even prep chef, or line chef, lunch chef, oh my God, sous chef, executive chef, owner, and, finally, "Chef" as part of my name (was I dreaming?), I must have been the "pre-chef."

Like a yeasty creation with a DNA recipe embedded in my soul's center still a mystery to my mind, I burped and yawned in a beer-scented mash, forming in a fashion that guided me in ways that seemed to have no map. I was a multitude, and I contradicted myself plenty. During the short time between school and what finally became my calling, I was a reluctant housepainter in Florida; a concrete sprayer in Kansas; a stoned, shoeless flower-seller in Honolulu; a carnival worker in the Midwest; and a sod layer, blues band struggler, roofer, small-time actor, and, most often of all, unemployed dreamer. I hitchhiked to California, then to Florida, then to New York, and then turned around and did it again. On the Big Island of Hawaii I was busted for "depositing rocks on a federal highway." I was simply tossing stones at a road sign waiting for a charitable soul to pick me up and drive me someplace else to look for myself. Sometimes I'd hitch going west and then, just to experience it, a buddy and I would cross the road at midday and head east. If we weren't into the conversation in the car, we'd say, "arrived," ask the driver to stop, and we'd get out. We weren't actually going anywhere. We were just *going.*

In May of 1970 I joined other fellow sojourners heading for Carbondale and the University of Southern Illinois (Southern had a long and enviable history as one of the best party schools in the U.S.) to attend a Woodstock-like rock festival that would span three days (sound familiar?). But just before the marijuana marathon of peace, love, and music took place, the National Guard tragically shot four students to death at Kent State in nearby Ohio, and our Vietnam protest days turned from playful dissent to bona fide kicked-in-the-balls, spat-on, hair-pulled outrage.

The festival was declared "illegal" and called off. Now there were thousands of angry kids in town so naturally one of President Nixon's fellow crooks called out the Illinois National Guard and imposed a 6 p.m. curfew. It wasn't even dark out but no one was allowed on the streets of Carbondale. When I was arrested I was sitting on my butt in a buddy's trailer drinking nothing stronger than a Coke. The Guard was further aided by "volunteers," which meant that scores of born-and-bred rednecks got to live out the fantasy of a lifetime and take on the "freaks." You couldn't have asked for a more beloved sport to be invented for these goons. When four of these guys tossed me like a half-eaten bag of Cheez-Its into the back of their borrowed squad car the theme song from *Deliverance* came into my head with all of the implicit fear my young heart had ever known.

After a night in jail followed by a Kafka-meets-the-writers-of-*The Dukes of Hazzard*-like hearing, I was finally done with that episode. And despite being handpicked by a Carbondale sergeant as "having absolutely been out there not only in violation of curfew but for destroying one of

Carbondale's telephone booths with his cannabis-induced rage," the judge dismissed me and the rest of us for lack of evidence.

Later that winter I worked in a factory in Illinois making picture frames. My job paid by the hour but the people I worked with were paid by the piece. (If you haven't heard of this practice before, it is actually called "piecework" and it doesn't promote the most collegial of vibes. In fact, it is one of the most psychologically twisted ideas to be perpetrated on the American worker and, thus, on to me.)

You see, to make a picture frame you need metal frames, of course, but you also need the backings, the variously sized sections of glass, corrugated paper of different thicknesses, plus staples, boxes for shipping, and so on. The wrong item or a missing component would slow down the assembly of each frame; that would mean fewer frames produced, and that would mean less take-home pay for my coworkers—and *that* would mean, if you were *me*, that you were swimming in a river of shit.

After I punched in, I'd report to an area of the factory where eight sweet-faced ladies sat at eight workstations all in a row. After unpacking their thermoses of coffee and bags of candies (fuel for boosting blood sugar levels as the morning wore on) the ladies waited for the 8 a.m. whistle to blow. The instant it did, I'd hear, "Norman! I need glass!" And I'd race feverishly across the vast factory floor in search of glass. Within seconds of staggering back with the correct glass (no "thank you" necessary) I'd hear my name screamed again: "Norman! I need cardboard!" And off I'd go in a completely different direction to the furthest reaches of the factory for cardboard. No one thought to make a list of, say, all the glass she might need for a morning's worth of orders. Nor, God forbid, did anyone think to create a "needs" form so I could gather *all* the cardboard for *everyone* in one trip, then do a staple run and collect *all* the staples *everyone* would need, or do an advance count of *all* the boxes required for shipping the fully assembled frames—*noooooo*—that might have made me more efficient and my job a little easier. No. I was their runner. And run is what I did.

"NORMAN!" I heard it on my lunch break. "NORMAN!" I heard it on a piss break. "NORMMMMMMMMMMMMMAN!" I heard it making love (but not in the voice of my on-again off-again girlfriend; the voices in my head belonged to the factory ladies!). I knew I had to get out before I crowned one of these poor women with the metal stool she sat on; before

I went in search of the psycho who (I imagined) had designed that factory, who (I fantasized) spent hours on an unseen balcony overhead, watching me, howling maniacally. So I quit.

I decided to hitchhike down to the University of Illinois where my oldest childhood friend, Wade, was still hitting the books.

I had a long flannel coat I picked up at a Salvation Army store and some high-topped leather boots (shit-kickers) and a thick red scarf to wrap around my face and neck. It was a March morning when I stuck my thumb out and headed to Champaign. March can be the month that will finally break you when you live up north. With December and January you have all the holidays and subsequent parties to take your mind off the cold. But then February comes along and each day is short, bereft of sunlight for all but an hour or two, and unremittingly frigid. March arrives and you begin the old deception game: you think any day now flowers will burst through the snow, the sun will melt the frozen lakes, and you'll be tearing off the galoshes, hats, gloves, sweaters, parkas, the chain-wrapped snow fucking tires and drinking beer just to cool the fuck off! But that day, dear suckers, is a long, long, long-ass way away. 'Cause it is only March. Wake the fuck up.

When I got to Wade's dorm he was there but he worked the reception desk to help defray the cost of his "leisure activities." After his jovial 280-pound ("but who's counting?" he would laugh) bear hug, he gave me his room key and I went up and lay on his bed with all my clothes on and fell asleep. We had met when we were only eight years old and shared countless childhood hours together. He had two brothers who were also a constant in my life growing up. We lived just across a creek from each other. Their daddy was our mailman.

Wade's oldest brother, Phil, was also going to school, or maybe he wasn't anymore and just dealing dope. Phil looked a lot like the lead singer and guitarist of Mountain, Leslie West. His Afro was a shocking affront to the folks who lived in the small town we grew up in. That was the idea, of course. He had a real attitude, that boy. A temper all of his life. He nearly beheaded me with a nine-iron when I called him "Chubby" one day. It was a good thing I could outrun him or I'm not sure I'd be here. But when he was sweet he was a whole different person, doing things like baking a cherry pie for you or pressing an album into your hands and saying, "I just had to buy this for you 'cause you are into this kind of music and you may not have heard of these guys yet."

Phil invited us over to his house for a party my first night. I never could handle the dope those boys could. I was never really more than a beer-and-weed type so when Phil gave me a Seconal I was asleep in like thirty seconds even though we were in the middle of a poker game. They stuck me on the couch and let me be. When I woke up the party was in full swing. There was even a plan afoot. It went like this: Two other brothers named Ray and Randy Paschen had a blue Ford Econoline. "Let's get the fuck out of here!" Part one of the plan. "Let's go someplace else!" Part two. "Steve's in Key West, isn't he?" (Steve was Wade's other brother.) The plan took shape. "Let's go!" The final plan.

So the Paschen brothers, a girl named Helen (from the party), and I got in the van and pulled out of Champaign and the snow and the dark and the gloom of never-ending winters. Randy scored a bag of "white cross" so sleep was completely unnecessary. When the sun rose we were already almost halfway through Georgia. The miracle of spring was unfolding before us at sixty-five miles per hour (top speed for the battered van) and with each passing county we felt as if we had one less care in the world. Helen and I became friends as the trip went on. We sat in the back peering over Ray's and Randy's shoulders as they drove into the gathering lushness of the South.

We stopped only to get gas and pee. With the white cross rolling through our brains we didn't need food. The afternoon sailed by and for the first time I learned just how long the state of Florida is. As we passed through Miami near sunset, the glass-and-steel buildings shone and glittered and glowed in the descending light. But our goal was still further south and on we rode. The Florida Keys back in the early 1970s were far less populated than today. In the northernmost islands of Key Largo you quickly lose the lights and pollution of the cities, and Helen and I stuck our heads out the windows and gazed up at the stars. The air was so different than any I had ever known. The sea was all around us now. In some places, the keys are not much wider than the highway itself. It takes more than forty bridges to arrive in Key West. The humidity and smell of the ocean propelled Helen and I together like some meteorological aphrodisiac and suddenly, quietly, we made love in the back of the van—unbeknownst to the jabbering brothers now passing a joint and stemming the rush of amphetamines that had gotten us down to the final island of the continent.

We got up from our play, our bodies now calmed, and stood leaning over behind the boys again, sharing the grass and watching wide-eyed as we pulled into Key West—for the first time in my life. It was as if the world seemed suddenly warm and fuzzy and giving. Was it the weed? Helen's body? Or was it this place at the end of America?

Deviled Quail Eggs

I always enjoyed deviled eggs growing up. But when I discovered the delicate little quail eggs in the markets, I felt it was time to offer a new version that spoke to my more kick-ass aspirations. Making "small food" is what we came to call preparing the amuse-bouche items on our menus. While operating Norman's—years after the events and restaurants covered in this book—I was frequently asked what I liked to cook, and I'd usually say, "I make the small food!" I bring this up not to get ahead of myself but to point to life's circularities. What could be a more apt illustration than eggs? And where better to do it than right here at the beginning?

6 quail eggs
¼ teaspoon Dijon mustard
1½ teaspoons minced red onion
1½ teaspoons minced sweet-and-spicy-style pickles
1 tablespoon mayonnaise
Tabasco sauce, to taste
kosher salt and freshly cracked black pepper, to taste

Place the eggs in a pot with enough cold water to cover and bring just to a boil. Lower the heat and simmer for 8 minutes. Remove the eggs with a slotted spoon and shock in iced water. When the eggs are cool, peel, and discard the shells.

Slice the eggs in half lengthwise. Carefully remove the cooked yolks without damaging the whites. Reserve the egg white halves.

Place the cooked yolks in a mixing bowl and mash using the back of a fork.

Add the mustard, red onion, pickles, mayonnaise, and Tabasco sauce and mix well. Season with the salt and pepper.

Stuff each egg white half with the yolk mixture. Garnish with freshly chopped herbs or extra onion and pickle.

Makes 4 small bites, appetizers, or snacks

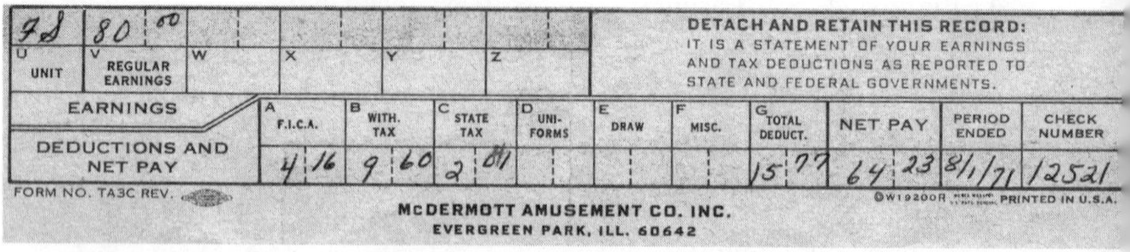

U UNIT	V REGULAR EARNINGS	W	X	Y	Z
78	80.00				

DETACH AND RETAIN THIS RECORD: IT IS A STATEMENT OF YOUR EARNINGS AND TAX DEDUCTIONS AS REPORTED TO STATE AND FEDERAL GOVERNMENTS.

EARNINGS

DEDUCTIONS AND NET PAY

A F.I.C.A.	B WITH. TAX	C STATE TAX	D UNI-FORMS	E DRAW	F MISC.	G TOTAL DEDUCT.	NET PAY	PERIOD ENDED	CHECK NUMBER
4.16	9.60	2.01				15.77	64.23	8/1/71	12521

FORM NO. TA3C REV.

©W19200R PRINTED IN U.S.A.

McDERMOTT AMUSEMENT CO. INC.
EVERGREEN PARK, ILL. 60642

A carny pay stub. It was a good thing we got to keep the money that fell out of people's pants

CHAPTER 2

Carnival Rides

The circus men knew no other earth but this; the earth came to them with the smell of the canvas and the lion's roar. They saw the world behind the lights of the carnival and everything beyond the lights was phantasmal and unreal to them . . . their life was filled with the strong joy of food, with the love of traveling.

—Thomas Wolfe, "His Father's Earth"

I RAN OUT OF MONEY IN KEY WEST and when I was down to the change in my torn jeans, I hitchhiked back to Illinois. My best friend at the time was a guy I met back in my junior year in high school at a pool hall called the Golden Cue. The Cue pissed off most of the parents in town when it opened for business, which made it that much cooler, of course. Back then our town was still a pretty little place with self-protective, old-fashioned values. A lot of the Catholic boys would show up at the Cue on Sundays dressed in jackets and ties for mass, when the manager opened up at noon. Aptly called "Kong," he was an apish, balding guy who wore thick glasses and stared sullenly at us as he stamped the cards that kept track of how long we used the pool tables. He seemed to live on Pepsi and caramel bull's-eyes.

My buddy's name was Geoffrey Lancaster. It wasn't too long before we started calling him "G-Baby" or just plain "G." We spent countless hours at the Cue playing pool, playing the jukebox and playing pinball. G and I were inseparable during our last two years in high school and we even went to our freshman year of college together. When summer came we got jobs together. Unfortunately they were mostly in factories. The first might have been the worst.

We started at Ball Brothers, the Mason jar manufacturers. My job was to shovel the countless broken jars that fell off the jerking rubber conveyor belt and shattered all over the concrete floors onto another jerking conveyor belt, located in the bowels of this hell, that shuddered and creaked to an incinerator to be melted and reformed. I was breathing glass dust all day and I could visualize all too well what it was doing to my lungs.

G and I fell in lust with two incredibly randy factory girls, which made the time pass quickly, for a while. But I was restless and one day I just split and took off hitchhiking around the country again, wanting to breathe something besides glass. I wasn't gone long. The road can be just as boring as a factory, especially when the money runs out. When I got back G and I hooked back up. His sister Mary was a wild one with pretty brown eyes and I had had a crush on her since the day I saw her in a long, rummage-sale-purchased fur coat with nothing on under it. (She didn't really show me, but she did.) She had a curly-haired boyfriend with rock star good looks, Tony, who was a few years older than us. We ran into him back at the Cue one night and he told us there was a carnival coming into town—and they were hiring. "No experience necessary." Perfect!

The starting wage was $2.55 an hour. The job was to help run the rides when the carnival was on and then help tear them down, pack them up, and move on to the next town when the gig was up. I started on the merry-go-round and G was on the Rambler.

The merry-go-round was the ride meant for the very youngest kids and was different than all the rest. The other attractions were for teenagers, adults, and older couples, strolling hand in hand, maybe trying to win a giant panda, maybe trying to be young again in the only Vegas they would ever afford.

I was not trained to do this job except for how to start the rotating machine and how to stop it. How I was supposed to place the children on the ride, take their tickets, or deal with the ones that were scared to death was all mine to figure out. The moms were usually without husbands, clutching children and purses, jockeying cigarettes from hand to mouth, struggling to help put their little ones up on the tall, hard, plastic, brightly colored fake steeds, with me standing ready to be sure Junior or Missy didn't fall three feet down to the worn wooden platform and risk being trampled by the four-legged "horsies." As the ride started and the canned carnival music of the past century swelled, the kids would grip for dear life the chrome pole that shot through what would have been the spine, saddle, and belly had it been a real horse. The moms would step off and track their kids for the duration that their fifty cents had bought them.

The management wanted to be sure they gleaned every quarter they could, so I had to be sure to take a ticket from each kid. It wasn't easy because most didn't know they were supposed to have a ticket and I'd typically have to figure out where mom had stuck it. It was always better if it was in a shirt pocket because if it was clutched in their little hands I'd risk terrorizing them by trying to unwrap their tiny fingers from that shiny pole that took them gently up and down as the world whizzed woozily around them.

I had worked that ride for a few weeks when one day we were setting up in a new town and G came running over and said, "Hot damn! They are gonna let you and me run the Tilt-a-Whirl from now on!"

The Tilt-a-Whirl has eight tubs that whirl in circles while riding on a rotating floor that spins at various speeds. Centrifugal force makes the tubs whirl around. Another mechanism on the floor of the ride causes the tubs to tilt up and down. In the center of the ride there is a protective fence of sorts that masks the giant spokes that give the ride its mechanical action. The motor was a gasoline-run engine with a long throttle that the operator pushed forward to elicit speed and then, of course, to slow it down when time was up. After a few days of running the thing we got bored holding the throttle in place and simply got a piece of rope and lashed it in place. It wasn't long before we discovered "Tilt-a-Whirl surfing." It was the fucking coolest.

G had shoulder-length hair with John Fogerty sideburns running down to his jawbones. He had a graceful way of moving without a scrap of fat on his body. I trusted his grace. I'd been in gymnastics since my mom introduced me to tumbling at the age of seven, so I knew a thing or two about balance myself.

Let's surf: The ride fills up with delirious folks who have been waiting to have their brains pushed backward in their skulls while their bodies are hurled like rag dolls for a three-minute trip to nowhere. It's hot, they've eaten all manner of carnival food, and, if we are really lucky, no one pukes. We start the ride and after a few revolutions are completed we throw the rope over the throttle, stand sideways to the spinning floor and kick one leg up, leaning way back to compensate for the next motion, and then step onto the inner floor. Immediately we are fully upright and standing on a narrow piece of the wooden decking which separates the now-spinning tubs. For one person to fit is not too hard, but we must keep our distance because as we go round and round—watching the world spin and faces fall in awe of our folly—those tubs can suddenly spin to where *we* are, which is at the exact center of where they *almost* hit, but which they are designed *not* to do. But nor are they designed for humans to "surf" on and they almost do hit, for God's sake! If one of those spinning tubs were to hit us we'd either be knocked into the pulsating, churning spokes in the center and be crushed in moments, or flung out into the carny yard, which was about five feet below and usually composed of asphalt or gravel. One was death and the other was shame—and pain.

After a while G and I managed to get this syncopation down so perfectly that we began to share the same wooden plank between the spinning tubs—really and truly insane! This put us as close together as two ice-skating dancers. It may have looked weird to see two young men holding each other around the waist, but it was no weirder than holding on to a person you are riding a motorcycle with at, say, eighty miles an hour. And we really didn't want to die. We just wanted to have fun and maybe impress some of the local girls who had come out to our little carnival, so we didn't really give a good goddamn. Whooeeee! We'd lean forward and back in rhythm to the force that propelled us in stoned harmony until it was time to end the ride and then I'd yell, "Ready, G? On the count of three: Go!" We'd raise our outside legs up and step off, take a few steps forward until the momentum released us and then untie the rope, slam the throttle to the closed position, and end the ride. We'd let the patrons off, take a quick check of the tubs, collect the next batch of tickets, load up the next group of riders, and do it all over again. Maybe it was exactly this rush that I found in cooking a few years later, working the hot line and riding the razor's edge of ecstatic accomplishment or violent chaos.

I was getting to know the carnival workers better. Larry was a wiry white guy out of Arkansas with receding hay-bale-blond hair. If I were to cast him in a movie I'd choose Ed Harris. Larry would have chosen an actor he was familiar with, like John Wayne. Larry and John Wayne had very little in common with each other except for their fine regard for drink. Larry said, "Let's you and me sneak out and get fuck faced while Lurleen is doing laundry in town."

Lurleen was Larry's wife. I don't know whose clothes she would have been washing since I never saw either one of them in anything other than the clothes they seemed to wear every single day. Lurleen wore a shirt that included an advertisement and recipe for making a Harvey Wallbanger, so it was pretty distinct. I was not yet twenty-one but I thought if I was with Larry I might be able to pass and jumped at the chance to go with him.

Larry had some of the worst-quality tattoos I'd ever seen, but he had a sense of humor about them. He'd gotten them in prison back in Arkansas where he'd done a six-year stretch for interstate auto theft. Six years for stealing a damn car. He described how the tattoos were "drawn" with safety pins dipped in ink then rammed repeatedly into the skin until the desired figures and words appeared. I studied one tat on his right calf as we walked to his car. It seemed to be a rooster on a hangman's gallows. As Larry expertly wheeled the car out of the carny parking lot he explained that it was, yes, a rooster on a hangman's gallows and he had it put there so he could "tell the gals" that he had "a cock that hung below my knees." I could sense that we were going to have a nice day of drinking.

We found a waterside establishment with a row of drinkers already engaged in mellowing out on a summer afternoon. The familiar sound of a Cubs game in the background added a comfortably lazy soundtrack to the afternoon. I tried to look nonchalant as I ordered a beer. Larry ordered a Seven and Seven. The bartender came back and gave him his cocktail but asked me, "Got a driver's license?" Larry looked at me hopefully for a moment. I reached for my wallet and pulled out a forged military ID I'd gotten from a friend. I wasn't even sure what the symbols or words on the card meant. I showed it to the bartender. Apparently it was enough to get him off the hook with the cops (if they came) and he sauntered back with the beer. He turned to a guy at the end of the bar, saying, "Hey, John, this guy must have been in the same camp as you in 'Nam." Now I gave Larry a look but he was lost somewhere between his drink and the friendly confines of Wrigley Field. The guy hopped up off his stool and came over. He knew I was a fraud and it wouldn't have bothered him if it had been a fake driver's license. But trying to pass as a vet from his unit made something in him snap, and Larry and I were suddenly out on the sidewalk blinking at the afternoon sun.

When we got to Lake Forest with the carnival, G-Baby and I were psyched for a good weekend, perhaps even a life-changing one! In the towns up toward the Wisconsin border we had a lot of fun with farmers' daughters and greaser gals. But let's face it, they had even less money than we did. And their fathers were onto us from the start. They could smell the carnival on us and they knew we were like they themselves used to be—young, horny, and looking for a night in the sack and nothing more—not at this age and certainly not in these circumstances. And these fuckers were not afraid, hell, they were ready to fight you. That would be fun for them! They were a world away from concerns about getting a call from some attorney if they scrapped with us. They knew we didn't have any goddamn attorneys or anything much else. We were just carnies coming into their town to feel up their daughters or more. And we were. But closer to Chicago, along Lake Shore Drive and such, well here was another world altogether! I was familiar with this world growing up. My mom worked in towns like these when I was in high school. She made her way in the rich town of Lake Forest quite nicely, as she was always able to do. She simply outworked—or outcharmed—everyone else.

The girls here were different. They had their own cars, they dressed up in more than jeans and flannel shirts, and they read books and even talked about them. And the money here—we had no way of understanding it, the privilege and power it implied. We were just simple midwestern boys who, within the context of our underexposed minds, thought if we could just marry one of the Lake Forest girls our lives would be new and golden.

The weather in Lake Forest that week of our carny run was magical, and the cool breezes floated deliciously from vast Lake Michigan over to the grassy park where we set up the rides. I was grateful for the drop in temperature because there are few jobs I have ever had that required the sheer physical strength of lifting those pig-iron heavy rides, section by section, and toting them into place. Breaking them down was a job we all liked a little more. Not only because it meant a three-day layoff until we went back to work, but when the rides were disassembled there was often free money to be found. It fell out of the riders' pockets and was called "the shakes." Sometimes I'd find up to $5, which was enough for a twelve-pack back then and nothing to sneer at.

Or a pizza! We lived on pizza. There was a place—and it's still there—called Bill's and no matter where in Lake County the carny set up, we'd borrow a car and drive to it. Bill's thin-crust pizza has the perfect balance of a pie that has known the hot bottom of an old oven that just kisses the edge of being overcaramelized, but it's not. And Bill's sausage comes from a European-style butcher shop down in Chicago with just the right fat-to-meat ratio. Bill's pizzas also have a mesmerizing, perfect left-right hook of crushed red pepper and fennel seeds, the licorice flavor of the fennel lacing in so beautifully with the tomato sauce. The mozzarella is soothing and filled our bellies that nothing since mother's milk has accomplished as well.

No food was sold at our carnival beyond cotton candy, popcorn, hot dogs, and Cokes. The polyglot marriage of ethnic foods that was so evident in carnivals and county fairs had dried up during this period in the early 1970s. We were too far north to have been lucky enough for a good soul-food entrepreneur to have joined us for a three-day gig, and the Hispanic community was churning out the intoxicating flavors of its foods below the still-uncrossed borders where they lived—and we didn't. It was a shame! It was a bland season during that little window of history.

There was a sort of a badass power we felt being carnies. It was a tangible excitement we brought to those towns that the local kids connected with first. They were overjoyed that something—anything—had come into their lives. They hungered for what was faraway that they could not afford, but, somehow, it arrived in the form of the visiting carnival. As dirty, hard, and poorly paid as the job was, the rush we got when the word got out that we were in town supplanted our needs for other things. Fuckin'-A! The carny is in town, ladies and gentlemen! It was about as close to being rock stars as we'd gotten to at that point in our young lives and we dug it.

The local kids from towns like Fox Lake, Roundout, Palatine, Mundelein, and Libertyville came to the carny lot as we were setting up. Some would ask us about the carny life. G and I invented tall and taller tales with each town. But some of it was true. We slept under the equipment trucks in our sleeping bags on nice nights and in my beat-up VW wagon when it rained. Each town meant new girls to shoot for. The other folks that worked with us became characters in our own made-up come-ons. We ate, drank, smoked, and hung out with our carny family, learning what made them become carnies in the first place and what they dreamed of doing. That part was real. As we worked from town to town G and I became more adept at not only assembling and disassembling the rides but we also learned something about the show-business world, knowledge that would be very useful when I got into the restaurant life just a few years later. We had a good run in Lake Forest that weekend, but the girls hadn't turned out like we hoped for. They saw right through us. They knew we had no money, no "real" cars, and no known future. We just had to deal with it.

We got the word to come back and do the breakdown at dusk. G and I returned just as the drivers were moving the trucks in place to start the load-out. The Ferris wheel had a guy wire staked into the ground in such a way that the largest truck couldn't quite clear the space to drive through. We couldn't easily reposition the wire, but if we could just move one of the swinging benches that jutted out about thirty feet up in the air, the truck could squeeze by. It rocked back and forth in the now gusting wind, almost mocking us. I always loved to climb and so I began to monkey my way up the outer frame of the wheel, hand over hand, until I was dangling in midair near the seat that blocked the way. I gripped the wheel's metal frame tightly with my hands and swung one of my legs out till I could hook my boots on the floor of the dangling bench, shoving it the few needed inches and allowing the truck to start down the drive.

I'm not sure what happened next. The world exploded. Maybe it was a nail in my boot but there must have been an electrical problem with the Ferris wheel's ground wire, because suddenly *I* was the connecting point of the entire electrical system for the massive wheel. My body surged, twitched, and sizzled with the current. I wasn't aware of it at the time but I was screaming bloody murder. My hands were clenched, locked in spasms. A voice screamed, "KICK! KICK! *KICK!* GODDAMMIT!" and something in my brain got moving: I swung both my legs up toward my paralyzed fingers and did a mule kick that broke me away from the life-sucking clutches of that fucking metal monster. My body immediately began to fall to the ground. My back hit the guy wire, scraping the flesh off me as I sailed earthward. It was as if a hot dagger was slashing away at me. This slowed me by a microsecond, just long enough for one of the carnies to catch my head as the rest of my zapped body thudded to the black asphalt. I remember lying there freaked out, watching Larry kicking the wheel's motor box furiously and cussing it out.

"Fucking piece of shit! Gonna sue these cocksuckers! Asshole mother!"

I remember lying there and knowing that I had to get out of this line of work. But, doing what? To where? For whom? What was my life? I certainly didn't know and as my brain pulsated G pulled me back up onto my wobbly legs and we went back to work, tearing down the carnival world we'd built before leaving the site as it was—a black asphalt slate on the edge of a small scrap of America.

Carny Corn Dogs

During the 1970s in the Midwest, carnivals and state fairs served up cotton candy, popcorn, hot dogs, ice cream, soda, and not much else. It would be several decades before they would become venues not only for entertainment and agricultural prize giving but also for the huge variety of ethnic and regional foods we enjoy and take for granted today. And after nearly being electrocuted on a Ferris wheel, it would be several decades before I started to appreciate and enjoy making my own Carny Corn Dogs.

- 1 quart oil, for frying
- 1 cup yellow cornmeal
- 1 cup all-purpose flour
- ½ teaspoon kosher salt
- ½ teaspoon cayenne pepper
- ½ teaspoon cracked black pepper
- ½ teaspoon ground cumin
- ¼ cup granulated sugar
- 4 teaspoons baking powder
- 1 egg, beaten
- 1 cup milk
- 1 cup buttermilk, or as needed to make a smooth, thick batter
- 6 wooden skewers
- 6 hot dogs, bratwurst, or Maxwell Street brand Polish sausages

Preheat the oil in a deep pot over medium heat to 350 degrees F.

In a large bowl combine the cornmeal, flour, salt, cayenne, black pepper, cumin, sugar, and baking powder. Stir in the egg, milk, and buttermilk, and set aside.

Insert a wooden skewer into each sausage at least two-thirds of the way up. Roll each skewered sausage in the batter, being careful to avoid the skewer, until they are well coated.

In the hot oil, fry 2 to 3 skewered sausages at a time for about 3 minutes, turning them several times, until golden brown. Drain on paper towels.

Serve with your favorite condiments. Mustard is my choice.

Makes 6 corn dogs

CHAPTER 3

The Fireside

Hainesville, 1972–73

I FOUND A HOUSE FOR RENT through a newspaper ad in a tiny northern Illinois town called Hainesville. The only things it was known for were a few antique shops and being a speed trap. It wasn't a mile in length and had a population of 120. (Most of them must have been deep in the woods because it didn't seem like there were more than thirty people living there.) At first there were just four of us renting what we called the "Hainesville House." Over the next few months there was a revolving door out front with up to eight of us living there at a time, plus any girls who might be currently enamored with one of us. (That would mean we might be so lucky as to have a clean kitchen, not to mention someone else to have a cup of coffee with in the morning.)

The local folks referred to our tribe as the "Hainesville Gang." We thought of ourselves more as a band of brothers. It was a time when we did a lot of hitchhiking, going places simply for the hell of it. But we could always come back to this place, no questions asked. It was our refuge. Hainesville House was a narrow, two-story wooden structure with two small cottages behind the main building. The second dwelling back from the highway was usually empty and that suited us fine because we would have driven just about anybody crazy with the parties we had on a near-nightly basis. A third cottage had a renter whose name was Pete. He looked like an ordinary old greaser who drove a beat-up Caddy, but he left us alone.

The way we found Hainesville House was through one of those free papers found all over America. You could be apartment hunting or looking for a boat, a car, a job, or almost anything. The *Advertiser* led us to many things back then. When I saw the ad it contained a phone number. A woman answered. I explained I had seen the ad and she gave me her address, asking me to come over and we could discuss it. When I got there an unusually good-looking blonde greeted me. Maybe not a movie star but easily TV pretty. I guessed her to be about forty. She told me to follow her out to the house she had advertised. It was what we could afford and so I signed the lease. She told me not to send the check but to drive it over to her every month. I told her I wouldn't mind. Her name was Mrs. Volé "with an accent on the é. It's Italian." It wasn't long after that we heard the story about her husband who was in jail for counterfeiting. It seems the printing press he made his bogus twenties on was buried in our yard somewhere. We looked for it but to no avail. So I needed to look for a job.

The *Advertiser* coughed it up: "Hot tar roofers needed." It had turned into early summer and I started work. God knows I was in need of a paycheck no matter the source. The foreman was a stern type who wore cop-like wraparound sunglasses and a baseball cap squeezed around his forehead. It was a shield against the blinding sun up on those roofs, but it also was his way of saying, "Keep the fuck out." And we did. The only name we ever called him was "Dark Eyes."

There were about nine of us on his crew. We mostly did commercial and public buildings. The dull drill went like this: I'd leave home at sunrise and drive to wherever we were working. We'd set up the ladders and begin by scraping off and disposing of the old roofing material. This work was so dusty that my nose would be caked and my eyes filmed over almost immediately. I had to shovel the roof rubble into a big heavy wheelbarrow. When it was full to the brim with broken tiles, loose pebbles, busted sections of tar, rusted nails, tree detritus, odd bits of glass and whatnot, I got a serious grip on the barrow's splayed handles, then gamely ran to the edge of the building, rolled it up a sort of gangplank and tipped it violently and suddenly *up* so the rubble would fall *down* into the gaping maw of the truck bed below. Somehow I acquired the strength, balance, nerve, and savvy to do this after some time on the job. But for the new guys, or if I was savagely hungover (which was one of the only ways to face this sad future), it was another story. Many was the time that I had to let the wheelbarrow go at the very last second or I'd have been pulled over the edge of the roof myself, plunging headlong into the waiting truck.

After the roofs were scraped, we brought in the black stove that held the hot tar. We'd lug the tiles and tar paper and nails and other paraphernalia up the ladders and then squeegee on the stinking, lavalike goo. The tar was not only noxious to breathe and skin-meltingly hot like napalm, it was fucking heavy. When stirring the tar around, my work gloves would inevitably get some of the black viscous gunge on them. As it congealed on my gloves my fingers would become only quasi-operational. The more I'd try to force my hands to work in the normal way the more they'd cramp, becoming barely usable claws encased within the thick cotton and rawhide shields.

Next was the actual laying of the roof tiles, and I must admit this was the one aspect of the job that appealed to me. I liked to create order with them, replacing the mess and stench with a neat pattern of rectangles. It had a tidiness to it that looked right. But that tar smell was the devil's cologne to me and I hated this job with a real passion.

Back in Hainesville we were partying a lot. We built bonfires in our driveway many nights, dragged our enormous stereo speakers outside, and cranked up the music. One afternoon we put up a huge sheet that we'd spray-painted with "Hainesville Welcomes the Rolling Stones!"

We invited all our friends and they invited all of theirs. Some folks driving by saw the sign and actually believed, or said they did, that the Stones were there. They must have been on even stronger dope. We didn't care. But the cops finally did and suddenly in the midst of everything they came rolling across our yard. We thought they had come to bust the party but they drove past our fire, our speakers blasting and all of us blasted, to Pete's house in the back. They pulled out the bullhorns and shouted for him to come out. He did and in moments he was handcuffed and tossed in the back of one of the cop cars. One of my "brothers" pulled out a camera and began to shoot pictures. Almost instantly one of the undercover cops, long hair and all, said, "Don't be stupid or you're going to jail with this fucker. We have over two hundred pounds of high-test weed of his and having you punks in the mix would be a nice snack for us. You want to go to jail tonight, do ya, punks?" Doin' the Dirty Harry thing perfectly. Fucking narc. Fucking longhaired narc. "But no, we would not like to go, thanks ossifer!"

Holy shit! Pete was a big dealer. He never tried to sell to us. Maybe he thought we were just nickel baggers and not worth going to jail for. The cop broke open the camera, took the film, and split. Party over.

We were working in the town of Libertyville. We had been hired to repair the roof on the high school. It was August, the hottest month of the year. We were early into the ten-day job when one afternoon the sky turned black. From up there you could really see. Big clouds began to push and rumble, and the searing heat of an Illinois summer day suddenly fell away. All of us worker dogs leaned on our brooms and shovels and stared as Mother Nature began to roll out her wonder. The drops of rain came very fat and slow at first. Our eyes widened and we tilted our faces to the world above us—and then it ripped! It was as if God had taken out a giant sword and slashed through a vast zeppelin filled with rain. It was a moving world of water. We threw our tools aside and nearly slid down the ladders. Everyone sprinted to their cars and trucks to get out of it—everyone except me. I rolled. I rolled and rolled around on the deep green grass of the high school football field. I laughed and rolled and rubbed the gathering mud on my arms. I didn't smell the tar anymore. I smelled the earth and it smelled like heaven.

When the rain stopped I was still lying on the ground. I had been pretending to make snow angels by swooshing the water in arcs with my arms and legs, when my arms hit his boots. I squinted up to see Dark Eyes. His body hovered above mine, upside down, blocking the sky. He said these words: "Van Aken, around here we don't need your kind." And that was it. Fired. I ran to my car and peeled out of the high school driveway. "Yippee! School's out!"

But when I got back to Hainesville House all I could think about was my next visit to Mrs. Volé and paying her the rent. I picked up an *Advertiser* from one of the neighbors' mailboxes and threw it on my bed, pulled off my soaking clothes, and took a hot shower.

When I got back to the paper I scanned the choices my future might hold. "Short-order cook. No experience necessary, $3.50 an hour." That's what it said. I reread it and realized that I might be going for it. "No experience necessary." That cleared me.

To be frank, I was ready for something else. The dope, beer, and tequila days and nights had me frazzled. Years earlier I had been a bit of a jock and a good student, but lately I was looking like crap and hadn't read much at all. I bought a car for a hundred bucks. The previous owner had painted it white with a paintbrush. It was slow and loud and the steering was sloppy, but it ran and it did have a good radio. My father was a used car dealer and growing up with him meant that I had lost any enthusiasm for cars, except the part about beating walking and a good sound system. For some reason I named the car "Babycakes."

I showed up for my interview wearing a V-neck sweater from high school. My hair was so long by then that it was easy to make a tight ponytail and conceal it behind my shirt collar down inside the sweater. I filled out the application sitting at the diner counter. The owner was a crew-cut gent named Jerry White. He and his dyspeptic wife had bought out Jerry's former partner, Tom. It was a family affair of sorts with the son working in the kitchen, too. Jerry was a stone drunk but I didn't know it. He came out from the kitchen to read my application and wash his hands there by the soda fountain. He wiped them on his white apron very thoroughly. He had large muscular hands and a smile that caused his eyes to squint shut when he laughed. He laughed more to hide his terrible shyness, I learned over time. He hired me and told me to start the next day. I drove Babycakes home and then, after a bit of thinking, went back out to a hardware store and got an alarm clock. I was starting as the breakfast cook at the Fireside.

When I showed up the next day I couldn't wear the sweater and they realized they'd hired a longhair. Back in 1971 that was a big deal, and not in a good way. But these folks struck a deal and they were going to live by it and see if I was a good worker.

Here's where my real working life began. I mean the cook's side of my working life. And it is a world unto itself, a world that conned me first with the smell of food. It is hunger that makes you crazy, whether it's one appetite or another. I was hungry for a lot of things. Later in my life people would often ask me how I came up with so many crazy-delicious dishes. I told them the truth. "I was hungry." They almost always think I'm just being facetious. But I'm not.

Henry Miller, Thomas Wolfe, and Jack Kerouac were great wanderers and who got awfully hungry on the roads they traveled. When I read their words I found a kinship when they described the meals they ate. While all of them were great eaters, none of them were cooks. I hadn't read a page of what it meant to be one, of what it meant to be going where I was going.

When you begin to work a line you have to get into the craziness or it beats you down. It is not a normal job. It's a brutal contest that takes place in a dangerous atmosphere. There is a whole language that must be learned. The men and women who commit to playing this game will not tolerate much in the way of mistakes. It means too much money to them. If you make the wrong plate on a party of four and have to start over, you have to face the wrath of the owner, your fellow line cooks, and, perhaps worst of all, the waitresses. The owner wants to turn the tables, the cooks want to turn the tickets, and the waitresses want to turn the guests, because that's where the money comes in. From the first set of cracked eggs at six o'clock in the morning to the last hamburger at midnight, the Fireside was one turning, cranking machine.

There were rhythms that became intelligible over the months. But in that first week it seemed like there was only one speed and it was breakneck. As soon as I got to work, I joined the owner's son and another kid just out of high school named Jimmy. Jimmy looked like Pete Townshend of the Who. He stuttered pretty badly. (My g-g-ggeneration, baby!) But Jimmy's speech problem was real. And what else was real was how fucking fast this kid could cook! That's why he was there first thing in the morning. Jerry needed Jimmy to get the jump on the day. Whatever speed you think you could find, Jimmy could find two beyond you. It kind of pissed me off that this younger kid could do so much more than me and in so much less time. But for some reason he liked me enough to help me learn.

There was no training manual and there was no cooking school. I just had to get in there and try to help out those who were more experienced than me. I would be grateful when anyone asked me to do a job that I could actually do. The fact that I got all the shit jobs was not lost on me, but it sure beat being useless.

I had found something I *wanted* to do. Desperately. I hated the factories and the concrete and the tar so bad that this one *had* to be the one. The work was hot and greasy and I was getting burned and cut every day and my nerves were assaulted by the waitresses' constant demands: "Ordering! Ordering! Ordering! Ordering!"

But each day I was getting better while fighting off many insane impulses. There were times I had to stop myself from just reaching down *with my hands* into a fryer's gurgling incendiary fat to get the fries next to the burger, bun, onion, and pickle, all arranged as Jerry decreed. I eventually learned to never trust that a pot handle hadn't spent an hour in the oven before I reached for it. I learned never to clutch anything metal without wrapping a doubled-up rag around it first. I learned which waitresses were fair and which were really pushy broads that even the other gals couldn't stand. I learned how to cadence the pace of my work. I learned how to flip two egg pans at once and do a million other short-order miracles that saved my ass from going down in flames. I became a short-order cook over the next few months and one day I finally looked up.

It was around four o'clock in the afternoon. I normally got done around 3:30 but something kept me later that day. The night shift was coming on. The women who worked in the daytime with me were all in their thirties, forties, fifties. They wore heavy black uniforms and white aprons with blue piping around the edges. My favorite of the Fireside's daytime waitresses was Miss Kitty. She was past sixty and wore burnt-red lipstick. She had worked there for over twenty-three years, longer than I'd been alive. The night-shift waitresses were younger and even included a few high school girls working part-time to help their families or to have enough spending money to cut into the dreary electives one finds in an empty purse.

I was in the kitchen talking to Jimmy and my old pal Wade who'd recently gotten a job cooking with us, too. We were stacking and wrapping roast beef for the night menu, apportioning them for the hot roast beef sandwiches to be sold during that evening's shift. A girl with brown hair pushed open the swinging kitchen door. She was young. And she had a young girl's energy. She didn't simply walk. She more danced a very powerful, soulful work dance. She dropped off an armload of plates with one hand and hung an ordering ticket with the other, picked up two saucers and cups as she swung back toward us, filled two coffee cups, and circled back to pick up the creamer in the reach-in box. She had such sass and confidence in her physical being. She was short, built like a gymnast. Her hair was pulled back and she had on a defiant amount of makeup. It put her on the edge of making her look cheap. But she was just young and it was her way of trying not to look like it. She bantered with Jimmy for a moment and then walked back out to set up her tables. Her body was driven by a set of hips that set off a rocket in my head. She hit the "out" door and I was almost surprised to see it remain on its hinges. Wade and I looked at each other and smiled like we'd just seen the same shooting star.

I began to work a little later each day but I didn't really know why until one night sitting back at the Hainesville House I got to thinking about that young waitress. I got in Babycakes and did something I had never done before. I drove back to the Fireside at night. I pulled up to a parking place that faced into the dining room and turned off the headlights. After a few minutes I could see. The place was crowded with the usual patrons. Some were having hamburgers or tuna melts. The AA folks were eating sundaes, chain-smoking, and drinking pots of coffee. She was in there. Her name was Janet. And I knew why I had come. I watched her move. I watched her smile. I watched her lift a tray and turn back to a diner and reassure him that she'd be right back with whatever he needed. I was falling in love with a high school girl through a diner window in Libertyville, Illinois.

It didn't take long, maybe three days. I asked Janet to hang out with me. Her girlfriend Kathy (whose boyfriend, Jimmy, was the cook at the Fireside) agreed to come over to Hainesville House after work one night. Luckily for me they came in two cars and when her friend pulled out of the muddy gravel driveway first I asked Janet to "hold on a sec." We talked and then she said she had to go because she had to be back in school the next morning. But before she closed the door on her little rusted, dented Chevy Nova, we kissed. We kissed again.

Over the next weeks we became lovers. I felt half in shock that I was with a girl so young but our physical relationship was impossible to stop. We were wrapped around each other. What we couldn't say in words we said with our hands, our arms, our legs, and our kisses. She grew up Polish Catholic with five brothers and two sisters in a modest home. It was right across the lake from where I was born.

One afternoon we were standing in the kitchen at Hainesville House, just hanging out and being silly, when I made a rude, sexually charged joke at her expense. She wasted no time and hit me right behind the ear. I had been balancing on one of the heels of my favorite cowboy boots when she delivered the blow and suddenly I crumpled over and fell. Wade dropped his joint on the kitchen carpeting by the gas stove and said, "Jesus! What a Whammer Jammer!" It was the title of a song by the J. Geils Band featuring a virtuoso harmonica riff. From then on her nickname by the Hainesville Gang became "Whammer," and she was in.

As spring approached so did a date that Wade, another Hainesville brother, Ricky Taylor, and I had made. Despite all the good things going on with the job and my love life, we had already made a plan to move down to Key West come March or as soon as we had about $500 saved, whichever came first.

Back then you could get what was called a "drive-away" car. When car dealers needed to get cars transported from a dealership in one part of the country to another, they would pay a driver a pittance plus gas but no overnight lodging. We had lined up to drive one of these cars from a lot in suburban Chicago to a dealer in Miami and we were waiting on the call.

Janet and I were getting along great. But she was in high school and I was not going to be a working stiff all my life. I had other plans! I liked the job and I liked the people I worked with. But Key West was calling me back and I wanted to join a band and maybe write songs for a living. Janet and I seemed to avoid talking too much about it. Maybe I thought, or maybe we spoke, about her coming south after she graduated in June? I don't remember.

But she had a surprise. One gunmetal-gray February afternoon when I got off work she was sitting at one of the tables in the dining room in her regular clothes, not a waitress uniform. She was talking to her pal Amy and another girl I didn't really know. I sat down and she told me, very matter-of-factly, "We're running away."

Dobie Gray was singing "Drift Away" on the jukebox. I know because it was my quarter and I'd played it for myself. But now here it was Janet talking about going. I couldn't believe it. She was just months away from graduation from high school. But she was done.

"What am I graduating to? It's not like I need a degree to wait on tables. And I hate it here. It's cold. I'm sick of winter. I'm sick of living at home. I want my freedom!"

"Where are you going to go?" I asked.

"Maybe Daytona."

I had been in the Fireside's dining room many times before in my life. I was born not far from it. My grandmother brought me here for one of my first restaurant meals when I was about five and we sat right by the ridiculous little fake fireplace this joint was named for. My father brought me here once when I was eleven and told me to order whatever I wanted. When I ordered the biggest steak on the menu he smiled and said, "I guess you have some of your old man in you after all."

He loved me but thought I spent too much time lost in books instead of sports, like him. When he died I was seventeen; I went to the Fireside during the wake for two snowy days and mourned him at the table by the fireplace. When I was working the carny I went to the Fireside with G-Baby after being up all night, still greasy and smelly from the work, and pulled the jukebox back from the wall so I could turn it up, pissing off the early-morning crowd. Now I was here again and marking another passage. As snakes slip their skins, we humans drop layers of protection as we grow until we are left exposed in one of the worst worlds of all, loneliness. The scuffed linoleum tiles offered no softness to my eyes. The song Dobie Gray sang had ended.

I was blown away. I had about three weeks' worth of work left before we would hit the road. I'd given my notice. Amy's mother, Laverne, worked there with us and just the day before she had raised her painted eyebrows and warned me that I was blowing a "very good job that any boy your age would be stupid to leave."

Janet had made up her mind. She stayed with me one more night. We made love and slept with our arms tight around each other. We hugged, kissed, and cried on the Hainesville porch when Amy and their other girlfriend pulled up. I didn't get it. I was the one who was going to leave and now I was being left behind. We held hands until Amy stepped on the accelerator and pulled us apart.

When I got to the Fireside that morning I had a very odd feeling. The place seemed empty without her even though she didn't work during the day. I sleepwalked through the breakfast hours. Around eleven o'clock, I remember the pay phone ringing in the kitchen. It was big, black, and loud. Laverne was talking into it. She looked around over her shoulder at me. Her mouth was drawn down tight at the corners. Her fake eyebrows twitched like a fishing line with something unknown at the other end. She wheeled around to me. "All right, Mr. Longhair. Where's Janet Amsler?"

I said, "I don't know."

She said, "Look, Mr. Amsler has a shotgun and he's coming over here to talk to you. That was Janet's mother on the phone and they found the note saying she was running away, going to Colorado for Chrissakes!"

Jesus God, I thought. *Wait until Laverne finds out her daughter Amy ran away with Janet.* Laverne slammed down the phone. The whole kitchen stopped. The world stopped. I really didn't know what to say. I didn't want her to quit school or leave home. Not yet. I wasn't really sure what I was doing except planning on getting back to Key West soon.

The phone rang again. This time it was Mrs. Amsler for me. I took the call. I still remember the ache in her voice. But I couldn't do anything about it. The dishwasher, Clara, scowled at me with her sunken black eyes and floury sagging skin. She looked away after a moment and stabbed her rubber scraper at some half-eaten eggs.

Where was my girlfriend? I really didn't know. Not for a few more days, at least. When Janet finally called I almost didn't recognize her voice. The usual excited energy had been replaced by a little voice with little to say other than she and the other two girls were not in Daytona, they were in Fort Lauderdale, where they had found jobs as maids at a motel.

The next week was taken up with getting the information on the drive-away car, packing up some stuff and storing it at my mom's house, and finishing work at the Fireside. And my Hainesville brothers had a lot of partying to do. Three of us were heading south and three others had decided to go to Alaska to work on the pipeline. (The wages that were being quoted up there were beyond belief!) The house was going to really empty out. Our hillbilly friend Herbert "Butchie" Mullins, who we had taken in basically off the street, was now going to be, along with another friend Ralph, the remaining holdouts in Hainesville.

"Save the fort, boys!" we hollered, "We may be back one day!!"

Wade, Ricky, and I picked up our car. Unbelievably, it was a Lincoln Continental Mark IV. We settled down into that plush white leather in our ragtag clothes and just laughed at the preposterous image of us in this car. We couldn't wait to hit the highway and get the fuck out of winter.

It was March, and as we drove through the day and night we watched spring greet us with each mile moving southward. When we got near Fort Lauderdale I picked out the postcard Janet had sent me from the motor lodge. The address was on the back underneath her few handwritten lines. I guess I surprised Wade and Ricky when I told them I wanted to see if we could find the place. Miami was still to the south and it was getting late. The dealership might not be open if we stopped for me. But they reasoned they could check out "Fort Liquordale."

It was dusk when we found the place. Wade stopped the big white Lincoln and I got out. A few tourists gawked at the three longhairs getting out of the luxury car and certainly imagined us as dope dealers. I had no idea where to find her. There were no cell phones or pagers back then. I went to the front desk and asked an older woman. She looked me over and stepped back as she said, "No. I have no idea who that is." I described her. "No."

I walked down the hallway and saw a maid. She spoke no English, and my Spanish was not good outside of a kitchen. But she seemed to know almost instinctively who I was looking for. She pointed to a room at the end of the hall far away from the pool. I knocked on the door. When it opened I gazed into a room that had a ceiling that might not have reached six feet. A king-size bed took up the room almost entirely. Janet was there sitting on the bed. Amy and the other girl were there, too. Janet looked surprised but she also looked scared and small. I asked her to come outside with me.

We crossed Highway A1A to the walkway that fronts the ocean. I asked her what she'd been doing. She told me they had simply worked the whole time and that they were being charged almost every cent they made just to live in that little room, all three of them sharing that one bed. I pulled her close and she cried for a moment. Her strong shoulders were shaking but I held her tight and she calmed. We listened to the Atlantic rolling in and we breathed in and out, feeling each other's warmth. She was only seventeen and a long way away from her seven brothers and sisters, her mom, her dad, her home. But we were together on this soft breezy night in Florida and somehow we were going to have to get to where that was the way it would be for a while. We held hands and walked, listening to the ocean.

Chef Salad for Miss Kitty

When you begin to work a line you have to get into the craziness or it will beat you down. It is not a normal job. It's a brutal contest, with a language all its own, and it takes place in a dangerous atmosphere. If you make the wrong plate for a party of four, and have to start over, you have the wrath of the owner (who wants to turn the tables), the other line cooks (who want to turn the tickets), and, worst of all, the wait staff (who want to turn the guests because that's who pays them). The Fireside's oldest waitress was Miss Kitty, already a twenty-plus-year veteran on my first day. She thought it very amusing that I chose salads for my staff meals when I "could have been eating meat." This one is so packed with protein I think she would have loved it!

For the salad:

1	romaine lettuce, inner leaves mostly, torn or chopped into bite-sized pieces
½	head lettuce, torn or chopped into bite-sized pieces
	kosher salt and cracked black pepper, to taste
4	ounces Swiss cheese, diced
4	ounces cooked ham, diced
4	ounces cooked chicken or turkey, diced
6	small radishes, trimmed and thinly sliced
16	grape tomatoes, cut in half
1	carrot, peeled and diced small
2 to 3	stalks celery, inner stalks mostly, diced small
½	cucumber, peeled, seeded, and diced
¼	pound button mushrooms, sliced

In a large bowl, place the lettuces, season with salt and pepper, and toss. Dress with the Parmesan-Ranch Dressing (recipe follows). Set aside for a moment. (If more than a moment, cover and place in the refrigerator.)

In another large bowl, place the cheese, ham, chicken, radishes, tomatoes, carrot, celery, cucumber, and mushrooms, adding just enough of the House Vinaigrette (recipe follows) to barely coat.

Makes 4 to 6 servings

For the garnish:

- bleu cheese (Maytag Blue is a favorite), crumbled, as desired
- 1 ripe avocado, sliced or cubed, as desired
- 2 hard-cooked eggs, sliced or quartered, as desired
- seasoned croutons, as desired

For the House Vinaigrette:

- pinch of kosher salt
- 1 shallot, minced
- ½ tablespoon Dijon mustard
- ⅓ cup red wine vinegar
- 1 tablespoon balsamic vinegar
- ½ cup canola oil
- ¼ cup pure olive oil
- ½ cup XVOO (extra-virgin olive oil)
- ⅛ cup sesame oil
- freshly cracked black pepper, to taste

In a bowl, whisk the salt, shallot, mustard, and the vinegars. Add the remaining ingredients (except black pepper). Season with pepper, and reserve until needed.

Makes 1½ cups

For the Parmesan-Ranch Dressing:

- 1 cup well-shaken buttermilk
- ¼ cup mayonnaise
- 1 tablespoon chipotles en adobo, pureed well
- 6 tablespoons sour cream
- 3 tablespoons finely chopped Italian parsley
- 2 tablespoons finely chopped chives
- 4 teaspoons Champagne vinegar
- 1 garlic clove, finely chopped
- 1 cup finely ground Parmesan
- kosher salt, to taste
- freshly cracked black pepper, to taste

In a bowl, place all the ingredients and whisk well. Taste, and season with additional salt and pepper, as desired. Refrigerate for about 1 hour. The goal is for the dressing to be thoroughly chilled and the flavors nicely melded.

To serve, lay the dressed lettuces onto each plate. Distribute the dressed protein/vegetable mixture among the plates evenly. Top with the eggs, avocado, bleu cheese, and croutons. Serve any extra dressing on the side, or refrigerate and reserve for another salad.

Makes 3 cups

CHAPTER 4

The Midget

Key West, 1973

WE RODE THROUGH THE LATE NIGHT catching the last Greyhound bus out of Miami. We were dead to the world after our thirty-hour drive from Chicago, and we collapsed onto the hard bench seats and made pillows out of our rucksacks. The small, silent community of fellow travelers only held my conscious mind for a few minutes. I tried to see who we were bound together with on this journey to Key West, but in the inky black-but-for-starlight night sky of the upper Florida Keys, my eyes struggled and then crashed into a few hours of heavy sleep.

We crossed over the keys whose names I would begin to know by heart over the years. For now they were exotic references to a land more sea than soil. The road stretched down like a necklace of concrete lying over the ocean's gently rocking body and tracing the trail of Henry Flagler's dream, a dream that became a reality with the building of a railroad that connected the mainland with the town of Key West over 150 miles to the south and west. His dream cost over $50 million and over seven hundred lives. The highway we were on that night had been built over the original rail bed, which was sent to its ruin in the horrific hurricane on Labor Day of 1935. Over four hundred bodies were recovered in the days and weeks afterward. Much of this "land" was not the kind of land I grew up on but outcroppings of coral reef and the calcified detritus of accumulated sea life. A great deal of it continues to be made of fill and marl. The land does not hill and drop. The highest point of all is a mere sixteen-foot perch on the rare "true" island known as Lignumvitae where giant mahoganies once loomed. Gone now, long gone.

Before that time Key West was the richest city per capita in the entire state of Florida; in 1913 it had the most residents of any town or city in the state as well—incredible, because the only way to get there was by boat. The four-mile-by-two-mile island town got its start in 1822 when it was sold in a Havana café by a gambling Spaniard named Juan Pablo Salas to an American gentleman named John Simonton (a man who had a surprising number of friends in the U.S. Congress) for the grand sum of $2,000. Seems that Salas had sold it earlier to someone else for a sloop valued at $575, but Simonton's connections eventually won the hand.

Key West boasted a deep harbor, which was the axis around which the island's economy swung. In the early 1820s, the town played host to fishermen and some minor pirates, but the businessmen of other port towns, like Mobile, saw the opportunity for wealth in mining salt. Slaves were brought in and, with self-interest at the forefront, Key West began a tolerance toward law that had not held much sway earlier. Gambling was not viewed as illegal and the Cuban lottery game called *Bolita* was pandemic.

The staggering wealth that was built in a matter of only a few decades came through the dubious profession of "wreckers," or those who salvaged the cargo of countless ships and boats that wrecked on the reefs and in the tortuous shallows that guarded and, in the process, nurtured the small island town into an economic miracle. Vast fortunes were made shortly after the turn of the century by Key West's version of robber barons. They would strike a deal with the owners and crew of the stranded vessels whereby the wrecker would get a cool 90 percent of the valuables salvaged and the stranded would get whatever remained. What alternative did the stranded have? Some of them ended up on this island for the rest of their lives, of course. Many of the grand wooden homes had been crafted by shipbuilders from the Bahamas. The taste for woodworking artistry reached a pinnacle in the ornate "gingerbread" style of the houses, some of which boasted plumbing plated with gold.

Even before the hurricane of 1935, Key West was already declining. The cigar industry moved up to Ybor City by Tampa, and a sponge fungus wiped out the other industry the town relied on. Then along came the Depression; on July 1, 1934, Key West declared bankruptcy and, in effect, became a ward of the state. It was now the poorest town in Florida and the grandeur became like that of modern Cuba: a feast of memory and faded fortunes. Perhaps this was, in part, my fascination for the place. Even then Key West had an attitude that basically shrugged its shoulders as if to say, "You win some, you lose some—at least we play."

We rode on, over Key Largo, over Tavernier (said to have been a corruption of the question, "Is there a tavern near?") and over the poetic-sounding Islamorada. (Try saying it softly aloud and you will know what I mean.) *Islamorada* is Spanish for "the purple isle," but it also could refer to the purple-shelled snail or to the many purple-blooming orchid trees and bougainvillea. We carried on south over Lower Matecumbe and Conch Key, Grassy Key, Marathon, Key Vaca, over the Seven Mile Bridge, which was where I woke as the bus nearly grazed a semitruck bound for the north at daybreak. We continued on to Pigeon Key, Bahia Honda (which means "wide bay"), Big Pine, Cudjoe (named for a long-gone "cousin Joe"), and then, almost 135 miles out to sea, headed almost due west as the light rose on the final shards of land: Big Coppitt, Boca Chica, Stock Island, and lastly, Key West—the end of the rainbow.

It was a six-hour ride in those days. The bus stopped at the Angela Street station. The Key West cop shop was the only place with a light on as we dragged our few belongings off the bus and stepped onto the island.

On our dazed, blinking faces might have been etched the outward evidence of the wonder we were feeling. More likely we just looked like three more stoned longhairs who were beginning to migrate to this island town back in the early 1970s.

From the first moments I felt different about where I now stood. The smell of the flowers is stronger here; the smell of the sea almost assaults you with her pungency; the quiet is of a place that seems to have turned her back on the locomotion of time as certainly as the death of the trains that used to scream into its heart, now and forever silenced by a force greater than man's sense of progress.

The sun edged over dim and slightly slanting homes that dealt with the tug of wind and water with little or no protection. Cats dodged our clumsy footfalls as we trudged along looking for the house Wade's brother Steve had rented at 524 White Street, where he said we could crash for a couple of weeks before we found our own place.

Steve was one of the finest athletes to have come out of our hometown. I met him the same day I met Wade, when I was about seven or eight years old. I played basketball with them and their brother Phil countless times growing up. I was usually paired with Steve because I was the worst among the four of us. But Steve could outscore his brothers in bursts of pissed-off Meadowlark Lemon-esque displays that left us chasing our tails. He led our high school team to several last-second clutch-shot victories that earned him a golden boy reputation. He always had a cool look and a slick style. He went to college on a football scholarship in Iowa but it was "high" times in America and Steve got into the drug scene. He was having a great time but he also decided to try and get on the supply side of the cannabis trade. He quit college and set up in a town just to the north of Diamond Lake. He had some parties and the cops busted one of them. He just managed to get off due to a warrant problem.

Steve decided to chuck it and headed to Miami where he chanced upon a biker in a Coconut Grove bar who declared that Key West would be a gold mine for him. He headed south and found his first home at the old Q Rooms, at the corner of Simonton and Fleming, for ten bucks a week. He sent a postcard to his brothers and that is how I found out about Key West. Steve was doing some light dealing back then—pot was his mainstay—but he'd launched a house-painting business as well, perhaps to show some legal income, even though he never took to the idea of paying taxes and such. A real Key Wester by some preternatural design.

Steve came home to the White Street house one afternoon spattered in paint a few days after we'd arrived and said to me, "Hey, weren't you just cooking to make a buck back in Illinois? There's a guy named Bud Man who runs the Old Anchor Inn and he is looking for a cook at a barbeque place called the Midget that opened in Old Town. Can't be too hard to make some ribs and burgers." Steve's enthusiasm was always a strong suit.

I walked down to the corner of Simonton and Greene Streets, met Bud Man, and he hired me on the spot. No application, no résumé, no stint as a *stage* (a French term for unpaid apprentice), no nothing. "Get an apron on and start cooking," he said warmly. "You'll be fine." I was not so sure. I'd cooked breakfast in Illinois. This was *meat*. And then Bud added, "Sammy will teach you the ropes. You'll be working the graveyard shift to start." I warned him that I wasn't much more than a breakfast cook and I didn't really know how to make barbeque and the like. He said, "That's all right. Just relax, kid. The people who eat on your shift are 90 percent shit-faced anyway."

Sammy became my chef, my teacher, and my boot camp drill sergeant. I was afraid of and fascinated by him. He was the head chef because he commanded it. Bud Man didn't cotton to hierarchy or authority of any kind and he imagined us cooks all working without a pecking order, aging hippie that he was. Sammy had other ideas, hippie that he wasn't!

Sammy worked with a grace I hadn't seen in the kitchen until I met him. The veins in his arms throbbed as if he were willing some kind of fuel from his brain to his limbs in an effort to get the food out of the kitchen as fast as he could. He was probably about sixty years of age when I came to work at the Midget. His skin was a dusty black when he was cold and drinking his first coffee, but an hour or so into the shift and his sweat turned his complexion into a slick of wet leather. He had ramrod posture and although he was not large, his chest showed the definition of a man less than half his age. His voice was a Satchmoesque rasp most of the time, but he said more with a look in many cases.

When it was slower I would cook and Sammy would "expedite"—a restaurant term which means to call out the orders to the cooks. However, what he called out would be far different from what had been scribbled down on the tickets by the waitresses, and he made me learn his language, a language he held on to from cooking days long ago. The Midget's menu had to be broad enough to handle the twenty-four hours of service we offered. Sammy would sit on a warped wooden swivel chair, smoking, when one of the gals would hand him a ticket. He'd peer over his large dark-framed glasses, looking for any mistakes first, and when he was satisfied her "dupe" (the paper duplicate of the order) was okay, he'd translate what she'd written to Sammy Talk.

He'd yell it out like we were half a mile away from each other rather than ten feet apart in the tiny kitchen.

"Adam and Eve on a Raft!"

After a few false starts I learned that this was to be two poached eggs on toast.

If he added, "And a slice of Noah's boy" my Bible study with the good Reverend Sammy would indicate the addition of a slice of ham, since Ham was Noah's son, obviously.

"One Shipwreck," he might add.

My mind raced as to what this menu term could mean. Did it have something to do with boat-shaped food? With great disgust, he'd shove the ticket in my face and I'd read, "Two scrambled eggs" and my education would continue in the only cooking school I would ever attend. Sammy was my first black professor.

Lionel and George were both nighttime bartenders and we cooked them a shift meal as well. When George worked Sammy would shout out his order to me. Typically it was, "Burn one!" It meant, "Put a burger on the griddle." If George made a thumbs-up gesture, it meant that he wanted the burger with lettuce, tomato, and onion and his ulcers were not fucking with him; then Sammy would wheel back to me and add, "Take it through the garden and pin a rose on it."

If George won at the track and was feeling particularly expansive it would show in a rare wide smile on his rubber mask of a face, and Sammy would boom, "Kid! Pop a Bun Pup on for Georgie!" But sometimes he'd mix it up and call out "Coney Island Chicken" and it was still the same hot dog as the bun pup. But it tickled him to see me wonder what it was until he'd either tell me or hop off his chair and show me how to make it right, "Sammy-style."

I'd clear out of his way but still watch from the back. How did this man make so few moves and get so much done? Just because he was cooking didn't mean he was done smoking, and I could see the thick white smoke curling around his black skin and up into the fluorescence of the bulb that illuminated our dark nights at the Midget together. He'd lay the cigarette on the windowsill and cut off a piece of a First Lady—a barbequed rib, which referred to the Eve of Genesis fame (not the aforementioned poached egg on toast) who was famously created from Adam's rib.

The rasp came out of Sammy's larynx somewhere, like coal cars shuttling up a mineshaft.

"Hey, you still watchin' me, kid? Good. You might learn something someday, though I doubt it."

Sammy grimaced tightly. Something didn't meet his approval in the slab of ribs he was sampling.

"Hand me Mike and Ike." These were also called "the Twins" and were really salt and pepper. He seasoned the pork with some rapid jabs a young boxer could appreciate, and tasted again. "That's better," he'd pronounce to himself. I wasn't sure which was salt and which was pepper. Maybe Sammy wasn't so sure either because if he wanted just salt he called out for Sea Dust. And by the way, in case you wanted to know, YumYum meant sugar. My personal favorite was "Gentleman Will Take a Chance." But it didn't inspire many takers. It was corned beef hash.

Lionel ate everything. He was short of stature yet movie-star good-looking and French Canadian. His accent added to his mystique. His hair was jet black and swept up into a quasi pompadour. Not some foolish Elvis-emulating construction for a man of about fifty, but maybe more like that of the craggy-featured handsome actor Richard Boone from the TV Western *Palladin*. He even reminded me of my own father.

Lionel had been on a drinking jag for two or three days when I got to work one night for my overnight shift. Old Town was quiet as it was June and much too hot for tourists. It was still about ninety degrees most nights and the heat from the charcoal grill burned into my back raising horrible blisters on my skin, a reaction I'd never had before. But down in the tropics I had no immunity and a lot of us Northerners suffered all kinds of skin ailments until our systems figured out how to recode. With no one in the place I walked out to the staff table. Back then there was no employee cafeteria or break room and it was accepted that the staff would often occupy a table where they could sit and smoke, snack, and drink coffee. It was always the worst table, the one immediately downwind from the charcoal grill in the Midget, where we passed our free hours when we could.

One day, a tall woman named Suzy I worked with asked me, "Norman, will you cook me some ribs? I'll share them with you and I'll pay."

I said, "You're a vegetarian, girl." I had been feeding her what could be found on a menu such as ours, and I was appalled at how much crap she ate to be one.

She said, "Wrong. Not anymore. My fucking boyfriend was forcing that on me, and I caught him in bed with another woman so I moved out last night. I want some damn meat!"

"Okay. Be just a few minutes. Meat it will be for Ms. Suzy!"

The barbequed ribs were truly great at the Midget, but when payday came we cashed our checks down the street at First State Bank and raced back to the little rickety restaurant to have the meal we'd been making all week long and lusting after: the Midget Burger—eight ounces of oval-shaped ground chuck with a crosshatch pattern scored into the top. Most crucially, the Midget Burger was cooked on hardwood charcoal on the outside grill. Real flames licked the meat and created the char that took us back to our primal selves. (It would be years before I'd be discussing them in terms of "the Maillard reaction" with the likes of Charlie Trotter, José Andres, Wylie Dufresne, Thomas Keller, and food science genius Harold McGee in Madrid.) Midget Burgers were served on appropriately large sections of garlicky buttered and toasted Cuban bread with caramelized onions that came off the ancient and perfectly seasoned griddle.

Incredible. Sexual. Redemptive.

We only had one dessert available, a Key Lime Pie that was made by a gal named "Sunshine" Smith. She delivered two pies on her bicycle each day. If we ran out, we ran out. She simply wouldn't make three because that meant she'd have to make two trips. A few years later she became Jimmy Buffett's business partner in a little venture called Margaritaville, so who can argue with her business sense now?

But Lionel worried us from time to time. One night he came to work looking like a zombie, dressed head to toe in black, standing for hours at the end of the bar. It was George's night, but Lionel chose to do his drinking where he worked. Loyalty. He'd smoke, then sleep standing up for long passages, awaken, then order another whiskey by tapping on the shot glass with the fingernail on his right forefinger that would have been the envy of a banjo picker. George didn't speak to him, but he was watching over Lionel, silently, waiting for him to either fall into a coma or erupt into a volcanic madness he'd occasionally witnessed during their twenty-odd years of tending bar together.

Around 5 a.m. Lionel appeared at our staff table and slowly took an empty chair. Suzy pushed our plates of now thoroughly gleaned pork bones aside. He said nothing. His head was large and bobbed like a cork in a very still river, his face a mask of numb, mute pain. He smoked holding his two hands in front of him with his elbows resting on the wooden tabletop. The smoke spiraled out into the humid air. After a while, Suzy and I resumed our casual chatter. About twenty minutes later, when we thought Lionel had finally had enough of this marathon and lapsed into a seated coma, he spoke:

"Have you ever been to Africa?"

Suzy and I exchanged sidelong glances. Is he talking to us or is this sleep talking?

"Have either of you [long gap of time] ever been to Africa?"

"No," we chimed, but not too loudly. This was weird and we were not sure if we risked waking him, which we deemed to be (possibly) dangerous. But he was awake. He smiled a twisted, down-turning sort of smile and opened his eyes into narrow, black, bottomless slits.

Haltingly, Lionel said, "I worked there as a . . . surveyor for Standard . . . Oil . . . for twenty-three . . . years."

This was the first whole sentence out of Lionel in what seemed like days. We were now mute.

"Twenty-three . . ." He seemed to trail off for good again.

Then he cleared his throat and said, "There was a priest I came to know there. Big fat, tall guy from Boston, like a football player but older. He took me around to show me Africa since we were the only two white people for hundreds of miles. He even spoke their language."

Lionel's words fell on us like stones, each one larger and heavier than the next. "He took me to a feast. It was a big-deal feast. The natives were drumming and painted up and they sat us at a long table to eat with them. The priest sat down next to me at this big long table." Lionel stretched his arms out to show us how long the table was and seemed disgusted that his arms couldn't reach fifteen feet in each direction to give us a more accurate idea. He shook his head at the uselessness of the situation. But he had things to say.

He said they passed a big platter of meat down the table and since they were guests they were served first, even before the chief. "I turned to the priest and asked him what we were eating. He just looked at me and said, 'Eat it. Eat it or we may be next.'"

Lionel tapped his nail on the empty glass and another whiskey appeared quickly.

He drained it and looked out at the quiet, empty street, past the beach and seemingly far out over the entire dark maw of the Atlantic Ocean until his eyes got to a little muddy village in Africa so many years ago.

He turned his gaze to Suzy and me. The usual rouge-brown eyes were now sunken black stars.

"We taste like pork," Lionel said.

"What do you mean, 'We taste like pork,' Lionel?" I asked after a full, awful minute.

"Humans. We taste like pork. Damn priest made a cannibal out of me." And he collapsed on the table. His head almost bounced. He was done now.

Suzy and I looked down at the rib bones and a fly that was circling and buzzing among them. We looked away.

When I cashed my next check I went back to the Greyhound bus station and bought Janet a ticket to Key West. I called her and told her of my purchase. I wasn't sure if she either believed me or wanted to come. In person she was always so cocky and full of joy, yet over that motel pay phone she seemed like another person and I hung up not knowing why.

But two days later I walked to the station and she climbed down the steep stairs of the bus. (At an even five feet in height most stairs were steep, and most of the world was tall to her.) She had a grocery bag with her few clothes in it. She took my hand and we walked down the streets of Key West together for the first time in our lives. Her long brown hair was pulled back under a kerchief but the longer strands caressed my hand on her warm, strong shoulder as we made our way to White Street where Steve was still letting me crash.

I wasn't sure how he'd feel about me bringing a girl into the place. I shouldn't have worried. When he met Janet he couldn't have been nicer and said, "Good timing, too. My girlfriend Debbie is making her famous Chicago spaghetti tonight. We can have a little dinner party to start you off in Key West the right way. You are gonna love it here in *Cayo Hueso*."

Janet asked, "What's a *Cayo Hueso*?"

Steve told her, "Oh, that's the old Spanish name for Key West. It means Bone Key."

I took Janet for a walk to show her around the area where we lived and how close the beach was. We walked down White Street past the M & M Launderette, past the Fourth of July (a restaurant where we ate some of our very first Cuban American meals), and on down to the White Street Pier, which gave us a view of the ocean, and then back to little Higgs Beach where we spent countless hours over the next few months. We walked over the sandy expanse past the brick walls of the East Martello Fort on the edge of the beach to the wooden pier. We caught the smell of french fries coming from a hamburger and hotdog stand. Hungry, we remembered Steve and Debbie's dinner was going to be ready soon so we headed back to the house.

When we got to the porch we heard a crash. Steve was in a rage and screaming at Debbie. Debbie's raven-black hair was flying around her head as she dished it back to Steve. Spaghetti sauce was bubbling on the rickety gas stove and big loaves of bread lay slashed open, coated with garlic butter. He picked up a hammer from a toolbox and shouted, "You want to give me a hassle? I'll show you how I fix things around my house!" And whack, he took out the kitchen window. Glass showered her bare feet. Janet pulled in behind me in total shock. I'd seen Steve's rages often since I was eight years old. He shot toward the stairs. He stopped by the mirror at the front door and turned back to Debbie. "You don't like what you see? Well, sweetheart, don't fuck with me, then. I'm the man!" He swiveled his torso halfway around then reversed himself, did a head fake, and smashed the mirror. For a grand finale he walked up the stairs and took out about four framed pictures along the way. Dinner was postponed.

We tried to be as scarce as we could for the next week until we found a place to rent in New Town over on Seidenberg Avenue. The Seidenberg house was soon crowded but it was the only way we could afford it. My pals Ricky and Wade moved in with us, as did Ricky's girlfriend Pam from Illinois. It was not long after that when a guy named Bobby we'd met at the Midget and his two female friends Cindy and Antonia moved in, too.

Ricky got a job as a carpenter and Wade joined me cooking at the restaurant. For the next few weeks Janet and I fell into the bliss of living each waking moment together, and the bliss of each nighttime moment sleeping together. Despite the tropical heat of Key West we slept with our arms and legs wrapped around each other all through the night. We had no air-conditioning but we did like everyone else and bought a big electric box fan and placed it on the floor at the foot of our mattress where it could offer some relief.

When I wasn't at work Janet and I walked the town and discovered its exotic charms. We fell in love with Key West and each other. The slow pace of lying on the beach, taking lazy swims at Higgs Beach, strolling through town, going to the little bars, shopping for our meals, eating some of the foods new to us in the Bahamian and Cuban restaurants—all became part of our new life. Many nights before my shift, we'd join in the "Sunset Celebration" that was just beginning to take hold in Key West. Locals from all over the island got together on Mallory Square in a free-spirited quotidian communal festival centered on the magnificent sun setting on another day. When the sun finally descended past the pretty clouds below the horizon, everyone clapped and hollered in appreciation for one more day here on this planet. Some of the clouds floating overhead were made from marijuana, of course.

Janet got a job waitressing at a seafood restaurant on Duval. The management kept asking her for ID because she was serving alcohol. She put them off for a few weeks and made some good tips, but got scared and quit. I continued working the night shift at the Midget, so while I slept on the sand in the shadows of palms Janet lay next to me, resting her head on my chest, a little girl living as a woman a long, long way from home.

It seemed our housing arrangement was destined to grow weirder by the week. The word was out on the mainland that Key West was *the* new place for the free-spirited young, and somehow we ended up with three more roommates. The sleeping arrangements got tight.

One of our roommates was known as "Billy the Sot," like Billy the Kid but his reputation was for drinking, not robbing and killing. I think it was Wade who rescued this damaged soldier of the post–Woodstock Nation. In the realization that with each new boarder everyone's rent went down by a nice percentage, we sort of shined it on. Billy set up a tent in the backyard, and, except for the noise he made stumbling through the house savagely wasted at night on his way to his sleeping bag, he didn't bother us. The other new boarders were a husband and wife from New York named Pablo and Linda. When you're only twenty-one it's hard to guess the age of anyone north of thirty-five, but even with my lack of skills I'd wager these two were forty and thirty-five, respectively. Linda was a Rubenesque woman with a sharp tongue, an intelligent wit, and a taste for partying. Pablo had sandy brown hair and beard, a strong physique from years of boatbuilding, and a taste for partying even harder than Linda. They moved into the room Janet and I shared, so we "redecorated" with clotheslines, tapestries, towels, beads, and sheets, which we hung to give us some cover at night.

It was mid-April and Janet's eighteenth birthday was at hand. I wanted to take her out to dinner. This was an expense we could not afford but from the very beginning of our life together we shared a passion for food and the allure of restaurants. There was a place in town that was easily deemed the most romantic, so I made a reservation at Louie's Backyard. We dressed up and I put a flower from the yard in Janet's hair before we walked the mile to Louie's, where the "backyard" actually was a small patio that looked right out onto the water.

Louie's was named for an Italian gentleman named Louie Signorelli. He had owned a few other businesses but this was the place for which he will always be remembered. The restaurant was, and still is, housed in a real home built in 1909 by a ship captain. It sits right on the Gulf of Mexico at the corner of Vernon and Waddell. Over time the restaurant has expanded but back then it held only ten tables. We had a dish of something we'd never heard of before called *bagna cauda* and we loved the creamy garlicky sauce for dipping our vegetables.

We ordered a bottle of wine and ate dinner holding hands. I was scheduled to work my usual graveyard shift so we lingered awhile and had a drink at the Afterdeck Bar. That night, a local musician named Jimmy Buffett was singing and playing for drinks. It was said he was cutting an album about life in Key West up in Nashville. We liked his songs.

The bartender that night was a local gadfly named Howard Paul. He was a notorious "flamer" even by Key West standards. Being gay was seldom a problem in this easygoing town. Howard was just such an incongruous combination of geekiness and flamboyance that he stood out. But he was no pretty boy—with his shaved, bony head, bug-eyed expression, fluttering hands, constant expostulations of mock horror and heavy-duty come-ons, most people were entertained by him. "Oh, *Howard*!" was a common reaction to one of his performances.

One of his stories—and Howard told it himself with Chaplinesque pathos—was of his decision to commit suicide. He was living at Louie's at the time, crashing on a couch in the upstairs office. It would have to rank as one of the world's prettiest places to end it all. The gently swaying waters of the Atlantic and the Gulf meet in the flat distance not far from land's end. The ocean floor remains shallow for a long distance. You can walk out into the water for fifteen minutes before it will come up to your chest. It is an ideal place to loll about but not such an ideal place to drown oneself. Still, Howard tried his best.

He felt unloved and so one morning he tied one end of a rope around his waist and the other end to a heavy cinder block and marched into the waters off Dog Beach alongside Louie's Backyard. He held the cinder block in his stringy muscled arms while having a last smoke, grasping the cigarette in his expressive lips that had given so much pleasure to others, but so little to himself. He strode forward, still only up to his thighs now, wondering why the world had no place for Howard. He told us (many, many of us) he began to cry just a little at that moment—and that's when he heard his phone ringing back in the upstairs office at Louie's. The peal of the phone struck him as a call of salvation! Someone! Someone! Wanted him! Someone was calling him! Howard dropped the cinder block into the water and slipped the rope from around his middle. He churned his white legs as quickly as he could, scrambled up the little rocks, and hurried up the stairs at the back of Louie's. The phone rang and rang and rang. Whoever was on the other end really wanted to talk to Howard! He picked up the phone and yelled into it, "Who is it? Yes! I'm here! Who *is* this?"

The voice on the other end was cold.

"Is this Howard Paul?"

"Yes!" he cried out again. "Yes! Yes! Yes! I'm *Hoooowaaaard!*—I am she!"

"Well, Mr. Paul, we are sorry to tell you this, but due to nonpayment we are cutting off your phone service as of now."

And the voice on the other end of the phone hung up.

Howard lived.

When her birthday dinner was over, Janet walked me to the Midget to work. We didn't have a car or even bicycles yet so we walked everywhere. This was a good thing as it gave us a chance to explore every lane, smell every flower, and hear the voices of the good people of Key West.

But one thing about Key West was as true then as it is now: keeping help is a bitch! When we got to the Midget, Suzy said, "Happy Birthday, Janet. And Norman, your dishwasher no-showed."

Fuck.

Janet followed me into the kitchen, put on an apron, and washed dishes and pots while I cooked through that April night, on her birthday, without complaint. The next morning we walked again, arm in arm, past the old Steadman's Boatyard and the barnacle-crusted and weather-beaten boats in the midst of a dance of repair and decay, over the Garrison Bight Bridge with the prettiest pink-and-yellow clouds hanging low in the cool of the dawn. We walked in the quiet until we got to our home and the sounds of about ten people sleeping off another night of Key West partying.

I woke near noon in a full sweat. For some reason the power had gone off and it was about ninety-nine degrees in our bedroom. I headed toward the bathroom to take a shower but it was occupied. I waited and to my surprise Wade and Pablo's wife Linda came out of it naked as the day they were born. Unbeknownst to me they had become lovers when Pablo wasn't around. Wade was happy and so was Linda with her big young lover.

Wade was big. He was big all our lives. He was a big teddy bear with long curly hair, a soft beard, and beautiful hazel eyes with long eyelashes. I loved Wade. No one ever made me laugh as much as Wade did. We met when we were in the third grade and were always together growing up. He was my constant companion on weekends when we'd stay at my father's house from the time I was ten until about fifteen. My dad was not around that much and Wade, along with my little sister Bet, had the run of what was my parents' home until they split up. We went to school together and played together. Now we lived and worked together. I was happy he was getting laid. He'd have to be careful, though. Wade was big; but Pablo, well, he was old and looked like he just didn't give a good goddamn.

Billy the Sot was living up to his name more and more with each passing day. He'd done some time in Vietnam and was an emotional basket case.

He had an odd way of dealing with it. Key West had been a service town for many years thanks to the presence of the naval base. When "Give 'em Hell" Harry Truman set up the "Little White House" in 1946, sailors and marines strode through the streets of Key West in their sharp uniforms and crowded into the rank bars. Three decades later, Billy haunted the same bars. When he was sufficiently pissed he'd challenge the marines to fights, calling them "pussies and faggots for killing for dirty Uncle Sam."

This didn't go over well and Billy would get the shit kicked out of him. I mean the living shit kicked out of him. He wore steel-framed glasses, not a great feature for a man begging to get hit in the face. His luxurious walrus mustache slightly hid the fact that he'd lost both of his front teeth, and in those days he wore his glasses with one lens still in working order while the other had been replaced with a patch he'd made by cutting out the front of one of his Camel cigarette packs and taping it where the missing lens was intended to be. His good eye was so black and blue and swollen from his most recent pugilistic efforts that he had to move his head from side to side to get any bearing on something as small as the keyhole to a door. Good thing he lived in a tent.

May became June and June sweltered on into the beginning of July. Each night at the Midget became hotter. My back was all torn up with the savage heat rash that was akin to leprosy. I was beginning to wonder if I had a sleeping disease, too. With the only cool coming at night, and me working through those few hours, I never could seem to sleep. I would finish my shift having to remove the coals from the huge barbeque grill we cooked the ribs on. I would take a large shovel and a metal garbage can or dented pail, remove the grates, and start shoveling the still-hot, dusty briquettes. But the dust would swirl and stick to my sweaty skin and plug my nose until I would have to walk out into the alley to catch a breath by the Dumpster—ack!—and start again. I would try to crane my face as far away from the heat as I could, but my arms are only so long. I carried the can to the street where it would wait for the next lucky working-class hero to haul it away.

Eventually, Pablo and Linda decided to move. Our restored privacy notwithstanding, the news was not all good because our portion of the rent would go back up. They packed up most of their stuff into their car but laid two open suitcases with Pablo's clothes in one and Linda's in the other beside their bed. On their last night we had a little going-away party at the Seidenberg house. We drank beer, played cards, and listened to WKIZ radio. At one point Linda somehow ended up on Wade's lap when Pablo had gone out for a pack of smokes. When he got back he shot Linda a look and she got up—slowly—her hands lingering on Wade's lap as she did.

Janet and I fell asleep around midnight. It was my night off and I was looking forward to a full night in the cooler hours, finally able to rest with my girl. Around four in the morning, however, we woke to a sound that was both familiar and yet very out of context. The tapestry that divided our bedroom into separate sleeping quarters was not, of course, soundproof. I peered under the fabric that hung from near the ceiling to about a foot from the floor. The sound grew louder, steadier, stronger, and even more familiar. Now I could see the outline of a male figure's shadow directly behind the tapestry and not two feet from our mattress. The sound continued. I could see the suitcases lying open. And suddenly the smell hit my nostrils. It was piss!

Then Linda's voice became the next sound, high, nasal, hysterical.

"Pablo!! Pablo!!! Stop pissing on my clothes!"

But the man was made of piss. It was a river of piss. He about filled that suitcase with a vengeance, swaying and wobbling from all the beer. He stood, wide legged, cock in hand and when he was done he walked out into the yard and fell dead asleep.

Janet and I had pushed our bodies up against the bedroom wall as far as we could get. We had mashed our pillows up against our mouths and noses. When it was over we got up and walked past Linda who was crying and swearing as she surveyed the damage. After a few minutes we walked out the front door and as we did we heard our bedroom window open. Linda hurled the suitcase outside in the direction of her husband's body. Now her urine-soaked bras and panties piled up on his naked chest.

"Fuck you, Pablo! Fuck you always and forevermore!"

Pablo slept.

I had to get Janet out of here. I had to get both of us out of here. But where should we go now? And how would we get there?

A few days later we were by the side of U.S. 1 with my canvas backpack packed with our few belongings. She stuck out her pretty thumb and I held a sign that simply read "Chicago" and we headed back to Illinois the only way we could. It was scary to hitchhike with a girl so young and so beautiful. The responsibility of making sure I protected her grew stronger after the very first ride with a flipped-out navy cat who had huge speakers in the backseat wedged between us. With Hendrix blaring, he was passing cars on the narrow bridges that no one sane would ever do. He admitted that he'd been "tripping all night." I lied and told him we were only going as far as Marathon (a mere fifty miles north of Key West) to stay with a friend. He was heading to Miami and roared back onto the highway as Jimi wailed.

We got a ride in central Florida from two guys who might have been a father and son, and who made me grit my teeth and secretly hold onto a camping knife in a pocket of my backpack.

The last leg we were picked up by a guy whose mother was the nurse at my grade school growing up. He was older than me by about four years and in the same grade as my older sister Jane. He was the heavyweight wrestler in our high school and he looked over his massive shoulder at Janet and me in our highway-bedraggled hippie clothes and said, "Aren't you Van Aken?" I said, "Yes." He said, "Thought so. You look different now. I'll drive you to your house." He knew right where I lived. We were back home all right. But before we got to my house we asked him to stop a few blocks away. We got out, thanked him, and walked holding hands the last little bit of the way taking in the beauty of this place once again.

Bicycle Sammy's Potato Salad

Everyone seems to put their own special stamp on potato salad, and my personal favorite was Bicycle Sammy's way. I've been making it for forty years with the unusual tang from the Creole-style mustard and the unexpected sweetness from the fennel. Sammy served his with barbequed ribs, but he told me that when serving it with fish or chicken he liked to stir in some cooked crumbled bacon in the die-hard spirit of a true pork lover. Sammy made it for a lifetime before he showed me how. Time tested. Like both of us, I suppose.

2 pounds new potatoes, scrubbed and cut into bite-sized pieces
1 cup mayonnaise
1 tablespoon stone-ground mustard (Sammy insisted, and I prefer, Creole-style)
2 tablespoons apple cider vinegar
1 teaspoon kosher salt
2 teaspoons sugar
¼ teaspoon cracked black pepper
½ teaspoon chili powder
¼ teaspoon ground cumin
½ cup diced fennel
½ cup chopped sweet onion
1 jalapeño pepper, stemmed, seeded, and minced
2 hard-cooked eggs, peeled and chopped
hot sauce of your choice, if desired

Place the potatoes in a 4-quart pot with enough water to cover. Bring to a high simmer over medium-high heat. Reduce the heat to low and continue simmering until the potatoes are tender, about 10 minutes, checking frequently. (Sammy would boil over if I cooked the potatoes too fast and "let the water come washin' in.") Drain well and allow them to cool somewhat, but not completely. Season with salt and pepper, lifting them gently to stir.

In a large bowl, combine the mayonnaise, mustard, vinegar, salt, sugar, pepper, chili powder, and cumin. Add the cooked potatoes, fennel, onion, and jalapeño, and stir. Add the hard-cooked eggs, and toss gently. Add the hot sauce, if you're using it, and stir once more. Cover in plastic wrap and chill in the refrigerator for a few hours before serving.

Makes 6 cups

CHAPTER 5

The Deerpath Inn
1973–74

WHEN I WAS STILL IN HIGH SCHOOL, my mom, Ruth Manderson, worked in a variety of restaurants around Chicago's North Shore communities. She was a single working mother with three children and she had to work as many double shifts as she could to make ends meet. Mama never complained although she had a recurring problem with herniated and slipped disks in her back and endured several hospital stays that included traction. There was no doubt the work was very painful for her, and despite her brave and sunny front we lived in a long period of extended economic uncertainty. When I think of those years I often remember my mother in her waitress uniform either about to go to work or finally coming home to a reheated dinner. I remember her smoking and counting her tips at the kitchen table, neatly rolling the nickels, dimes, and quarters into the paper coin rolls she'd get from the bank so she could deposit her heavy, but meager, earnings in our family account in town.

Our maternal grandmother, "Nana," was widowed by this time and she came from New Jersey to live with us in the small house my father, Harold Van Aken, had bought just before we ran away from him. My mother and father had a tempestuous relationship veering between mutually awestruck love to bitter, object-throwing (her), door-smashing (him) violence. My sisters and I tunneled into our bedroom and cried. I was nine. Sides were expected to be taken. It was a no-win scenario and I had nightmares of imaginary courtroom scenes where a satin-robed judge expected me to pick one of my parents over the other. He asked me black-and-white questions but all I could see had the color of hurt.

When Mama had had enough of Dad's dalliances and the fights, she'd load my sisters and me into one of the cars he'd brought home from his used and new car lot and roar back to her parents' home in New Jersey. The middle-of-the-night trips took place when I was four, seven, and eight. In a rare period of reconciliation, Dad gave the little house to Nana and my older sister Jane, and when we finally came out of hiding during that last awful, lonesome summer, Mama, my younger sister Bet, and I moved in with them.

I really didn't put together why my father had a difficult time with my mom, or with relationships in general, until after he died. Or maybe I was simply getting older and able to think of him as a flawed human being instead of my superman father. He was a superman in strength and humor and he was also a very good businessman in a tough field who worked tenaciously his whole life.

I am not sure when I first heard that he had been adopted by our grandfather, Carl Van Aken. But my dad first heard about it when a relative nonchalantly said something at a family gathering as if it were a fact known by all. He was about sixteen, and the shock and confusion it caused him must have been awful. I know he adored his mother and he loved the man who he'd always thought of as his flesh-and-blood father. "Grampa" and my dad worked side by side as car dealers until my dad died.

Carl Van Aken came from Michigan to rural Ohio and fell deeply in love with my grandmother, Dorothy Circle. This was at a time when many men of that generation would have shunned the young mother. He was a gentle and wonderful man whom my mother, brother, sisters, and I adored as we did our grandmother. "Gra," as we kids called her, was born in 1900 and my dad came along in October of 1915. The family heard stories in the ensuing years as to who my dad's biological father really was, but it was only a guessing game. Whoever it was abandoned the unwed young woman to fend for herself. There were times I felt a disconnection with my last name, but it fell to my father, and at a tender age, to bear the confusion and failed trust that I wish I could have loved away.

Living with Nana turned out to be salvation for me because she was the first person in our family to lead me to the world of books and ideas beyond what our little town had to offer. Nana grew up in the Chelsea section of New York City at the turn of the twentieth century. Her father, John Quinn, was a theatrical agent and Nana, Janie then, lived in the colorful world of Manhattan's Lower West Side. Through her father's work she came to know many of the biggest entertainers of the day: Al Jolson came to their home for dinner, Buster Keaton played with her, and she took on a lifelong passion for music and the theater, opera in particular. Many afternoons, as Bet and I walked up the short but steep hill toward home after school, we'd hear her belting out an aria in Italian (which she spoke not a word of) at the top of her lungs accompanied by one of her old 78s at full blast.

As I grew up, from awkward adolescence into a young man, Nana pushed me, spoiled me, and guided me in ways I only wish most children could know. Nana was regal. All my friends were smitten with this wise and imperiously mannered grand woman who somehow made us all feel smarter, more capable of becoming something special. She told me once in her high, clear voice I can still hear, after she had made a batch of scones that I liked immensely and told her so, "Of course you would like them, Norman." (I was named for her husband and her son, who died at the age of twenty-four from kidney disease.) "Your great-great-grandmother was the baker for Queen Victoria when she took her summer holidays in Scotland." I believed Janie Margarita Quinn Manderson. I believed her always.

It was Mama who provided the other lessons—those of work and courage and humor, of never quitting. One of the jobs she had during the late sixties was at the Deerpath Inn in the ultrarich town of Lake Forest, Illinois. She had moved on from waitressing and was now the hostess of the inn's restaurant. It was a role that suited her very well. During that time she came to know the Deerpath's permanent residents, around two dozen people with enough money to live anywhere in the world they wanted but chose the familial and comforting tradition this place was imbued with. The inn was modeled after the Manor House, a timber-and-stucco Tudor home built in the 1450s and located in Chiddington, Kent, England. Mama also got to know the entire restaurant crew and became lifelong friends with some of them.

My sisters and I loved to visit Mama during those years. We'd even go for an occasional Sunday brunch with Nana, my sister Jane driving us from our small town to this bastion of luxury. We sat in the Garden Room and the light that poured through the windows seemed to dance on the magnificent spread of food that tempted my adolescent body in ways that I'd never experienced in our cafeteria at Mundelein High. I wondered where they found such gigantic and luscious strawberries and blueberries! Huge platters of pancakes and waffles were made to order, their sugary richness filling the room. I hadn't known the pleasures of fish growing up in the Midwest, where seafood was neither as prized nor as common as on the East Coast, where Mama and Nana came from. But they got me to try it, and smoked salmon, smoked trout, and shad roe entered my world. The white-uniformed chefs stood before seductive platters of honey-baked hams and steamship rounds of beef waiting for us to order how they should pile our plates. After all, we were Ruth's kids and they *loved* my mother. It may have been there, in the Deerpath dining room in 1968, that I saw a truly broad spectrum of foods for the first time in my life, and I was awestruck by how much I loved the look and smell and variety before me.

When Janet and I returned from Key West, I applied for a job at the Deerpath, marveling once more at life's cosmic circularity. It was 1974 now and Mama had gone to work at another restaurant. I was twenty-three, a number I took as my luckiest. When I wrote on the application that the inn's former head chef back when Mama still worked there referred me for the job, I secured an interview. The general manager was quite puzzled to see the unkempt creature in front of him, wondering, I'm sure, how I could ever have crossed paths with, much less associated with, the former head chef of this hallowed establishment. But, as is so often the case, they needed someone in the kitchen and they needed him now and badly. So I was hired. I quickly came to see how the few intervening years had changed the Deerpath Inn for the worse.

I arrived around two o'clock in the afternoon each day. My battered black Volkswagen was broke and so was I, so fixing it would have to wait. I hitchhiked in to work all that summer so my arrival time was subject to the vagaries and compassion (or otherwise) of others. I usually arrived in the high chaos and tidal roar of the lunch rush hour. Chefs, waiters, the cocktail girl, the cashier, bartenders, every fucking one of them, lost out of their minds, were screaming in at least four languages. It was always like a bad day at the United Nations. This restaurant world took some getting used to. It was bizarre and I was not yet battle hardened to it. That would come. But for now here's what it looked like:

The Filipino grill man, Juan, would be elbowing the Scandinavian fish chef, Thor, out of his way to puff up his Florentine omelets under the one-thousand-degree broiler. It's a great trick and one that most home cooks don't know. We didn't know it back at the Fireside. Instead of making the omelet using only the heat of a bottom burner and letting it do all the work, you can do the first part of the omelet on the stove and then lay in the filling ingredients and thrust it under the heat of the broiler. In a few critical seconds the omelet "blows up," expanding in size and fluffiness and looking extremely "come hither" to the diner. The chef grabs the omelet pan and rolls it using gravity to render the now rotund egg package onto the preheated plate with the softest plop. If it's a Florentine, he ladles on a nutmeg-spiked cheesy Sauce Mornay and, like most places at that time, a sprinkling of paprika, which tastes awful when used that way but looks enticing. Thor's greatest single achievement (in his mind) was to bodycheck Juan at the most critical moment so the Filipino's ascending omelets were burnt to blackness and he'd have to begin his work anew.

Thor would peer over his granny glasses that were eternally sliding down his pale nose in a slick of sweat at the mounting snowstorm of ticket orders and mutter to no one in particular, "I'm gonna stick a knife in this dick some day." Which dick, I didn't know; we were all uniformly dicks to Thor when he was in the rush.

Eddie (we all called him "Bigfateddie" like it was all one word) was from Philadelphia and the only guy on the line I could not understand. I had better luck understanding the Korean fish cutter. A word from Bigfateddie here and there, but that was it. Just enough to keep me trying to follow his trail but that trail broke off under the food he was pushing into his face. His voice was very high, a Jerry Lewis–like high. His head was small and seemed to float above his towering Macy's-Day-parade-float-sized body like a helium balloon bobbing around on a stick. He wore

Buddy Holly black-framed glasses and wrapped his apron around his massive middle like a sheet. The apron strings were forever coming undone and he was forever retying them but never seemed to notice it happening. It was his one-man dance, his hokey-pokey. Bigfateddie was the guy who taught me how to use a French knife. I'll always be grateful to him for that. He did this by having me slice boxes upon boxes of button mushrooms. He taught through gesture and pantomime due to that crazy shorthand language only he spoke.

Maybe Thor could understand more because he would always tell BFE to "shut the *fuck* up." Eddie worked in the cold pantry (what the French call *garde manger*). He must have consumed five pounds of shrimp and crabmeat each day. Polar bears eat less. I can't think of his face without seeing white flecks of crabmeat or an errant shrimp shell plastered on part of it.

The executive chef, a Frenchman who had won some medals for cuisine in Paris long ago, usually retired in the midafternoons with his newspapers, cigars, and Burgundy to his private quarters upstairs. Sometimes he would reappear for the dinner shift but by then I'd be so buried in work I'd be too weeded to care. He was an unknown planet to me. He spoke to me only once and it was in a variety of French that was not taught at school. (Apparently, I had violated his mother or done something equally egregiously stupid.) He delivered his invective standing on the steep ramp between the kitchen and the dining room while folded over at the waist so he could thrust his Panavision-wide, white face directly in front of mine and vent on me in full surround sound. When he was satisfied that I knew I was dog shit, or worse, American dog shit, he marched woozily up to his small apartment above the restaurant. I never understood why this man ruled our lives.

The kitchen was built below ground level and had no windows. With all the other chefs napping after the lunch shift in the bunkhouse they lived in behind the restaurant, the hours between three and five o'clock were dark, dreamy, and quiet.

I spent many of those afternoons with a kind, funny, and dying Japanese man named Tokio Suyehara. Toké was the head chef whose name I had put on my application for the job. A friend of my mother's from the 1960s, Toké had stomach cancer and he no longer had the strength for the job. Food, his greatest pleasure, was denied him. His body shrunk down to a boy's size with only his head, feet, and hands left large.

Toké and I had chores to do in those midafternoons, making vast pans of the inn's famous creamed spinach or potatoes Savoyard, peeling shallots and garlic, slicing the Dover sole's lemon garnishes, which meant carefully sprinkling paprika on one hemisphere and chopped parsley on the other, laying them on half-sheet trays and covering them for service. We accomplished these tasks quickly so we could sit in the chef's office and drink his imported teas and talk. He and his family were forced into the Nisei camps in California during World War II, and he told me all about that strange chapter in American history from a side I had not heard before. Sometimes, when Toké was feeling up to it, he would raid the walk-in refrigerators and make me some incredible dishes he knew from his travels throughout Asia.

On doctor's orders he ate big bowls of ice cream or drank shakes to try and put some weight back on, which frustrated him because he missed his own spicy, aromatic, textured cooking. I was learning why with these meals and felt bad for him. He shook it all off with a smile and downcast eyes, revealing nothing that resembled defeat. I remember him out in the yard picking dandelion greens in the softening late-spring sunlight one day before I left that job (never to see him again but in his coffin), bringing them in and making us a little sesame-oil-and-soy-dressed salad with them. Who knew that you could eat weeds? I thought it was inspired.

By five o'clock in the afternoon the other chefs would be returning to work after their breaks in the bunkhouse (for those who could sleep), or from listening to ball games on a tinny little radio, or getting in some letter writing back to old countries or old loves (who had forgotten them long ago), to work the dinner hour.

The big news of the day was kidnapped Patty Hearst's "conversion" from heiress to Symbionese Liberation Army poster girl. Maybe because we were in such a wealthy town it fascinated us that one of these rich guys' daughters (who dined here) might betray all that privilege and run off with the likes of one of us. We could dream. Unlike many Americans, who rarely talk politics with their coworkers, the European chefs took on the subject with a passion and followed the developing story as avidly as a soap opera. When the Feds went in and blew up that house we switched our fantasies to safer stuff. Now we wanted her caught. The rich girl was not Robin Hood anymore.

The restaurant changed rhythm dramatically between the hours of four and six. The dishwashers had lifted the mats, swept and mopped, cleaned a thousand dishes and hundreds of pans, taken out the laundry, and reset the cutting boards. Usually the Italian would be back first, whistling and bragging about a midafternoon conquest (mostly imaginary) and readying his station, which was the meat grill. His name was Michelangelo but he asked us all to call him Mike. Mike envisioned himself as a real lady-killer. And who knows? Sometimes he did come back with a badge of lipstick smeared on his freckled face. Who could understand what the waitresses went through in that place and that time better than the cooks? Those women, jockeying food up and down that ramp for hours on end, dealing with the infinite requests and complaints from the guests, needed to curry a little flirtatious favor with the chefs just to survive: "Mrs. Hobbs needs the eggs taken off her chef salad. Can you help me fast, honey? Mrs. Hobbs is up my ass today, as usual." Who would blame her for using the bait of sexy, teasing charm to try to get someone to just fucking "do it" and help her make some tips today? It was brutal work. The female servers had to wear high heels and lift to shoulder height huge plate-laden trays that nearly equaled their own body weight.

Mike liked to show off for me. He tried to teach me style. He had very pale green eyes and wore his hair slicked back. He'd cadge some filet mignon out of the meat cooler and season it with a prized olive oil from somewhere near his birthplace. (I thought his hair smelled just like that olive oil.) He would make a salad with vinaigrette and torn, toasted bread and then hurl the bits of raw meat directly on the stove's "flat top" which is like a solid piece of stone (like a driveway) that's heated up to a blazing temperature. He'd flip the meat around a few times, stabbing it with a huge butcher's fork, and then scoop it onto our salad. We'd eat standing up salting the meat with each bite. He stood with one foot out to the side like a ballet dancer and school me further on how to move in a kitchen, how to "work-a-nice." It sounded like a phony impression of a typecast Italian, but that was the way Mike would say it, with the palms of his hands upturned, his elbows pointing downward and his shoulders shaking with an ironic shrugging laugh. I couldn't help laughing, too, and enjoying our different worlds united by this salad and this place in life called the Deerpath Inn. He laughed harder once I was laughing, "Mike [he spoke of himself], he make-a-you laugh, eh? That's good! Let'sa laugh and eat-a-this good meat, kid. Let's work-a-nice tonight, too, eh. I show you."

The other chefs came in one by one and soon the staff meal was coming together, which always seemed to make the cooks momentarily pleasant. Maybe it was the wine they gulped in coffee mugs. (Everyone on the floor knew but they never ratted on the cooks or they'd have had one helluva time getting their food later.) In fact, one of my chief jobs back then was going to the little liquor store a few blocks down to pick up the beer and whiskey and hide them behind cases of lettuce or the prepped escargot dishes. The chefs took bottles from the restaurant's cooking wine inventory, which the owners allowed under the naïve assumption that that would be all that was drunk. They assumed wrong. Some chefs drank the Chablis right out of the Shrimp de Jonghe, leaving the shrimp, butter, and parsley, quite literally, high and dry.

I was learning so much. Restaurant cooking was very different in the U.S. back then. In fact, there were two distinct periods of restaurant cooking in America before the modern era, roughly 1975 to the present. In the first period, beginning shortly after WWII, the entire restaurant profession experienced a golden age that lasted until the mid-1960s. With the country getting economically stronger at that time, more Americans were traveling, and many were former soldiers who had tasted the authentic food and wines of France and Italy and were now eager for more. Magic was in the air and the surge of restaurants turning out extraordinary food and excellent service blossomed across the country. In restaurants from San Francisco to Chicago, Boston, and New York, Americans were finding a recreation of some of the finest European cuisines and of France, in particular. Even First Lady Jacqueline Kennedy hired a French chef, René Verdon, at the White House, thus the dinner parties of Camelot had a distinctly French accent.

Following the assassination of President Kennedy, through the Johnson years, the heartbreak of Vietnam, and the shame of Watergate, the whole grand show slid into a corrupted imitation of *haute cuisine.* Nixon sneaking Margaux into his glass while his guests drank plonk would have been in perfect sync with the cynicism a waiter on a typical floor staff would manifest by the early 1970s. Oh, you could still see the old pattern on the tapestry of classical French cookery at the Deerpath. The names were still there—Veal Oscar, Tournedos Rossini, Sole Bercy—and there was an occasional rivalry that flared up between the cooks—the French vs. the Italians vs. the Asians, with young Americans on the very bottom.

The restaurant life just killed me, twice a day, every day—first lunch then dinner. I knew that I had to get out before my ability to be the only thing I ever considered worthy of being died.

But the family business, selling new and used cars, was even more out of the question for me. I had made that decision at age nine when my father was shot and pistol-whipped and my then twenty-one-year-old brother was nearly murdered in an attempt to save him. The shooter was a guy from whom Dad had recently repossessed a car. The guy had stopped paying. Dad was not someone to do that to. It was a horrible summer, visiting my brother in the hospital twice a week with my grandparents and watching the gash in my father's skull slowly heal. Then and there I took myself off the list of the next generation Van Aken to be a car dealer.

But if I wasn't going to sell cars (like Dad) or work in restaurants (like Mom), where would my path lead me in this life? I decided to escape to someplace where it was going to be sunny and fun again. I could go back to Key West, but we'd only been gone a short time and there were other places to wander, other mountains to climb!

So I decided to go out to Colorado. "Go west, young man!" My old friend Joel was living in Greeley, wherever that was.

Toké's Tokyo Beef and Mushroom Bites

Though he has long since passed into heaven, Toké remains an inspiration to me. He had a poet's soul when it came to creating cuisine but a soldier's fearlessness as a cook. He would slash off a section of beef tenderloin, rub it with canola oil–slicked fingers, aggressively season it, and toss it right onto the French flat top. It would sear in nanoseconds on that thing. Then he'd make a zesty marinade featuring a pantheon of Asian ingredients I had scant knowledge of in those early days. Tasting his food made me want to know all I could.

For the marinade:

½ cup loosely packed cilantro leaves
1½ to 2 tablespoons chopped serrano chilies, stemmed, seeded, and minced
4 cloves minced garlic
4 tablespoons light brown sugar
3 tablespoons fish sauce
1 tablespoon soy sauce
1 tablespoon dark roasted sesame oil
1 tablespoon mirin
1 tablespoon minced ginger, packed
8 scallions, white part only, trimmed and sliced
½ teaspoon cracked black pepper

In a bowl, place all the ingredients and whisk well to combine. Set aside.

For the beef:

12 ounces filet mignon, sliced into wafer cuts, about ½-inch thick
kosher salt and cracked black pepper, to taste
canola oil, as needed

Season the steaks with salt and pepper.

Heat a large sauté pan over medium-high heat. (It should be consistently hot.) Increase the heat to high and add enough of the oil to liberally coat the bottom of the pan. Sear the beef evenly on each side *for no more than 30 seconds.* Remove the steaks from the pan immediately and place on a plate to cool. When the beef is completely cool, trim any uneven edges and set aside. (Save the trimmed-off bits for a snack or to add to a salad.)

Strain the marinade into a bowl, reserving the liquid. Pack the remaining solids around the cooled beef squares and set aside.

For the mushrooms:

1 ounce shiitake mushroom caps (*note*: caps only)
canola oil, enough for sautéing
salt and pepper, to taste
squeeze of fresh lime

Slice the mushroom caps into quarters, add to the marinade liquid, and soak for about 20 minutes. Stir once. Lift the mushrooms out of the liquid and reserve in a separate bowl.

Heat a nonstick pan and add the canola oil. Add the mushrooms and sauté until they are just soft. Remove the mushrooms to a plate and allow them to cool. Season with salt and pepper.

In another saucepan, add the reserved marinade liquid and reduce over medium heat until the marinade is syrupy and about 2 liquid ounces remain. Remove from the heat and allow it to cool.

To serve, arrange the beef on a platter. Drizzle the reduced sauce over and around the meat. Add the mushroom caps. Serve with a squeeze of fresh lime, as Toké instructed me to do. That last zing of acidity is truly key.

Makes 4 servings as an appetizer

CHAPTER 6

The Holiday Inn

Greeley, 1974

JANET AND I DECIDED TO SPLIT UP. Maybe the fear of commitment was becoming too real for me? I don't know. When the Stones' song "Angie" came on the car radio one day and I told her it sounded like us she wrote me off as a lost cause. So after a short time hanging out with Butchie (who kind of suggested I was fucking up) and a few of the other Hainesville Gang (who probably thought that now Janet was fair game for them) I stuck out my thumb and left for Greeley, Colorado, and a reunion with my old friend Joel. He was going to school there and there is no place better for shaking off the commitment blues like a college campus.

Joel and I had known each other since high school where we both were jocks *and* heads, a very narrowly populated category. We got to know each other really well when we spent our sophomore year in college together attending (not much) the University of Hawaii in Honolulu. You couldn't know a sweeter guy than Joel, and he took me right into his home in Greeley where I crashed on the couch. But Joel's girlfriend and I didn't get along. I was having a tough time sleeping and she seemed to want to join me on that couch, but it would have ruined my friendship with Joel. I went through my little bit of money and when it came time to go to my cousin Hank's wedding back in Illinois I hitched home. Short trip, but I got to know Greeley a little. I had hair down to my ass and a beard that predated ZZ Top. If I were employable anyone would have been hard pressed to figure out at what.

One of the newer Hainesville brothers, an artistically minded guy named Paul, and I hatched a plan to hitchhike to Alaska and join three other Hainesville brothers who had gone north in 1973. Paul was a nice change to hang around with. His paintings were startling and large. His characters looked like something out of the imagination of Nikos Kazantzakis. He was a former wrestler in high school but, like many of us, was flowering out in the reaction to the times. Paul had a fully grown Alaskan malamute named Pahuska (which meant "longhair," the Indian name for Buffalo Bill Cody). We hitchhiked with this massive creature, three longhairs looking for a way west. I'll be damned if rides didn't come more quickly with Pahuska.

We stopped in Greeley to see Joel and hang for a few days. His girlfriend had moved on so no hassles there. But I was getting a little tired of having Pahuska in the backseat with me stepping on my legs, my lap, and especially my balls as the young and muscular animal traversed the car's narrow quarters seeking a new view of the passing countryside. I studied the Rand McNally map and Alaska looked further away than Mars. Greeley was starting to look good.

One morning we went to Sambo's Pancake House. During those years, Sambo's and IHOP were my go-to places for filling up the massive void in my stomach and doing it as cheaply as possible. A stack of three steaming buckwheat pancakes with a full complement of syrup and butter could do the trick for next to no money. Add an endless cup o' coffee and it was a better world. It was with that sated feeling I walked out the door of Sambo's with Pahuska tied up and waiting in the shade of the restaurant's awning.

Paul was unleashing the dog from outside the pancake emporium when a big white Caddy stopped and a burly gent motioned me over. I thought, seeing our backpacks, he was going to offer us a ride. A Caddy is a good way to see America, but I couldn't imagine he would want Pahuska's claws gouging his fine white leather seats. And I was right. He was the owner of a concrete business and what he actually wanted was some young, strong, and probably cheap labor. When he offered ten bucks an hour and free room and board I was in! Paul was not. We both knew what was coming. The distance that remained to get to Alaska was nearly incomprehensible, especially given our mode of travel. Paul and I said adios and the next morning I found out that the Caddy owner's concrete business was not in, or even near, Greeley. I was in the passenger seat of a very heavy concrete truck going very slowly to a town in Kansas, a part of the country I'd never been through with a fifty-year-old man I didn't know.

Normally the drive from Greeley to our destination would take about seven hours. But when Will (the driver) picked me up at the Sambo's parking lot in his diesel truck and headed south, I realized I was in for a much longer ride. The diesel fumes made me nauseous and each acceleration, even a slight one, required a gear change, which in turn made the lumbering truck lurch drunkenly. We then went nearly due east on U.S. 70 until we hit western Kansas, then dropped south again, stopping our journey a short hop away from Dodge City. It was nearly eight o'clock at night.

Will turned out to be a pretty cool guy who once wanted nothing more than to be a great rock-and-roll drummer; in fact, he claimed to be known throughout Colorado for his ability to play the drum solo from the top radio hit of all time, "Wipeout," faster and better than anybody else. But his dreams of rock-and-roll glory fell way to mortgages and a failed marriage or two.

When we got to Garden City, Kansas, Will pulled the rig into a Holiday Inn parking lot. This is where I'd be staying during the job. The actual worksite was in Holcomb, which had no hotel. When I got settled into my new abode I went down to the pay phone and called Hainesville House. By the next morning, brothers G-Baby and Cary, the crazy redheaded Texan, were on their way out to join me in Kansas.

Holcomb was famous for one thing: the Clutter family murders made famous by Truman Capote's book, *In Cold Blood.* It was eerie to pass through the tiny town and imagine the magnitude of the lurid crime committed there. Truman Capote (whom I would cook for and watch stroll around Key West a few years later) must have been about as out of place a bird as ever flew into the Kansas sky. We drove over to the outskirts of town where we learned the brute strength required for spraying concrete, my newest rung up the ladder of success.

During the next weeks G, Cary, and I got to know the Mexican laborers with whom we shared the job. We were lower on the hierarchy than they were. They already knew how to lay, accurately measure, create the forms, and spread the concrete. We didn't so we had the chore of managing what looked like fire hoses but actually jetted wet concrete instead of water.

We were building pit silos, which are supercheap conveyances for cattle feed. The concrete came out of the back of the concrete truck, but instead of being dumped into wheelbarrows and shoveled into forms, it was siphoned into a machine to which hoses were also attached. We would each aim a hose at a "feeder" fitted with metal mesh that captured the wet concrete and formed the grain bins. The feeder would cough and splat and "choke" on stones or other crap caught in the slurry and then we'd have to wrench the hose free and try to dislodge the impediment before the concrete hardened up and wasted the hose. Lifting those hoses, aiming them fully loaded thirty to fifty feet in the air, was heavy work to be sure, but digging the hoses free was a real ballbuster.

The work was crushingly hot and so dusty my teeth would cake over and my nose would get as jammed as one of those infernal hoses. One of the few moments of relief, which provided an almost hallucinatory happiness amid the blinding blue of the western Kansas sky, the dull ache of our sledgehammer-shaken limbs, and the desperate hunger of grunt-labor appetites, were the chorizo-and-scrambled-egg-filled tortilla sandwiches the Mexican workers so graciously shared with us. I believe that it is the communal sharing of food in this very rustic way that laid the foundation for me to not only become a chef but to become one who was inspired by the down-to-earth foods of Latino and Caribbean people, and one without a sense that European food is inherently better. Hell, sex wasn't any better than these tortillas! Not after six hours of wrangling concrete in the western Kansas outback.

Despite the good times we had at the local karaoke bar drinking away our wages and watching Cary become a local hit covering the tunes of Three Dog Night, we could only handle living in a hotel room for so long. We ditched the job, left a marginal paycheck behind, and headed home to Hainesville.

I found out that Janet was still living with her folks. I surprised her down in the basement where she was doing laundry. We kissed and knew that we were terribly in love and wouldn't be apart again.

I bought a black Volkswagen Beetle from my mom's boyfriend for $150 and drove out to Greeley with Janet. She had wanted to go to Colorado and "see some mountains," so we did. It was April and we headed west in the little car with our belongings in the backseat. The starter was messed up and whenever we had to stop for the night or for a meal we had to push start it and I'd jump in and pop the clutch. But we made it. This time in Greeley we had our own bedroom.

I needed to find work and, in short order, I was "short order" again. Once again I'd be tying on the apron! I was hired as the breakfast cook for the Holiday Inn in Greeley. Janet got a job as a checkout girl in a supermarket. We couldn't use the VW, because until I got the starter fixed it took two of us to start it, so Janet hitchhiked to her job and I rode a bicycle to mine. We managed to get a basement apartment right off the UNC campus. Our Hainesville buddy Butch got the Colorado itch too and came to live with us. I was happy to have the twelve-string-acoustic-guitar-strumming hillbilly from "West-by-God Virginia."

Butch was the salt of the earth. Every day he hitchhiked with Janet so she wouldn't be doing that by herself. Janet would say it was not necessary and that she could handle herself if there was any foolishness. Butch would counter with, "'If' is the biggest word in the whole dang dictionary. If! If! If! Why, if a frog had pockets he'd keep a knife in 'em to keep the snakes off his back." This was usually followed by a loud, full strum on the twelve-string as if to say, "Court's closed." And then he'd hitch back home and repeat the kindness when her shift at the grocery store was over. Janet loved Butch and always was happier when there were more mouths to feed, so Butch had a home, too.

Greeley is a pretty town. They say the sun shines on average of three hundred days a year. I think it might. Another "natural wonder" of Greeley is the smell, the only thing that kept us from staying there for a long time. Greeley is located very near the huge cattle farms of Colorado, and you could almost set your watch by what time of day or night it was based on when the cows would shit. Where was John Cameron Swayze? The town was as awash in the smell of dung.

But being a breakfast cook means that the first smell you are aware of each day is of your brain. It's on fire from the moment the fucking alarm clock rings you out of your warm bed and you look out at the black night sky and know that you are already fucking late! You were late before you went to bed. You were late before you moved to Greeley. You were late before you were born. And you never, never, never were going to get your prep done before the hordes would descend on you and the tickets for breakfast would be flying out of the waitresses' order pads like the birds attacking Tippi Hedren.

When you punch the time clock you are late and you hate, hate, *hate* anything or anyone standing in the way of you getting the exhaust fan on, your ovens fired up, the eggs for the omelets cracked, the first sheet pans of bacon cooked, the pancake batter made. There is a stereotype about cooks being prickly; it is not wholly untrue, yet it is exaggerated. But if you cross a breakfast cook before he or she is less than midway through the morning shift, you might as well grab a pit bull by the balls.

Because once you do get through the last order of eggs over, or a Western, you crack that first beer, drain it and, *voila,* your attitude is more than on the mend, hell, you can even joke around, maybe even flirt with that waitress who fucked up your whole ticket board earlier with some asshole order for a salad, for fuck's sake, at breakfast!

Some of the waitresses, still in their thirties, who (though being eight to twelve years older than the likes of me) could mind-fuck you with their serious, no-bullshit work attitude during the rush, then pour on the charm, stick a hip out or cross their legs with their stockings sliding just so, and make you wonder. Are you flirting with me, Mrs. Robinson?

But then it was back to reality, as we had to get the line set for lunch.

Around that time every day the chef would come in. Chef Fred Boomer was, after Toké and Sammy, the next in line as one of my culinary mentors. He stood about five and a half feet tall, unless you counted his hair—a fabulous Fabian coiffure that replaced his former navy-issue crew cut and added three inches. It was golden, perfect, and styled high atop his pale white face. He wore creased blue jeans and shiny black cowboy boots. From a distance he looked much younger due to his trim physique. But his face was lined and leathered up close. His eyes were as blue as some colors you might find in an orchid, but they looked crushed and broken as if hit by a whiskey bottle, which they were almost every night.

Fred was, poor soul, another one of my great teachers and also another one of the great chef drunks who missed the era of "celebrity" chefs. Cooking was still looked at as a dead-end job, the result of a destructive and pitiable life, not even a profession back then. But Fred wasn't alone; hell, he wasn't really a minority in that department.

When he walked in the back door of the Holiday Inn each day, no one had to tell you he'd arrived. A curl of cigarette smoke presaged any visual sighting. He pulled off his sheepskin coat and hung it over the back of his chair. He didn't have an office, just a table that stood against the wall by the deliveries door. He didn't have to look, either. He would just cock his head, like he was hunting in some deep woods. If there was the right "sound" to his kitchen he knew he didn't need to run over and put out any "fires" by helping me cook for some unexpected rush of customers. He could start to make his specials in the back.

I hated it when he had to help me. It meant that I'd failed to do my job, but worse, his egg yolks broke over and over again. He got the shaking under control about an hour after he got in, but not at first. And the waitresses got mad at me when they saw Fred's ruined, running yolks. He seemed to not even see them. He flew into the fray blindly. They couldn't say a word to him. He was the chef, after all! But they knew their tips would shrink if they carried these fractured meals to the floor. I would try and shore up a "bleeding" yolk with a wedge of American fries but usually to no avail.

When it was over he went about making the one thing that Fred Boomer may have still liked about the world: soup. It was even written on the menu: Fred Boomer's Soups. It was the only fame he ever knew; but you'd see him put his heart and soul into making his soups and you knew it was a recognition he didn't need. It was probably a bone the management threw out to him in lieu of actual money or something as cherry as an office for the man.

When you learn to cook in the military, Fred explained, you also learn order and precision. You also learn to cook for thousands, which reinforces the order and precision. He babied those soups in a directly inverse relationship he had with eggs. He was so careful, so meticulous, it seemed a form of religion, like an ornate Shinto ritual with the vegetables being cut just so, the potatoes gleaming white, the tomatoes at the peak of ripeness, and the stocks, Lord a-mercy, how he babied those stocks! Like he was nursing a child back from the brink. I watched him from afar, agog, amazed that this shit-kicking ex-navy Jack Daniel's–swilling cowpoke cared so much about something so motherly as soups.

One night he crashed his truck on the way home from the Dew Drop Inn, the Greeley bar he holed up in every night after the dinner rush was over. He got two black eyes and broke both arms. They were in matching casts. He couldn't dress himself. He couldn't comb that magnificent hair. He couldn't drive. Even smoking took the help of another person now. But most importantly, he couldn't cook.

So he turned to me. The Fred Boomer soups were *not* coming off the menu. If Fred allowed that, it might mean the management had something to hold over him. He worried that they might love to cut his salary out of the mix and find somebody to do his job more cheaply.

"It happens all the time in this fucking screw business, Norm!" he'd warn. "They always eighty-six a chef when they feel a sous chef can take over!" He knew it wouldn't be me. He knew that I was already thinking of my next place to live. So he trusted that eventuality and taught me to make his soups. I just had to make them until he could get the damned casts off his arms. I worked while he sat on the edge of his small desk commanding me to follow his instructions and to keep his cigarettes lit and making regular trips to his lips.

While he healed, I learned to make his soups and I'm sure I'm the first person, and maybe the only person, he ever taught. His soups reflected his world travels with the navy. It was something quite astonishing to see soups like his in this little Western town. He taught me the curried Mulligatawny, classic lobster bisque, and the simple perfection of a proper chicken noodle. A navy tour through Greece brought on the exotica of an avgolemono with its bright lemony notes and satisfying chicken-stock backbone, brick-red tomato soup with basil he grew on a windowsill, gooey and soul-warming French onion, a brilliant and authentic borscht, and a smoky split pea loaded with falling-off-the-bone country ham that I would give ten bucks to have a bowl of right now. I asked him every dumb question anyone has ever asked trying to unravel the mysteries of Fred's soups.

"Why do I have to cut the vegetables so evenly if people are gonna crush them in their teeth?"

"Why do I have to caramelize the onions so slowly when I make the French onion?"

"Why do I have to pick through the split peas and look for little stones when there never was even *one* complaint about fucking stones?" I, of course, never said "fucking" in front of the chef, not in reference to one of his soups at least. He might have cracked my head with one of the casts.

The only answer my questions ever received was a withering look of such palpable disgust I came to hate my stupidity and wondered if I'd ever overcome it. After two months we had run through Fred's repertoire and I had learned more about soup and, by extension, stocks (information that would one day lead to a mastery of sauces) at the side of this broken-armed ex-sailor in a town that smelled like the ass end of a barnyard. It was good.

Winter began to slide down the mountaintops and into the once sunny valley town. Each morning before the sun rose Janet got up, made me a pot of black-as-the-ace-of-spades espresso, and tied my long hair back into a braid that I'd finish with bobby pins when I got into work to shove under my hated chef's hat. The bicycle ride was an increasingly frigid drag and now that Fred's arms had healed I no longer was learning shit, just flipping eggs and going home to watch *Star Trek* reruns with Wade (who'd now joined me in the kitchen at the Holiday Inn) and Butchie, on the sagging yard-sale-purchased couch at the end of a working day.

We hung an "Engine for sale" sign in the little Laundromat where we did our clothes. A farmer came by and saw the crippled black Volkswagen. He offered us $200 for the engine. That was $50 more than we paid for the car. Jackpot! Now we had enough money to go back to Illinois and try something else. Butchie's car still worked, so the four of us piled in and headed east. Things got hairy when we were pulled over in Lincoln, Nebraska. There were many empty beer bottles on the floor of the backseat, but somehow Wade bullshitted his way through and the cop let us go. Wade could charm the pants off anybody. Good thing the cop didn't search the glove box. Butch had a fat lid of Colombian weed and fifty white cross tucked away in there behind some eight-track tapes. He picked up the twelve-string and sang in his warble:

There's a river in my brain
That sometimes flows the way it shouldn't,
And though I've tried to dam it
When the river roared I couldn't.
As of late, I've found a way
To sail inside your heart,
I've learned to ride the river flowing
But I have to learn the crossing part.

U.S.N. Mulligatawny Soup

Many Americans were introduced to this Indian soup (which means "pepper water" in Hindustani) while watching the Soup Nazi on *Seinfeld*. The man who introduced me to it was Fred Boomer, under whom I labored at the Holiday Inn, and who picked up an amazing array of soups during his travels with the U.S. Navy. I loved the spices and how they could disguise the infamous manure scent of Greeley, Colorado (look it up, if you don't believe me), if only for the period of time it took to enjoy a bowl.

For the soup:

4	ounces unsalted butter
6	ounces uncooked bacon, diced
½	sweet onion, thinly sliced
1	Scotch Bonnet chile, stemmed, seeded, and minced
2	cloves garlic, sliced thinly
3	tablespoons minced fresh ginger
¼	cup Madras curry powder
1	cup unsweetened apple juice
½	cup celery, diced
½	cup carrot, diced
½	cup fennel, diced
2	Granny Smith apples, peeled, cored, and diced
2	tomatoes, peeled, seeded, and diced
¼	cup fresh lemon juice, strained
1	cup uncooked converted rice
	kosher salt and cracked black pepper, to taste
1	quart chicken stock, warm
1	(14-ounce) can coconut milk
2	cups heavy cream
2	cups cooked chicken, shredded or chopped into bite-sized pieces

In a large pot, place the butter with the bacon and gently cook until the bacon is just cooked through but still soft. Add the onion and continue cooking until golden brown at the edges. Add the chile, garlic, and ginger; stir well. Add the curry and continue cooking, stirring constantly (take your eyes off it at your peril!), until the mixture is quite fragrant. Add the apple juice and continue cooking until the liquid is reduced by about half.

Add the celery, carrots, fennel, apples, tomatoes, and lemon juice and continue cooking for another 5 minutes. Add the rice and season with salt and pepper. Add the chicken stock and increase the heat, bringing the stock to a simmer. Stir one more time. Reduce the heat to low, cover, and allow it to cook for about 15 minutes. Check the rice and when it is fairly soft, add the coconut milk and heavy cream. Simmer for another 5 minutes. Add the chicken, stir, and season to taste. Reduce the heat to low to keep the soup warm.

For the eggplant:

10 (¼-inch-thick) slices eggplant, skin on, salted, and weighted for 30 minutes on absorbent toweling
blended oil, for cooking

Thoroughly rinse the salt from the eggplant and pat dry. In a preheated skillet, add the oil and cook the eggplant in batches until they are nicely golden on each side. Reserve as you cook. When all the eggplant is cooked, cut each slice into small squares and add to the soup.

For the garnish:

toasted unsalted almond slices, as desired
toasted unsweetened coconut flakes, as desired

Makes 3 quarts

Ruth and Harold Van Aken on their wedding night in 1950

With my sister Jane on the steps of our family home in Illinois

With my childhood best friend, Wade Harris

Janet Amsler's high school photo

The drive-away car in the parking lot of the Fireside. Wade's standing on the right.

With Janet at a Key West party

Back in the red truck, leaving Key West again

Irish angel Danny McHugh

Port of Call chef/owner Philip Mascia

Working the hot line at the Port of Call

With baby Justin on Olivia Street

Janet and baby Justin

Shaking hands with Tennessee Williams backstage after our performance of *A Streetcar Named Desire*

With Gordon Sinclair

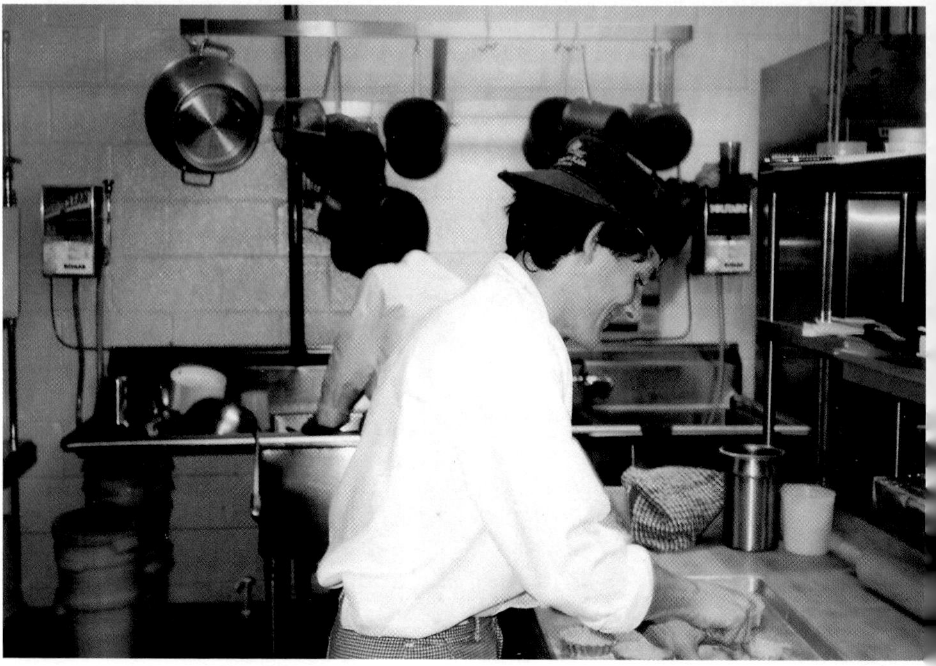

Charlie Trotter prepping at Sinclair's American Grill

From left: Don Yamuchi, Charlie Trotter, Suzy Crofton, Gordon Sinclair, me, Celeste Zeccola and Carrie Nahabedian

CHAPTER 7

The Gale Street Inn

Diamond Lake, 1975

WHEN WE GOT BACK FROM COLORADO the big news going around our little town of fifteen thousand was of the new restaurant being built on the opposite shore of the lake where we lived with Mama and Nana.

Living on Diamond Lake was such a lucky thing for me growing up. I had a childhood filled with days of swimming, climbing trees, playing in the fields and forests around our home with the Harris brothers, my sisters Jane and Bet, and other neighborhood kids. Diamond Lake lapped my mother's lawn and we had French windows that we could open up in warm weather and luxuriate in the gentle breezes coming off the lake. Even in winter it was a kind of heaven. We only had to slide down the snowy hill behind our little home and we'd be ice-skating or ice-fishing in no time. My older brother Buddy would drag me around the lake behind his motorcycle on a sled or we'd go tobogganing behind the Dutch Mill Tavern.

When I was sixteen I got a job across the lake at Ed's Beach where I was a lifeguard there one summer. We sometimes swam across the lake for Cokes, burgers, and candy bars at Ed's and then swam back. You just had to watch out for the motorboats and water-skiers. So while the big new restaurant was being built, memories of earlier times caused me to wax nostalgic and think that cooking there might be my destiny, a Diamond Laker by birth.

It was a handsome building with huge plate-glass windows looking out on the water. There was a pier and an area outdoors for a little beer garden. The specialty of the house was going to be barbequed ribs. Janet and I both loved ribs because her dad, Irv (who had come to be my pal—the threat with the shotgun long in the past), made the best ribs I'd ever had. Janet and I applied for work there just before the Gale Street Inn opened. The family that ran it was Greek out of Chicago. I was too green to know what that might mean but over time I came to find out that the owner was a hard-nosed, up from the streets, tough son-of-a-bitch named George Cholis. Even his son, Peter, who worked with us, was not spared Big George's fury if he thought we were not working fast enough or if we wasted food in any way. But that was later. In the early days of opening a restaurant there is a kind of glow. While there is madness there is also a very resonant esprit de corps that seems to take place in restaurants from humble greasy spoons to French five-star seekers. Here we were in the solid middle and all having a good time unwrapping the new equipment, plates, and glassware, setting up the bar, hosing down the still-new floor mats, testing the recipes, and doing food tastings for the staff.

I was hanging out at Janet's family home a lot. Her seven brothers and sisters shared a small house across the lake from where I grew up. She was a middle child, so she mothered the babies and was the little sis to the older siblings. Her sister Pam was one year older and a very beautiful girl, too. She was more bookish than Janet, and shy.

The grand opening of the Gale Street Inn brought hundreds of folks from as far away as Chicago, where the family's original restaurant was located. The mood was contagious and I took to the job with a fervor I hadn't known before. Janet got a job as a waitress and looked so cute in her sailor motif uniform, which was meant to go with the nautical theme of the place.

I'd never worked in a new kitchen; this was now my fifth restaurant and at age twenty-four I really liked the feel of it: brand new stoves, walk-in refrigerators, and drawer-style reach-ins for food storage close at hand so we didn't have to move more than a few inches to get at stuff.

There were four of us on the hot line. A good load of the work was made easier because diners at the Gale Street were directed to the new salad bar, a fake boat stocked with big bowls of various lettuces as well as (of course) cottage cheese, pickled peppers, cooked garbanzos, the all-important bacon bits, cucumbers, bell peppers, tomatoes, croutons, six different kinds of salad dressing, radishes, beets, raw onion, chopped eggs, carrot curls, even raisins and sunflower seeds. No one in Diamond Lake had ever seen such a thing, and it was included in the price of a meal! This new innovation was prepped during the day; the waitresses took out the bowls, crocks, tongs, spoons, and forks and were taught how to replenish it. Each night we served more and more guests as the good people of Diamond Lake, Mundelein, and all of Lake County fell in love with the place. It was exciting to be a part of such a hit! The owners were unable to contain their joy.

The restaurant business was a cash business back then. The only person Big George trusted with the money was his "cousin," Bob. Though not really related, Bob had worked with George for over twenty-five years. He was George's only confidant and he also counted the money. If the little office door by the kitchen was closed, you knew to stay away and did not dare open that door. On one occasion the head cook, Jerry, asked me to get the keys to open the delivery gates so a truck could haul away the french fry grease. Bob had to let me into the office to hand me the keys, and when I entered it reminded me of a "count room" in a Vegas casino (the way they're shown in the movies, anyway). Twenty grand in bills lying on a desk is quite a sight. I nearly swooned. I went back and told Jerry.

He said, "Bob let you in during the count? Jesus, he must be slipping. George would wring his neck. I've worked for these stingy bastards for ten years coming up and they have never let me in on that scene. Oh, I know what this place hauls in. It's plenty. One of these days ol' Jer-Bear is gonna open up his *own* rib joint! Americans love ribs, crazy for 'em and I have the Gale Street recipes."

As a cook, as a chef, sometimes about all you have, the only thing you walk out the door with, is what you can stuff into your head. The money dries up as soon as it's made: rent, mortgage, food, gas, insurance, auto, vices, women, vices, women. It goes. There is no parachute. If you quit or you're canned, you go with what you've learned and then hustle to find another gig. Savings? From where? From what? Jerry was living proof. Most every chef I ever cooked with was a guy who barely had the coat on his back and a shitty car to get back and forth. They drank. Lord, did they drink. And I was getting a taste of that with my older pal Jerry in the trenches of the Gale Street Inn in the summer of 1975.

Jerry got the waitresses to start bringing me vodka tonics—like his. I switched to gin, "G and T, please," as I couldn't stand the aftertaste of the vodka. We had our coffee cups and every hour or two we'd shove them forward to where the gals picked up the dinners and they'd slide 'em back. By the end of the night we'd be sliding a little, too. But we were having fun. Jerry was teaching me how to be a broiler man while I painted buckets and buckets of baby back ribs night after night.

The Gale Street purchased their desserts ready-made from someplace. The waitresses had the job of cutting the cakes and pies and scooping out the ice creams. Simple.

I started on hot apps like baked onion soup, pizza bread, and coconut shrimp. Another guy who they brought in from Chicago named Ralphie worked the rib grill. Jerry was the broiler man. Although he wasn't called the "chef" he had the most complex job of tending the steaks and chops broiler. In a place like this, and in the multitudes of restaurants around this time, the broiler man was the top dog. In a French place it was the sauté guy, but in a steak, chop, and rib place, this is where the real fire was.

I liked Jerry. He was a sweet-tempered, balding-just-a-little-on-top white guy also brought in from the city. He was mellow and when the tickets started flying in he'd just hum along to himself arranging the steaks in a system that let him know where he had his "rares," his "misters" (medium-rares), "mediums," and "well-dones." He slid the big broiler back and forth on its coaster and adjusted the grate like a gearshift on a Shelby GT Ford Mustang, going up and down to get more char or to slow things down if need be. That wasn't often because as summer advanced and the word got around we went from three hundred covers on a Saturday night to four hundred. Ralphie had to get back to Chicago, and that's when Jerry suggested to management "Norman is ready to be our rib guy."

It meant a fifty-cent-an-hour raise and working next to Jerry. Janet was making good money out on the floor. She was a great waitress and could move at light speed. The Gale Street dinner patrons were neither big drinkers nor big spenders. Wine was not even a consideration in terms of sales volume, but many nights she was going home with what it would take me three nights to make. She made that money waiting on a huge number of customers.

Jerry was no matinee idol; sort of a cross between Fredo Corleone (from *The Godfather*) and George Jones, but he had a very sweet charm. He was married but that didn't keep some of the waitresses from flirting with "Jer." He was the main man in the kitchen and his power was as potent as musk oil. But while he enjoyed the attention he never fucked around. I could see his cheeks redden when a waitress named Jill would set his drink down and give him a little glimpse at her ample cleavage. But it went nowhere. He'd pack up a bag of ribs or chicken, some leftover rolls each night, load up his muffler-dragging convertible, and head home to the wife, whoever she was.

The rib broiler was its own world. You didn't nor could you have cooked anything else on those two sliding racks of steel. A slab of ribs is roughly a foot and half long if it has been precooked in the oven. That's the way the Gale Street did their ribs in such volume. They were, essentially, precooked. That is a sin by most true aficionados of barbeque cookery. Every single expert will tell you to cook them "low and slow" over hard charcoal from start to finish. But they were not cooking for Big George. He wanted numbers! The customers wanted the soft falling-off-the-bone and heavily sweetly sauced version and they wanted them badly. The to-go orders became a whole new revenue stream once we opened up that opportunity to our guests.

Now the reason I mention the size of the ribs is that at one and a half feet long and about four to five inches wide, you can fill up that broiler fast. With three hundred customers, with almost half ordering ribs, you had to be flying to keep up with the demand! But we kept getting busier. The place in Chicago made a bunch of money and that's how they were able to afford building this one. But the number of guests in Chicago would top out at about two hundred. This place was clocking toward four hundred now and with the private party room downstairs just starting to kick in there was a feverish lust growing in Big George's stony Greek eyes.

At the end of each night I had the grimy job of taking the entire rib broiler apart. It was astonishing to see how much gunk, carbon, barbeque goo, shit, and funk could accumulate on a broiler in a single day. I used a flat-bladed shovel and shaved a reddish-black mass into a steel garbage can. It was ten times the mess of cleaning the barbeque at the Midget back in

Key West. But at least I wasn't alone and it wasn't six o'clock in the morning. When we were done I'd go outside by the lake and walk into it in my chef pants and, depending if Janet was done waiting on tables yet, take a swim in Diamond Lake.

When she finished, we piled in our car and most of the time she had to drive home. I was catching up with the older cooks I'd been learning from. I was learning to drink like a chef.

With school out for the summer the families were bringing their kids, lots of them. In that area there was a phenomenon of really big families. The town of Mundelein was at one point the "fastest growing community" in America according to the U.S. Census. I don't know how that is possible because the population never reached twenty thousand, but maybe it was a household average. Mundelein was a strongly Catholic enclave and the families did their best to bring more little Catholics into the world. Janet came from a family with eight kids and there were families with ten, twelve, even sixteen kids—the Kick family had twenty-two! My sister Jane married a Jaroch boy and they had thirteen. There were a lot of kids. And George Cholis discovered another thing to love about his new location in Diamond Lake: kids loved ribs, too.

By early August we had now eclipsed the seemingly impossible number of five hundred guests on a Saturday night. George and Bob bought new cars. I painted ribs and Jerry flipped more and more steaks and chops. The bartenders were making a fortune and so were the waitresses. I was getting slaphappy, painting the open-pit barbeque sauces on that stacked and choking grill packed with more and more pig meat. We served six hundred people the third week in August and had seven hundred on the books with the party room fully booked for the last weekend of summer.

The whole restaurant was intent on doing it. "C'mon seven hundred! Let's do it!" When school started back up the next week we all knew this would be the last shot at doing a number like that. Jerry arranged for his wife to come in for dinner that night with her sister. Wow. The mythical wife was going to finally drop in! This was Jerry's big night. No one in Gale Street history had worked the broiler on a night doing a bigger number. We warmed up like athletes. We stretched and did a few deep breaths and leg lunges and yelled a few "Yahs!" at each other! Kind of joking but kind of meaning it, too—if this was our ball game let's win it!

Janet and all the waitresses were scheduled in. In fact, every employee that worked at the Gale Street was on the schedule that night. It was our battalion and as the first guest arrived we sent the food flying out of that kitchen. Jerry's wife and sister were asked to come in early so that they would be out of the way when the really heavy prime-time period of eight o'clock was upon us. After dinner she was escorted into the kitchen. Jerry's wife had huge red hair, bright lipstick, faux pearls, and a blue dress and she must have weighed 250 pounds! My eyes bugged out of my head. Her sister was even bigger. They were introduced to us by Jerry. The sister pointed directly at me and said, "I'll have him for dessert! He's gorgeous!!!"

I drained my coffee cup cocktail, not knowing what to say to Jerry. The sisters went back out into the dining room and Jerry turned to me, understanding my perplexed face, and said, "Beautiful, isn't she? She's big, I know it, man. I just like my women that way. There's a whole lot of butter in my bed, little brother, that's all I can tell you." I motioned for another drink and got it.

The night now kicked into an unusually early vicious gear I hadn't experienced before. It was only seven o'clock and we'd neared two hundred guests. I was hurling the ribs on and painting them as fast as I could. I had to keep refilling my barbeque sauce bucket. I had nowhere to put more ribs. I painted more furiously. Jerry hummed and sweated, proud to be there with his woman seeing him center stage!

The August heat was pressing in through the screen doors. The smell of barbeque was beginning to argue with the gin. The eight o'clock rush was on us now and we could actually hear the roar of guests in the dining room. The waitresses were nearly running in and out of the kitchen, some of them hurriedly restocking the salad boat. Even Bob was toting lettuce at one point. Big George, dressed in a light blue blazer, white pants, white belt, and white loafers, handed out menus.

I painted and flipped ribs, tossing them on my cutting board and slashing them into the full- or half-rack orders, piling them on a mound of fries and setting them under the heat lamps.

"Four hundred!" a hostess screamed as she ran into the kitchen to find a waitress.

"Five hundred!" another hostess now hollered. It seemed like less than a moment later. But time was not real. It was all distorted, from the pace, the heat, and the work and, of course, the alcohol.

Usually one waitress was assigned to get Jerry and me our drinks on any given night. But in the chaos and pregame there were two if not three of them who lined up the beverages.

"Half a league, half a league, half a league onward," Jerry was laughing as he quoted the Tennyson battle poem.

Ten o'clock came and with it came our six hundredth guest. "More sauce! More ribs from the back!" I screamed out to a dishwasher who knew what to do. There was so much meat on Jerry's broiler it didn't seem possible he could keep it straight. But he had his wooden markers with little cows on them and he stacked the steaks and chops up like fucking cordwood. All I had to do was paint precooked ribs, turn them, and not burn them and I was nearly drowning.

That paintbrush with barbeque sauce was glued to my hand now. My shirt, pants, apron, and sneakers were splattered with the red elixir of life these folks could not seem to get their fill of. What in the world was I doing here? I couldn't stop myself. I looked over at Jerry squinting into the roiling maw of his broiler. I flipped the bowl of barbeque sauce on my head to look like a helmet and saluted him. Sauce ran through my hair and over my face. Jerry's eyes bugged out.

"What the fuck are you doing, man?" he yelled. "We are about to break seven hundred!"

But I was gone. Grinning and blasted, I walked directly out into the dining room. They say I was yelling, "You really like this fucking barbeque shit, don't you, people?"

George was at the end of the bar and he just looked at the bartenders. In his day he'd seen it all and in less than twenty seconds I was out the back door, down by the docks, and tossed into the lake I was born on the other side of. I didn't quite make the 700 Club.

Gale Street–Style Slaw

The grand opening of the Gale Street brought customers from as far away as Chicago where the family's original restaurant was located. The mood was contagious and I took to the job with a fervor I hadn't known before. There was a salad bar—or, more accurately, a salad boat—and, of course, there was cole slaw. But it lacked the snap and spice my palate craves. (You can always tone down the vinegar and cayenne, if you like.) This recipe falls right between a creamy and a drier kind of slaw. To make it creamier, add the mayo. This classic and refreshing side dish is also a terrific condiment layered on burgers and grilled sausages.

¼	head green cabbage, finely shredded
½	red or yellow bell pepper, stemmed, seeded, and diced small
½	sweet onion, diced small
2	stalks celery, diced small
2 to 3	radishes, diced small
1 large or 2 small	carrots, grated
¼	teaspoon fennel seeds
¼	teaspoon cayenne pepper
1	tablespoon kosher salt
1	teaspoon cracked black pepper
3	tablespoons sugar
2	tablespoons blended oil
5	tablespoons white vinegar
½ to ¾	cup mayonnaise, as desired

In a large bowl, mix together the cabbage, bell pepper, onion, celery, radishes, and carrot. Add the fennel seeds, cayenne, salt, black pepper, and sugar. Add the oil and vinegar, toss, and allow the salad to sit for 10 minutes. Drain; discard the resulting liquid. Fold in the mayonnaise, mixing well. Cover and chill before serving.

Makes 3 cups

CHAPTER 8

The Fox Lake Country Club

1975–77

SCENE: Outside the jail, a woman is lying in the back of a car smoking.

ARLETTA: Why, we always thought you was strong enough to carry it. Was we wrong?

LUKE: I don't know. Well, things are just never the way they seem, Arletta, you know that. A man's just gotta go his own way.

—Frank Pierson, *Cool Hand Luke*

AFTER PAINTING MY HEAD with barbeque sauce, I needed to stop, take some time, and reassess what I was doing with my life. Advice to self in the mirror: "Get out of the restaurant world, sport. You are losing it!"

Janet was worried about me and maybe even wondered if I was ever going to grow up. I just had no clue now. I wanted to go to the equivalent of Walden Pond and regroup. Now there's another way not to make a buck. But money seemed irrelevant in the surging tide of uselessness I was feeling about myself. I was lost as to where to go, what to be, how to deal with the world around me.

One of our neighbors was a lovely older couple who'd come to the peaceful shores of Diamond Lake to retire. My mom, who almost never met a person with whom she could not find some sort of common ground, went over to meet them shortly after they moved in. She shared a smoke with the husband and gave him a quick history of the community while the wife made coffee for the three of them. Their name was Prezell and, as it turns out, their son had just been promoted to a new job. He was now president of the Fox Lake Country Club. My mother told them I was looking for work. And as quick as you can yank-start a lawn mower I was hired. I was hired to cut the golf course lawns.

This would be my answer to Walden?

Since Janet and I had taken up residence with my former brother-in-law, Chipp, in the town of Volo, very near Fox Lake, it seemed an almost predestined stage in my life.

None of the assorted characters I worked with at the golf course had graduated from MIT or CIA, to be sure. They were mostly white boys who'd managed to stay out of jail most of the time. Nobody took the job seriously. In fact, we took it like a sentence you might be handed for some unbelievably dumb victimless crime. We were the kind of guys who would goad one another to eat fifty eggs, like in the movie *Cool Hand Luke*, although I'd say half the boys working with me wouldn't have known that classic.

We even had a boss straight out of *Cool Hand Luke*. His handle was "Karn," short for Karney. He was a three-hundred-pounder who had dark circles under his eyes, heavy jowls, buckteeth, bib overalls, a limp, and a set of keys that he carried like a jailer. He did not enjoy our sense of humor.

Each morning we'd receive our assignments.

Karn, from his clipboard, sitting on a golf cart, Styro of Dunkin' Donuts coffee, gut hanging:

"Elmer." (Karn talking all stern-like.) "You mow the fairways."

"Vincent. You get the rough." (Karn missing short, curly-haired Vinnie's mock salute.)

"Van Aken. You got the traps." (A shit-eating smile coming up on his donut-frosted lips.)

And so on.

The traps meant that I was going to be driving a speedy grass-munching machine that could spin on a dime, cut in and out like a dancing barracuda, and make me about as dizzy as a loon. But that was bad news as far as I was concerned. Give me the fucking tractor and let me space out on the fairways, for God's sake! I've got some thinking to do. Who am I? Where the hell am I going? I'm twenty-four and there's s'posed to be "so much more," right, Neil? But somehow Karn didn't trust the idea of one of us thinking and so I was the sand-trap man many days that late summer and fall.

Janet got a job in the dining room at the Fox Lake Country Club. Besides being a public golf course there were some middle-income residential housing developments springing up in the area. Along with the golfers and retirees, weddings brought in a fair amount of business and once again she was working for tips.

I'm sure that some afternoons, looking out of the big plate-glass windows facing the ninth green, she could see her mate spinning around in the lawn mower and wondering if he was getting any better. She held on to me, we saved a bit more money, and we found a place to rent of our own. It was a falling-down faded-white wooden house on the edge of Pistakee Bay. Fifty years ago I'm sure it was a beautiful place with broad windows facing the bucolic waters. Janet fixed it up like she always did. We had towels and sheets in a designated linen closet, dishes in the cupboards, food in the fridge, and our stereo set up. No TV. I got a fishing pole but only picked it up once.

I just went through the motions that summer. If my fate was to be a golf course grass cutter, I'd be one, and when the day's work was done, I'd join in the same after-hours pleasures of my coworkers. That meant drinking at a bar called John and Angie's. We called it, for no good reason, the J and A Gay Bar. It was a drinking man's bar. Fox Lake was a drinking person's town for that matter. At the J and A we were allowed to run a tab. My hourly wages were increasingly going down the pisser at that bar. I'd taken to drinking gin and tonics and beers to the point that when I got home I'd be asleep by dark. I woke up all too often on the floor of the kitchen, the front yard, or in the back of my pickup truck outside the J and A unable to drive home.

As Thanksgiving approached the golf course was going to close for the season. They wouldn't need us lawn jockeys for the next seven months and that would mean no work, no money. Jobs were scarce and it wasn't like I had a bunch of different payable skills.

The Prezells' good son and president of the Fox Lake Country Club, Dan, came up to me one afternoon in mid-November and said in the flat midwestern accent that some folks really had, squashing down hard on the a's, "Your ma told us that you've done some cooking in the past. We could use a hand with Thanksgiving, and if it seems like a good fit with you and Chef Jeff, you might be able to work through the winter with us cooking dinner."

A kitchen job again? Oh my God! What crimes did I do in a former life to merit this role again? But I didn't have the strength to say no, nor did I have a plan B.

The chef thought he was a gifted kitchen god and a real lady-killer, too. He was living with a woman in Fox Lake and balling the one girl who worked on the golf course with the rest of my lunatic buddies. Or at least he bragged that he was.

He was certainly more experienced than me at cooking, having grown up in the business making breads, rolls, and pastries at his parents' European-style bakery in the center of town. So I was basically his grunt boy even though we were probably the same age. He worked days doing the ordering and prep. I worked afternoons and nights doing the line work.

The Fox Lake Country Club was out in the sticks, especially if you were not golfing and only coming for dinner. So from time to time Chef Jeff conjured up a special dish that he thought (or hoped) might make the place a kind of dining destination, or, as he put it, a dish that was "cruise boat chichi." One such item was his take on a shish kabob. Oh yeah, here was his passport to an exotic realm. The waitresses, Bunny and Marie most nights, would dab a thick cotton ball in a nasty amount of lighter fluid, shove it on the end of the lamb skewers, and light it with a Zippo. The acrid smell would have shaken a dog's resolve to sample that meat, but it didn't faze our solid midwestern audience (my people). The gals walked through the dining room to approving smiles in their matching red-and-white-checked blouses and white stretch pants. Chef Jeff was long gone and not there to take his bows.

The snow howled outside and drifted in vast sheets over the mute fairways and greens of summer. Aside from a dish or two the menu was simple. The gig was straight ahead. Come five o'clock Tuesday through Thursday I'd cook alone. On Friday and Saturdays, a high school kid would come help me through the rush.

My mom sent me an envelope. There was only a newspaper cutting inside:

"FEB 14th Funeral Services for Tokio Suyehara. Born October 28, 1923. At Rest: Feb. 11, 1975." Service would be at Scanlon Funeral Home, 2907 N. Clark St., Chicago, at 8 p.m.

I thought back to those days at the Deerpath and it sent a shiver down my spine. I don't know if I thought of Toké as "my chef" then. Hell. How could I? I didn't think of myself as one. We drove down to the city on a dark and cold night. Mama was there with her great friend and coworker, Janice. The funeral parlor was filled with Japanese family members and the multicultural mix of the restaurant trade people who worked with him for so many years. Everyone was very sad and respectful. For such a quiet man it spoke strongly to me. I thought of Toké as we stepped out into the snowy, grimy dark streets of Chicago. I thought of him all the way home in a swirling snowstorm. I thought of him picking dandelions.

From the beginning of January until mid-April, I was mostly alone in the Fox Lake kitchen at night. That solitude and confinement made me feel quite abandoned at first. The games and fucking around and drinking and getting wacky with fellow cooks wouldn't be the escape route now. It was just the menu and the line: salad, grill, and a few burners for a sautéed dish or three. I cooked the shish kabobs along with pork chops (garnished with red apple rings), a club steak (served on a sponge of white toast), frozen, pan-cooked head-on trout (in a quick lemon butter sauce with pine nuts), and Chicken Parmesan (in a homemade red sauce). I also made the house salads that came with dinner, heated up the Parker House rolls, and scooped the ice cream on the hot apple pie.

Don't put it down. It was where I was going to night school. I hadn't even heard of culinary universities and the like yet. I hadn't read a cookbook yet. I hadn't read a magazine on cooking yet. I didn't choose to be a cook; cooking chose me. And so I did what the tickets instructed me to do in the order and tempo of how they came in. I learned to move more economically to get the work done. I learned not to burn the pots and pans because *I* was the one who was going to be washing them at the end of the night. It is amazing how you can learn to cook with fewer pots when you wash them yourself—and burn them? It ain't happening.

I washed the dishes between the rushes of tickets. It was a small and practical kitchen. I learned how to grill and that alone is a world-class art. Even on that crappy gas grill I learned to use high heat while moving the meat as little as possible in order to create the delectable char on a good steak. There weren't really any elaborate sauces to learn, and that was a blessing because I'm sure they would have been some odd concoctions. That said, the fried perch came with tartar sauce and we made our tartar sauce from scratch. Getting just the right note of acidity to cut through the emulsion of olive oil and egg yolk is a cornerstone in all kinds of great sauce making. Eventually, I would learn much more about the alchemy of sauces, but alone in that kitchen, tasting and prepping and cleaning through that long winter, I learned lessons about cooking that would never have come any other way.

A change started to come over me. One night, after a tearful session with Janet who was wondering what we were doing, where we going, I asked her to marry me in the house on Pistakee Bay. We were standing on the middle landing of the staircase—where you can either turn and go down or turn and go up. We were in each other's arms. We went up to our bed, and she said, "Yes."

She said, YES!

We set the wedding for June. We were married in a little park right behind the house I was born in. You could see Diamond Lake shimmering in the distance. Janet had a white bridal dress she picked out with her mother and I wore a Western-style suit with a string tie.

Wade, Ralph, and Butchie came to the wedding. Wade was my best man. We had our reception at the Legion Hall up in the town of Ivanhoe. A band named the Embers played wedding songs until some of my musician pals took over the stage and we went at it. One of Janet's neighbors who did some catering made the food, sort of a Polish Italian combination of goods. Janet and I made our wedding cake, a little lopsided, delicious, and chocolate. When the reception was over Irv slipped me a hotel room key to the Hitch Inn Post Lodge so we could have a night at a "nice" hotel. We couldn't afford a honeymoon that year so we just went back to work at the club.

The months flew by and another winter came and went. I stayed in the kitchen. The following April, Chef Jeff went on vacation for two weeks and when he did Dan Prezell said, "Well, Norm"—midwesterners routinely feel it unfriendly if they use your whole name, so I was often Norm and Janet was Jan—"you are our chef for the next two weeks!" He smiled a well-meaning smile and shook my hand.

And now what? I wondered. Did that offer me some kind of creative license? And what if it did? What did I ever create in a kitchen?

Easter was the next week and we would be doing a big brunch. I asked Dan what the menu was since the pinhead had left on his vacay without letting me in on this detail. Dan said, "Jeez, I guess that's up to you, Chef."

What did he call me? I'd been cooking five years and nobody ever called me "Chef."

I got home and told Janet about the turn of events. She and I sat at our kitchen table and began to talk about ideas for our vision of a great Easter brunch. I pulled down one of my notepads I used to write my little poems and stories on. I wrote at the top, "Easter Brunch," and something was suddenly "busy being born," instead of the other way around.

The next few days included the ordering of the foods we would prepare, the prep, and finally the big day, Easter Sunday.

Janet and I had gone to the Grayslake Outdoor Drive-In Theater back in late November and the last movie they showed that year before winter shut them down was *Rocky.* We sat in our car with the heat on and watched the tearjerker turned uplifter. Corny (sort of like Janet's obsession movie *It's a Wonderful Life*) but true and powerful just the same. Here on Easter Sunday by six o'clock that night I felt like I was bouncing up those steps like Rocky Balboa.

Goddamn, what do you know? I *liked* being called "Chef."

When Chef Jeff returned he looked pretty chagrined at the changes. I'm not sure if it was my newly found confidence or the fact that he was going to have to actually do some work because now Janet and I had a little money and we were finally taking our honeymoon in Key West. And this time we had saved up enough to fly there.

Flame on Shish Kabob

The "flame" here is not from chilies. It's unlikely our gentle guests at the Fox Lake Country Club would have tolerated truly fiery flavors back in the day when I cooked for them. The flame was all for show. One of the "girls" (as all the female servers were called regardless of age or status) would dip a cotton ball in nasty-smelling lighter fluid and shove it on the end of a metal skewer, then set it alight just before grabbing it from the pickup window. The bobbing flame and acrid aroma was always a head turner. But please don't try this at home!

For the lamb:

	4-inch wooden skewers, as needed
4	garlic cloves, minced
2	teaspoons kosher salt
1	tablespoon curry powder
1	tablespoon coriander seeds, ground
2	tablespoons fresh, chopped thyme
½	tablespoon freshly cracked black pepper
½	cup blended oil
2	tablespoons lemon juice
	kosher salt and cracked black pepper, to taste
2	pounds boneless lamb, loin or shoulder, cut into bite-sized pieces (totaling about 60)

Place the skewers in a bowl, add enough cool water to cover, and set aside.

In a bowl, combine all the ingredients, except for the lamb, and mix thoroughly. Add the lamb and toss. Cover with plastic wrap and marinate in the refrigerator for at least 2 hours.

For the vegetables:

1	red onion, peeled
2	yellow bell peppers, stemmed, seeded, and ribs removed
2	red bell peppers, stemmed, seeded, and ribs removed
	canola oil, as needed
	kosher salt and freshly cracked black pepper, to taste

Cut the onions and bell peppers into bite-sized pieces. Barely coat with the canola oil, and season with salt and pepper.

In a pan over high heat, sauté the vegetables until they are nicely charred. Remove to a plate and allow them to cool.

For appetizers, place 3 pieces of lamb, alternating with vegetables, onto each skewer. Add more lamb to each skewer if you are serving as an entree.

Preheat the grill or broiler. Add the kabobs and when quite hot, cook to the desired degree of doneness, about 4 to 7 minutes, turning as necessary. Serve over rice or with warm Indian naan.

Makes 18 appetizers, or 6 entrees

CHAPTER 9

700 Duval
Key West, 1978

Banana bread, banana bread.
Get your fresh, hot banana bread.
Don't blame me when it's gone.

—Frank Baing, a.k.a. the Banana Bread Man,
who sang while selling his loaves each evening
at the Sunset Celebration on Mallory Square

IT WAS ONLY JANET'S THIRD TIME on an airplane of any kind. When we arrived in Miami and got on the tiny Air Sunshine plane to Key West her sometimes green, sometimes blue eyes were as big as saucers. (The airline was called "Air Sometimes" by the locals.) We held each other tight the whole way and tried to ignore the incessant drone of the engine. As we descended we looked out of the bobbing aircraft and saw a hand-painted sign on a faded gray building. *Bienvenidos a Cayo Hueso!* it read. "Welcome to Key West!" And we already felt like the time would be too short here and go way too fast.

We wanted to surprise our friends so we took a cab from the grandiosely named Key West International Airport to the Old Town section of the island. We rode in the Five Sixes cab, named for the 6-6666 phone number painted on the doors (you still only needed to dial five numbers in those days) down Duval Street, cut left on Angela, right on Whitehead, and right again onto the minuscule, tucked-away Aronovitz Lane. The cabbie thought we might be lost going to such a dilapidated address with our "tourist" luggage. This clearly was no typical hotel for honeymooners. We were as white as one would expect of two kids who'd just spent the past winter in northern Illinois. But the sights and smells of Key West once again intoxicated us more potently than any herb or brew.

We spent the next week forgetting winter in Fox Lake. But as the final days of our honeymoon approached we sought some way to stay in Key West. We decided to go down the lane to the Green Parrot Bar. The open-air saloon had drinkers in it from morning until late. I ordered a beer and declined the Happy Hour offer of three shots of tequila for a buck. I had cut back on the drinking. Beer was all for now.

One of the guys we were staying with on Aronovitz was my old Hainesville brother, Ricky Taylor, who, along with Wade, I'd come to Key West with in 1973 in the big Lincoln. Ricky was a carpenter now. He'd been working on a restaurant just across the street at 700 Duval. It was on the corner of Angela, just kitty-corner from Pete's Fish Market. He came into the Parrot, got three shots lined up with a Busch backup, and said with his Alabama-born accent, "You want a job?"

He pulled a long slug of cold beer from the Busch longneck, then ordered two more from John the co-owner and bartender. Ricky slid one of the beers to me. He continued, "Cuz if you do want a job, you ought to go talk to the guy I've been building this restaurant for, man. The chef he hired landed his ass in the Key West jail last night and they found out he was wanted in Michigan on some breaking-and-entering beef. That place is s'posed to open in less than a week and the owner is fucking flipping, man. His name is Lou, big white guy with glasses and a bad comb-over."

I walked Janet back to the house on Aronovitz and headed over to the newly refurbished restaurant. Four years earlier it had been called the Shipwreck Lounge, a good place back then for live music and topless dancing. Janet and I went there a few times when we had first explored Key West together. I found Lou, just as Rick had described him, sitting on a barstool sampling a Planter's Punch out of a Mason jar. I explained why I was there and that I cooked. In less than twenty-four hours Janet was heading back to Illinois on a plane and I was heading with Lou to his other restaurant in Fort Myers to learn the recipes with which this guy was going to try and win the hearts of Key West.

We left Key West in Lou's big white whale of a Cadillac El Dorado on a beautiful morning. It was different to be riding the Florida Keys in a car instead of a bus. We rode lower and closer to the water, and the smell of the salty air seeped in through the air vents. After completing the ride north out of the keys he turned left and headed across Alligator Alley in the early afternoon. Seminole Indians worked hand lines along the roadside culverts as if time had stood still. I watched alligators pushing off the banks and marveled at the aquatic wonders of my new home state.

I crashed at Lou's house for about a week as I learned how he made items like Shrimp Lou. (The secret ingredient was Cheez Whiz.) I was so delirious over the chance to have a job and leave Chef Jeff and the cold world up north that it didn't even really faze me. "Yes. I see, Lou. I melt the cheese into the jug Chablis with the precooked shrimp and mix quickly using chopping motions with my tongs. Got it."

I rode back to Key West on a Greyhound bus, glad to be away from Big Lou and his shortwave radio shtick. Lou had made his money as a radio deejay on the Gulf Coast of Florida and no man was ever more in love with having a microphone in his hands and near his golden-toned voice than he was. The CB radio craze had just struck the country and Lou was talking endlessly. He had the entire CB lingo down. His handle was "Cycle Daddy." If you said something to him like, "Does this lobster dish get Cheez Whiz too?" the answer would be "That's a big 10-4. We'll be 10-10 [hanging out more or less] on this 9-9 [CB radio channel]" or some such trucker mumbo jumbo. Lou had a monster Honda Gold Wing motorcycle. He wanted to ride it down to Key West and store it there. No way was I going to ride on the back of that bike with my arms wrapped around the big fellow's gut. I lied to him that I had a severe fear of bikes. He nodded condescendingly and was so happy to finally be opening up the Key West restaurant he sported for my bus ticket. I picked up a few souvenir T-shirts for Janet from some tourist trap in Fort Myers and got on the bus and to our future. Meanwhile Janet was driving down with Mama and our little black mutt,

Smokey, in our now year-old red pickup truck listening to a Linda Ronstadt tape with her cover of Roy Orbison's "Blue Bayou" over and over again. A great friendship was growing.

Mama stayed a few days. She had her own job to get back to. Janet and I found an upstairs apartment to rent on Varela Street just off Truman Avenue. Truman is what U.S. 1 turns into when it reaches the last mile markers into Key West; it's the end of the road that starts in Kent, Maine. The fact that it ends makes some of them crazy, I guess.

Along with our other household items, my books, and our clothes, Janet had brought my ten-speed bike from Illinois and that's how I got around. No one rides a ten-speed in Key West. It looks stupid because no one is in a hurry. The bike of choice is called a "conch cruiser" and you sit upright, usually with a big wire basket between raised handlebars. But my old ten-speed still worked, had a light on it, and I could park it right next to the kitchen door, so I rode it. The pickup truck sat on Varela for the entire time we lived there. I don't think I even started it once that year.

Our neighborhood radius was tiny. Janet walked to Fausto's grocery on White Street and we had our morning *café con leche* and Cuban toast at the M & M Launderette. Many mornings we'd walk down to the end of White Street pier and look at the calm and immense ocean stretching out toward Cuba and the Caribbean.

It was a blur setting up that kitchen at 700 Duval. I lived on chocolate milk and still lost fifteen pounds the first month. I was too hot to eat any food during the fourteen-hour shift so once I got home I'd get Janet and we'd go out to IHOP at one or two in the morning when my core body temperature dropped enough for an appetite. I'd pack away a big plate of pancakes with two sunny-side eggs on top. Janet thought I had given up meat entirely, and it was a time when I actually thought about going vegetarian. A lot of folks in Key West were into it and I wondered if it might be a healthier way to live. Janet was a midwestern girl and she was having none of this hippie rhetoric. She had sausage or ham with her pancakes and waited for me to come to my senses.

The heat was a physical opponent of those working in the kitchens of Key West and would remain one for all the years I cooked there. But this kitchen was more extreme than any other before it. I wore a thermometer around my neck one night I worked the grill and it climbed to over 120 degrees in that corner. No wonder I was dissolving on the rubber-tiled floor.

But I was dead set on making it at this position. It was my first shot at being the head chef, and my days were filled with a mixture of terror and joy. I had to hire a staff, locate the best vendors, and figure out how to make Lou's food. I hadn't worked with actual recipes before and it was a little like playing a board game with the rules Lou had worked out in Fort Myers. He hired a general manager who reminded me a little of a young Charles Bronson from the movie *The Great Escape*, only a bit smaller in size. He had a beautiful girlfriend named Toni and she became our first hostess. They hired the mostly female floor staff and trained them on everything from how to describe the dishes to the guests to how to refill the big salad bar "boat" that was a dominant feature of the somewhat nautically themed dining room. (Gale Street memories all over again!) It was the "salad bar era" in American dining.

Finding cooks in Key West was a different world than the one I'd experienced in Illinois. Then again, I hadn't much experience of any kind when it came to hiring anybody. Oddly, everyone I hired was older than me. Rick Lutz had been one of the original bartenders at the fabled Chart Room Bar at the Pier House Resort. He'd had enough of drunks whining about life's betrayals and decided to go behind the scenes into the prep kitchen. I asked him why he didn't want to be a bartender and work in the air-conditioning. He laughed and said that Lou had built "the world's smallest bar in the world's drinkingest town" and he wouldn't subject himself to it. I wasn't sure if I understood the point really. The Chart Room was not exactly a ballroom, either. It was hot and sticky in our breezeless prep room. But Rick knew what he wanted and who was I to argue? I needed a prep guy.

Another was a chef who had worked most summers in Providence, Rhode Island (a sort of sister city to Key West), but was now a full-time resident. He was heavy, hairy, and he sweated like a leaking fire hydrant. He was also officially out of his closet and often too hungover to work thanks to his fondness for Kahlua-and-cream drinks. The big gun I hired was a square-shouldered, bearded, ponytailed bruiser named Ron Truax. He had bright green eyes and owned a Harley that he'd ridden all the way from his home state of California with his girlfriend Janice on the back.

Janice was a cook, too, but she and Ronnie had agreed not to work together after trying it and hating it in the past. Ron's voice was part Wolfman Jack and part Jack Palance. He should have been the head chef because he knew a lot more about cooking than I did then and he commanded the respect of everyone, including Lou. But by then Ron had signed off on the climb up the so-called ladder of success. He made about $50 less a week than I did but he worked about half the hours. He'd figured out that his road to happiness was much more entwined in his Harley, Janice, and fishing. Not unlike many of the residents of Key West he was going to enjoy his time in paradise. But his intelligence also kept him involved.

Like many of the old men I worked with at the Deerpath, Ron had seen and tasted some really great things and he wasn't just taking up space on the hot line with me. Ron worked sauté. The sauté station is the one that many chefs love the most. It is the station that involves the most connection with sauces, considered the apotheosis of being a chef. With Lou's school of gastronomy forced on us we didn't have much reason to know more than the world of cocktail, tartar, and, yes, the white wine and cheese goo that formed the crux of the cuisine at 700 Duval. But Ron started talking to me about making a few sauces, and I wanted to learn more. One day I remember him changing in the back entranceway from his T-shirt to a short-sleeved cook's shirt and telling me that if I wanted to learn more about cooking maybe I should go back a few steps and take a job working as a line guy at the Pier House. The Pier House was the beautiful hotel located right on the ocean at the foot of Duval Street. Ron said they had a new chef there from New York and that the energy was pretty real. As a Californian he had a way of saying things—he didn't sound like he was faking it.

"They probably will have you chopping the vegetables for the"—and here he said a word I had never heard before—"mirepoix for a few weeks but eventually you might get to learn the next steps of a saucier."

"What in the heck is meer-a-pwah?" I asked him.

Ronnie let out a loud cry, "Oh Gawd!" Wolfman Jack–style. It was like a rock guitar player hitting a power chord. "Oh Gawd!" I never heard anyone say it so loud and with so much shock at the (fill in the adjective) wonder, idiocy, humor, doubt, anger of whatever the situation was being discussed. "Oh Gawd! You don't know what *mirepoix* is and you are the chef of this place? Oh Gawd!"

One afternoon, in the circus of all this, I felt a large shadow slowly sheathe the throbbing tropic light that flooded through the kitchen screen door at that hour. It was like when you're diving in the ocean and a very large fish swims behind you. I stilled. Then came this voice. It was a booming bass singsong with Bahamian inflections:

"Hey. Hey. I'm Frank, the Conch Salad Man. I'll sell you the world's best conch salad and you can sell it to your customers." It was more Samuel L. Jackson than Bill Cosby's Fat Albert.

Without knocking he pushed open the screen door and came in holding a big white pickle bucket brimming with his conch salad. Conch salad is not what normally is understood as a salad. It's more of a gazpacho-like creation. He reached in, scooped some up, and thrust a paper cupful at me. I tipped back a mixture of finely diced conch, tomatoes, red onions, Scotch bonnets, bell peppers, celery, citrus juices, and herbs. The flavors of the sea were in there, too. I really began to look at him now.

His heavy, black-framed, saltwater-stained glasses were held on with fishing line. His hands were thick, meaty, and marked from heavy labor. He wore canvas shoes, navy-issue pants, and a white T-shirt. A long gold chain around his neck was the only adornment, and it drew attention to the nasty scar along his collarbones.

He pulled out another taste for each of the other cooks and waiters who were working nearby. He sold us his conch salad every week for the next few months. That was until I came in early one morning and found him in our prep room cutting up our tomatoes and vegetables and charging us as if they were his.

One of the waitresses was pretty sharp. She learned Lou's cheese-laced repertoire faster than the other girls. But she was fast in other ways and pretty soon Lou's star waitress had shacked up with half the hot line. I was too weak to even think about those things. When you first get to Key West after living up north you spend equal parts of your life adjusting to the heat, the viruses, and the hangovers. One afternoon she strolled back in with a former cook, a married guy that she had made pussy crazy. Her dyed red-blonde hair was burnt by what obviously were a few days of lying on the beach and getting wasted. She stepped up in front of the hot line and offered to show the boys and me her new tattoo. She lifted her skirt and next to her panties she pointed to it. The skin was raised, bruised, and comic book colored. "Forty bucks," she crowed. Ronnie shouted back, "That's nice. How much for the tattoo?" She flashed him a smile, gave him the finger, and took the married man with her.

I had gotten my fill of pancakes finally and now I wanted something more. I found a place to eat on Duval. It had a sign out front that read "Café Expresso." Little did I know when I entered this tiny restaurant only searching for some of the "Cuban speed" to power me through another sixteen-hour day that I would be walking into one of the most important restaurants of my young life.

The place was small even by Key West standards. There was seating only at the counter and just barely enough room to squeeze by the folks on the stools to get a seat at all. I was alone and there was but one seat left of the twelve, so I took it. I sat next to two Cuban fishermen on my left who were drinking beer and each eating a huge plate of very thin steak I came to learn later was called Palomilla steak. A man in his late fifties sat on my right. His hair was graying and he wore glasses and an elegant guayabera shirt. His hands were large and soft and he was reading a thick book as he waited for his food. I could smell the very pleasant scent of a man's cologne on him. I usually don't like to notice cologne on a man but his was an ancient sort of barbershop smell of soap and botanicals. His hair was neatly combed back and a leather satchel was at his feet. It held newspapers written in Spanish and English. I studied the menu and the chalkboard specials wishing I were fluent in two languages, too. I had become a soup lover during my Colorado days at the Holiday Inn and ordered the Caldo Gallego as a starter from the woman who was the cook, waitress, cashier, and cleanup person all in one.

The man on my right saw immediately that I was not only new to the island but the language, the food, the history, everything. I was just a young man who might have well been sitting in a joint a world away in Thailand as here at the southern tip of America. Key West was like an exotic country, not part of the United States.

He had warm brown eyes and he asked me if I liked Cuban food. I said, "I don't know. It smells good in here, though."

He said, "That is a wise response, but it is clear you need to learn a great deal. Do you live here?"

"I just got a job as a cook." I was not confident enough to use the word "chef" yet. "And I'm trying to make it here, yes."

He said, "I live in Miami but I am from Colombia and I like to come down here and feel the different world of Key West. My wife, Beba, is from Cuba and I've learned a great deal of the food of Cuba from her. It is a complex story. Do you like history, young man?"

I said that I did and he began to speak in a low and fluid manner:

"Let me tell you about the food you are about to eat in this unprepossessing little café. You should know where food comes from and why it is so unique if you are going to cook food for a living. Cooking is a very noble profession. Please keep in mind this is the only art practiced under the pressure of time to regale the taster a pleasure as fleeting for his palate as it is lasting in his or her memory."

I had not ever heard this said so convincingly or aristocratically. He continued: "The Yoruba people were, after the Bantu, the second largest ethnic group brought on the slave ships during the abhorrent Middle Passage from Africa to Cuba. They were from now what is southwestern Nigeria, a country roughly twice the size of California and located on the botanically equally rich western shores of Africa. The Yoruba either brought some of the native ingredients with them or adapted to the produce they found. From the period of time between 1820 and 1870, close to twenty thousand of these richly cultured people were torn from their land, their families, and their gods to work the sugar plantations, since Europeans had developed an insatiable demand for sweetness in their diets. Nigeria is one of Africa's most ethnically diverse countries so its peoples are open to new foods much in the same way a person from, say, New York or Bogotá would be (the latter referred to his native city). The different foods available depend, of course, on the season. The season before the rains, which arrive in March, is called 'the hungry season' when food is scarce, for instance.

"This bold woman who is cooking for us and speaks a tongue you cannot understand could be akin to one of the *orishas* or minor gods, of which there are dozens after the main god Olodumare, one of the many facets of the African religion simply lumped into the broad category here as Santeria. The slaves were not permitted to practice their own faith, and the master's whip was a steady and brutal reminder of that ecclesiastical intolerance. The slaves adapted to this like they had to adapt to so much by simply and cleverly grafting the names of the approved saints like the Virgin Mary or Saint Barbara with those of their true religion. Voodoo head shrinkers and the overstated business of sacrificial animals like the goat were blown up to purposefully belittle another race's form of spiritualism. Don't we good Christians kill a turkey in the name of devotion each November? Hah!"

He dabbed his chin with his own large cotton kerchief and he marveled momentarily at the deep stain of curry it left on the white cloth.

"Certain foods are equated with specific orishas. The black-eyed peas I am so fond of reference the orisha Oxum, who corresponds to the Virgin Mary, while Xango, corresponding to Saint Barbara, is the orisha of okra."

He ordered a beer and the proprietress, Gloria, walked over with her huge hips thrusting in her orange stretch pants. Her gold-capped teeth and rough, tied-back hair now seemed different to me. I marveled at the grace and strength of her body. Her back and neck looked as strong as a man's, but her breasts and her ass were as curved and giving as perfectly ripe papayas. She set the cold beer down in front of my new teacher, and he looked appreciatively after her as she returned to the little kitchen. Celia Cruz's voice could be heard from a small radio over the dish sink.

We had talked, or I had listened, now for so long I felt embarrassed not to know his name. He seemed to read my mind instantly and said, "Since you are wondering, my name is Mr. Z. It's actually longer than that but that is what you may call me. What is yours?" And I told him. He said, "Strong name and its connotation helps me understand what a different history you hail from and why this is so new to you. Don't be put off by it. You will find the world a much more delicious stew if you have the brains to stick your spoon into all of it."

The foods on my plate now were more than sustenance or flavors, good or bad. They were an edible form of the vast shifting happenstances of human histories. He warmed to his subject, looking at Gloria as she bobbed her head to the drums of ancient tribes and seeing me take in his expertise like a thirsty sailor.

"According to the oral histories, each and every person is protected by one of the orishas from birth, sort of like your guardian angels. Gloria could be guided by a deity such as Yemayá, the great Mother Goddess whose majestic maternal energy is that of the great ocean, or perhaps the deity Ochún, whose power is seen in the snaking movement of river water.

When I watch her walk I could believe it to be either," he said with a devilish sparkle in those warm brown eyes.

"When you receive food that is made by hand you receive the energy of the person who made it. This modern mechanization of food, processing, preserving, packaging, freezing, microwaving—bah!—such methods remove the *soul connection* and the *energy*, the *vitality*, the *aphrodisiacal power* of food!"

The phrase "made by hand" held fast in my mind, as I tasted the mesmerizing flavors of a caramelized plantain that was given a kiss of key lime and embraced by slowly cooked red onions that had also suckled in some of the black beans' juices.

Gloria came back out of the kitchen, and Mr. Z reached into the left front pocket of his guayabera and retrieved a massive cigar. Her eyes lit up and she revealed those gold-capped teeth again. He laid the Montecristo in her hand and she took a plate and put the cigar on it. She retrieved a bottle of Havana Club from underneath the counter. She uncapped it and poured a few drops of the vanilla-scented rum into both of her palms and rubbed it lightly into her skin. She then cut the cigar at the mouth end with her pitted carbon knife and dipped the cut into the bottle ever so gently. She pulled it out, struck a match and inhaled deeply, her bosom rising as she worked the bellows of her lungs. The bluish smoke filled the little café and when the cigar was properly lit she sauntered back into her kitchen and stirred her iron pots.

I said, "She is so distracted by your cigar. You could easily walk out on the check."

He turned on his stool and looked at me to see if I would do such a thing, peering right into my soul. He saw that I would not but still felt compelled to drive home another point in his lesson for me today. He said, "First off, I am a gentleman from a good family and was not raised to steal. Secondly, and you must learn this, the world of food and wine and hospitality is amazingly small and if you were to burn the proverbial bridge by doing such a stupid thing you would never be able to cross it again unless you were able to rebuild it, not an easy task. It is so easy to do the right thing. Why be a fool as well as a cheat is what I am saying. Make allies, be honest, be fair, and your life as a cook will be infinitely better. You do that and one day you will even become a chef."

The time had gone by so fast I hadn't realized that I was now going to be in the weeds back at the restaurant. When I went to pay up at the cash register near the front door Gloria waved her hands and said, "He pay." I looked back down the counter and Mr. Z had slipped out the back door. I hoped I would see him again one day. I went back to the kitchen at 700 Duval and started looking at the food and the menu in a different way. I had been made aware of the differences in what I was doing as a chef and what glorious Gloria was doing as a cook, and I was shocked at how little I knew.

One of Lou's treasured recipes was batter-fried shrimp made with Bisquick. I decided to refuse to make it with this stuff because I had some notion there were additives in the packaged batter that were unnecessary. I wanted to devise a "pure" batter that would not have them. Plus I wanted the coating to have some of the spice and flavors I was getting from the Santeria café. The Bisquick batter stuck to my hands, and one night I lost my gold family ring in it and had to search the Dumpster to try and find it. It became a symbol of the stupidity of this food.

Lou found out about this transgression from one of the older cooks (who wanted my job) and came to the kitchen to see if it was true. I admitted that I had changed the ingredients to one of his recipes. His white face reddened in a way I'd never seen before. I asked him only half seriously if I was going to be fired.

"That's a big 10-4," he said, slipping into his CB jargon to create distance between us.

Now *I* was red.

"Copy that, Cycle Daddy!"

I let the screen door slam behind me.

"Guess I won't see you on the flip-flop, Lou!"

Now growing a little punchy with the realization I really was fired.

"Guess I won't see you in Shakey Town!"

He looked at me through the mesh as I ripped my ten-speed away from the back of the building and rolled away.

"Yeah Lou, guess it's time to put 'the hammer' down!" I shouted over my shoulder going down Angela Street pushing hard on the pedals, moving faster and faster now, just to get away from the fucking Bisquick.

"Guess we won't be a-huntin' 'Bear' no more!"

The Jar Cocktail

This is, of course, a version of the classic Hurricane. There was *not one thing* about the owner that was original when it came to recipes, so no one was surprised he gave it a name of its own. His response was that it was served in a jar and he was "not a fan of storms." He certainly was a fan of these babies. He had one for breakfast every day I worked for him.

- 2 ounces dark rum
- 2 ounces light rum
- ½ ounce freshly squeezed lime juice
- ½ ounce freshly squeezed lemon juice
- 1 ounce freshly squeezed orange juice
- 1 tablespoon simple syrup
- 1 tablespoon grenadine
- 1 ounce passion fruit puree
- orange slice, for garnish
- maraschino cherry, for garnish

Combine the ingredients (except for garnishes) in a cocktail shaker over crushed ice, and shake like crazy. Pour through a strainer into a Ball or Mason jar. Garnish with a fat orange slice, and if you are not looking to live to a hundred, a cherry.

Makes 1 cocktail

CHAPTER 10

The Pier House

Key West, 1978

CHEF: From Late Latin *caput* (head). Ultimately from Indo-European root *kaput* (head), also the origins of the words *head*, *captain*, *chapter*, *cadet*, *cattle*, *chattel*, *achieve*, *biceps*, and *mischief*.

—Sharon Tyler Herbst, *The New Food Lover's Companion*

SINCE I'D BEEN FIRED from my job at 700 Duval, Janet and I were broke again. I'd submitted some applications for employment around town but nothing was panning out. I was lying on the floor of 1401 Newton Street in our rented home, another in the long list of homes we rented in those years. If we could save $50 a month, we would pack up all our worldly possessions into our red pickup truck and move three blocks or a mile. There wasn't much more island to move to on tiny Key West.

I lay there in a state of turmoil, watching dust motes in the slow air swirl like shifting stars in the lazy afternoon sunlight streaming through the large front windows trying to figure out if I should sell our truck. Apart from hitchhiking again it was our only means back to our families in Illinois if it all came down to that. I had just sold the camper shell that covered the truck bed to make the last month's rent. I got $300 from a Stock Island shrimper. Maybe I could sell the truck's tires for another short-term fix? Then hopefully get a job, and replace them? Maybe it was time to give up the dream of making ends meet in Key West and go back to Illinois?

I heard a scuffle of feet on the steps and saw shadows. There was a knock. A guy with a New York accent asked, "Do you see somebody laying on the floor in there, Hookah?"

Another guy answered, flat and nasally, "Nah. Let's go get a beer before we have to go back to work and Chef figures out why we volunteered for this gig in the first place."

I jumped up and opened the screen door. It turned out to be two chefs from the Pier House Resort, one of the places in town I'd applied. The thirsty one's name was Hooker (I never found out if it was his real name), and the other was a strapping black-haired guy with an Amish-looking chinstrap beard (no mustache) named Allan Katz. We didn't have a phone at our house so they had to come over to find me. Allan pressed a scrap of paper into my hand and told me to call the Pier House: "Ask for Human Resources and tell them you're coming in for an interview before they give the job to someone else." He had a kind face, and I felt a wave of hope. I hustled three blocks down to the pay phone outside West Provision Meats on White Street. Someone on the other end of the line said, "Why are you breathing so hard? Slow down, honey. Come in tonight around 5:30 and talk to Chef."

Ronnie Truax, from 700 Duval, was in my head when I walked up the driveway at the end of Duval Street. I wondered, *Do they make "meer-a-pwah" here?* I still didn't know what mirepoix was, how it was spelled, or how it was used but, due to Truax, I felt it had to have some mystical power to make godlike food. It was not a word in my first cooking boss's vocabulary at the Fireside. Nor was it in Fred Boomer's back in Greeley at the Holiday Inn. The chefs at the Deerpath might have used it but it fell on my deaf ears. It took the gruff Ronnie Truax, a.k.a. "biker chef," to awaken me.

It was about five o'clock when I walked into the kitchen. I wore long pants and tucked in my shirt. I felt like it was time to take myself more seriously. I held the application in my hands waiting by the wall where the hallway from the outside intersected with the kitchen. The chef's office was on my right and the butcher's station was to my left. A white-haired man was expertly portioning out plump red tenderloins and tying them neatly with butcher's twine. A sallow-faced, skinny young man with a tragic haircut peeled shrimp and tossed them nonchalantly into an iced bowl on the opposite side of the butcher block. I would learn later that they were father and son, Nino and Luciano, from Italy via New York City.

The chef's office door flew open and Chef Annie Donovan roared out of it: "Yes! Yes! *Yes!* I will look at your fucking cake now. Jesus! I don't have ten arms. I'm the chef of this goddamn zoo and I have to deal with these nonsense fucking time cards and all of the rest of this accounting *bullshit!* Fucking bean counters are gonna destroy me and my cuisine for that fucking matter!

"Where is it? Where is it? Where is the fucking GODDAMN fucking cake?"

There was a tall, round chocolate cake sitting on the stainless steel table. The pastry chef cowered and pointed at the cake. I had never seen anything like this before. They were actually going to *taste* the food and assess the value of it *before they would allow it to be served*. This was the first required tasting I'd ever witnessed. I was clearly beholding a new level of thinking and caring about cuisine.

Chef Annie's eyes were a beautiful deep green and set into a face that was as pretty as any parent could hope for save for a dramatic scar that was born in a teenage year. It must have been traumatic for her. She had bright, shiny black hair, delicate hands, and those otherworldly eyes. When she smiled you felt privileged to go along. But if she scowled and the light caught her scar it was a visage both menacing and effective. All these chefs would stand one day in her judgment. Now it was the pastry chef's turn.

Annie grabbed one of the white-haired butcher's knives and washed it quickly of its blood in the sink. She dried it on her apron, turning it against her legs. (Not even Nino the Italian bull dared to speak of his knife now.) She cut a perfect wedge out of the cake and flipped a piece onto a plate, took a fork, and slowly placed the piece in her mouth and chewed. She appeared thoughtful and looked far away. Maybe she was back in the CIA and thinking of how they had taught her to taste, what to look for. *Was there mirepoix in there?* I wondered. I think I had posited mirepoix in my mind in what would eventually become known as umami, the fifth taste. But at that moment I didn't know pâte from pâté.

Annie's face stopped the chewing movements. She spit out the unconsumed cake bite into a half-empty coffee cup and coughed.

"It's fucking dry! Did you even bother to taste this cardboard abomination, Sandra?"

And with that she took the big blade and backslapped the whole cake into the garbage can at the edge of the table.

"We can't serve that shit here."

And she stomped her way back into her office saying to Allan on the way, "Of course hire that guy with the tucked in shirt by the wall. What's there to think about? Just do it! Tell Klausing he can help cook fucking breakfast if he thinks my labor cost is too high. We are in the shits for breakfast help. He works with Betty. He's the breakfast cook, number two position, under her."

I'd cooked breakfast in Greeley at the Holiday Inn so I thought I was overqualified for the position but it was my way into this kitchen so I was intent on doing whatever it took. I wanted to get a glimpse of this "mirepoix mystery." Maybe they used it at breakfast.

The day started before sunrise with a man named Marvin. Even in the cool predawn hour he'd be sweating just a little, a fine glow around his eyes and shining on his broad forehead. His bangs hung down in an unevenly cut line some Duval Street barber had perfected for him. It was always the same. His mustache was getting salty but it was still full and walrusy, wrapped around the cheap skinny cigars he favored. Some mornings, while chaining up my bicycle, I'd see him parking his boat of a lopsided Olds convertible in the parking lot, finishing a beer discreetly veiled in a brown paper to-go bag (pinkie finger extended) and swinging his long legs and ample frame out to work the breakfast service.

"Hey, babe," he'd say with a soft New England accent, using his hip to push the car door shut.

"Hi, Marvin, how you doing today?"

"Marvelous," he'd say. And if he got lucky last night it might be followed by "Simply marvelous."

Marvin was a professional waiter. He was not on his way to star in a soap opera, or become an underwear model, or open a string of hair salons up north. He waited on tables because it gave him happiness, some money, and a human beehive he hummed along in just fine. He lived with another man in a tidy little conch house, and they may as well have been the Mertzes with the domesticity they enjoyed. Childless, bickering but clearly meant to stick it out through the whole 'til-death-do-us-part plan.

There was a different feeling during the hour before breakfast in the Pier House. It was quiet then. The sun was not up and the darkness of the ocean dominated the floor-to-ceiling windows of the dining room where I'd go to get my coffee. There were usually only three servers. One was a woman named Martha who was about four and a half feet of mean and with a face that belonged on a Roman coin. She had an adult son and she spent a lot of her money keeping that head case out of jail. A few years later I caught him and a buddy robbing our home. I threw an ice chest at him as he was scaling our back fence and broke his foot in the process. Had she known this was a part of the future I'm sure she would have stabbed me.

The other servers were a rotation of whomever the food and beverage manager wanted to punish. Typically, it would be some young man who'd just started working there and hadn't learned an iota of what his job required. It was hard to say whom I'd rather not see in my window with a returned plate, Martha or the new meat. I'd never see Marvin in my window with a returned plate. The concept didn't exist with him. He didn't make U-turns in his Zen of waiting tables. Magically, his guests were always happy, their food was prepared exactly as ordered, and they left the Pier House feeling, well, marvelous! It was a state of being he spread to the world around him.

The other waiter who got punished from time to time and made to work breakfast was an atypical fag named Daniel. Don't be offended by me saying the word "fag." Please. The boys said it about themselves when they weren't saying "homo." It was their way of taking control of a word I was taught was awful. "Fag," "homo," "pussy" were all simply what they used to free up the hate and distrust they got in places up north. In places not Key West. Only one of the guys actually made me nervous about forcing themselves on me in some way: Daniel.

Daniel was not like the other waiters at the Pier House. Most all of the waiters were rail thin with neatly cut hair. Daniel was muscular with a long, curly brown-blond leonine mane. His face was deeply tanned with a dark brown Fu Manchu mustache. He was, indeed, a "Macho Man."

"Fuck or fight?" Daniel said to me the first time I saw him. The word "fight" came out with a singsong quality and it took on an extra measure or beat; sort of like "fy-yite," with the inflection going up just a notch. Part question, part statement.

"Fuck or fy-yite? Either way, I like them both, so what's it gonna be, new kid? What's it gonna be, cookie?"

"I'll knock you down," in the same singsong.

"I'll knock you down," walking up to my area of the kitchen now.

"I'll knock you down," he'd repeat staring at me through the ticket window.

"I'll knock you down and suck your dick. Fuck or Fy-yite?"

Marvelous Marvin would sail past Daniel, rolling his eyes and saying to him, "I saw him first. Keep your mitts off that one. He's spoken for."

As breakfast ended and the lunch waiters began to arrive the kitchen began to get loud. I never looked forward to that time. Even though the hell of cooking breakfast was ending the greater chaos of lunch was imminent. Marvin would saunter over, his ever-present dish towel draped over his left shoulder, lean over my cutting board with a devilish leer, and say, "Whyn'tcha come over to my house tonight, babe? We'll have a few drinks, a good time. Whatcha say?"

"No thanks, Marvin," I'd say for the umpteenth time since I met that lovable coot.

"You'd throw rocks at your old lady after one night with me!" he'd chortle and head down the hallway to have a smoke by the pier and wait for his first lunch table.

Even though Betty may have needed my help she didn't want it and she didn't pretend to want it. She'd been through too much already and she was tired. She was now finished with the breakfast duties and in a few minutes we'd both start to get ready for lunch. She sat on a hard metal stool and let her big, heavy black boots slide off her socks and thud to the cement kitchen floor.

"Tiiiiiired dammit!" she'd say. The "dammit" word coming down like she was whipping a towel on the counter to kill a fly. Whap! "Tired!"

Betty was born in Key West, and she grew up in the Bahamian section of town. Her life as a girl was carefree and easy compared to this. She was olive black with green eyes and a slightly unkempt Afro. She had been married to a cop for fifteen years, but it ended badly and now she was like so many women who end up alone, forced to be the sole support of herself and her children. She worked hard and her body was feeling the pain of it. She wore those big black leather boots untied. Her hips were huge and bulging in her black stretch pants.

Working with Betty meant doing things her way. It was understood from the beginning. She told Annie, "Look, that young white bread fucks up my rhythm one mornin' and I'm walkin' down that hallway goes outside and you can find me at Two Friends drinkin' and him cooking the damn breakfast." Samuel Jackson could have taken elocution lessons from Black Betty. Annie impaled me with a look that told me she agreed. So whatever menial job Betty didn't want to do went to me. "Got it, chump?" Annie wasn't really asking a question.

I took the Danish hams out of the cans and cut them up for omelets and scrambles. I'd cut the bell peppers and onions for "westerns." I cracked her half a case of eggs, passing them through a china cap to catch any shells. I cooked the sheet pans of bacon and dealt with the blasting heat of the ovens and the hot grease that could boil the skin off your hands. I iced her beers and stuffed them under the romaine leaves in the walk-in cooler. And I helped her cook. It took time. It took patience. It took humility but slowly, ever so slowly she let me step in and help. She had been burned too many times by previously assigned helpers who had only lasted a few days or weeks, and then all the time she spent training and talking to them was for nothing. I could see it. And because I could see it and I stuck it out she came to like me. She even mothered me a little.

If a big batch of the Pier House's version of conch chowder went bad, and it did at least once a month, she'd protect me from the elderly Cuban dishwasher, Mr. Herrera, who would come screaming after me swearing in his rapid-fire Spanish as if I had sabotaged him. He knew that the spoiled soup was supposed to go down the dish machine's garbage disposal. The garbage men would revolt if you threw that nasty brew in the Dumpster. It was uncanny to see how that soup would be sitting on the floor *boiling* with no fire under it. It was that volatile. No Alton Browns were there to explain the phenomenon to us, but any fool could see this would kill you if you ate a spoonful.

Betty could even be flirtatious. After the breakfast service was over and she'd had a tall cold Blue Runner beer she'd walk dramatically away from the hot line and then, about ten feet out, look back at me and say, "I know you're looking at my big, beautiful ass, white bread. Hey! Don't it look like two pigs wrasslin' under a blanket, Norman? Hah! Caught you! Caught you, didn't I?"

But she taught me, too. She taught me speed through efficiency. If you watched her you probably couldn't tell. She seemed to be moving slowly, without a care in the world. The tickets could be plastered up and down the line and Betty moved with the steadfast rhythm of the salty waves outside. She didn't holler or slam plates when it was busy. Oh, if a waiter made a dumb mistake on a ticket she'd maybe slam a plate just to sort of wake him up, but not during the normal course of the job. It looked to me like she was just cruising along.

But when you stepped on the line and joined her and divided the tickets up and you took half and she took half—then you'd see. She could cook circles around anyone else, man or woman, in that kitchen when it came to breakfast. It was a one-woman ballet and she left me in the dust. She would cook all of her tickets and then reach over and take a third of the tickets still on my side, give me a little shoulder roll, and then we'd finish the rush. She was proud of her skills and I was just lucky to learn from this Bahamian woman on those mornings in Key West in 1978.

The Pier House made an important contribution to the city and its very economic future. When the navy pulled out of Key West in the mid-1970s, the crucible in which the economy was forged cracked again. The tourist industry was dormant until a man named David Wolkowsky turned a one-time fish market at the end of Duval Street into the low-key but elegant Pier House Resort. This was a marked change: for the first time in years well-to-do Northerners had a place to camp out in comfort and style in the funky island town. It also became a haven for the moneyed gay population that was steadily growing—and staying. Times were changing once again in Key West, and David Wolkowsky was a major force in the turning tides of those changes.

The great hotel owner could have had his meals in a penthouse suite overlooking the ocean opposite Christmas Tree Island. He could have commanded the dining room's center table every night (which he did, but only occasionally). And he could have gone aboard a powerful speedboat and taken it over to his private home on nearby Ballast Key with a few chefs and waiters and had us prepare a feast for him there. But as often as not David would order dinner and eat it in the kitchen while seated on a cheap stool or some milk crates at a makeshift table fashioned from a sheet pan inverted over a garbage can. From there he'd survey the meals being cooked, looking up at us from his hooded eyes, seeming happier than ever.

I was tired of cooking breakfast by then and the money was pathetic. My pay stub for the week of March 29 said I had worked thirty-five hours at a total gross pay of $148.75, with a net of $125.45. I hadn't realized it, but if I had simply spoken up earlier I might not have had to tell Annie I was going to leave the Pier House and look for a job elsewhere, if there was no position for me other than breakfast. I was shy about asking for either a raise or more opportunity from my bosses back then. I thought they would simply see my value and reward me—or not. So when I told the chef I'd be leaving she said that the grill station had just opened up and she'd move me to it immediately. No more predawn alarm clocks! I was ready for that. And she gave me another fifty cents an hour! Little did I realize back then that I was becoming a cook and a valued worker after all by those above me in the hierarchy.

When you learn to cook the way I did, you must learn from others. Without culinary school there is no other way. You use your previous skill set and try to get stronger with each new set of tasks at each new workstation.

To reduce the learning curve and speed the process (and make the process less brutal) it is wise to try and make friends with the cooks next to you. My first day on the grill I met Danny. Danny became my next teacher. He'd worked the grill already and was moving up to the much more esteemed position of sauté line cook. The guy I'd replaced went simply missing in action. It happened all the time in Key West, so there was a short period of time when Danny had to work both grill and sauté and he was glad to see someone, anyone, coming in to make his life less insane. I learned over time that everyone wanted to keep Danny from getting his Irish up.

Danny stood only about five foot, five inches and couldn't have weighed more than 115 pounds. He had an athletic body; no amount of beer ever seemed to give him the paunch and no amount of cigarettes seemed to wind him. He could and did work at light speed! He spoke in a rapid New York fashion and in short order helped me learn the ropes of working the grill. We became great buddies and for the first time in a long time I was working with someone who showed me how much fun cooking could be. I would do anything to help Danny and in doing so he taught me how to make hollandaise, brown sauce, and veal saltimbocca, but best of all Danny McHugh finally broke down the mirepoix mystery for me!

Now I knew that it was a French term for a collection of vegetables used to make a variety of sauces and soups. I would speed through my afternoon prep so I could make the mirepoix for Danny, which in turn, freed him up to show me more and more new stuff so that I would not only be able to work the grill but one day move over to sauté if they made Danny sous chef. He wanted the position and of course he wanted the money it meant. We all were just trying to find a way to move up the ladder in the Pier House kitchen. Now I was no longer breakfast cook number two, I was the night-shift grill guy and I liked the feeling.

Jimmy Buffett was beginning to become a national star at this time. We'd all been kind of astonished to see the guy who played for free at Crazy Ophelia's and the Chart Room just a few years earlier was now playing on our ratty kitchen boom box. One evening Tom walked in and handed Danny a ticket and said, "This is for Jimmy Buffett." Danny was not the kind of person to give a shit that anyone famous was in the house. It was a surefire way to get Danny moving toward getting his famous Irish temper up.

But Danny waited and played it coy this time. I kept waiting for Danny to tell me when he was ready to fire Jimmy's food but he kept pushing the ticket back on the fire-board. Finally, Tom came back and said, "Hey, Danny, where's the food for table ten? Where's Buffett's food? It's been over twenty minutes, Danny!"

Danny looked like a penitent choirboy for a moment at Tom. Then he started to sing, bending the lyrics more than just a little:

So sorry Jimmy Buffett
Looks like you'll have to tough it
Cuz me and Nor Man/Grill Man are
Wasted away in Margaritaville
We are looking for our lost shaker of salt!

Tears of laughter were falling from under Danny's glasses now. He fell to the floor and his small legs shot up and down kicking the air as he held his sides. "Hey, Tom! Tell him it will just be a minute and [now singing again] the shrimps are beginnin' to boil!" Peals of laughter shook out of the little man lying next to my grill. I could see that we were going to have a lot of fun on this hot line for a change.

It was a well-known fact that Danny liked to take his pants down. When he was happy or pissed or faking some mock (mostly) "fuck you" to authority he'd unsnap the button and, like releasing a shade, they'd sail down over his skinny Irish white legs (almost a girl's legs) and he'd turn around, bend completely over, and moon whomever. If he was drunk or really revved up he'd go in the opposite direction and whip out his cock and shake it at the offending party. This part was nothing like any girl's. It didn't go with his little body, yet there it was, the one-eyed trouser trout. But Danny was straight all the way. To my amazement some of the waiters had never seen Danny's full-frontal performance and yet the word went around that he might possess something the floor staff could, at least, judge.

The dining room manager was a thin guy named Jamie Conahan. Jamie's girlfriend was a great-looking, fun-loving platinum blonde named Ann Harlow. She was working down the street at a restaurant I was starting to hear some amazing things about. Jamie was a riverboat-gambler sort of a guy who loved a good game, a good story, a test of wills. One night after work at the Beach Club bar, Danny dropped his trousers to protest some happenstance from earlier in the evening, plus the generally poor management (his opinion) running the floor at the Pier House. That complaint was aimed at Jamie and, for a moment, so was Danny—from the waist down! Jamie found the gesture more hilarious than threatening and the next day he suggested a cockfight of sorts.

Jamie explained that there would be no violence in this contest but gambling would, most assuredly, ensue: "Let's see who's got the biggest dick on the staff, Danny. The waiters are willing to put up five bucks each. C'mon. It would be a huge win if it's true and you, little straight Irish rascal that you are, were to win."

Danny was puzzlingly reticent.

"Why would I want to look at a bunch of gay boys' weenies?" he asked.

Jamie was nimble: "You don't have to look if you don't want. I will be the impartial judge. Since I run the dining room and assign these dancers to the good or bad stations they are not going to argue with me as to the outcome."

In a former life Danny was a trader on the stock market back in New York City. He did some fast calculations. Ten waiters were on the floor at that time.

"Make it twenty bucks a head!" Danny demanded, smiling at his own joke.

"Great! I'll only impose a 5-percent cut as the agent, of course!" Jamie added.

And so the show was on. After pre-service on Friday it was agreed that the cockfight would commence before we opened for dinner. In the spirit of the game Allan informed us he would make the staff meal that night. No one volunteers to make staff. What with the chore of simply getting your own station together each night there was already too much work. On top of that you had to make do with whatever was going to feed us without poisoning us, and Chef Annie did not want her food costs to suffer. And then you had the caustic review of the meal by the waitstaff that took this freebie as their ordained right each night and they expected a five-star meal. It was a strong group when you put them all together. If they were sufficiently unhappy with one of our efforts, they were known to come back to the hot line after a bitch session out in the cool of the dining room and boo us while we cooks ate in the kitchen standing up!

But Allan was giggling as he went about the task that Friday. The waiters respected Allan. He was one of the first chefs I ever met who had graduated from a cooking school. In fact he, the former chef, Waldy Malouf, and the current chef, Annie Donovan, all graduated from the Culinary Institute of America and it was, in part, how they all came to work down in Key West, that and through the efforts of Mr. Wolkowsky. The Pier House was truly a powerhouse of culinary talent, with Annie at the helm. She was also the first female *chef-de-cuisine* I'd worked under. Annie continued to be one of the most mercurial humans I'd ever known. I kept my distance from anything that might tick her off. And once I got a glimpse of what Allan was creating, this certainly qualified.

When the front-of-the-house waiter and floor manager meeting was over around 5:15 they all would burst through the kitchen door like Huns with their knives, forks, and plates in hand and jockey for the center position at the pickup table from which Chef Annie would be slapping the guests' dinners in an hour or so. She was back at her apartment during this hour resting up for the night ahead. We'd set the sheet pans and mixing bowls down and the frenzy would begin.

This night began in the same way, but when the troops stampeded in looking for their meal there was nothing on the table.

Grumbling and anxious voices began to fill the kitchen. Allan silenced the room.

He took on a mock German accent. "Vee vill haff order!" he shouted, unable to suppress a Cheshire cat smile. He pulled a pan out of the oven and held it so high no one could see what was on it. Then he set it down so all could see the enormous phallus-shaped meat loaf Allan had sculpted. You could hear the proverbial pin drop.

Tom, the most senior waiter, spoke first, "Oh, it's me!" doing a perfect Paul Lynde.

Danny dashed over and dropped a big blob of mayo on the tip. Peals of laughter filled the kitchen, and the ladies skipped out to enjoy Allan's ode to meat.

Tammy (his gay name) worried, "I don't know if this meal will make my baby fully unfurl or not for the contest." But he was hungry so he ate.

Allan had made another meat loaf for us line guys so we could eat, too. It was an excellent meat loaf. *Had he learned this at the Culinary Institute of America?* I wondered.

After the staff meal Jamie corralled all the waiters outside near the Dumpster where, behind the tall wooden gates, the contest would take place.

"We better hurry, boys!" Jamie advised. "Annie will be back from her tryst with the salad chef by six!" It was well known she was now fucking the garde-manger chef and he was using her to get coke, an increasingly popular drug in Key West.

Everyone who wanted to be in the contest was lined up now. Jamie had set up two sawhorses with a big piece of plywood stretched across them. He had one of the dining room tablecloths on top.

Jamie, basking in his role—all he needed was an eye patch and a bull-horn—made the call:

"All right, then. All who are able, come to the table! Okay lads and lassies, it's cock-a-doodle-do time!"

Each waiter placed the pride of his loins on the tablecloth.

There was one woman who worked the hot line with us. Her name was Mary and she was one of the most beautiful women in Key West. One of her eyes was green and the other was blue. She had soft blonde hair and a delicately structured face that evoked her Scandinavian blood. When you looked at her still-so-youthful face, you found that you longed to look at one eye and then the other. She had a high, little-girl voice, but the things that came out of her mouth betrayed her talent as a spirited line rat who could cook alongside the rest of our ragtag lineup. Mary determined it was her job to keep Danny happy and fully capable of representing the kitchen. She had two children, both nearly grown and living in Virginia. I think Danny was her new mothering project.

Since it was because of Danny that the contest was taking place he got to go last. There was one person senior to Jamie Conahan and that was the restaurant manager, Mr. John Klausing. After graduating from a world-class hotel school in Switzerland, John came to Key West with his wife and settled in Old Town. He was a nice man who liked to do as little physical work as possible. It wasn't that he didn't know what was supposed to be done. Clearly with his training and background he was light-years ahead of anyone else in Key West except, perhaps, the Frenchman, Chef René, who owned Le Crêperie down the street. John suffered from the shakes when he was upset, so when things in the restaurant didn't go according to the rules set out by Escoffier his arms and hands would tremble. John told Danny and me a story from his past when he worked at the Savoy in London. His arms wavered as he pointed in each direction of our Key West kitchen trying to explain the vastness of the kitchens at the Savoy and how big the staff was.

"We served over ten thousand meals a day! There were eleven butchers! Can you grasp that? Listen. There were two Arabs that worked there and the only job they ever did was to peel hard-boiled eggs! From sunup to sundown every day they peeled eggs! Oh yes!" he would add with his voice rising, as if somehow we were prepared to object to this fact. We weren't. His head bobbed up and down and his double chin shook.

Mary was rubbing Danny's shoulders while he looked out over the sparkling ocean drinking a Molson and sucking on a cigarette. "Are they all out now, Mary?" Danny asked, letting out a long cloud of smoke.

"Yes, Danny, they sure are. Pretty maids all in a row," she said, sounding just like Marilyn Monroe.

It was, of course, at that moment that Klausing appeared outside in the Dumpster area. He just backed up against the wall and said nothing, shaking. There were ten penises lined up on the sawhorse table. Later some of the waiters complained that it was the sight of Klausing that caused some shrinkage, but that would never have changed for who won.

Danny turned and looked at the competition on display. Being as short as he was his waist barely cleared the tabletop. Mary helped him drop his pants. (That was the first time he ever needed help with that!) He pressed his body against the table's edge, pulled his cock out below it, and began to inch it onto the table's surface, paying it out like a rope.

The waiters' eyes got wider with each uncoil.

Danny said, "Look, you deviants. I'm only going to show you enough to win."

And win he did, leaving all to wonder how much more the Irishman had down there.

In 1978, the menu at the Pier House was what might be described as "international." The "New American Cuisine" as we know it today was still a few years off. But the groundwork was being laid and—with no real conscious intention—it was being laid, at least in part, in this kitchen at the end of U.S. 1. There were some key forces at play. Continental cooking was recognized by the American hospitality industry as being very important if you wanted to attract wealthy travelers and diners. So we served dishes like Beef Wellington, Chicken Chasseur (French for "hunter"), and Sole Veronique (extravagantly prepared with peeled white grapes), dishes I was very happy to be learning because I felt they were classics and thus important to my expanding repertoire and budding evolution as a chef. And some of the chefs Wolkowsky hired had the background and know-how to execute these dishes in the time-honored manner.

David cared deeply about quality and Nino was a case in point. Nino had been born in Italy and learned in the classic European way, coming up through the ranks of the grand hotels of Rome, moving on to Paris and London, and eventually working with luxury cruise lines. That brought him to a position in a New York temple of haute cuisine and to the attention of David Wolkowsky. David was entranced by the white-haired Italian and hired him away to Key West to replace a French chef named Paul who'd moved to Fort Lauderdale to open up his own restaurant. David hadn't checked so thoroughly on Nino's capacity for the English language, so instead of a fully capable head chef he had a vastly overqualified butcher.

This brings us to the other source of talent that David was tapping well before much of American restaurant management ever heard of the place, the Culinary Institute of America. David was in on the ground floor of this wellspring of bright, young, and desperate-to-pay-back-their-tuition-loans crew. These talented cooks brought the winds of change with them and were eager to forge a more global style. As Americans, they had grown up outside the heavy imprimatur of the European culinary worldview. Thanks to them we developed several dishes that nodded to the Far East, the Middle East, and even a few with roots in Africa. The rules were changing.

But the most striking dynamic was that David also had a fascination and a love for the flavors emanating from and through Key West itself. He once flew to New York City with a Key Lime Pie on his lap to take to his aging mother. We didn't stop with that old yet beloved confection. David's celebrity friends were coming for the fun in Key West—Leonard Bernstein and Truman Capote among them—and we were introducing the local Key West catch to the New York cognoscenti, who had never tasted conch before. We did a grilled swordfish and served it with the extraordinary treat that is caramelized plantains. We served spanking-fresh snapper ceviche. The second-favorite soup on the menu was black bean. I'm sure David had had it at the legendary Coach House in New York and commanded us to put it on the Pier House menu.

At this time—and possibly for the first time—classically trained chefs were communicating with local people. This dialogue shifted the culinary zeitgeist and gave birth to the New American Cuisine, which was nurtured, championed, and refined by the creative geniuses Alice Waters, Paul Prudhomme, Mark Miller, and Wolfgang Puck. The seed was also sown in the mind of a young grill cook from Diamond Lake, Illinois.

It was at the Pier House that I began to piece together the vast puzzles of sauce making. Pots of varying sizes would be placed on the hot line's "piano" (essentially, a large, flat, stove top). Some pots were large, say for chicken stock; some were small, say for a sauce Poivrade (a venison stock reduction). Some sauces required the larger, flat rondeau pans (used for the secondary phase of sauce making.) *Why did some sauces get mushrooms and some not?*

I wondered. Which herbs were right and which wrong? The rules seemed fairly immutable but since I had not been to culinary school or read any cookbooks or worked for a chef who had taught me these things, I just kept watching, asking the occasional questions. Sometimes Nino would answer; sometimes he would just curl his lips and expose a row of teeth to make me shut up. He'd trump that body language by reaching directly into a raging oven and pulling out a flat steel pan with his fingertips to show me that they were burned for so long and so thoroughly that he had no feeling in them anymore—and that I would never be as tough as him.

Hooker was the sous chef at the Pier House. He had one name and that suited both him and us. Simple. As with many people in Key West, one name was enough. Danny knew Hooker stood between him and the sous chef job and detested him because of it. It made me less likely to like the guy, too, I admit. One time Hooker was leaning against the big Hobart mixer near the door of the chef's office. He looked as if he could fall asleep at any moment. Annie came out of her office and Hooker feigned interest in some papers on a clipboard. She asked him what he was going to make for a special tonight. He pressed his long fingers against the bridge of his long nose and said, "Veal. Veal with a velouté at the base, maybe some peas and pearl onions. Dunno exactly."

Annie, apparently satisfied with this culinary chalk talk, went back in her office. I walked over to Hooker and said, "How do you know that term you just used, 'velouté'?" I had been around Hooker now for a few months. Knew he was from Wisconsin. Knew he was not one to do a damned thing that would raise a sweat and here he was talking over my head.

He said, "I went to the CIA, the Culinary Institute of America, just like Annie and Allan. Maybe you ought to go to school."

"I can't swing that kind of tuition, man," I said.

"Well," Hooker replied, "why don't you read?"

"I do read, Hooker. I read a lot! I read Dostoevsky! I read James Joyce!"

The frustration of not knowing this term "velouté" and the fact I couldn't afford to go to school was really starting to piss me off.

"Yeah. But do you read cookbooks, Norman?"

Hooker had me. Nailed. I had been cooking for a living for seven years and hadn't read a book on the subject. I was soaking it all in, or using the on-the-job-training method.

I found my voice after a moment. "Like whose cookbooks?"

"Like Beard. James Beard. That would be good."

"Never heard of him!" I shot back. Not yet willing to give him the satisfaction of thinking that he taught me something.

I stopped that afternoon at the bookstore on lower Duval and bought James Beard's *Theory and Practice of Good Cooking.* Wade came down to Key West again and got a job working as a bouncer/doorman at an outrageously successful (and outrageous in many other ways) bar/nightclub called the Monster, just a block away from the Pier House. I was surprised that Wade would work at this place but he was always one to get along and find humor in all kinds of situations. What I didn't know was that what he also found was a steady supply of the drug that would begin to take over my oldest childhood friend's life—cocaine.

Cocaine was the drug of choice in Key West. There were others, and alcohol was never far behind, either. But coke cut across all lines (so to speak). It was like the salt air—it was everywhere. But it wasn't cheap and it turned people into very needy animals: straight, gay, male, female, young, old. When the coke was plentiful everyone was beautiful. When it ran low folks got desperate. Wade ran the door, and the party boys would often pay him in coke versus the cash entrance fee. It was "stepped on." He'd let ten guys in for a bag. He drank for free. Wade always hated the taste of alcohol. So he drank rum (151 proof) and Cokes. It added up and then it started inevitably to subtract. The most popular song I think I heard in that place was Gloria Gaynor's "I Will Survive." Listening to Springsteen's "Streets of Fire" on my stereo at nearly full blast to get myself psyched up for work became an everyday ritual for about a month thanks to a massive lightning bolt that came out of a hot summer sky and fried the main electric generator somewhere up north. In the aftermath we learned that power was going to have to be rationed for an unknown period of time. In reality, the city officials had no plan, which meant that we could not plan.

We'd be cruising along, doing prep or lunch or dinner, and suddenly the power would fail. As soon as the huge overhead ventilation hoods stopped sucking out the furnace-like heat of the still-functional stoves, we'd turn off the gas in the now pitch-black kitchen, leave the tickets hanging on the pass, abandon our stations, our customers, and our duties, and run down to the Bull and Whistle Bar on the other side of the "no power zone" of Duval Street. We'd load up on two or three beers, watching and waiting until the power was restored. Once it was, we would run back to the kitchen and resume cooking. This often occurred just as the dinner rush was peaking and so the dining room, still adequately lit by the summer sun (even at eight o'clock), would be full of customers who were still drinking but not getting fed and becoming damaged in the process. We had the old tickets to fill (the ones we'd left hanging), then suddenly the machine that spits out fresh dupes would come clackety-clacking to life, fully loaded with new orders taken while the power was down. The board would look like a New Year's Eve ticket board while Annie was screaming like Lady Macbeth for us to get moving.

Billy was a young kid with a massive Afro who had come to work with us. He was a short, rubber-bodied guy who almost seemed to be dancing when he was merely walking. He was helping out in the salad department when the power went out and was in the process of making a huge batch of bleu cheese dressing. When power was restored he went over to the big Hobart mixer with a five-pound bag of bleu cheese crumbles. Somehow the machine's speed button had gotten moved from the lowest setting to the highest. Billy leaned over with the cheese-filled bag and hit the "on" switch. Ten gallons of sour cream, heavy cream, vinegar, and bleu cheese erupted from the Hobart's bowl and draped Billy's entire body, lodging in a glorious apex upon his newly whitened and cheese-pungent Afro. He looked like a living flocked Christmas tree, his big brown eyes like twinkling twin bulbs emanating from within. From then on he was called, "Billy Bleu Cheese."

I decided to leave Key West and see what might be waiting for me up north. Janet and I were still living hand to mouth and I knew it wouldn't be long before we would want children. We certainly couldn't afford them on a line cook's pay. So we loaded up the truck and said good-bye to our friends with the sense it would be a long time before we would see them again.

When we got back to Illinois we moved back in with our brother-in-law Chipp. I quickly found work. The first place was called Sacha's (prophetically subtitled The Lazy Gourmet). I hadn't realized exactly how lazy Sacha was until I had been there about a month, but even with my limited skills I knew this place was cutting all the corners it could and I would not learn to be a sous chef there. So I found another job, this time at a place called the Barn of Barrington. When I applied they sent me home to study the menu. It was in French with English translations. I was very excited that perhaps at last I was going to get a higher education. I felt so positive about it I called Chef Annie and read her some of the menu items: Loin of Lamb Clamart, Sole Meunière Mont-Bry, and Rice Cakes Pompadour. She confessed that even she had no idea what these dishes were and advised me to "learn all you can!"

But when I got to work, the first thing I saw cued me to the possibility that the menu and the reality of what was happening in the kitchen were distinctly out of touch with one another. I was directed to the garde-manger station. (At least they were identifying the workstations in French.) A young woman there asked me to slice the hard-cooked eggs to garnish a salad. I asked her where they were and she held out a long plastic-covered salami-like item. I was curious and sliced off the end. It turned out to be a concoction that someone had made with egg whites and egg yolks and somehow shaped into a tube so that, the girl explained, as she wrestled the lid off a commercial salad dressing, "you could get perfectly even slices of the egg on the salads and no one had to eat the ends."

I wandered over to the grill station and met a guy named Ray. I asked him if he would be making the sauce Foyot for the tenderloin dish I'd read about on the menu, and he said he'd already made it two days before. Foyot is a cousin of sauce Béarnaise and cannot be made more than an hour or two in advance or you risk spoiling it. I knew that I had to move on from this place, too. I faked a need to use the restroom, slipped down the stairs, and ran out to my car.

I thought about enrolling at the CIA. Maybe it was the only way to move up and past this world? I called Chef Annie again and asked if she'd write me a letter of recommendation. She said, "Fuck that! You know I went to that fucking school, Norman. You know how to cook more than those kids. You just need some other shit I can show you. Come back to the Pier House. I'll make you my sous chef."

Suddenly, I was excited again!

The Meat Loaf Contest

The Pier House Meat Loaf Contest was inspired one fateful afternoon by my dear friend Danny McHugh. But it was most decidedly *not* a culinary head-to-head but a head-to-head of another order altogether. This one involved men and a kind of out-gunning that belongs safely in the chapter named "The Pier House" and far from the world of recipes!

For the meat loaf:

2	tablespoons blended oil
1	large sweet onion, diced small
1	large carrot, diced small
2	tablespoons roasted garlic oil
½	pound mushrooms, sliced
2	tablespoons roasted garlic, mashed
¼	cup tomato paste
2	tablespoons Pick-a-Peppa sauce
2	eggs
1	pound beef chuck, ground
1	pound pork, ground
½	cup Panko crumbs
½	cup buttermilk
2	tablespoons fresh thyme, chopped
3	tablespoons fresh oregano, chopped
1	tablespoon kosher salt
1	tablespoon cracked black pepper
	bacon strips, enough to line loaf pan
	kosher salt and cracked black pepper, to taste

In a pan over medium-high heat, add the blended oil, onions, and carrots. Sauté, allowing the vegetables to caramelize. Season with salt and pepper and remove the vegetables to a bowl.

To the same pan, add the roasted garlic oil and the mushrooms, and sauté until the mushrooms are cooked through. Season with salt and pepper, remove from the heat, and allow them to cool.

In a small bowl, whisk together the roasted garlic, tomato paste, Pick-a-Peppa, and eggs. Set aside.

In a large bowl, combine the vegetables and mushrooms with the ground beef and pork. Add the remaining ingredients, except for the bacon, and mix together. Line the bottom of a loaf pan with the bacon strips. Place the meatloaf mixture atop the bacon strips, patting and smoothing into a loaf shape. Top with the glaze (recipe below).

Bake in a 350 degree F oven for approximately 1 hour, or until the internal temperature of the meatloaf reaches 135 degrees F. Allow it to rest for about 10 minutes. Serve, or refrigerate until cool before serving, preferably overnight.

For the glaze:

½ cup ketchup
2 tablespoons dark brown sugar
½ teaspoon dry mustard

In a bowl, combine all the ingredients and whisk until smooth.

Makes 6 to 8 servings

CHAPTER 11

Shit Happens

IT WAS 1978 AND I WAS FINALLY a sous chef! I still worked a line position but I was moving up, albeit in a world of absolute chaos. I was at the Pier House in Old Town, Key West. Key West at that time was not the well-adjusted, rehabbed, corporately correct, child-safe, real estate gold mine it has become.

Nonetheless, we loved the raffish, piratical, barely legal town that it was. We ran to it like children run to an ice cream truck, like hobos once chased freight cars. It was idyllic, illicit madness.

On this particular morning, however, I woke up in agony, struggling to open my throbbing eyes. It was immediately clear that the day ahead was not likely to go smoothly. Not surprising, really, considering the day before had been the annual Tequila Races. (The city put an end to them in the early 1980s.) The race started and finished right at the Pier House, an event so well attended that the throng of contestants spilled out of the Chart Room bar and onto the deck by the pool. It started with a shot of tequila; afterward, each contestant had to jump into the pool and down a second shot just as he got out. Two shots. No big deal. But then you ran to the edge of the small beach and received a third shot. You swam a short distance to a raft—another shot. Then you got into a small Hobie Cat and sailed out about a mile to a buoy, where you were handed your next shot. Then you sailed back to the raft, anchored, and, that's right, drank another shot. Back to the pool for another shot and finally, back to the bar for the last shot. The person with the fastest time to do all of that won. Beautiful. Even if you didn't race you got caught up in the spectacular insanity—there was no avoiding it.

But the next day, I pressed an ice bag to my head and lapped at my café Cubano like one of Hemingway's dazed polydactyl cats. I was not savoring the idea of going to work. But as any kitchen rat knows, a hangover is not a reason to call in. You work in pain or, if unavoidable, still drunk.

After a while, I managed to stagger out the door and climb onto my moped. Of course it was drizzling. The city was gloomy and quiet. While cradling my second café I hit a pothole. The moped bucked and hot coffee splashed against my lap, soaking through my pants. I cursed and flung the little foam cup away. A moment later, I lurched into the driveway at the very end of Duval Street, where some unfortunate soul was busily rooting through the Dumpster to see what might be salvaged. He threw a hamburger box viciously aside. I hustled past without a word.

Lunch was just starting to pick up in the main dining room. Tom was waiting tables, as he had been doing since the resort opened. He was attending a family from someplace like Madison, Wisconsin. Mom, Pop, Buddy, and Sis—they were all putty in his flowing hands. Tom had an incredible way with children, and what could make parents happier than their children actually enjoying themselves while trapped in a restaurant with Mom and Dad, happily eating food they'd never heard of? Apparently, Tom had won swimming trophies back in his native Michigan, a reliable icebreaker when waiting on tables like this one. Soon they'd be ordering more food than they could possibly consume.

Meanwhile, things were getting noisy at the pot sink. Trixie was late again. Ah, Trixie, how shall I describe "her"? Think of Janis Joplin as a man, wearing Buddy Holly glasses that were perpetually fogged up, even in bright sunlight. But she worked hard, even if she was out all night workin' harder. (I saw Trixie arrive in a limo on more than one morning.) So without old Ms. T, that meant brother Clyde was tossin' two loads and he was not happy about it. His boom box was approaching a volume he'd never get away with if we didn't need him crankin' on the dirty pots, pans, and dishes. I could hear Clyde's favorite song, the Commodores' "Brick House" from across the kitchen. Hell, I could feel the bass line.

Clyde did a three-sixty, swatted his dishrag at a pot rack, and sang along. He winked knowingly as the salacious lyrics bounced around the kitchen walls.

My hot line buddy Danny McHugh waved me over. He wanted me to join him in the "Rosie Trick." There was a young lady who worked in what were the shortest cutoff blue jean shorts imaginable. And, oh yes, she had the figure to cover the bet and cash the check, and then some. She was amazingly good natured and seemed oblivious to our petty mischief. Danny yelled over to the dish room, "Hey Rosie! We need a stack of plates!" Rosie gently pushed her large-framed aviator glasses with the back of her hand, guided her long brown hair behind one ear, and picked up an armload of plates. She strolled over, her rubber flip-flops gently slapping the bottoms of her feet, to behind the hot line where I worked the grill and Danny sautéed. She set the plates on the edge of the stove. As usual, Danny and I both pretended that we were far too busy to come away from our tasks to be of help to her. She reached up to put the plates away, arching her back as she situated them high on the rack, four or five plates at a time, and on each occasion having to stretch her body ever higher over the oven. Eventually, unable to resist, Danny pretended to drop something and sank to his knees to take in the view, relishing it with all the pleasure of a prisoner receiving a cake on Christmas morning.

Meanwhile, the Commodores' "Brick House" continued to pound on my ragged nerves.

Some of the waiters had two names. One was their straight name and one was their gay name. I come from a very small town in the Midwest, so a lot of this was new but oddly okay with me. Marvin would tease me at least once a week, "One night with me, baby, and you will throw rocks at your old lady!" But he was like an uncle to all of us, one we loved and watched over. He'd had some seizures and if the owners found out they might have eighty-sixed him. Makes the touristas jumpy, they'd reason.

"Tammy" was reading the *Key West Citizen*, the local newspaper. He was standing near the pantry when I heard him shriek. This was not the type of shriek you cry out when you're fearful, as if a car were suddenly swerving out of control and into your lane. No, this was the shriek of a game show contestant who had just won the big money prize, "*So come on down!*" A team of waiters rushed over. "What? What? What?" they demanded. Trembling with excitement, Tammy pointed to the paper, where it announced that the Philippine fleet would be docking one of their ships at Key West for the entire weekend. Estimates of over five hundred sailors on shore leave! Tammy looked up, an angelic glow wreathing his finely featured face, and beamed, "I just adore seafood!" He clutched the paper to his chest and marched out the door to see whom else he could share this joyous news with.

I glanced at Clyde, still blasting "Brick House." His vibe was beginning to get to me. I think I saw him toss a newly emptied bottle of Miller High Life into the trash. He looked at me like he was "just working man, just working."

At the time, we didn't have an in-house pastry chef; Annie had fired her. Nino (the butcher) would make the Zuppa Anglaise Cake, the pantry girls would make the Key Lime Pie base, and so on. I took on the task of making the meringue for the pies and topping them with a towering stack of sugary goo, then glazing them in the blast furnace of a hot oven. It was just after I set the batch of six pies in the oven when Danny signaled me over. I beat a path to Danny's side and caught another installment of the Rosie Trick in all its refinement. Danny and I high-fived each other. That's when I heard Betty, the breakfast cook, laughing wickedly. I looked at her with a dumb "whaaa?" expression. She pointed to the oven with her sixteen-ounce Busch beer can and cackled, "You fucked up the pies, Ace." The glory of Rosie's perfect bottom faded instantly as I raced back across the kitchen and flung open the doors on the rickety Blodgett. It is a bit of a miracle to see pies literally on fire. *En* fucking *fuego! Dios Mio!*

Six cylindrical spires of flame danced in the maw of that oven. The heat spanked my face hard. I pulled the sheet pan out, trying to keep away from the key lime infernos, whipped around, and dropped the pan on Nino's butcher block. I yanked a long spatula out of the knife rack and quickly slashed off the smoldering meringue tops in an effort to salvage the bottom of the pies and the graham cracker crusts. The tops hissed like burning ships sinking into the sea as they met whatever was in the garbage can at that moment. Beef blood? Fish heads? I swore at the dilemma unfolding in front of me. "Shit, fuck, dammit to fucking hell!" It was eerie how it almost seemed to be occurring in slow motion. Some faces looked on in horror and some of the crew was slapping their knees, doubled over laughing. You could count on it with this team.

That's when I snapped. I ran over to Clyde's noisemaker and yanked the cord out of the wall. "That's it, Clyde! No more fucking Commodores today!" I'd never had the balls to face him down before that day. But Clyde knew what crazy looked like and he was starin' at a face full of it at that moment. By now Tom was nearly finished serving lunch to our young family from the Midwest. He had managed to get Mom and Pop to order an extra round of daiquiris and he felt confident about a sizeable tip. He decided to reward himself. The main waiter station was situated so that the waiters could watch the guests arriving or leaving from behind a chest-high wall. As the family happily strolled out, they could see Tom bent over, apparently engaged in some task. Since they'd forged such a wonderful bond, the family called out, "Bye, Tom!" Tom suddenly snapped upright, startled by the proximity of their voices, and by the stimulants now hitting his brain.

Normally the family wouldn't have been any wiser, with the plate hidden well out of view. But when Tom bobbed up to jovially wave them out, the plastic straw was still stuck up his nose. The family wrestled with this grotesque image, momentarily trying to make sense of it, and then fled down the hallway and out into the streets. Tom was confused as to why they had reacted with such horror, until he bent down again, and the little mirror showed him what they'd just seen. He yanked out the straw, composed himself, thought for a moment, and then did "just one more tiny bump since I'm here" plus a "freeze" for good measure, before shimmying back to his tables.

I finally got out of work around 10 p.m. and I needed drinks. Plural. You could always count on the Full Moon Saloon back then. At that hour it was just beginning to happen. Danny and I sat down at the horseshoe-shaped bar and started to unwind.

Buddy D. was bartending. He introduced me to a singer/songwriter who was down from his home state of Alabama, the same place Jimmy Buffett was from. His name was Keith, a nice guy, and he got a real kick out of the food and restaurant rap Danny and I were filling him in on. He invited us to go over to Buffett's place and see what was going on. They'd been working on a song for most of the afternoon and maybe we could listen in. No *problemo*, my new friend. Buffett's? Sure. Let's go give Jimmy a hand. Why not?

Another guy was at the house when we got there, an excellent bartender as well as one of the island's most heralded cocksmen. Chris was a mellow

Vietnam vet whom I could never imagine being at war with anything other than a stubborn zipper. By now Jimmy had most of the lyrics down and most of the melody, too. But the opener was where he was still seeking his muse. It was a song about the odd twists and turns of life. Jimmy and Keith made up nonsense words or just hummed to fill in the gap and then moved on to the part they were happy with. That's when I fell out of Jimmy Buffett's window. First Jimmy, then Chris, and then Keith came hotfooting it around to the waterside of the house. Danny stayed put and continued to drink. Chris lifted me up and clapped me on the back to get my lungs to open. Then he reached delicately into my shirt pocket and plucked out my moped key. With motorized transport safely out of the way for the evening, we climbed back up the wooden stairs and Chris fixed fresh drinks. Jimmy picked up his battered Martin and found the notes from before. Words came now and he sang them with a golden smile, "Shit happens. . . ."

Tequila Races Salsa

The annual Pier House Tequila Race is vividly recounted in detail in this chapter. This deceptively simple salsa was developed in homage to the unforgettable event after the city brought it to an untimely end. In addition to being the perfect host to your favorite corn chips, it's also a lively accompaniment with grilled fish, baked chicken, or boiled shrimp.

2	medium tomatoes, skinned, seeded, and diced small
⅓	cup sweet onion, diced small
1	jalapeño pepper, stemmed, seeded, and minced
1	teaspoon minced garlic
2	tablespoons cilantro leaves, roughly chopped
1	tablespoon Spanish sherry wine vinegar
1	teaspoon lime juice
1	(liquid) ounce XVOO
½	teaspoon kosher salt
½	teaspoon freshly cracked pepper

In a bowl, mix together all the ingredients and set aside for about 30 minutes to allow the flavors to meld. Serve with your favorite corn chips.

Makes 1 cup

Port of Call menu. This was my best culinary education to date.

CHAPTER 12

The Port of Call

Key West, 1979

ALLAN KATZ CALLED ME about a month after he left the Pier House and all he had to say was one short sentence: "We make beurre blanc to order, Norman." His uniquely warm version of a New York accent buzzed in my ear like a bee. I missed cooking with the big guy and I knew I was missing out on learning from him, too.

Over at the Pier House we made big batches of beurre blanc (the French term for white butter sauce) with three pounds of butter. Sometimes we'd make a basic beurre blanc and then divide it in half or thirds and flavor them two or three different ways. Beurre blanc was the basic "flat white paint" that was used to sauce many (too many) fish in those days. It can be a temperamental sauce, especially in the roaring heat of a Key West kitchen and can "break" if it gets too hot. (When exposed to warm temperatures, the delicate liaison between the acidity of the vinegar and/or citrus juices and the creaminess of the butter tends to break down, ruining the sensuous "mouth feel" for which it is renowned.) For that reason it took an experienced hand to make it amid the hustle and bustle of a kitchen putting out two hundred dinners a night, and it was easier to make a big batch and then not have to deal with it again. That was not the mindset at Philip's Port of Call, however.

If there was one restaurant that finally made me want to cut the shit of the wandering, partying, and "what-am-I-gonna-be-when-I-grow-up?" whining and succeed and become a serious chef, it was the Port of Call. I'd been cooking for over eight years and I'd had enough of the clowns, cowboys, and ruined, drunken chefs. I wanted to get to what I was just starting to realize could be on the other side of the next hill. I'd heard about the talented Chef Philip Mascia and of his restaurant's popularity. The place was packed every night with Key West's "in crowd." Port of Call was a mini version of New York's Le Cirque or Elaine's. The famous and the infamous dined at the Port of Call. Philip was the "chef-patron," which was what some of the chefs in France called themselves; the idea of being one myself one day began to wave its hand in front of my mind's eye and say, "It's now or never."

Philip hired Allan to be his sous chef and, though Allan took a pay cut to work at the Port, he explained that the knowledge he would gain would quickly justify the cost of leaving the Pier House. "Hey," he laughed, "I paid a ton of money to go to the CIA and I've already seen more stuff here in a month than I saw in the two years at Hyde Park and the Pier House combined." I had moved up to sous chef at the Pier House and the money was starting to help pull Janet and me out of the trenches. But beurre blanc to order? Hmmm.

For the second time Allan came over and told me there was a job for me, if I was ready to rock and roll. Allan looked like he'd been through boot camp, but he had a look in his eye of a crazy kind of happiness, too. This time it was going to be at the near-mythic Port of Call. A position was open. I gave my notice at the Pier House.

I was fucking scared to enter that kitchen. To compensate I tried being a bit of a joker on my first day. Philip smiled from time to time, but I didn't know it was a wary smile. On the second day I accidentally knocked into the hot line table and a bottle of Marsala shattered right where Philip was working sauté. Philip flew into a rage. Allan turned even whiter than his normal shade and I think he feared for his *own* job because he was the one who had gotten me in the door. But the fury passed, and I went about learning the Port of Call way. I was the salad and dessert maker now, not a sous chef anymore.

We did it all there. Unlike the Pier House, there was no designated prep department, butcher department, or saucier. We received the fish in the alley behind the kitchen. I flipped a board that hung from chains on the alley wall and cut the fish before it went into the reach-in cooler. There was no walk-in fridge, just some reach-ins. As a back-up, we also had a household refrigerator in a back closet behind the dirty linen bags, its door held shut by the weight and stench of that linen. It wasn't fancy, but it was functional. Still, there was an artisan's atelier feeling to the Port of Call kitchen. The tools there were all carefully chosen. It was the first time I had seen professional-grade saucepans for almost every sauce made in the kitchen. Unlike all the other places I worked, this was not a battered hodgepodge of broken or beaten-up cookware. It was almost like entering a Williams-Sonoma store, except the Port of Call's tools had been used and bore the patina of that use proudly. The kitchen was clean and logically organized with products and supplies arranged with near-military order.

Philip was the most natural cook I had ever seen to that point in my life. When he made food, its flavors spoke more clearly, more joyously than any food I'd ever tasted out of a pan. The colors and aromas were vibrant, clean, enticing, and exciting. I loved to watch him and maybe help him a little, if he let me after he'd come back to the kitchen from a swim or a nap at home with his pregnant wife. He wore shorts and white socks, construction boots, and a short-sleeved dishwasher shirt rather than a chef's coat. He draped a bib apron over himself, which accentuated a healthy gut, the gut of a fully satisfied chef-patron. Philip was becoming my role model! He had his own little place, small and manageable, and was doing *his* food *his* way. The Port only had about forty seats. Perfect for Janet and me one day! Was this possible? Did I just think that? Was I becoming a chef?

The Port of Call kitchen was small but efficient. There was a single door to the dining room with a small window in it so waiters would not smash into each other as they went in and out. As you entered the kitchen from the dining room the first area was an island station. There was very little room on the waiter side but that is where the espresso machine, silverware, and wine glasses were. The cash register was off to the right. If you came around the island to place an order you squeezed in on the left facing in, past the dish/pot sink and the sink we washed the bushels of spinach in for our signature spinach salad. Spinach did not come prewashed in those days and that sink and I spent a lot of time together. The servers would stand at the end of the short two-man line near the back door and place their orders by calling them out. They didn't yell. They spoke as if announcing a train arrival. The message was important and Philip made sure everyone gave it the attention he wanted it to have so we could successfully fill each order.

"Ordering! One Spinach Salad, one Port of Call Salad with Sauce Piquant, one French Onion Soup and one Stuffed Avocado followed by two Veal Chops, one Rack of Lamb and one Fish and Fruit."

Philip would take the ticket and place it over his workstation. At the beginning of my time there, Allan was next to him and I worked the pantry. Over the course of the next two years I'd learn to work the other two stations, butcher the fish, make the sauces, and, during the winter tourist season, I took on the role of lunch chef. I learned so much at the Port. But let me not get too far ahead of myself. It started like this: I was becoming a devoted reader of *Gourmet* magazine and was excited to go down to Valladares newsstand on Duval to buy it each month. Valladares was a fantastic place with newspapers from all around the world and magazines devoted to literature, painting, photography, and even the emerging new category of food writing and photography. I would lie out on our little back porch before work and fry my hide as I underlined whole passages and made margin notes in the restaurant reviews. *Gourmet* covered the very finest restaurants in New York and San Francisco, only occasionally branching out to other locales. But it was in New York and San Francisco where the greatest chefs were doing the most amazing cooking. I couldn't even dream of financing a trip to visit these places with Janet so I imagined I was there, in those dining rooms, eating the "grande cuisine." And I wanted to immerse myself in these ideas more and more.

I stayed committed to my morning reading then swam in the ocean for a mile off the Pier House beach, riding my bike over from our place on Seidenberg Avenue. I was getting very healthy and strong from the regimen and took to eating large salads or steak tartare sandwiches on toasted whole-wheat bread when I'd get into work around one o'clock in the afternoon. The pull of the salt from my swim would be drying my skin by then and I'd go into the public restrooms and take a birdbath in the sink, washing my hair with Dr. Bronner's and rinsing myself off outside with the hose we'd use later to clean the cutting boards, before going into the still-quiet kitchen to begin my nightly salad prep. I wanted to be alone. I didn't want to fuck up in front of Philip. That was for sure. I also could pretend the Port was mine.

The restaurant was located on Front Street. Since Key West was not originally linked to the mainland by road or rail, the only way to get to the island used to be by sea. Front Street was the first street of Key West. The famous Sunset Celebrations took place right behind the restaurant, and on many evenings we could hear the shouts go up when the sun made its final descent to the ocean. Will Soto would be doing his tightrope act. The Cookie Lady would have two piles of cookies, one with marijuana and one without. Our dishwasher was a guy Philip brought down from Pennsylvania. He rarely missed a batch of the "reef cookies."

Philip got the money to build the Port of Call, in part, from a Pennsylvania buddy named Brian who had gotten a settlement after a factory accident in which all four fingers from the knuckle joint on his left hand were cut completely off. Brian worked with us, too, from time to time but his drug of choice was quaaludes and we knew we'd be cooking without his assistance when he took the first one (of several) of the potent depressants on any given evening. He was a great guy, very intelligent and Philip had taught him to cook well. But the 'ludes took over.

After a while Philip stopped cooking with us every night and started joining in the party life of Key West. He was taking in lots of cash from the restaurant and his wife couldn't track it. She loved her husband but knew him well and watched him like a hawk. They'd been through a lot together, coming from Philly to own and run the Port, and she was pregnant. She could be tough, but Philip was wily. He started to buy cocaine. The rumor was that he bought it from the Port of Call's bookkeeper.

Allan decided to go back to New York with his sweet wife Denise, so Philip brought in a Belgian-born chef who had worked there the year before and had returned to Key West. I got to move over to Allan's position and help the returning chef. His name was René. A Brazilian guy named

Aloysio, a busboy who could have been a kick-ass waiter but his English wasn't quite good enough, became the new garde-manger, or "salad slut" as we were called in that position. I loved working with Al. He made the nightly cleanup chores we faced fly by, turning them into more of a contest between us instead of the drudgery they would have been for most cooks. We cranked up the little tape deck with some Brazilian music he had and samba'd our way through the tasks. We'd finish by mopping the floors, drying them with our bib aprons, and crawling out the door backwards on our hands and knees like deck-swabbing sailors of olden times. John, the Port of Call's manager, would walk around from the front door and lock the doors each evening. I would get back on my bicycle and ride the quiet streets of Key West with my little taped-on flashlight bobbing in front of me as I made my way home.

René's approach to cooking was not all that different from Allan's or Philip's. But he had a very different sense of humor about the dishes we made at the Port of Call. It was not so much an out-and-out hatred (the way I came to feel about Lou's dishes at 700 Duval) but a real sense of the absurd. René had been classically trained abroad by European chefs and at the Adolphus Hotel in Dallas, from which he'd just come. But he had not gone to any school that offered the American international style of cooking, so it was not part of his repertoire. He cooked and thought in French. He was openly sarcastic about such Port of Call creations as Fish and Fruit, a dish that called for egg-battering a delicate yellowtail snapper, sautéing it in clarified butter, and then topping it with a pan sauce made with lots of butter, cinnamon, currant jelly, and a mix of bananas, papayas, and mangoes. It was a festive dish that even children could eat, not that we had many kids dining at the Port. Another dish he disdained was the Baked Stuffed Snapper. Whenever a waiter called out the order René would make a face. After a while I got to know him a little better and asked why he didn't like the dish. (It was a sandwich-like construction made with two thin, perfect pieces of the freshest local snapper filled with a crabmeat mixture bound with mayonnaise.) He looked at me as if I had just asked him the stupidest question on earth.

"Hot mayonnaise? Hot mayonnaise? I have never heard of anything so disgusting. Only an American would come up with hot fucking mayonnaise and put it on a poor defenseless snapper. Bullshit! Same as the oyster dish he makes us serve. Oysters Remick? What the fuck is that? Another dish he concocted? Oysters with a sauce made with ketchup and topped with cheese. Ugh!"

The criticism was over my head at the time, but I did think that René should loosen up a little. And another thing, he knew all of this before coming back and taking the job *again*. I was getting a little steamed at him by this time because I wanted this to be a job we were all proud of. I felt a new emotion in that kitchen. I felt honored to work there. I felt like I belonged to an elite corps. I may have been not much more than a private but I was in the service of something I would do battle for. But René taught me one of the most valuable lessons I ever had in a kitchen. He taught me about something that I must have been born to love.

One day Philip improbably ordered in some fresh calves' liver from the only local meat purveyor in town, West Provision Meats. He was down at the Pier House's Chart Room bar when it came in. Philip was there more and more now. René opened the box and clapped his hands. "Oh boy. Can't wait to see if we are doing this with fruit or ketchup!" I ignored the remark and he let the sarcasm fade, too. He took the two livers and placed one in the reach-in cooler. The other he expertly peeled, cleaned, and portioned.

"Let me show you how I like liver prepared," he said.

In a few minutes he had laid out some beautiful broad slices of the vibrantly red meat. He dusted them liberally with seasoned flour and set them aside. Then he heated a black steel pan and put in a slick of bacon fat. He had some chopped shallots, Italian parsley, and cold butter on the cutting board in three small bowls. When the pan was quite hot he slipped in the calves' liver. The blood-rich aroma scented the air. He quickly cooked both sides, being sure to leave the liver rare to medium-rare in the middle with a nice little crust on the outside. He set the meat aside to rest. He wiped out the same pan and now added the butter and shallots. When the butter was just turning a foamy hazelnut color he splashed in a bracing measure of Spanish sherry wine vinegar and poured it over the meat. The smell of that vinegar was magical! I'd never experienced the "brightness" of vinegar and the woodsy tones it brought along with it. We stood there between the stoves and the cutting board and tasted the food. It had a balance that I found to be perfect, and it helped me form a thought process that would become part of my first cookbook. The seeds were sown with that heavenly smell of the vinegar knifing into the fat of the sweet butter and the earthy aroma of cooked shallots.

Over the next few months, I became a much better cook. I was becoming so much more precise. When we picked up a two-top or a four-top René and I would work in absolute sync to be sure that the food came up in unison and that all the textures of the sauces were as they should be. The plate rims were carefully wiped clean and the servers were expected to know where "six o'clock" was on the plate so they could serve each dish as it was designed to be presented.

I wanted to show Philip I was even more serious about becoming a better chef and asked him if I could make a new dessert from time to time. He was so hard to get to know and had built a wall around himself, but occasionally the light would pour out of his deep brown eyes and he looked like he might shed a tear. It was that kind of look that he gave me when I asked about the desserts. I was on a flat salary, and he knew that meant I was going to have to come in even earlier to do the desserts. But he toughed out his emotion and simply said okay.

I had purchased Gaston Lenôtre's *Desserts and Pastries* at the same Duval Street bookstore where I had obtained my very first cookbook the year before. The book was laid out in a way that allowed the reader (cook or lay person) to know beforehand how complex or simple the gifted Parisian pastry chef's creations were to make. I had chosen a simple enough jelly roll cake, or so I thought. It called for making a genoise cake but, despite the straightforward instructions, I found it more mentally taxing than I'd imagined. But after long, secretive hours working when neither René would be there to mock me nor Philip would be there to make me nervous, I made a pretty reasonable version of the dish.

Philip came back from an afternoon of drinking at the Chart Room and I showed it to him. He pulled back the parchment paper to see the spongy rolled cake with the raspberry jam inside. He grabbed a knife and a small plate and cut off a slice. The powdered sugar topping caught in his thick mustache as he placed a hefty forkful in his mouth. He never even took off his sunglasses. Standing there in front of me he smiled and made a nodding motion with his head. He walked out. But the powder already on his face—not the sugar from my cake but what he'd snorted earlier at the Chart Room and in his El Camino—was running around in his brain faster and with a tighter grip than anything else in those days.

Summer wore on and the Port of Call slowed down. Restaurant revenues were always feast or famine in Key West. With summer's heat pushed into the danger zone we worked in our swimming trunks and put cold towels around our necks as we cooked. There was a "survivor's pride" we took in not wimping out and going up north as did many Key Westers in August. Then one afternoon something happened that made me wonder if we should have. September was just a few days away and we were officially in hurricane season. Even though I had lived in Key West off and on for years by then, I had never taken the threat of hurricanes as serious and real. It seemed to me that the likelihood of one hitting our tiny island would be like throwing a baseball from one side of a stadium to the other and having it hit a specific seat in the grandstands. What were the odds?

My lack of awareness came to a rattling end as the news reports of the storm's progress crackled over the TV and radio. It was suddenly a scary movie. Key West was uncharacteristically a beehive of activity for this time of year. Local folks were racing to buy plywood, batteries, water, canned goods, and everything else you might need to get through a big storm. Our home on Seidenberg Avenue was not much more stable than a tent. There were holes in the walls large enough for a bird to fly through. If a huge wind were to come at us, what good would some plywood do? Still, we tried to get ready. I cut down the coconuts, as I was advised, so they could not "become lethal cannonballs."

The days and hours before a hurricane were something I'd never lived through, and I watched the old-timers who had lived in Key West all their lives to see if I could detect just how bad this would be. From what I could tell the "conchs" were taking this one, dubbed Hurricane David, very seriously. And, like its biblical name, this one was taking on biblical proportions. Many folks began to see the steadily approaching storm as payback for the "sins" that made Key West notorious. There were those who warned that this was "God's way." We went to work the day before the storm and waited to see if our island was in David's crosshairs.

John went to the Chart Room and asked Philip what the plan was. Philip must have been clear because when John returned he told us we had to put every single bottle of liquor, box of pasta, wineglass, pot, pan, ash-tray, fork, napkin, steak, candle, can of snails, and everything else into the lockable storage area on the side of the building. Even for a place as small as the Port of Call, this would take many hours. We did the best we could. Janet was back at our home doing whatever she could. Philip remained at the Chart Room, watching the television.

I finally told John around nine o'clock that night that I was going home. If Philip wasn't going to be there to help board up his own restaurant I had done all I was going to do! John was a man who conveyed the weariness he had with the world in his sad green eyes. He gave me that look but he realized I had a wife to be with. So I jumped on my bike and raced home. An hour later John, on his way home, stopped by our house where we were building a small fort around our bed and said Philip had come back and went into a rage that I wasn't there to finish service. I told him, "Too bad." I knew I was quitting. John didn't even try to talk me out of it. I think he wanted it to hurt Philip in some way and maybe wake him up to the fact that he was in danger of losing it all, losing the Port of Call.

The next morning we woke to see that the storm had skirted us well to the north. Some of the so-called feeder bands had mildly strafed the lower keys and there were some large palm fronds littering the ground. A neighbor's garbage cans were blown into our front fence. But the air was marvelously clear and alive as if a miracle had occurred. One had, but I was out of a job once more.

Janet and I walked out into our little yard. She looked up at me, still in her bathrobe, held me tightly, and said, "Hey. You'll find another one. It's all right. We're safe."

Oysters Remick

This was one of the recipes that caused immense friction in our little Port of Call kitchen. Not that anyone would actually confront the owner—that would not fly. Philip never did anything obvious, like a Gordon Ramsay, and yell. He would look *through* folks with eyes older than Sicily, and nothing more would need to be said. Case closed. But a young French chef I otherwise very much enjoyed working with named René scrunched up his face at the idea of this dish. "Hot mayonnaise? Hot fucking mayonnaise? Only an American could think of something so bad." I liked them, but hey, *I'm* a fucking American.

1	cup mayonnaise
¼	cup Heinz chili sauce
1	tablespoon Dijon mustard
2	dashes Tabasco sauce, or more, as desired
12	fresh, raw oysters
2 to 3	slices bacon, cut into 12 (1-inch) sections
½	cup Panko crumbs
1	tablespoon Italian parsley, roughly chopped
	lemon wedges, for garnish

Preheat the broiler. In a bowl, combine the mayonnaise with the chili sauce, mustard, and Tabasco. Set aside.

Shuck the oysters, then replace each oyster back into the deep side of its shell. Reserve the oyster liquor for another purpose.

Spoon the mayonnaise sauce over the oysters until they are nicely coated. Place the oysters on a heatproof platter. Top with the bacon slices and cook under the broiler until the bacon is just cooked. Remove, sprinkle with the Panko crumbs, and return to the broiler just long enough to toast the crumbs. Remove from the broiler.

Sprinkle the parsley over the oysters. Serve with the lemon wedges as well as more Tabasco on the side.

Makes 2 generous appetizers, more as a snack

CHAPTER 13

Chez Nancy

Key West, 1979–80

WORD TRAVELS FAST on the little rock of Key West, and the word was that the lady who was the living embodiment of the restaurant Chez Nancy was looking for a chef. The day I went to speak with her was the first time I'd been to the address. It is amazing to me now but back then we lived and worked within such a tight circle of geography. Everything we needed back then—groceries, bars, beaches, the newsstand and bookstore that fed my passion for reading about this beckoning world of haute cuisine, the bakery and *café con leche* spots—all were within a short walk or bicycle ride from our crumbling yet cozy cottage home back on Seidenberg Avenue. It had been but six years since we had lived just a few blocks down the road as longhaired, free-spirited hippies. Now we were a married couple working hard for a living.

So I cranked up the red pickup truck we bought as a wedding present to each other back in Illinois three years earlier. It was the first time I had even started it in months. When it chugged to life I headed up the boulevard to the Ramada Inn, home of Chez Nancy. The restaurant had windows looking out over the shuttling traffic of U.S. 1 and the Gulf beyond. But its setting was really quite isolated from the charms of Key West compared to everywhere else I had been. This restaurant was on Key West's only highway, for God's sake.

Nancy did not conduct an interview as such. She greeted me somewhat stiffly in the lobby of the Ramada Inn and told me that I'd be "on trial for a week or so." She was the polar opposite of Philip with a wardrobe that bordered on the severe as well as the regal. She might have drawn her inspirations from Nancy Reagan and Margaret Thatcher; their politics were certainly kindred. She even wore a pearl choker that day. She had a nice smile but something seemed to keep her from sharing it. She lived in a suite on the second floor of the two-story hotel that her husband had made as "Palm Beach" as possible. It had a balcony from which she could come out and keep an eye on the business of the lobby below. The restaurant had been built as an addition to the hotel. The walk-in cooler was actually a truck that was stationed outside the building in the parking lot. You had to go through the small blue-tiled and latticework-featured dining room to get to it. There was no back door to the kitchen—not a safety feature.

It was approaching Christmastime when I started working at Chez Nancy. The busy tourist season would be coming, so I needed to "make my bones" quickly with this gig. But I was still just forming. I wasn't even a tadpole yet. My dishes were a mishmash of collected things. I could really only copy what I'd been shown. I'd been cooking nine years now and I had been nowhere that was well known or classically grounded. I hadn't worked for a "name" chef, nor had I ever spent a day in a cooking school. Perhaps Nancy didn't interview me because she knew that the real test of my mettle would come from the waiters of her namesake.

The Port of Call had a nice mix of men and women. Some of the men were actually straight. Well, one for sure and maybe two. That was a rare average in Key West. At Chez Nancy there were no female servers. Each waiter had been with Nancy for several years at a minimum. They knew the Chez Nancy style. It had kept them well funded and they certainly didn't want to see me mess with the formula. I was probably doomed, of course. I was falling in love with a new dish every day and I was desperate to make it. I didn't want to cook the same menu as the chef before me.

When those first nights of service were over I could tell that the waiters were mulling me over. Nancy had stayed clear. Perhaps she'd gone on a wine-buying junket to France. She made a point of telling me what a shabby collection of ridiculous Californian wines we had at the Port of Call. I didn't know a thing about wine at that time. I drank beer.

Janet was now twenty-four and had decided she preferred tending bar. She liked to get to know the guests and being in front of the regulars may have appealed more to a girl who came from a family of ten. The extended sense of family a bartender can feel is more than many servers can. There are steady customers in the dining rooms. But for day-after-day-steady customers, a bar is the place to be.

The La Concha Hotel is one of the most notable buildings in Key West. It is in the middle of Duval, Key West's main drag, and rises a comparatively daunting six stories! The La Concha was built in the Spanish architectural style in the late 1920s by local businessmen. When Hemingway steamed in from Havana for the first time, it was the first thing he saw. In *To Have and Have Not* he wrote of it appearing so tall in contrast to the other buildings on the island.

Tennessee Williams lived there in the winter of 1947 before buying his own home. It is believed that he wrote the early drafts of his most famous play, *A Streetcar Named Desire*, while at the La Concha. The great playwright enjoyed a cocktail party there thrown in his honor by actress Miriam Hopkins. To his delight many of the guests were naval officers in dress whites and tight pants. He cooed that all the navy boys seemed to be walking to the tune of "Managua Nicaragua," a popular song of the era.

The place to hoist a cold one or nurse a strong one was on the top floor of the La Concha. The bar, of course, was called the Top (short for the Top of La Concha). Janet applied and was hired. Fishermen, shop owners, the county sheriff, drug dealers, lawyers, local pols, real estate wizards—all found the panoramic view offered a preferred vantage point from which to eye the world below, whether through the large windows encircling the bar or through the bottom of a rocks glass.

There was a small kitchen that turned out the kind of menu you might find between the ninth and tenth holes on a golf course. The cook's name was Bob and he was falling into the bottle pretty badly. The Top was not a tourist bar back then. It didn't really market or advertise itself as such, but every now and then some Bermuda-shorts-wearing sunburned sport would wander in with one of the fishing guides he'd been out with on the water all day and ask Janet one of her favorite questions: "So do you actually live in Key West?" Not having a sarcastic side, she couldn't bring herself to say out loud what she was thinking: "No. I live in Georgia and drive here each morning." So one of her regulars like skinny Roby or scruffy Heavy Duty would josh the guy for her. Family. Then Heavy would return to argue with another patron, "Hell, I've wrung more salt water outta my socks 'n you ever sailed over, cocksucker!"

The disco balls were spinning at the Monster and the Copa for the gay crowd but the straights loved the music, too. So the Spottswood family, owners of the hotel, created a bar called Fitzgerald's in the grand hotel lobby. I guess it was chosen to evoke the Roaring Twenties and cater to the more conventional dancing and coupling. Janet took a job there, too, and soon was dividing her time between the Top and Fitzgerald's at each of the opposite latitudes of the La Concha. I was glad to see her enjoying herself with a joyous bunch of coworkers while making great tips, of course. Between my salary and her tips, we were able to fix the truck and start a small nest egg. But I didn't like the fact that she couldn't get home from work until dawn from the disco. I hated sleeping without her. I worried about her being out in Key West or, even worse, the Boca Chica bar, where she and her Fitzgerald pals went because it was the only place that stayed open after all the other bars closed. When you get off work at three or four o'clock in the morning and you are a bartender it's hard to go home and simply fall asleep. The adrenaline is rocking your brain and so the after-hours places fill up with the professionals.

But I didn't have to worry long about her keeping that schedule. One night, when she wasn't on the schedule for Fitzgerald's and I had gotten home from Chez Nancy, she sat beside me on our bed and told me, "We are having a baby." And the world became a universe bigger.

Janet kept her job at the Top but the late nights were over. She was home when I got home and we waited and felt the growing bulb of life getting bigger. Through the fall and winter I kept going to work on the boulevard with pieces of my growing cookbook collection accompanying me. In the kitchen it was a lonely time of study again. I felt something like the isolation I had experienced when I was at the Fox Lake Country Club. I had my small crew but they waited for me to give them their prep lists, which I formulated from what I was trying to absorb in the works of chefs like

Michel Guérard and his book *Cuisine Gourmand*, along with *The Nouvelle Cuisine of Jean and Pierre Troisgros* by the brothers of Roanne. These were my two bibles at that time and I tried to follow their scriptures literally. When the instructions for a dish said, "Keep the fish warm in the oven with the door open while you prepare the sabayon," I'd wince and try to figure out how I'd do that and not have the tickets piling up on me.

The books were written for cooking at home but I had no other manual or teacher. My heavy Henckels chef knife or a "b-and-b" plate held down the pages. My three-man kitchen crew handled the salads, most of the apps, and the grilled items, but I was the sauté, the saucier, the expediter, and the ordering person. This was the first restaurant at which I began to have pre-service meetings. At five o'clock each day I'd come out of the Chez Nancy kitchen and into the frilly dining room with the wrought-iron chairs covered in pale blue cushions. I'd sit down on one of those cushions and tell the waiters what the specials were going to be that night. The language of my menus resonated with the words I'd been learning from the French masters. I was able to finally convince them that I could help them make even more money than the chefs who had toiled in the kitchen before me. They began to fall in line more and more. But the locals were also beginning to come out to the boulevard and taste the dishes we were offering at this little island restaurant. Some were calling Chez Nancy the "Port of Call North" and described it as: "Maybe a little more 'Frenchie,' but you don't have to beg for a table."

Someone who noticed was my former employer. Nancy came looking for me in the kitchen one day. She looked both angry and amused. She had the ability to portray both of these emotions simultaneously like no one I'd ever known before. She found me outside in the walk-in bringing back a load of food I was gathering for another afternoon of prep. She held a letter in her small, strong, porcelain-white hands. The wind gusted in from the Gulf across the boulevard and blew her long heavy skirt against her firmly planted legs.

"I have a letter from a lawyer and it's about you," she said. My heart jumped up into my throat.

I had hated the word "lawyer" since I was a child. They always made me think of my mother and father getting divorced. I didn't have any faith that if a lawyer was involved it could be a beneficial thing.

She held out the large white envelope from the law firm of Morgan and Hendrick. I recognized the latter name from the man coming into the Port of Call. He came in a lot.

The letter warned me that Philip was aware that I had "stolen" many of the signature dishes from Port of Call and that I was "causing him injury to his business by serving them at Chez Nancy." I looked up from the page thinking that my days were ended and that I'd be looking for a job and now with Janet in the second trimester of pregnancy. When I looked at Nancy this time she was smiling radiantly. I didn't get it. She wasn't mad. She wasn't scared. She was delighted that we'd pissed off Philip and his lawyer, and that her restaurant was now getting some tongues wagging in this town, something that she'd always wanted. She was smitten. Chez Nancy was getting attention now. We were even in a mini scandal, of sorts. It was a drug to her. It was a vindication of her vision as well. Suddenly we were on the same team. She put her arm around me and marched me back into the dining room. She ordered Veuve Clicquot Champagne and we toasted to Chez Nancy!

It was a big shock and it emboldened me. I threw myself even further into my work. Nancy bought me a few of the more classic French tomes. She learned I did not have either *Escoffier* or *Larousse Gastronomique*, and so the row of books grew broader across my little wooden desk. My Gallic fervor was growing in leaps and bounds! Everything French! We were cooking the classics! We were avatars of "La Nouvelle Cuisine," too! I would show Philip! I could see Chef René at the Port sneeringly laugh at the conceit of Fish and Fruit. This was payback time. He had told me I would be fired if I left and now he's trying to cow me with his lawyer? Hah! Look at my menu now, Philip! Salmon Escalopes à l'Oseille Troisgros and Tournedos of Veal à la Crème de Ciboulette. We were sailing out of your Port of Call and into the belly of "La Mère France"!

One of the books Nancy gave me was *The Auberge of the Flowering Hearth* by Roy Andries de Groot. It was a small, inauspicious-looking book to behold, but it changed me and helped me in fundamental ways. Mr. de Groot's work tells of the time he spent at a French inn in the town of St. Pierre-de-Chartreuse, Savoy. The inn was run by two women who created their menus entirely from locally produced foods, including fruits, grains, vegetables, dairy, livestock, and game. Every dish they served was made almost entirely with their own hands, from aperitifs made with herbs gathered on the grounds of the auberge, to game birds shot then roasted to perfection on a spit, to rustic yet exquisite tarts made with fruits harvested by hand. It was the single most perfect ideal of what I would want a restaurant of mine to be.

More customers were coming in and the reservations were starting to grow past 9 p.m., then 9:30. I convinced Nancy to allow us to try a little entertainment in the dining room to encourage a late-night crowd. My friend Warren had formed a musical duo with a girl named Perry and had become the afternoon band at Sloppy's. They were getting really good, and since we were friends they cut us a great price and played Friday and Saturday nights. The Chez Nancy experience was really blossoming. Not exactly my *Auberge* yet, but it was a start. I dreamed of reaching for an ideal—I would seek to create a restaurant that would become an integral part of an artistic community, a place to feed not just the body, but also the soul.

Janet was just a month or so from delivering our baby when I learned that my Pier House mate, Danny McHugh, was out of a job. I spoke with Nancy and she let him spend a few weeks with us, not only to help him out but also to give everyone a small vacation. He would also spell me here and there while Janet and I hunted for a new place to rent. Our home on Seidenberg was a shotgun shack with only one room and a bathroom hidden by a bamboo wall and door. We hung a blanket from a wire over the side of the bed facing the front door for a bit of privacy. The washer and dryer were on a porch outside next to a banana tree.

Having Danny in the kitchen with me again was fun. He was intrigued by my new "French mode" and he jumped at the chance to butcher the new cuts of meat I was putting on the menus. Danny was a very skilled butcher and I learned a lot from that little Irishman. But he was never better at anything than he was at finding a good place for a drink and conversation after work. One of our favorite places, and that of many workers from most of the other restaurants and bars, was the (Original) Full Moon Saloon on the south side of United Street.

Rick Lutz, former prep cook (among his many trades) from 700 Duval, had taken over the kitchen, and he created a fish sandwich that was just the tonic and ballast needed for a night of drinking with Danny. Rick made his fish sandwich with a batter of Bisquick, buttermilk, and cracker meal, and topped with Sysco cheddar bought in the loaf style. Evidently he found a use for Bisquick that worked. The Full Moon Saloon Fish Sandwich was irresistible to almost everybody. Another plus was that Rick kept the kitchen open until at least 3 a.m. so many of the cooks, waiters, and others congregated at the Moon and joined some illustrious newcomers who had found their way to Key West. Hunter Thompson and Jim Harrison could be seen at different tables. So could Thomas McGuane.

One of the Full Moon's most loyal drinkers was a jack-of-all-trades named Phil Clark. Phil had tended bar with one of the Full Moon's owners, Vic Latham, back at the Chart Room when it first opened at the Pier House in 1971 and Jimmy Buffett was just beginning to strum his guitar there. Phil was already a fully fledged Key West character and boasted of such accomplishments as allegedly dating Lauren Hutton (pre–modeling career) and living with the Mamas and the Papas on the beach at St. Thomas for a spell. There was always a seemingly endless parade of humanity to make Key West colorful, but Phil was one of the greats. Some years earlier Jimmy wrote one of his very best songs, "A Pirate Looks at Forty," which is mostly, they say, about Phil Clark.

One night at the Full Moon Saloon it was Danny and I who were doing the looking. As we were in the middle of enjoying a couple of massive Full Moon fish sandwiches, Phil stood up at his place at the apex of the horseshoe-shaped bar. Miss Vicky had been serving Phil for almost twelve hours by then and had little doubt that, with his in-between trips to the bathroom and the coke plate stashed in there, he could party for twelve more. The manager/bartender/co-owner John-John was there, too, keeping an eye on all, but as usual he was nearly mute. Maybe Phil had a bladder issue that night, or maybe something emotional had snapped because he proceeded to pull out his manhood and piss a glorious golden arcing stream over the bar, high into the smoky air, over the gap between the bar and the bottle rack and directly onto the large silver Full Moon Saloon cash register. He swore something incoherent about Vic owing him some money from a Captain Tony card game and then fell backward over his chair onto the floor and to sleep. Another night at the Moon was over for me. I had a pregnant woman to lie next to.

Danny came home with me after work on the night of May 7 and we had a few beers. Janet was making a lot of homemade breads at that time and Danny loved them with a wedge of soft cheese. I had a bad toothache coming on, and Danny advised me that I should have a few snifters of brandy and to "leave it soak on the gum, Nor-MAN." I obeyed his counsel. Perhaps I overdid it. I woke up at my desk with a cookbook opened under my face. Danny had gone. Janet was shaking me. "Hey, my water broke." I was useless. I headed for the bed, but she said, "Oh no you don't. You aren't sleeping in those soaked sheets. I'm stripping that bed now." She steered me to the couch and spent the next few hours reading her magazines, making lunch for me (part of the Lamaze training), and quietly waiting. Around dawn she shook me again. "We have to go to the hospital now." This time I got it.

After all the Lamaze classes it was like a well-orchestrated script. Still, it's an out-of-body experience. We drove out to U.S. 1 and stopped at a little store and bought the hard candy Janet would suck on during the contractions. We pulled up to the emergency room and I guided her down from the high perch of our truck. It was so odd to see my little girl so big! She was all baby. Her five-foot-tall body seemed nearly round and she moved so carefully that it wrenched at my heart. I was your typical, nervous, first-time father.

The three nurses at the front desk saw this in an instant and quickly took over and got us into a room. There we waited and tried our best to follow the Lamaze method. It was around 5:30 when we were finally taken into the delivery room. I had a Nikon camera I had been using to take pictures of various subjects of interest to me: churches, barbershops, and the little lanes of Key West. When the miracle of our baby was upon us the doctor looked at me as I was staring at the tiny, sticky, creature that had just come out of my wife, and he said, "You going to use that camera, amigo?" I had to actually watch my hands to get them to make the camera work.

It was just after six o'clock and the streaming sunlight was soft and heavenly. Two assisting women pressed our baby boy's feet against an ink pad that made the indelible marks on his birth certificate and in our memories, or, consciously, at least in mine. Janet was so dazed and justly out of it after hours and hours of labor. But she smiled, her eyes closed, her brown hair lay wet and limp from her sweat on the white hospital pillow. Finally, the pain of childbirth, a pain that would probably kill most men, was over and she could begin to breathe without grimacing or crying out.

They moved us out into a single room and someone took pictures of me wearing the hospital gown and surgical hat and mask and the dazed expression of a "Daddy, day one."

That night Warren came by and picked me up. We got properly toasty and went to Sloppy Joe's. Since Warren was part of the band no one said a word to us when we got onstage and I took the mike to announce to the world that *JUSTIN WADE VAN AKEN WAS NOW A MEMBER OF THE WORLD!* I'm sure the crowd at Sloppy's was not only duly impressed with my shit-faced sentiment but ready to drink to just about anything.

We brought Justin home the next day and all seemed fine. But we learned that his bilirubin counts were whacked and he was turning yellow with jaundice. Our doctor told us to lay him out in the sun to get his levels to "bounce." It didn't work and he had to go back into the hospital. They put him in a special light box and shot him up through the spine. I was a basket case but Janet was nearly preternaturally calm. Janet's mother had been a nurse for thirty years and it was the best way to face these things. I tried to be strong but I was jelly inside. The treatment worked, and two days later we were moving baby and all into a new home with a carpeted, quiet bedroom for our boy and a loft for Janet and me to sleep in. I had room for a desk in our living room and my cookbooks fit on it perfectly. There was even a wall shelf to expand the collection when we could.

The house we moved into was on Olivia Street in the center of Old Town. It was in a row of similar shotgun-style homes built for cigar rollers or spongers in years gone by. Our home was painted a sunny shade of yellow and had a porch in the back just off the compact but nice kitchen. Across the street was the Key West cemetery.

The cemetery was a perfect place to take Justin when he woke up crying, not from hunger, but being new to the planet. In the quiet of that resting place there was no one to hear him but me when it was my turn to calm him. When he finally (gratefully!) fell back to sleep and I held him against my chest and walked in the gentle breezes of that peaceful, timeless place I felt as if I were in someone's arms as well.

But it was a bad time for my old friend Wade. We had feared for a while that he was going to jail. It was certain his brother Steve was going because he was over thirty when he was busted. I had lost touch with Steve in the few short years since he had been kind enough to give Janet and me a place to stay. He'd become like a character in a movie, another person in Key West living under an alias, keeping under the radar. He went by various names, ones that appealed to his comic-book sense of drama, but we called him "Cuban Steve." He was with an island-born woman named Rosa whose family seemed connected to drug dealing, too. They ran a little coffee bar and snack shop but that wasn't buying them the big cars they drove and gold rings they wore.

Rosa was a hotheaded Latina and neither Janet nor I wanted to be around her. Steve and Wade had fallen into the web of dealing with their oldest brother, Phil. He was, to my mind, the instigator of their operation, the reason the boys had gotten into this dangerous business, and I didn't like it. And I was afraid of it. The coke talk, the false identities, the coke whores that befriended Wade and mind-fucked my pal—it all weighed on me. I wanted things to be simple again, the way it was when we were kids. I really hated that Wade was facing jail time. When he was busted Janet was still pregnant and we tried to give him hope for acquittal and told him we were going to name our baby Justin Wade if we had a boy. But hopes were dashed and the two brothers were sent to prison in Ohio. They had been caught with over four hundred pounds of marijuana and Steve would also do more time for discharging a firearm. I don't know where his head was. It was as if he was acting out a movie. Steve could be wild as a kid but this was off the hook. He had shot up the house of some guy who tried to screw him on a drug payment.

Steve went to a very tough prison in Mansfield, Ohio, where the movie *The Shawshank Redemption* was filmed. Wade went to a correctional facility in Lebanon, Ohio, for younger offenders. They each were sentenced to six to eight years. Without parole. Our Justin would be in grade school before he'd know his uncles. And the uncle with whom he shared his name, Wade, would be nearing forty fucking years of age.

Larger dramas were unfolding in the country at that time as well. The long and tortured conflict between Fidel Castro and the U.S./Cuban exile community turned into a much larger battle. Castro was a master at thumbing his nose at Washington politicos, and the island ninety miles off Florida's southern tip became a major headache to the Carter administration. It was a real dead-on assault to normalcy in the streets of Miami when the Mariel boatlift brought hordes of Cuban nationals to the shores of Florida during those first months of our son's life. It created problems in Key West, too.

The situation erupted in mid-April of 1980, when several Cubans drove a truck through the gates of the Peruvian embassy in Havana. Who knows why now? The Peruvians refused to release the gate bashers to Cuban officials. Why the fuck would they? What would Fidel do but throw them a party? With his own twisted logic, Castro announced: "Anyone who wishes to leave Cuba can now do so." The Cuban American community saw what they took as a "break for daylight" after the long dark vigil waiting for Castro's fall and they organized the now-famous event. Throughout May and June Key West's Garrison Bight Marina was filled with thousands of boats of every size and type trying desperately to take advantage of this temporary hole in the "Tropical" Iron Curtain. Shrimpers were now dealing in human cargo. Pleasure cruisers arrived at the docks packed with hungry, ocean-ravaged but grateful refugees. The boatlift endured the bad luck of an early hurricane season. Ferocious storms sunk both vessels and dreams on each end of the dangerous albeit short crossing between the harbors of Mariel (just west of Havana) and Key West. The tide of human need—need for food, shelter, clothing, medicine, and safety—created a modern-day crisis seldom seen on American soil.

One of the great (and unfounded) fears was that Castro only allowed thousands of his people to leave Cuba in an aquatic version of the Trojan horse. The proponents of this idea claimed El Maximo Lider was sending inmates from Cuban prisons and mental hospitals in order to wreak havoc on the health care and law enforcement capacities of Florida. However, the U. S. Department of Justice calculated otherwise and stated that of the 125,000 refugees, only 2 percent were convicted criminals. This was all, in the end, basically beside the point because the influx of these refugees into Miami transformed the entire city with a force and swiftness that is impossible to quantify. It was a diaspora that was a portent of things to come from the tropical paradise ruled by a latter-day feudal king. A king that would, like all kings, learn he was not a god.

If I had what is called, in the vernacular of classic French cuisine, a "sous chef" at the time, it was certainly a very sweet guy named Greg. I resisted giving my coworkers and employees titles of rank. I still clung to my "hippie ethics" and it took years for me to change. I was "Norman" at work, not "Chef Norman" or "Chef." Back in the sweatbox kitchens of Key West we were all working together to make great food. Bicycle Sammy would be scowling at me for this silly lack of decorum, but old habits die hard. Greg loved to work and he was loyal to the *n*th degree both to me and to the vision of what we were trying to accomplish. Being a gay man, he was also a vital conduit into the psyche of our waitstaff and was able to tell me what "the boys" (his term) were thinking and how to nudge them forward in step with our goals.

Even though Nancy and her husband, Chuck, were the owners, and Chez Nancy was specifically her dream and essentially a separate entity, the hotel crew eyed us with barely concealed disdain. Each night at the end of service when all the tickets were in and we were done with the mopping, wiping, storing, and ordering for the next day, I'd say good night to Greg and the others and bring the food-smudged, grease-spattered tickets (the only written record of what the waiters had ordered and we had cooked) to the bookkeeper over on the hotel side. I never took the time to tally those tickets myself. It was all I could do to work twelve to fifteen hours a day Monday through Saturday, come home to wife and baby, and lie like a comatose dog on the beach or in our bed on Sunday. Let the bean counters be bean counters, I reasoned. I wanted to simply be a chef.

Greg was the straightest gay guy I had met yet in my life. He had a wife, for instance. A female one. Her name was Jeri. And Greg and Jeri kissed. They didn't kiss on the lips but they did kiss with true fondness for one another. I was heartened to learn of the never-ending capacity of people to weld a fitting and mutually exciting life together. They had figured out what worked for them. And there was no doubt that Jeri wanted Greg to sleep only with her. I assumed it was for the age-old reason that many, if not most, humans crave a monogamous relationship. But a new fear was menacing our island.

HIV and AIDS had arrived in Key West. And when they did, the twin goblins of fear and paranoia went to work. "How did you 'get' AIDS?" was the swirling question. And on a more sinister note, "Who is 'getting' it?" One thing was certain. Our waitstaff was starting to disappear one by one. Each month somebody else was simply gone without a trace. Pretty soon, words like "gay plague" and "biblical scourge" were being whispered—and then not whispered. Eventually, needle-sharing drug users also fell victim. There was an "end of days" atmosphere pervading the island that was hard to reconcile with our own *Auberge of the Flowering Hearth* ideals. So Jeri wanted Greg to stay faithful for another reason. She wanted to live and share her life with this very beautiful man, and she had every right to hope so.

When Janet and I had a chance to take a one-week vacation in August, Greg took over in my absence. It was the slowest time of the year, yet on the night we returned I dropped Janet off at home, unloaded the luggage, and simply had to go to Chez Nancy and see how my crew was doing. It was approaching 10:30 p.m. and I knew the kitchen would be pretty much done. When I arrived Greg was walking back from the hotel side where he'd gone to drop off the night's tickets. Something was brewing. I could tell by the speed he was walking down the glassed-in hallway that connected the hotel to Chez Nancy's dining room. When he saw me his eyes were blazing and his high forehead was covered with a gloss of sweat.

"What's up, Greg? You look like you've been shot out of a cannon."

"I need a drink," he stammered.

There was a lounge just down the stairs from the dining room and the bartender working at Chez Nancy at that time, Sam, was behind the bar. I knew he wouldn't care if we grabbed a drink. Technically I was still on vacation. Greg was another matter. Greg ordered a margarita ("make it a double") and I asked Sam for a beer. Sam was bright and could see that we had an agenda, so instead of chatting us up he served the drinks and we sat at a low table by the back wall with Greg facing me and me facing the bar.

"Spill the beans, brother. Spill them before you burst."

Greg drained half of the tequila drink.

He had a voice that went up to a higher octave when he was outraged by something and now it came out that way: "I can't belieeeeeve what I just heard. I can't believe it. I can't believe it. I can't believe it!"

He sounded like a cuckoo clock announcing some demented hour of doom.

"Well, clue me in on what you can't believe, Greg, because it sounds like you have some serious mojo up your ass."

"They are going to fire you," he said.

"Excuse me?"

"When I went down there to Accounting the door was open and the new manager that Nancy just brought down from Provincetown—the ugly cow named Wendell, you remember? He offered me your job! Said it was obvious we don't need Norman with you (ME!) doing such a fine job this past week."

"What did you say?"

"I couldn't speak. I just laid the tickets down, left the office, and that's when you saw me coming down here."

I carefully tore the label off my beer bottle and pasted it on the cocktail table. A seal or a sign? "You did good, Greg." I had seen this game before and I was finally seeing (and understanding) some of the patterns to this business. It's a simple gambit. Hire the sous chef to replace the chef once the chef makes a good reputation for the place. Salary of chef goes away. Sous chef makes a little more but not nearly so. More money for the bosses.

"Gotta ask. Do you want my job?"

"Not without you. We have a nice kitchen and I know I'm not ready to be 'the chef.' Not yet anyway."

"Will you help me do something then, Greg?"

"Name it."

"Will you help me fuck up Wendell?"

"Ewwww. Gross!"

"I said fuck up, not fuck."

"Oh, sure!"

"Good. I know this is his greedy head scheme and he's trying to impress the owners. Let's see how impressed they are when they find out what that jack-off wanted to accomplish tonight."

"Sam, two more please of the same. And add a shot of Stoli for me."

I led the way back to the kitchen. Our dishwasher, Big Don, was the only other person still working. His thick spectacles were fogged up from washing the floor mats. I pulled out all my lovingly made sauces, soups, marinades, and terrines from the coolers and then Greg and Big Don got it. They knew where I was going. If those management bastards wanted to have Chez Nancy without me they certainly were not going to have the very life's blood of my efforts, and down the garbage disposal they went. Glug, glug, glug.

"Ciao, Nancy!" No. Actually it was, "Ciao, Wendell!" Nancy I would miss. She had given me some really great books. I pulled back into the spot I had left an hour or so earlier on Olivia in front of our home. I went inside. Janet was upstairs in the loft with the electric fan doing its best to blow out the late-August night's air. I went into the dark, cool quiet of our baby's bedroom and quickly fell asleep on that soft carpeting.

When I awoke our son was standing in his crib underneath the gently dangling mobiles hanging from the ceiling and bobbing in the current of the large Hunter fan above us. He looked down at me on the floor with his beautiful blue and intelligent eyes, eyes that held a question: "Where will you work next, Daddy?"

Smothered Pork Chops Adobo with Onion, Orange, and Fresh Pineapple

I grew up in a community in northern Illinois that experienced one of the first large migrations of Mexican families in the early 1970s. You almost couldn't help but learn about chilies and other Latin flavors in that era, and I was a fan. When one of my dishwashers made some adobo for tacos one day, we quickly cobbled this baby together for a staff meal. The servers' stony hearts began to warm. . . .

For the adobo:

- 1 clove
- 10 black peppercorns
- 1 teaspoon cumin seeds
- 2 bay leaves, broken
- ½ teaspoon ground cinnamon
- ½ cup of roasted garlic, well mashed
- 8 ancho chilies, seeded, stemmed, toasted, and softened in water
- 4 chipotle or morita chilies, seeded, stemmed, toasted, and softened in water
- 1 teaspoon finely minced oregano leaves
- 1 teaspoon finely minced thyme leaves
- 1 teaspoon kosher salt
- ¼ cup Spanish sherry wine vinegar

In a dry skillet, toast the clove, peppercorns, and cumin. In an electric spice grinder, combine the toasted spices with the bay leaves and cinnamon to a fine grind.

Combine the ground spices in a food processor with the roasted garlic, drained chilies, oregano, thyme, salt, and vinegar until they are thoroughly and evenly combined. Reserve.

Makes a little more than 1½ cups

For the pork chops:

4 pork chops, with some fat around the edges, thick or thin cut
2 tablespoons blended oil

Paint both sides of the chops with the adobo paste, and let stand 30 minutes. In a large nonstick skillet or frying pan, heat the blended oil until quite hot. Carefully add the chops, one at a time, searing each side. Remove the chops to a separate pan and place on a rack.

For the onion sauce "smother":

2 tablespoons of butter
2 cups of sliced sweet onions, loosely packed
1 tablespoon of all-purpose flour
1 cup freshly squeezed orange juice, room temperature
1½ cups chicken stock, heated
squeeze of lemon
1½ cups fresh pineapple, cut into julienne strips

Drain the used cooking oil from the skillet, but leaving any adobo residue. Add the butter. When the butter is melted, add the onions. Stir well and cook until they begin to caramelize, about 5 minutes. Add the flour, stir, and continue cooking for 1 minute. Add the orange juice, stir, and continue cooking until it has reduced by more than half, about 3 minutes. Add the chicken stock, and cook down to 1 cup or less, another 3 minutes, stirring frequently, especially as the sugars condense and the flour tightens. (Be patient: allowing almost all the liquid to evaporate will make the sauce nicely intense. The nonstick skillet will help.) Remove from the heat and keep warm, or rewarm when needed. (The smother can be made a day in advance.)

Place the seared chops in a preheated 400 degree F oven and cook until the pork reaches an interior temperature of 145 degrees F. (The timing will depend on the thickness of the chops, so a meat thermometer comes in handy.)

Remove the chops from the oven and allow them to rest for at least 5 minutes. (The resting time will bring the interior temperature up to the safety zone of 160 degrees F or higher.)

Squeeze a little lemon, if desired, into the onion sauce. Plate the chops, spoon the onion sauce over them, and garnish with the sliced fresh pineapple. Serve with white rice.

Makes 2 to 4 servings

CHAPTER 14

The Port of Call (Reprise)

Key West, 1980–82

THERE IS A SYSTEM OF communication down in Key West the locals call the "coconut telegraph." It is the way the word goes out and there is pretty much instant communication as to what has happened, often while it's in the midst of happening, all over the freakin' island. It is true and has been noted before, and yet, like a parable of Jesus or a line from *The Big Lebowski*, it bears repeating because so few seem to act on, or at the bare minimum, take heed of it. Here it is: The restaurant world is insanely small (bars are included in this maxim). Everyone knows everyone, and if you think they don't, just have something happen to you and the bag boy in the grocery store or the little lady who seems to speak no English and who sits next to you on a bus ride to your dentist will wink and tell you the most intimate details of it. Take that equation and boil it down to the size of a pimple on a bug's ass and you have the Key West scope of it. So it came as no surprise that Philip had heard about my contretemps with my most recent employer.

What was stunning to me was that he called me and asked me to come back to the Port of Call. Philip was not known for forgiveness. He was known for being a hard-ass from Philly with Sicilian blood in him. And even though he fired me in a coked-out moment, I thought he'd never see it as "his bad."

He was sweet and playful on the phone and I was out of work and desperate. The combination was compelling. This time I'd be back, he explained, as the lunch chef. He wanted to try and see if he could create some more business by pulling in revenues from the upcoming winter tourist season that would start with the newly dreamed up Key West pageant to paganism: Fantasy Fest.

He also said I'd get to help write the menu! No one had ever had that much creative license in Philip's domain before, and since lunch had been dropped last spring, there was no staff left so I could hire whomever I wished, as long as they could work for an amount Philip was willing to pay.

Working lunch meant that I could spend more waking moments with Janet and our baby. And it also meant I could indulge in one other notion that had been in my heart since Nana had shared with me her passion for the theater. Because there was a new one called The Red Barn being fixed up on Duval Street.

The first thing I did was to convince my buddy Warren to come work with me. He'd never worked in a professional kitchen before but he was ten thousand volts of high-powered energy. I also got Billy Bleu Cheese to come in from the Pier House to make the salads and desserts. Billy worked at the front counter and Warren worked at my side.

The lunch menu at the Port was a major stylistic break from the food I had been cooking at Chez Nancy. I turned my back on hardcore French cuisine. Perhaps it was a rebuke for the way I had been treated. But it might also have had to do with an invitation I'd received through the mail to "discover the great cooking of the world" through a new series of books called *The Good Cook, Techniques and Recipes*. It was published by Time-Life Books, which had done other series on subjects as grand as *The Civil War, The Old West*, and *Seafarers*, all of which I'd enjoyed.

This series was to be edited by Richard Olney, a culinary paradox in that he was from the Midwest (hmmm . . .) yet was considered a beacon of extraordinary cooking abroad. Each book would cover a specific category: there would be a whole volume dedicated to eggs, another on pork, another on sauces, then sandwiches, desserts, poultry, lamb, and so forth. The complete set would number about two dozen books, and be shipped bimonthly. I could see from the brochure that the books would be lavishly illustrated with scads of step-by-step how-to photos. It would be like a college extension course. As the books arrived new menu items began to fill the plates and bowls at the newly opened lunch at the Port of Call.

One of our best customers of the restaurant was Roddy Brown. The coconut telegraph dossier had it that Roddy had been a noteworthy child star in theater productions back in his native Virginia. The way I got it was that his mother was a superb actress and Roddy had followed her onto the stage. It was a story not unlike that of another actor whom I admired with so many others of my generation, Marlon Brando. Brando had gone to high school in Libertyville, Illinois (the town I was born in), as had my older brother, Buddy. In some ways between that albeit tenuous association and my nana's theatrical background I had a bit of an eye for performing, too. I was still writing stories and songs, and I had written a full-length country-rock opera that was lying in a drawer under my old copies of *Gourmet* waiting for a moment to find a way out.

Even in the rich mix of powerful characters of Key West, Roddy Brown was memorable. He was more alive than most people. His green eyes were dazzling with a dancing incandescent energy that transmitted humor, energy, intelligence, and a flair for living life to the fullest. I didn't know him well enough to talk to him at first, but as a loyal guest of the Port's he came to know me, and one day he asked me if I had ever done any acting. I told him I hadn't except a small part in a high school production of *Our Town.* He told me that he was in the process of cocreating a new theater in town and their first production was going to be *A Christmas Carol* by Charles Dickens. I think he added "by Charles Dickens" more because he liked the flow and sound of the words than to compensate for a lack of education he might suspect of me. He asked me if I would help him out and play the very simple role of Mr. Fezziwig. The character only had two lines, he reasoned. "And I'll pay you fifty bucks." I was in.

The next play Roddy had selected (he announced with no small drama to the opening night crowd of *A Christmas Carol*) would be *A Streetcar Named Desire.* The audience roared its approval, but many tongues were wagging during intermission with a more cautionary view. It was a bold move to stage a play of such fierce and ranging emotions with such a young repertory group. Roddy answered the problem by calling on some former colleagues from Virginia to handle the key roles. I was excited and for a few short weeks I began to wonder, again, whether being a chef was not for me after all. Look at my chef-patron drinking and getting wasted at the Chart Room. Was that always to be the inevitable scenario for a chef? Janet held Justin and looked at me with wordless wonder, once again.

The flyers were posted around town announcing auditions to be held in a building across from Fausto's Food Palace. The entire Key West theater community massed for their shot at portraying one of Tennessee Williams's bruised yet compelling characters. *I* brazenly auditioned for the starring role of Stanley Kowalski. Though the casting director allowed that I had given a strong reading I had nowhere near the experience to handle the Brando role. It went to a vastly more experienced guy named Kirk who chewed up the scenery and embodied the brute rage the audience craved. I got to play the upstairs neighbor.

It was a fascinating experience to be involved from the earliest days of rehearsals through the entire run. But I came to see up close that the bullshit warring, petty grievances, and endless jealousies and squabbles that infest the theater community were not for me. Once *Streetcar* reached its end I told Janet that I was going to recommit to cooking "all the way."

Tennessee Williams was still alive and had a home in Key West. To our amazement he came to the final rehearsals just before opening night. Whatever he thought of our little Key West community theater he was gracious enough to keep to himself.

Perhaps even more incredibly, he threw a cast party for us at the end of our run at his home on Duncan Street. We all arrived in a state of natural, but still quite heady, intoxication. It was one of those occasions when, no matter how many famous people you may have met, or will meet in the future, you knew you were with someone whose work will continue to matter centuries from now. In your mind you begin to say things to yourself like, *I'm in Tennessee Williams's driveway. I'm in Tennessee Williams's kitchen. I'm in Tennessee Williams's washroom splashing water on my face and looking in the mirror that looks back at Tennessee Williams.*

There was absolutely nothing to drink at the party but gin. There was nothing to eat either, except a bowl of potato chips. I found some tea bags in a cabinet and began brewing some tea. While the water boiled I went outside and searched the immediate neighborhood. I quickly found a tamarind tree and snagged some of the beans. I stripped off the bark and strings and scraped the stickiness into the water with some sugar. (Bicycle Sammy had shown me this once.) After a few minutes I strained the tamarind and sugar water over the tea bags, stirred in some ice cubes, and put it in the freezer.

When I turned around he (HE!) was standing directly in front of me. "Whatever on earth are you making, my boy?" he drawled. I was worried that he was angry with me for messing around in his kitchen. I said, "Some tamarind iced tea. Would you like a glass?" He smiled charmingly at me, then looked down at the floor, and, while still looking down, held out a Tom Collins glass at arm's length. I filled it half full with ice and began pouring the tea. He motioned me to stop with his other hand. I stopped and he reached around me, his face brushing my arm, and picked up the gin. He topped his glass off with the alcohol and stirred it with a gold letter opener while gazing fully at my face. He tipped back this newly created cocktail and drained it, smacking his lips with that universal sound of approval. Then he set the empty glass down, leaned over, elevated himself on his toes, gave me a little peck on my forehead, and then rejoined the cast out by the pool.

I heard the voice in my head say it: *Tennessee Williams just kissed you on the head, pal.*

I made myself a drink.

When the party was over we got into Warren's pickup truck. We decided to go have a few more drinks at Sloppy Joe's. Why not? The world was our oyster!

The gin I'd drunk with Tennessee began to hit me after my first beer, and it wasn't long before I passed out directly on the bar underneath the various framed photographs of Ernest Hemingway. I hadn't had gin since the Fox Lake Country Club days and I should have stayed away from it. Janet and Warren danced to the rock-and-roll band for a while and finally came and rousted me up from my nap.

We headed back arm in arm for support to Warren's truck parked on Greene Street. Some guys were walking toward us and suddenly one of them whipped around and shouted something at me, something like: "It was you that did it, wasn't it?" He grabbed me by the shoulder. I had no idea what the hell his problem was and I broke free from Janet and Warren, lunged woozily, and tried to brush him aside. He wheeled around in a 360-degree loop and slashed through my black satin party shirt into the side of my left forearm with a switchblade. Janet jumped between the attacker and me as I tried to swing with my right. Warren reacted like lightning, picked her up, and hurled her into the cab of his truck as I fell to the ground. The thugs ran down Greene Street into the noisy mass of revelers at Sloppy's.

Warren pulled me up and lifted the sleeve of my shirt. Seeing the long gash spurting blood, he cinched a bandana around it and expertly tied a sharp knot. A cop car arrived, lights going wild and officers asking us what the hell just happened. We told them, suddenly sober. The cops told us to jump in their squad car then made a quick sweep down lower Duval Street looking for the asshole who slashed me while Janet kept my arm elevated, but it bled anyway.

In a parking lot behind Sloppy's, Warren yelled out, "That's them!"

The policeman driving pointed to some guys by the back wall of the bar. "Those guys?"

"Yes, yes!" Warren hollered. The cops looked at each other and groaned. It turned out the "culprits" were some undercover officers helping in the search.

The cops let us out of the car and told us to get over to the emergency room on Stock Island: "Get him sewed up."

So we headed to the hospital just a few miles to the north. We knew we'd be there for a while. Warren pulled into a gas station at Truman and White and picked up a cold six-pack.

I read the *Citizen* the next afternoon with seventeen stitches in my left arm and a mammoth pain that invaded my entire left side. An excerpt read, "Van Aken mistakenly identified two undercover policemen as his assailants." Perfect. I'm slashed, stitched, and in the paper for seeming stupid.

I got a letter from Wade on March 10, the day before his thirtieth birthday. His handwriting was neat and his sentences clear. He told me that I was lucky to have Janet and Justin, that my karma was good and that I deserved it, and that he loved me. (I wish he could feel that we all love him and have it help him always.) He also told me that Phil felt really bad and how I should realize that Wade had himself to own up to and hoped I would realize his older brother had a heart of gold.

I spent the next month wondering what I'd do with lunch ending in May. That is when René gave Philip notice and Philip asked me if I wanted to be head chef of the Port of Call. It was like my mother would often say to me: "In life you will find that one door closes and another one opens." She had faith by the bucketful.

I got back into my life as a chef with renewed determination. I was reading even more, buying a new cookbook whenever we could afford one, and thinking more and more about the hows and whys of cuisine. It really got into my head, and for about three months that winter, I entered a phase of sleeping and dreaming I wouldn't wish on any cook. It went like this: I would come home from work, cross-eyed from exhaustion, but seemingly blank in my mind. I'd fall asleep almost immediately. Around 1 a.m. the dream would begin: The ticket box would rattle and spit out the first ticket of the night (the first one we had cooked in real life back at the Port). "Ordering! Two

Caesar Salads, one Onion Soup, one Conch Chowder, followed by two Rack of Lamb, one medium, one medium-rare, a Fish and Fruit, and a Veal Chop!"

And that was only the beginning. It didn't end until we had cooked every single dish all over again. It was a three-hour dream. I'd awake drenched to the bone, the sheets soaked and clinging to me. I would then rise and walk a dead man's walk into the shower and let the water calm my fevered brain and soothe my aching limbs. Then, and only then, could I crawl back into bed and find the peace I needed so badly.

Of course, as head chef I had to take on new responsibilities. My least favorite had to do with personnel. I had long known the instability of finding reliable help in Key West. I had sprung more than one guy out through a bail bondsman after having to explain to an owner that if he didn't come up with the bond money their restaurant wouldn't be opening that night. But the more daily wear-and-tear excuses gnawed at me, too. What was so hard about it? We could all have some fun after work and still make it the next day, couldn't we? And where did these folks find the money for rent or drinks or the phone company? Weren't they living in the paycheck-to-paycheck world we all were citizens of? How could they take off so much work? The near capper came for me one morning when Billy Bleu Cheese called me at the Port saying, "Sorry I'm gonna be late. Actually if you want to know the truth I may not make it for lunch at all."

"Why the hell not, Billy?"

"I'm fucking this chick and she's hot."

The final blow came when I unlocked the restaurant one morning to get the place ready for lunch to find Philip passed out on the floor of the dining room. His keys lay beside him with a large sum of cash strewn like leaves at his feet. Summer was coming, and I felt that if I kept this up, living in this town, I'd end up on a floor like my talented but tortured boss. I had learned so much from him but maybe the biggest lesson lay before me. If I thought the pressure of running a little lunch crew in this town was rough, what would it be like if I took on the job as head chef one day? Maybe the time to get out was now—while I still could.

This time I gave Philip notice. He tried to sweet-talk me out of it but Janet was eager to get back to Illinois and share Justin with our families. I missed the summer and fall seasons. Maybe that is where the next big chance for me would be after all. Mama flew down and got Justin and flew back with him. Janet and I loaded up the red truck and it was "So long Key West! It's been good to know you!" We headed back to the sweet and uncomplicated Midwest, with no job but we'd figure that out when we got there.

Tennessee's Streetcar

When I turned around he (HE!) was standing directly in front of me. "Whatever on earth are you making, my boy?" he drawled. I was worried that he was angry with me for messing around in his kitchen. I said, "Some tamarind iced tea. Would you like a glass?" He smiled charmingly at me, then looked down at the floor, and, while still looking down, held out a Tom Collins glass at arm's length. I filled it half full with ice and began pouring the tea. He held out a "stop" sign with his other hand. I stopped and he reached around me . . . his face brushing my arm, and picked up the gin. He topped the Collins glass off with the alcohol and stirred it with a gold letter opener, now gazing fully at my face. He tipped back this newly created cocktail, drained it, and smacked his lips with that ancient sound of approval. Then he set the empty glass down, leaned over, elevated himself on his toes, and gave me a little peck on my forehead and then rejoined the cast out by the pool.

I heard the voice in my head say it: *Tennessee Williams just kissed you on the head, pal.* I made myself a drink. This one was created by master mixologist and author of *The Modern Mixologist* and *Vodka Distilled*, Tony Abou-Ganim.

1 tablespoon egg whites
1 ounce fresh-squeezed lemon juice
1 ounce Tamarind Syrup (recipe follows)
3 dashes Angostura orange bitter
2 ounces Tanqueray gin
2 ounces Fever-Tree ginger beer, chilled
lemon slice, for garnish
mint sprig, for garnish

In a pint mixing glass, add egg whites, lemon juice, Tamarind Syrup, orange bitters, and gin. Add ice and shake vigorously to blend and emulsify the egg white. Strain into an ice-filled Collins glass and spritz with chilled ginger beer. Stir to mix. Garnish with the lemon slice and mint sprig. Serve with straws for the Southern ladies.

Tamarind Syrup

2½ cups water
½ (wet) tamarind
2 cups sugar

In a pot, bring the water and the tamarind to a boil. Add sugar, reduce the heat to medium, and stir until the sugar and tamarind are dissolved. Simmer for 15 minutes; remove from the heat and allow to cool. Strain the mixture through a large sieve to remove solids, and refrigerate syrup until ready to prepare drinks.

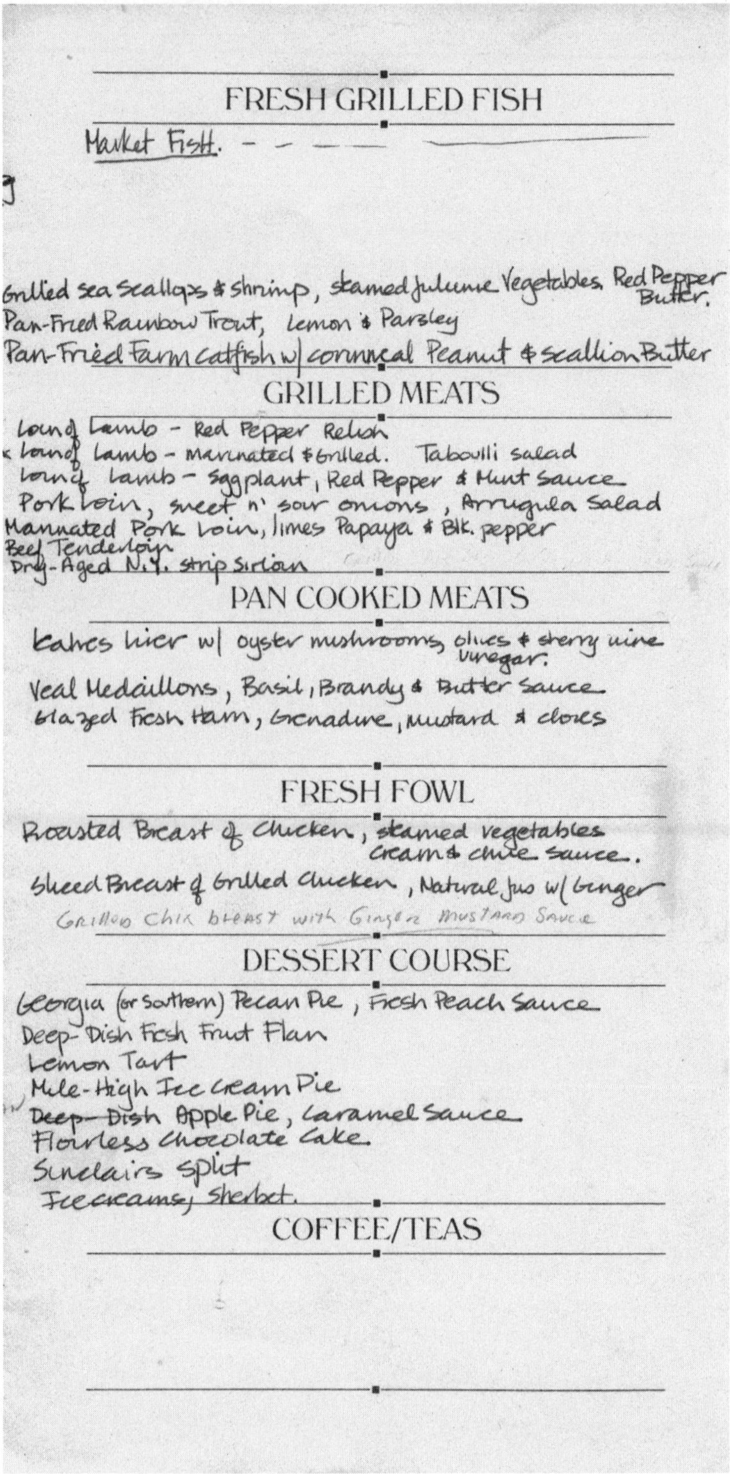

FRESH GRILLED FISH

Market Fish. — — —

Grilled sea Scallops & shrimp, steamed julienne Vegetables, Red Pepper Butter.
Pan-Fried Rainbow Trout, Lemon & Parsley
Pan-Fried Farm catfish w/ cornmeal Peanut & scallion Butter

GRILLED MEATS

Loin of Lamb – Red Pepper Relish
Loin of Lamb – Marinated & Grilled. Taboulli salad
Loin of Lamb – Eggplant, Red Pepper & Mint Sauce
Pork Loin, sweet n' sour onions, Arrugula Salad
Marinated Pork Loin, limes Papaya & Blk. pepper
Beef Tenderloin
Dry-Aged N.Y. strip Sirloin

PAN COOKED MEATS

Calves liver w/ oyster mushrooms, olives & sherry wine vinegar.
Veal Medallions, Basil, Brandy & Butter Sauce
Glazed Fresh Ham, Grenadine, Mustard & cloves

FRESH FOWL

Roasted Breast of Chicken, steamed vegetables cream & chive sauce.
Sliced Breast of Grilled Chicken, Natural jus w/ Ginger
Grilled Chix breast with Ginger Mustard Sauce

DESSERT COURSE

Georgia (or Southern) Pecan Pie, Fresh Peach Sauce
Deep-Dish Fresh Fruit Flan
Lemon Tart
Mile-High Ice cream Pie
Deep-Dish Apple Pie, Caramel Sauce
Flourless Chocolate Cake
Sinclairs Split
Ice creams, Sherbet.

COFFEE/TEAS

Sinclair's menu. We purposefully sought to create a New American Cuisine at Sinclair's.

CHAPTER 15

Sinclair's

Lake Forest, 1982–84

EVERY DAY IT BECAME CLEARER to me that I was now the primary breadwinner for our baby boy. When he shouted "Daddy!" I was the happiest I'd ever been. And we were, the three of us, so lucky. Justin was almost two. It was time for me to find my way to make it safe for him even though I still didn't know quite how to do it. He looked at me with his big blue eyes as he tore through the world of discovery a child embarks upon whether Mom and Dad are ready or not. His mom was ready. She was a natural. And he was additionally surrounded also not only by the supernatural love of his maternal grandmother but maternal great-grandmother as well. The prince of Diamond Lake! We read him *Mickey in the Night Kitchen* and he loved it!

I spent the majority of daylight hours for many weeks that spring in my mother's backyard. I was digging her a series of terraces that cascaded down to Diamond Lake. She had transformed the same piece of ground where we had lived in what was called the "Spanish House" into a beautiful, new wooden home with big glass windows and a fantastic porch. But the yard was impossible to use and enjoy without risking a straight drop down into the lapping waters of the lake. I had railroad ties delivered to the side of the property and I dug that hard clay and heavy mud in an attempt to beautify the landscape but also to burn off the energy my body was used to draining in Key West kitchens.

I had put out my résumé around town but no restaurant needed my help. So I dug. I positioned huge stereo speakers toward my work site and treated the neighborhood to a lot of Lightning Hopkins and Muddy Waters. One afternoon Janet's voice came cutting in over the din of my music and mudslinging: "Norman! A man named Gordon Sinclair is on the phone!"

I remembered the name from a collection of restaurant menus from Chicago, there might have been fifty of them, each with a photo of the chef or owner. One of the restaurants was a place downtown somewhere called Gordon—not Gordon's—but Gordon, like it was a person. I remember looking at the photo of the man the place was named for and getting the oddest feeling of connection. He wore a very unusual sport coat ("natty" might be the word for it). It had stripes. He looked like he could be on an album cover. Not the typical sober-looking conservative suit for a Chicago businessman. And something in his face looked so empathetic. When Janet called out his name—as if it had been preordained—it changed the trajectory of my life.

When I got to the phone he asked, "Can you come to Lake Forest and meet me next week? We are almost done with construction on Sinclair's and I'd like to get your thoughts."

I had no clothes for this interview. My Key West days had eliminated all but the most basic clothing needs. I was advised, very strongly, by my mother to go to Langworthy's in Libertyville and buy a pair of slacks, a white shirt, and at least a sweater if not a sport coat. "A sport coat?" I muttered. "Yeah, and maybe a dickey to go with it all." But Mom knew I had to get the job, and she told me I could put the bill on her account until I got back on my feet.

It was a beautiful day with gusts of wind roaring off the mighty lake. I got there more than an hour ahead of schedule. To pass the time I walked around the perfect little town. I had been there before, God knows. The Deerpath Inn was just off the main square and the hours working with Toké came to mind as I waited to meet the man staring so intently, so sagely, from the magazine.

I passed by the tony clothing shops of historic Market Square and looked down at my schoolboy threads and wondered if they'd be okay. Three men passed by me as a rush of wind rolled in. One of the men was wearing a cape! A cape like Sherlock Holmes might have worn. I caught a glimpse of his profile as he shielded his face from the sweeping onslaught of wind and leaves. It was Gordon Sinclair! I was sure of it. He strode on. I decided that I should just go to the restaurant and wait for him. I didn't want to be late.

I drove the truck over to the corner of Forest and Westminster. My pickup joined those of the construction workers who were still installing the kitchen equipment, laying the terrazzo tile flooring, and installing the banquettes, bar, and booths. The men ignored both me and my V-neck sweater as I paced around the empty dining room.

Then, with another sweep of his cape, Gordon Sinclair walked into the dining room through an unfinished hole in the wall! It was startling! He wore a black fedora and a finely checked suit, tan pointed shoes, and driving gloves! He tore off one of the gloves and walked briskly over to me while extending his hand.

"Norman! How good of you to come! Let's look at the blueprints!"

I was dizzy. How did he know who *I* was? He pulled off his cape and fedora and set them on a table. Fred Astaire was the only man I had ever seen move like that. And it wasn't in real life. Was it? It was happening very fast now.

He spread out the blueprints on a section of plywood set over two sawhorses. His silver cuff links shone out of a baby blue silk shirt. His pocket square dallied out of his breast pocket.

He showed me the dish table and the pot sink and their proximity to each other.

"I think on slower evenings one gentleman dishwasher could wash both the dishes and the pots, don't you, Norman?"

After I squared the notion of a person being referred to in such a genteel way as a "gentleman dishwasher," I croaked something like, "Sure. But I am certain the chef would have his opinion on that."

He looked at me with the steadiest "Paul Newman–blue" eyes (as he would later describe them himself) and said, "I thought YOU were going to be my chef!"

I rolled my eyes over the new kitchen. Maybe it was through divine maternal intervention that I found the moxie to say, "Yes, sure, Mr. Sinclair. I am!"

"Oh, don't call me 'Mr. Sinclair,'" he said, looking at me with his warm, smiling round face. "It makes me feel old! Call me Gordon."

Since the restaurant was still under construction and there had been the typical delays, Gordon explained that I would need to come to Chicago each day and help him plan the menu, get to know the purveyors, and such. I couldn't imagine driving my pickup to his elegant restaurant and parking it near the Cadillacs and Lincolns every day. But then, as if on cue, I heard the Lake Forest train's whistle blowing and I realized I could drive the truck to Libertyville (just a stop or two to the north and close to my home) and take the train to work each morning and back again each evening. I would be a commuter.

I had never lived in a city before except Honolulu for the six months I went to the University of Hawaii back in 1970–71. This was a new adventure, one that both scared and delighted me. Going into Chicago, the "city with big shoulders," was a real turn of events for me. And with the turning wheels of the commuter train came the turning thoughts that Gordon Sinclair propelled in me.

I arrived at Union Station every morning about ten. Thank God for restaurant hours; even though I was there to work in his office, Gordon had to work evenings in the restaurant "being Gordon," so he wouldn't arrive until about eleven. Gordon treated me as if I were an equal in his project. I don't know where he got this egalitarian ideology but I was digging it. There were new books and menus each week that would be on his shelf and he told me I was "free to peruse them." Peruse them I did.

To my great good fortune one of the books was *The Chez Panisse Menu Cookbook* by Alice Waters. I liked her face and her winsome smile on the book's back jacket cover. She seemed to be inviting me to join her on a mission. Any doubts or fears I had were cast aside as I fell under the spell of Berkeley's revolutionary restaurant. I loved the book! I loved it in many ways. I loved her reminiscences of special nights, special menus, and special events. It was a real confidence builder because she admitted that even though she succeeded in accomplishing her ideas *most* of the time, there were nights at Chez Panisse when there were fiascos in the kitchen and disasters in the dining room to deal with. Her words were emboldening, empowering to me. And the *Auberge of the Flower-*

ing Hearth sensibility seemed to be more fully integrated at Chez Panisse than any restaurant I had ever heard or read about in America.

The Menu Cookbook was part cookbook and part manifesto. It called for intelligence and connectivity to nature in ways intimated in the works of Elizabeth David and even James Beard, but in a more fully realized and imploring voice. Ms. Waters conveyed both a sense of perfection and a striving for the utopian ideals I had been searching for. I wanted to make Sinclair's in that fashion!

Gordon showed me other ideas from his travels that excited me, too. He brought back a menu from a new place called Spago in Los Angeles. The chef was the theatrically named Wolfgang Puck. The chef drawings replicated on the menu's cover were very much like ones that I was making to show my cooks how I wanted something plated. Maybe I was onto something! Maybe there was a kindred spirit afoot here. The Austrian-turned-Californian chef's food bespoke of a real pride in American regional ingredients. I suddenly wanted (and needed!) to find Maui onions and Santa Barbara spot prawns! Puck's food also embraced Asian aesthetics, and my memories of Toké at the Deerpath Inn came rushing back to me with the power of what-could-I-do-to-show-homage-to-him in this beckoning new sensibility of American cooking and cuisine. I wanted to make a sizzling catfish and serve it with dandelion greens.

Gordon raved about the simplicity of Spago's décor, how it was so inviting rather than intimidating. Gordon was the most modern of restaurateurs. Had he opened his original Gordon restaurant in New York instead of Chicago, I'm certain he would have been as famous and lionized as Sirio Maccioni, if perhaps with a more cutting-edge crowd. His skewered sense of humor and droll wit were just the antidote to too much passion. Gordon was being interviewed by a reporter for the *Chicago Sun-Times* one day in the dining room and when the journalist asked for a definition of this New American Cuisine, I waited alongside the newspaper man with real anticipation—waiting for this eloquent and dapper man to give the defining answer, if not an all-out apocalyptic one. Gordon said in his nasal Michigan accent, "Oh, I guess now we put the sauce *under* the meat and fish instead of *over* them." But that was just Gordon making sure that the media's klieg lights were not only trained on the food but on the whole grand spectacle of it, and on the whole grand yet sweet spectacle that was Gordon Sinclair.

Another influential and instructional book I found on his shelf was *The Four Seasons Cookbook* by the owners of the landmark New York City restaurant of the same name. Within its pages, Swiss-born chef Seppi Renggli presented some of the most modern dishes I had ever read about. The notoriety of the Four Seasons restaurant also signaled a return of the celebrity patron, the heydays for which were the 1930s and the 1950s. Except that now celebrities enjoyed being photographed not only with owners but also with the *chefs*—a total departure from the past! These were heady times for the New American Cuisine movement. I felt that I could be in the vanguard, with Gordon Sinclair as my "knight exemplar" or maybe "knight errant," in search of the culinary version of a new Holy Grail.

In August we opened Sinclair's. Gordon had to submit to some last-minute haggling by the "decency board" of Lake Forest. He had had local artists create a faux classical panel (actually, a detail of a famous painting) for the back wall of the dining room that dared show, among other things, a woman's breast.

"This travesty of morality will not be allowed in Lake Forest, Mr. Sinclair," the board warned. "You can have that down on Clark Street, in the seedy section of town your restaurant is in, but not [saints preserve us!], *not* here, not in Lake Forest! This is a family town, Mr. Sinclair."

Gordon found out that the specific problem was not the breast per se, but the real offense was showing a nipple—the part that delivers nourishment (an irony entirely lost on the board). So he had his carpenters and electrician mount a lamp to cover just the banned areola. He had outfoxed the board. The breast remained and the campy sense of sexuality that defined Gordon's downtown was actually even funnier and much sexier.

The painting itself referenced a Dali-like surrealism rather than the solemnity of old Europe. I once asked Gordon what he thought I should shoot for when plating a dish because he had complained that my plating was just too formal. So I asked, "Can you give me a clear example?" He pulled on the lapels of his double-breasted jacket and stared down at my dish. Then he looked up and said, "It should be familiar and timeless, like the Mona Lisa. But I want her to have a little strand of spaghetti peeking out, just a little, from her lips."

The restaurant opened and I found myself thanking God every day that I had the good luck to hire a young woman named Carrie Nahabedian. You see, I really didn't have the skills to be in this position. What I apparently had was the right astrological chart! I didn't know it at the time but Gordon had a chart done on each of his prospective chefs. I had been given a glowing (and surprising to me) letter of reference by my old employer from the Pier House, David Wolkowsky. But what shooed me in was the divination of the stars. But those stars weren't there to illuminate me, and I was suddenly in a kitchen putting out food that would be compared and held up to the rigors of a much more sophisticated audience than I had ever known in Key West. Part of it was Gordon's reputation but another significant factor was the fact that Sinclair's in Lake Forest was not really owned by Gordon Sinclair but by local resident and near billionaire, Marshall Field IV.

Gordon was on a first-name basis with Marshall and his attractive and unaffected wife, Jamie. The Fields brought the blue bloods of North Shore society to Sinclair's and thus the descendants of America's great industrial dynasties became regulars at our restaurant. They often supped with us or with the likes of Chef Jean Banchet at his restaurant Le Français in nearby Wheeling. Banchet was a protégé of the legendary Chef Fernand Point of La Pyramide, who was considered by many to be operating the finest restaurant in America. *Bon Appetit* magazine put Banchet on its cover, and Point's book, *Ma Gastronomie*, would become a bible for many chefs.

To be sharing a venue in such proximity to Banchet's, knowing that guests would be coming to us after dining at the great Frenchman's place, was a task so large and beyond my abilities that I nearly shivered at the steepness of the learning curve I was on. But fortunately for me, Carrie was far more experienced at these altitudes. Also fortunate was the fact that I was still too naïve to really grasp the breadth of the chasm between my skills and Banchet's!

Carrie had actually worked at Le Français, and one night she took me over there to borrow some fish after we had had a particularly heavy night. I got to tour the walk-ins and saw the game hanging and aging in the coolers. I even snatched a wild morel mushroom as we were leaving and stuffed it in my pocket. I had only read about them and never tasted one. When Carrie asked me what I was eating as we pulled out of the gravel driveway I told her. She pulled the honeycomb-textured mushroom directly out of my mouth, hurled it out her driver's side window, and scolded: "You have to wash them to get rid of any mites and cook them first or they can make you sick as a dog!" She has also worked for one of Chicago's greatest restaurateurs, Jovan Trboyevich of Les Nomades, as well as one of its most beloved chefs, Leslie Reis of Café Provençale. Word has it that Carrie was the very first female chef that Banchet hired. She had the scars to prove it, but I soon realized that she could dish it out, too.

Carrie was born to be a chef. Maybe more than any person, male or female, she was born to be the kind of chef a true ball-busting but sick-with-talent French chef was supposed to be. She got it. She understood it. She reveled in it. She had cream and butter in her DNA. She knew so much about cuisine that it was nearly daunting. She knew how to see talent in young cooks and how to either coax or kick it out of them. She was a raven-haired, dark-eyed woman of good Serbian stock.

She knew she should have been Gordon's chef, I'm sure. But she was dealing with the old realities, and sexism was still very much entrenched in the system. As my sous chef, she stood by my side as I raced to learn techniques and how to use products I had never seen before. I would have been buried in the rich soil of Lake Forest if she hadn't come to join me that summer.

We had a good team but we were charting new waters. I loved Carrie's strengths with the classics but she sensed we needed to find a way to express this rekindled interest in American flavors and foodstuffs. She was actually bored with the same old canon of dishes and I think that is another reason she signed on with me.

One day a young man applied to work with us. I had just arrived to work and had not yet changed into my whites when he entered the kitchen. His skin was soft and pale and his hair hung evenly over his forehead. I would have guessed him to be about eighteen, perhaps from Lake Forest High. He asked one of the dishwashers to see the dining room manager. The man he asked spoke no English, so I told him, "If it's for a front-of-the-house position, the manager isn't here yet."

He said, "Oh, you work here? I thought you were a delivery guy."

"Yes. I am the chef. What's your name?" I asked.

Something seemed to startle him. "Chuck," he said. But then he bolted out the door.

A few nights later I recognized him at our pre-service meeting with the dining room staff. He was in a busboy uniform. I gathered he'd gotten the job. Then a month or so later he came into the kitchen around 2 p.m., well ahead of when the floor staff was required to punch in. He came up to me and haltingly asked me for "a job, any job, in the kitchen." I informed him that we were currently all staffed up. He left without a word. The young man came back the very next afternoon and I gave him the very same answer. This continued for a week.

Finally Carrie came over to me after the seventh rebuke and said, "Let's give him a shot. He really wants to work in the kitchen." I said, "Where do you think that skinny little guy could work, Carrie? He looks like the Lake Michigan wind could carry him out the door."

Carrie said, "I'll put him in garde-manger and see if he can handle it. If he can't he's gone, but I think I see something in this one." She had been right about the pastry chef we hired, a girl named Suzy Crofton.

So the young busboy started to work in our kitchen. I asked him his name again the day Carrie brought him up the stairs in a cook's shirt and apron. He said, "Chuck." And then he stammered, "Well, actually, my name is Charlie Trotter, but everyone calls me Chuck."

"All right, Chuck," I said. "Let's see if you're cut out for this side of the restaurant world. You have an excellent coach named Carrie. Let's see what you got."

During the 1960s, Chicago, and the whole of the North Shore, experienced a steadily growing influx of Hispanic workers, primarily from Mexico. I consider this one of the most fortunate fates of history. The early interaction I had with the Mexicans in my life helped create my appreciation for their food, their humor, their character, and their work ethic. The restaurant business would have been humdrum and listless if not outright doomed without them. Even though I loved it, getting others to take in stride the long hours, the intense heat, the emotional tension—the whole lot of it—was not easily accomplished. As the head chef one of my biggest jobs was finding the hands to do this exhausting work.

The Hispanic restaurant workers had a different attitude than many of my Anglo fellow travelers in the profession. And the beautiful thing was that if I needed to hire another person I didn't have to place an ad because there was always another family member or neighbor to call on. In a short period of time I had Santiago, Carlos, Ray, and our hardworking *telenovela*-handsome pot-and-pan man Roque. Carlos started as a dishwasher; by the third day he asked me if he could learn to cook and by the fifth he was making hollandaise. Santiago was Superman on the fish grill. Our menu was set up so that we could offer about six different catch-of-the-day specials, simply grilled, and served with a choice of compound butters. They were immensely popular and he often had thirty fillets getting flame-licked to perfection at a time. Santiago could not have had more than 110 pounds on his five-foot, ten-inch frame. He had holes in his sneakers and his jeans barely hung on to his hips, but in the middle of the rush he never went down.

I was learning about and buying ingredients that were being featured in the emerging southwestern food movement. Dean Fearing, Robert Del Grande, Stephan Pyles, Mark Miller, Anne Lindsay Greer, and others were becoming well known for their creativity in fusing Mexican and other Latin-based cuisines with classically European preparation methods. Jicama was new to me and I learned how to use it from Roque, with Ray translating. I was also greatly expanding my chilies larder with their help, and before long the staff meals were migrating to the restaurant menu in a slightly more dressed-up form. Everyone was happier. The Mexican staff saw their native dishes served right alongside the French and Italian standards. Exciting experiments like these would eventually inspire places like Frontera Grill as the new world of fusion cooking expanded and evolved. At Sinclair's, we were in the vanguard. We sensed it, so we dug in, played with it, and had fun with it.

All my reading was having another effect on me: I was turning into the chef as professor. I held "pre-preservice" meetings with our kitchen crew, gathering them around 2 or 2:30 for a capsule reading on what I'd been studying. (I often made copies of particularly important pages for them to take home and absorb.) I would pull out my steadily weathering copy of A. J. McClane's *Encyclopedia of Fish Cookery* and share his erudite insights into, say, pompano (a fish I'd known well back in Florida): "The silvery slab-sided pompano is one of the spookiest fish in the ocean. It's not uncommon to see a pompano 'walk' across the water in a semicircular course around a running boat, and the fish may even pancake over the surface the way children throw a flat stone to watch it skip."

I felt these readings helped open their minds to the great texts we all could learn from. Janet bought me a copy of *Japanese Cooking, A Simple Art* by Shizuo Tsuji for my thirty-second birthday, and my knowledge of the complex and exotic cuisine of Japan deepened further. Would I ever go there and see these fascinating dishes and techniques firsthand? I realized that traveling would have to wait. So all through the summer and fall of 1983 I cooked and served my take on New American Cuisine.

My favorite fish purveyor, Roy, at the time called me and asked if I would consider buying a turtle. When he rang our kitchen bell I saw his little boy first, a child of only four or five, standing on the creature's back. The most striking things about the turtle were its eyes, resembling the ash of smoldering cigarettes. It looked mean and its beak looked menacing. Roy explained that his boy was astride a diamondback terrapin that had been obtained legally (Gordon would be pleased) in the Mississippi delta the day before. I asked him if the turtle came with butchering instructions and Roy laughed, shook his Harpo Marx hairdo, and presented me with the invoice. "I sold another one to a guy who owns a Thai restaurant downtown. You are the only other person in the area I could think of that might take this one. I'd suggest asking him how to cut the critter up but he only speaks Thai!" Roy pulled his two-legged critter off the newest living member of our kitchen, hoisted the youngster onto his own back, went out to his truck, and drove away.

Everyone in the kitchen came over and surrounded the turtle. They all had the good sense to stay away from the beak. I had seen turtle on menus in Key West for years, and I'd seen live turtles at a popular tourist spot called the Turtle Kraals. But I'd never cooked one, much less been taught how to clean it—after killing it. I decided to act quickly before I overthought the whole thing. There was a husky young man named Kurt working with us, and I asked him to grab one side as I grabbed the other. We barely had room to scrape past the stairway that led down to the basement, which housed a gleaming, tiled prep kitchen as well as the small office I shared with the general manager. We landed the turtle on a catch basin of the stainless steel sink. The waitstaff had arrived in the middle of this hubbub and joined the crowd of onlookers. The decibel level began to approach Times Square on New Year's Eve down there: "Are you actually going to kill him?" "Where did you get him?" "Is it a 'him'?" "How do you tell?" (We discovered later that he was, in fact, a she.)

I was torn with doubt, but I firmly believed that, as someone who consumed the flesh of animals (and by "animal" I include fish) it is important that, once in a while, the veil of deceit should be removed and one should perform the "final act" oneself. I am sure I could (probably) not kill a cow, but I felt that it was time for me to face the fact that when I order meat I am asking someone to kill it for me. I needed to take the knife in my hand and see how my conscience felt when the killing was done and dinner was served.

It is not rocket science, so say the poets. We all know how to finish a life. Making it respectful and not grisly was my goal. I thought the way to do this was to be humane and neat. It was not easy with the howling mob of cooks, busboys, waiters, and utility staff watching my every move, voicing their opinions and waiting for the axe, as it were, to fall. Kurt helped by first goading the turtle to do what it is born to do—snap. Kurt grabbed a broom and held the handle an inch from the terrapin's face. The turtle chomped down on the oak with ancient savagery. Santiago and Carlos steadied the body of the beast and I took out the longest, sharpest, curved blade I had and held it over the turtle's neck. Its jaws were still clamped around the broom handle. Its neck seemed to be stretched to its furthest extent. The entire pack of humans was huddled around me with all eyes zeroed in on that primeval head waiting under my knife. I said a short prayer under my breath and bore down with a swinging, slicing motion, and suddenly the head and body were separate!

Yet the head did not fall to the sink as planned. No. It hung fiercely to the broomstick; its eyes, still open and smoldering, gazed skyward. No one spoke. Kurt took some butcher's twine and tied one end to the turtle's tail and the other to the handle of the Hobart mixer a few feet away. In this way the blood would drain into the sink and at some point (we hoped) the head would drop, the turtle would ascend to turtle heaven, and we would decide what our next steps would be in this eternal act we call survival of the species.

One by one, as if in a funeral processional, everyone took a last look at the turtle and then slowly, wordlessly marched upstairs and on to the routine duties of getting ready for a night of service. The turtle was left alone. I turned off the lights, as I was the last up the stairs.

It was a good night, and though we had no private party we did steady business. Around nine, in the middle of the last rush, the kitchen door swung open and Gordon walked in dressed as perfectly as ever. He waved to me with his hat and motioned that he was going to the office downstairs (to check the numbers, no doubt). I was expediting that night and my perspective allowed me to watch Gordon descend the stairs, turning on the fluorescent lights on the way down. An instant later he was back at the top of the stairs, screeching, "What is in the sink, dear God?"

He didn't wait for an answer. He bounded out the back door, jumped in his Mercedes, and fled to the safety of Chicago.

After we cleaned up the usual end-of-service mess, iced the fish, wrapped the "mise," and stored it, it was time to deal with the next cycle when you buy a living thing to cook it: butchering. There was no Internet to consult, no cookbooks on the subject, no old sailors or Caribbean fishermen to ask. We hoisted the turtle back up the same stairs we had taken him down six hours earlier. To my surprise no one wanted to stay and help me do this. But then Kurt said he would, provided he could keep the shell as a keepsake. I said "Sure. Take it." I'm not the great white hunter. I view the custom of mounting dead fish and birds and mammals on the wall as an odd bit of behavior leftover from the past. I grew up with men who prized their taxidermy, but it never made sense to me to take a once-living thing and stuff it in an eternal pose no matter how lifelike. The eyes were glass and they were lifeless.

The first thing to do was to remove the shell. It was as large as one of the round aluminum sleds I rode down snowy hills growing up. It was not so hard to detach it, but once we had done so there was a mass of biology before us like I had never imagined! The diamondback terrapin is known for its delicious eggs and the nearly translucent spheres, as large as my fist, we discovered must have been immature eggs. With no previous experience we plodded on, removing the four appendages. We grimly realized that for all of the weight of this turtle, the parts we could actually use were the legs. Our net entirely depended on our skill at culling the meat from them. We stood as still as surgeons. I started drinking beer. Kurt was a born-again Christian and water would have to do for him.

I started by placing one of the legs, including the foot and fleshy toenails, directly in the middle of my cutting board. I sized up its structure, trying to discern where the largest harvest of meat would be. I mean, people had been doing this for centuries. I had to believe there would be a rich reward for all the effort. I placed my left hand on the leg and slid my boning knife into the flesh. It was at that moment that the leg disconnected from the turtle, which had been dead for six hours, jerked. Kurt and I stared in disbelief, wondering aloud if the other had just seen what we each thought we'd seen! I had not only seen but also, most definitely, felt the leg move. My resolve to know the full measure of being a carnivore began to falter, but my inquisitive nature propelled me on to finish. Kurt and I worked on for another hour finally netting about six pounds of meat. We had no idea what to do with the eggs, guts, and other unknown, unidentifiable viscera so we buried the lot. Kurt washed the shell and took it with him. I packed the turtle meat into my area of the walk-in, drank one last beer, and drove home.

I slept fitfully. Since my Port of Call days I've twisted and wrestled around with ideas in the requisite lunacy of dreams. Sometimes something useful comes out of the nocturnal pageant, but more often than not it's a mishmash, so in the cold light of dawn I turn to my dream sheets (composed when truly awake) or my books. For turtle, I went to the man Craig Claiborne proclaimed the "panjandrum—the greatest authority and practitioner of Louisiana cookery," Paul Prudhomme.

His book *Louisiana Kitchen* was already in my possession, though it had just come out. Today, my first-edition copy is faded and roughed up from decades of use and yet Paul's picture on the cover portrays a man in full power. He begins his turtle soup recipe with this line: "This is a dish for a special occasion." I followed the recipe like a Vedic text and to this day it is one of the best things I have ever tasted. It was more of a sacrament than soup. I almost never did what I did with that soup. I brought some home for my wife, my mother, and my grandmother to taste. I didn't feel it was stealing from the restaurant. I felt it was my responsibility. I felt it was in my blood.

Winter came and with it came a job offer to return to Florida with a big new project of Gordon's. Janet was no longer homesick; she was now sick of winters! We endured the final Illinois cycle of snow, ice, wind, sleet, dead car batteries, and snow tires. Another spring arrived and we packed up our car and our child and headed south, once again. Justin was on his first car ride to Florida. We stopped in Cincinnati to see my Hainesville brother, Butch. I called his mother's home to make sure it was okay that we drop over as it was early in the morning. I wanted Butch to see how Justin was growing. But his mother told me on the phone from our hotel room, "Butch is dead, Norman. I'm sorry. I thought you knew. He shot himself with his handgun over that girl he wanted to marry. She was cheating on him. He killed himself sitting in his truck right out in the driveway." Then she screamed. I heard a male voice in the background. The connection was lost.

I hung up. Janet and little Justin were hugging me. I couldn't control my tears. "What's wrong, what's wrong?" Janet pleaded. Justin repeated his mother's words. "What's wrong, Daddy, what's wrong?" When I caught my breath I whispered the words Butchie's mother had spoken. But I had to lie to Justin. It was too much weight for a child. It was too much for us but we had to bear it.

We got in our car and continued on to Florida. I thought of many things as I pressed down on the accelerator. Unable to think about our beautiful hillbilly friend any longer I began again to think about creating something new. I began to think of my life as a chef. I wanted to create a life's work that brought happiness, and I finally was beginning to understand the full measure of what a restaurant can be and how it can fit into the very culture of America.

Gordon Sinclair helped provide a real place for me. I was actually going to Florida this time with a job! I was going to be chef of Sinclair's American Grill in a town called Jupiter.

Gordon's Artichoke Fritters

The original chef of Gordon—the one who launched its success—was a guy named John Terczak. John had a great imagination and an edgy lifestyle that complemented the seedy patch of Clark Street where Gordon Sinclair launched his restaurant in the late 1970s. Gordon had tons of style, and though this dish would not fly in today's "farm-to-table" times, he made sure this appetizer became a must-have for the famous and infamous of the era. John served it with sauce Béarnaise, but for home-cooking practicality the tarragon flecked aïoli works nicely, too.

For the batter:

1	cup all-purpose flour
1	teaspoon baking powder
1	teaspoon cornstarch
	kosher salt and freshly cracked black pepper, to taste
1	cup milk
1	egg
1	teaspoon olive oil

In a bowl, combine the flour, baking powder, cornstarch, salt, and pepper. In a separate bowl, combine the milk, egg, and olive oil. Whisk into the dry ingredients. Set aside to rest for about 30 minutes.

For the fritters:

3	cups canola oil
5 to 6	(1 small can) artichoke hearts packed in water, drained, and cut lengthwise into quarters
	cornstarch, for dredging

Heat the canola oil to 375 degrees F. Lightly dredge each artichoke heart in the cornstarch, then drop into the batter to coat. Place the battered artichoke hearts into the hot oil and fry until they are golden brown. Remove; drain on paper towels. Serve with the aïoli (recipe follows), or as desired.

Makes 4 to 6 servings as an appetizer or snack

For the aïoli:

1	egg yolk
½	teaspoon Dijon mustard
	warm water, as needed
1	tablespoon roasted garlic, mashed
1	cup pure olive oil
1	tablespoon fresh lemon juice, plus extra, to taste
1	tablespoon tarragon leaves, roughly chopped
	kosher salt and freshly cracked black pepper, to taste

Place the egg yolk, mustard, and ¼ teaspoon of water in a nonreactive bowl. Add the roasted garlic, and combine. Slowly add the olive oil. As the emulsion thickens, add the lemon juice a few drops at a time, until all the oil and juice are incorporated. Add a little water (not much!), as needed, to thin to the consistency of the aïoli. Add the tarragon leaves, and season with salt and pepper. Set aside for serving.

Makes 1 cup

On the deck at Louie's Backyard, which overlooked the Gulf of Mexico. *Photo courtesy of Richard Watherwax.*

Grilling in the Napa Valley

With my friend and business partner, Proal Perry, in the Napa Valley

In the MIRA kitchen. *Photo courtesy of Richard Watherwax.*

With Chef Paul Bocuse

At the stove at Hoexter's Market.
Photo courtesy of Donna Ruhlman.

In the a Mano dining room

Plating at a Mano with Randy Zweiban

With Justin at a Mano

A family of chefs: Janet, Justin, and Norman Van Aken

With Julia Child

Emeril, Charlie, and me. *Photo courtesy of Dr. Lee Smith.*

The Triangle cooking at the James Beard House

With Emeril Lagasse

With Charlie Trotter at the Beard House

With Ron Wood, Charlie Watts, and their wives

CHAPTER 16

Sinclair's American Grill

Jupiter, 1985

I DIDN'T REALLY GIVE much thought to where we were going next. We had come to trust Gordon, and my experience with Sinclair's was the most professional and career propelling I'd had up to that point. There certainly had not been much to compete with it. But it was a good time in our lives, and Janet and I were elated to be getting out of the winters of Illinois and back to the sunny Florida climate that had so spoiled us! Key West was not too far down the eastern coastline from the town we were going to live in: Jupiter.

What strands of fate have pulled me to these coastal places? From the small and womblike shores of my idyllic Diamond Lake to Key West and now to Jupiter, which protrudes out into the frothy Atlantic further than any other geographical point along the entire state of Florida. There is, of course, a lighthouse there. It sticks its sandy brow out into the vast wetness to watch and guide passing ships. It has been a beacon of safety since about 1550. Sailors have planned their voyages with this point in mind when crafting their routes to Central and South America. Aged maps illustrate as much with the Spanish word for point, *punta*, on them. Would it be a beacon for me? Would it be a launching point?

The project was Bunyanesque for me, especially compared to any place I'd worked before. The property was built around 1975 and was owned by the same man who owned Sinclair's in Lake Forest, one Marshall Field IV, from a family known for truly Paul Bunyan–sized accomplishments. The town of Jupiter is located twenty-five miles north of Palm Beach and I have no doubt that Marshall (as he asked me to call him) purchased the hotel for a song. Jupiter, you see, was in the sticks. (I'm from the sticks, so I know sticks when I'm in them.)

How in the world did he and Gordon imagine that anyone from up here in the hinterlands—far from the mansions of Palm Beach, far from the growing wealth and evolving sophistication of Fort Lauderdale and Miami—would come to Sinclair's American Grill? A lighthouse couldn't help them find it.

But for the time being I couldn't concern myself with marketing issues. We had two kitchens (a regular kitchen and a banquet kitchen) to build, a staff to hire and train, and a menu to create and source. I was now the executive chef of a nine-story, 160-room hotel that was smack-dab on the ocean at the very end of the prosaically named Indiantown Road in a town called Jupiter.

As is so often the case, Jupiter got its name thanks to a fuckup by the non-Spanish-speaking English. The Spanish fucked up the Indian words and then the English fucked up the Spanish ones. You might not be able to look that up in *Webster's*, but you can count on it.

When the Spanish explorers first started arriving around 1565 they came across the Jega (or Jaega) Indians. The Indians living along the inlet and the Loxahatchee River called themselves the Jobe, so the Spanish called the waters on which the Indians sailed the Jobe River. Two hundred years later the English came along, settled the town and began trading. To their ears, the word "Jobe" sounded like the Roman god Jove, also known as Jupiter.

It would still be almost forty years before Henry Flagler would build his "Iron Ship to the Sea" and connect Palm Beach to Key West, but railroad construction was already well under way by the 1890s. When Jupiter was connected by rail to the towns of Juno, Mars, and Venus it was quickly dubbed the "Celestial Railroad" by a writer for *Harper's New Monthly Magazine*, and it gained a little notoriety and attention. But the attention wouldn't last. Venus and Mars were little more than loading platforms and Venus could only boast a population of one man and two cats.

In 1985 Jupiter had a nearly celestial calm about it. The old-timers in Jupiter had come to tolerate the large hotel before we got there, since it was not yet attracting much business. They wanted no part of the glitter and wealth of Palm Beach. They would have truly hated Miami's exploding population and appearance-obsessed culture and they would never have approved of bawdy, irreverent Key West. They were nature lovers, and Jupiter was still a beautiful, pristine oasis providing natural habitat for abundant wildlife: foxes, owls, raccoons, bobcats, otter, deer, wild pigs, panthers, alligators, snakes, and turtles. One of the only activities offered to guests at the Jupiter Beach Hilton was a nocturnal walk on the dunes to observe the nesting process of turtles. Out in the waters of Jupiter, in the Loxahatchee River, and in the Intracoastal Waterway, dolphins and manatees cavorted in their peaceful, intelligent way.

But as humans our way to respond to this godly place seemed to favor pouring concrete on it and attracting tourists to come and spend their money in it. The state of Florida wouldn't exist without these charms. Marshall Field IV was our developer, and he was pouring millions into the hotel. He felt we'd done a good job in Lake Forest and now he was entrusting us to do the same for his investment in rural Jupiter.

For the first few months Janet, Justin, and I lived in a hotel room. There was no kitchenette and so we lived out of Igloo coolers and cooked on a hot plate or went out to the nearby Jonathan Dickinson State Park and had picnics and barbeques. Justin was four years old and not in school that summer. The kitchen was closed to guests so it could be entirely rebuilt, as were the dining room and new banquet areas. So we drove our car around Jupiter and Palm Beach and tried to get to know the area.

The general manager for Sinclair's American Grill was the same guy we had in Lake Forest, Rick Carbaugh. I also was able to relocate one of the best cooks who ever joined me in a kitchen during those years, Ed Hale. Ed had married a Hainesville girl so we had another connection. Her name was Pam Molidor, now Pam Hale.

Several other members of the Sinclair's team migrated south from the North Shore. They, like us, longed for year-round sunshine and to be a part of the excitement of opening up a new resort. We banded together—Gordon's commune.

Gordon came down often during the build-out. He was intimately involved with all aspects of the design of Sinclair's American Grill, not only because it had his name, but because he enjoyed building things. His excitement and involvement spilled over to me and I was beginning to understand what it meant to be not just a chef but a restaurateur, as I was now watching Gordon do it.

The hotel had been operating since 1975 so there was an entrenched group of employees already in place when we landed. We were, even before we arrived, suspected of being wild and woolly city types who were going to run riot over the settled, happy life the staff had enjoyed for a good number of years. And maybe it was a good thing for them to worry about. We, and I count myself as perhaps the most ardent of all, wanted not to be known as a *Hilton*—ugh! What a tired appellation that conveyed to me! I wanted the hotel to be known as the home of Sinclair's American Grill. I was getting a real taste for being on a national stage, due in no small part to Gordon, my ever-expanding library, and the opportunities for culinary cross-pollination that came with new colleagues and new cooking experiences.

So we were, in the beginning, a house divided. On one side we had the fabulously hip character in Gordon who had gotten in tight with the fabulously wealthy Marshall Field IV. On the other side we had the hotel management, who wore name tags, drank endless cups of awful coffee, and ate happily in the employee cafeteria. The general manager insisted we all call him "Mr. Stone." It was hard to take after calling Gordon and Marshall by their first names. But Mr. Stone turned alabaster if anyone on staff called him Jerry. Hell. I didn't consider myself "on staff." I was the chef of Sinclair's American Grill and we were about to make history! Or so I dreamed. One day the phone rang in our room and the low tones, jazz-like bursts, and lulling cadence of words I would come to know intimately undulated through the line.

"I hear you are opening up a new place with Gordon again, outside Palm Beach somewhere, right? I was wondering if you could use a hand maybe?"

We had placed an ad for twenty-five cooks in the papers, and for all twenty-five positions, only four applicants showed up. We were in a real jam.

"Yeah, man!" I couldn't control my enthusiasm for another Sinclair's "grad" to join us. "Yeah, Chuck. Come on down!"

About a week later Charlie Trotter (still Chuck) rolled into Jupiter after a nearly nonstop three-day marathon from San Francisco where he'd been cooking with the great Californian legend, Bradley Ogden of Campton Place. Charlie couldn't find the hotel entrance, tucked away as it was under a leafy canopy behind the tennis courts. He called me from a nearby 7-Eleven pay phone. I jumped in my little black car and roared into the parking lot. He lay fast asleep in the driver's seat with a filthy road-stained white golf visor sheathing his bearded, sunken cheeks. There were about thirty empty coffee cups littering the foot wells of the Volvo's backseat and rumpled newspapers lay plastered with the sticky remains of chocolate bar wrappers on the passenger side of the car. He snored softly, angelically in the brilliant midday heat. I walked inside the 7-Eleven and got two Heinekens. I came back out and pressed the cold beer up against his face. He woke, smiled, and we started our thing once again.

Gordon had a big design budget to work with and he brought in his trusted guns, guns he could never have afforded when he started with the quirky original Gordon on Clark Street. But after the success of Sinclair's in Lake Forest and flush with Marshall's money (along with Marshall's pride in doing things right) Gordon was able to help design a spectacular "theater kitchen." Jutting out into the dining room, the new kitchen imitated the topography of the land pushing out into the ocean just beyond the dunes. On one side of the V we had the hot line. On the other we had the salad and dessert stations, or cold line, and at the apex we had two large wood-burning Aztec grills we'd brought in from Texas. Immediately behind the grill and equally center stage we had installed La Broche rotisseries imported from France. The glossy marketing pamphlets showed chickens, quails, ducks, rib roasts, pork roasts, and even pineapples and eggs (!) spinning away in munificent glory. We would do them all and more, we swore! I asked Ed Hale to set up that station. But there was a practical design flaw: we didn't realize that when the chef was stationed between the grills and the rotisseries while they were operating at full force, the temperature could about roast the man. Ed's flaming red hair seemed to have an aura around him and he quickly lost the winter flab so many of us got in northern climes.

Charlie didn't so much ask to take over the cold side as much as it was his condition for coming aboard. He wanted to have a sphere that was all his own to guide, shape, and make his "camp." I realized later that this was pure Charlie. He was, in effect, creating the groundwork for making his own kitchen. And while we had a menu that offered all the prerequisite dishes one would hope for, there were also experiments that Charlie had in mind. Smoked pasta was presented. We had a small water smoker in the receiving zone, and Charlie would be out there with a lump of carefully handmade dough in the early morning mothering the nearly impervious mass into accepting the aroma of hickory or apple or mesquite. Later, when he'd ask me to taste the cooked noodles he'd cut from the flour, egg, and water dough, I had to tell him the truth: "No, Chuck. I really can't taste the smoke in the pasta now that it's been cooked in water and drained. Why don't you smoke the tomatoes and see how that works?"

And so he did. He would go into the most intense way of "knowing" every ingredient. It was fascinating to watch and I wanted to be a part of it with him every step of the way, but I was continually torn away to administer to the multifarious needs of the resort. Charlie would make requests for ingredients, and when I'd do the dreaded job of inventory I'd find our dry storage area or walk-in coolers suddenly filled with whatever field of study he was into that week. More than anyone I'd ever worked with before or since, Charlie shared a passion for the books I was reading. But reading about new ingredients and cooking methods was not enough for either of us. We wanted to make them ours! I lived, in part, vicariously through him, caught as I was in the endless succession of banquets, room service, breakfast service, and the never-ending battle of staffing. But there were moments, usually in the afternoon (in a way, like the time I spent with Toké), when we got together and went over the new books we treasured, conspiring to put new dishes on our menus. One of those was *The Cuisine of Fredy Girardet*, a slim volume that would inspire Charlie to visit Girardet in the Swiss town of Crissier. (Many years later Charlie would take me to a luncheon that Girardet cooked for us himself in his home!)

We also read *The Three-Star Recipes of Alain Senderens.* I spent time under the spell of Penelope Casas's *The Foods and Wines of Spain*, thanks to the Latin influences of my years in Key West. I underlined passages in the *Arroces* (Rice) chapter and taught our team Ms. Casas's philosophy that "unknowing diners . . . have come to believe that paella is basically a seafood dish accompanied by quite ordinary rice when, in fact, the opposite is true." My Spanish flavors began to emerge while Charlie's French leanings became even stronger.

But perhaps more than any other cookbook at that time it was Paula Wolfert's *The Cooking of Southwest France* that caused us the most study. In the works of Girardet and Senderens there was little background or philosophy. You read the recipes and gazed at a few pictures. (Back then neither photographs nor drawings were deemed important. In fact, few cookbooks had either.) Ms. Wolfert's books were not illustrated but she was a writer and an incredibly good one. She could make you "taste" the food and understand the culinary goals of the region.

The book was dense with information and we pored over it like Talmudic scholars. We deepened our understanding of Escoffier and learned of the lamentably unknown and wrongfully overlooked chef and teacher Andre Guillot. In a short, eighteen-line paragraph, his method of making sauces, which he called "stratification," forever changed our views on this ancient art. We had already banished roux (well nearly—I still used them for béchamel but I hid it from the other cooks for fear they would want to use them in other sauces where they no longer belonged). Instead we followed the scripture therein! We would, as Ms. Wolfert guided, start with an acid, follow with a rich protein, and finish with some fat through a series of rapid reductions to arrive at lighter, more clearly defined, and complementary sauces than the hoary, lumpy old goo of days gone by.

And so that winter we made cassoulet from her recipe, which included headnotes that ran five pages of text! We loved this woman! We made duck confit and a replication of the Toulouse sausages, we obtained the very beans Paula Wolfert advised us to use, and we got them from the mighty purveyor list she so generously shared in the back of this epic work. She quoted the legendary French gastronome that went under the pseudonym of "Curnonsky," a man of whom it has been said: "Was to be found wherever imagination triumphed over conformity." Curnonsky himself said, "A great dish is the master achievement of many generations."

The sacrifices and the efforts required for any achievements were an endorphin rush for us! We made Ragout of Duck Legs with White Onions and Prunes and Roast Shoulder of Lamb with Anchovies. Charlie prepared a Cold Confit of Pork with Green Beans and Cabbage. Ed made Barbequed Spareribs on our wood-burning grills, but he followed Wolfert's recipe and did them in the style of the Languedoc.

Once in a while, Charlie offered to watch Justin for Janet and me. It was great to have the time to get out on our own for a date. The town of Jupiter was so lonely for us, and we tried to get away from the totality of enterprise that the hotel demanded of me and to get to know the place. But back then it was like being in Nome, Alaska. We went to a movie and found a place for pizza and a couple of beers afterward. But we couldn't find any fun in town, and we weren't up for driving down to West Palm as the younger workers were prone to do. Being married and parents, our gusto for that kind of partying had fallen by the wayside. We decided to go back to our little rented bungalow and see how Charlie was doing as a babysitter.

When we turned the key to the front gate and crossed the small patio we could hear the TV and see the lights were on. But when we got inside we couldn't find Charlie or our boy. Losing calm a bit, we power walked to the pool area. No luck. We walked back to the house to recheck and then we heard muffled laughter from the small toolshed right by the front gate. We found Charlie and Justin holed up in there. Later Charlie explained that it was Justin's idea to hide from us. They both were giggling at our worried faces.

"How could I turn him down?" Charlie asked. "The little rascal is so darn convincing!"

All through the spring and early summer we tried to find a way to craft a menu that suited our desires and energies as evolving chefs in this new era we felt so lucky to be in the midst of. But the diners at Sinclair's American Grill almost never ordered our more creatively daring dishes. (Why didn't they get it?) They wanted Caesar Salad, Crab Cakes, Fettuccine Alfredo (the traditional nonsmoked version!). They wanted lean (no fat, no rib-eyes) grilled steaks (strips or tenderloins only) cooked medium-well if not well, roast chickens, and baked fish ("paprika is fine, paprika is better!"). In short, they wanted what they were used to ordering before Marshall Field IV and his $5 million renovation of the Jupiter Beach Hilton. And the banquets were where the money hummed, churning out Prime Rib, or Herbed Chicken and Mashed Potatoes for four hundred. But I was not giving up so easily on my new way of doing things. One night, I blocked the staff elevator door open to improvise a temporary pickup station as close to the dining room as possible. There was a particularly large group that night and they had spent big money on their dinner. I was intent on serving them Roast Rack of Veal, and I was equally intent on carving it to order! It was just havoc. About a hundred of the guests had been served when the emergency bell started to wail, warning of surefire disaster unless *whoever* was holding up the elevator *damn well let it go!* I just told the boys to "step on it" but when you have three hundred more mouths to feed it doesn't happen in a snap.

The word got to ("Call me mister, dammit!") Stone and that word was passed onto Gordon. He flew down a week or so later and we had a come-to-Jesus meeting about where we were and what was expected of us. The honeymoon was over. The restaurant wasn't breaking even and the only way we made up for it would be on these banquets. Gordon was saddened, but he was a businessman. He asked me to conform, but by this time I was considering it might be time to end my long relationship with my boss and mentor. I was sick of the wars between the hotel and the restaurant. There was another big party coming in, lots of government officials, and I promised Gordon I'd do a "normal" menu and not commandeer the elevators again. He gave me a cashmere-softened hug, dabbed his blue eyes with a polka-dotted pocket square, got in his rented sports car, and put-putted out of the driveway.

The banquet was preceded by what must have been the entire southern branch of the Secret Service. Suddenly the Jupiter Beach Hilton was awash in dark-suited, shiny-shoed, somber men who spoke into their sleeves and lapels.

Around this time, Burt Reynolds and *Dukes of Hazzard* star Catherine ("Call me Cathy!") Bach, dined at the restaurant. Burt was from the town of Jupiter and had created the Burt Reynolds Jupiter Dinner Theater a short cop-car chase down the road. (When we first got to town it was our sole hope for some local culture.) Burt finally came in and had dinner with the crew of whatever show he had Ms. Bach in. They (Burt and Cathy) were polar opposites. She was sweet, flirtatious, joyful, impetuous, and alive, everything a starlet should be. Burt was morose, monosyllabic, and bore the look of a man who has just witnessed his shiny new, just-off-the-lot Corvette getting keyed. The only time he brightened was when dessert was served. He favored our Mango Ice Cream and took cartons of it home. I asked Karen, our lead server, if he appeared to be happy. She replied, "I guess, but apparently he'd left his tip money back on his ranch."

The play Cathy was in ran only two weeks, but she came to dinner almost every night and we went out to a West Palm club the night before the huge banquet and danced until the place closed. (She was not only wearing her "Daisy Duke" shorts on TV!)

The security team was already swarming all over the Jupiter Beach Hilton when I got to work at 11 a.m. the next day. I felt like hell but I felt good, too. The image of Cathy Bach dancing picked up my mood and somehow it was the perfect antidote to all the serious G-men skulking around our kitchen.

We were in the final throes of prep for the party. The banquet room was filled with eagles, swords, banners, red, white, and blue bunting, and a huge blowup photo of the latest aircraft carrier that the manufacturing company had completed for the military cause, a truly near-Roman spectacle. Our guests included George H. W. Bush and Alexander Haig. (Haig was the one that wore his ardor without disguise.) But there is a certain, near-cardinal rule in the hospitality business: there are no politics inside the dining room to create a wedge between the servers (I include those of us cooking) and the served. We are as neutral as Switzerland during the show.

We peeled their shrimp, filleted their fish, carved their birds, sliced their steaks, and served the Key Lime Cheesecake they requested. I went back to the office to change and meet up with my new thespian buddies (including the darling Ms. Bach) for a drink at a joint down the street that was just hick enough to be considered cool by the otherwise jaded Hollywood characters who were part of her entourage. I slipped off my whites and pulled on a black shirt. Being color blind, I have always opted for simple clothing matches. I headed out the employee exit and listened to the air curtains whoosh, momentarily knocking out the din of the partying warriors within the Jupiter Beach Hilton.

Outside it was quiet and the tide lapped along the seemingly infinite Florida shoreline. I took a moment and stopped on the lawn of the hotel and gazed up at the night sky. I looked for the Big Dipper and found it. Then I found Orion and was happy that the three little stars offered their symmetry to my eyes in this chaotic world. It was at that moment that a really big guy grabbed me from behind. His arms suffocated any movement—I may as well have been in a straitjacket—and when, I think, he sensed or felt I was unarmed, he let me down. There were three others all in suits around me. "What are you doing out here?" they barked. Being scared shitless, the power of speech evaded me. That didn't work in my favor and the guy grabbed me again and now pinned my arms behind me.

"Leaving work," I finally grunted.

"What do you do?"

"I'm the chef of this place!"

One of them held a flashlight up to my face and then pulled out some folder with photos of all of us who worked at the hotel. Creepy. Yet I was relieved to see my photo there with my name and position.

"Why are you wearing all black?" they asked.

"It matches," I replied.

"Get out of here!"

"I'm gone. I am so gone!"

And thirty days later I was.

Daisy Duke's Papaya Ice Cream

Charlie Trotter got his first job cooking in a kitchen with me in 1982. He loves to try and reverse reality by "recalling" with mock gravity, "I remember when I gave Norman his start . . . he was working as a truck driver. . . ." and so on. But the fact is after that first year with me and my crew in Lake Forest (where we were blessed with the incomparable Carrie Nahabedian) Charlie headed out to California to attend cooking school and work a few jobs. I pursued an opportunity back in Florida, and as one thing led to another Charlie asked if he could come back east and "maybe help run garde-manger." I happily agreed. He arrived bristling with 1,001 ideas and recipes, and this simple—and simply delicious—ice cream was one of them.

By the way, it was named for Catherine Bach's character, Daisy Duke, one of the unforgettable characters in the television series *The Dukes of Hazzard.* She was doing a play across the highway from the resort that was home to Sinclair's American Grill and loved this ice cream. So much so that when she wasn't able to come over and enjoy it in person, she had it sent to her dressing room.

Equal parts by liquid volume:
- granulated sugar
- heavy cream
- papaya (or mango or any fruit desired) puree

Place all the ingredients in a food processor and blend thoroughly. Pour the blended mixture into a container, cover, and freeze.

Once it has frozen, serve garnished, or not, as desired.

Makes as much ice cream as you desire

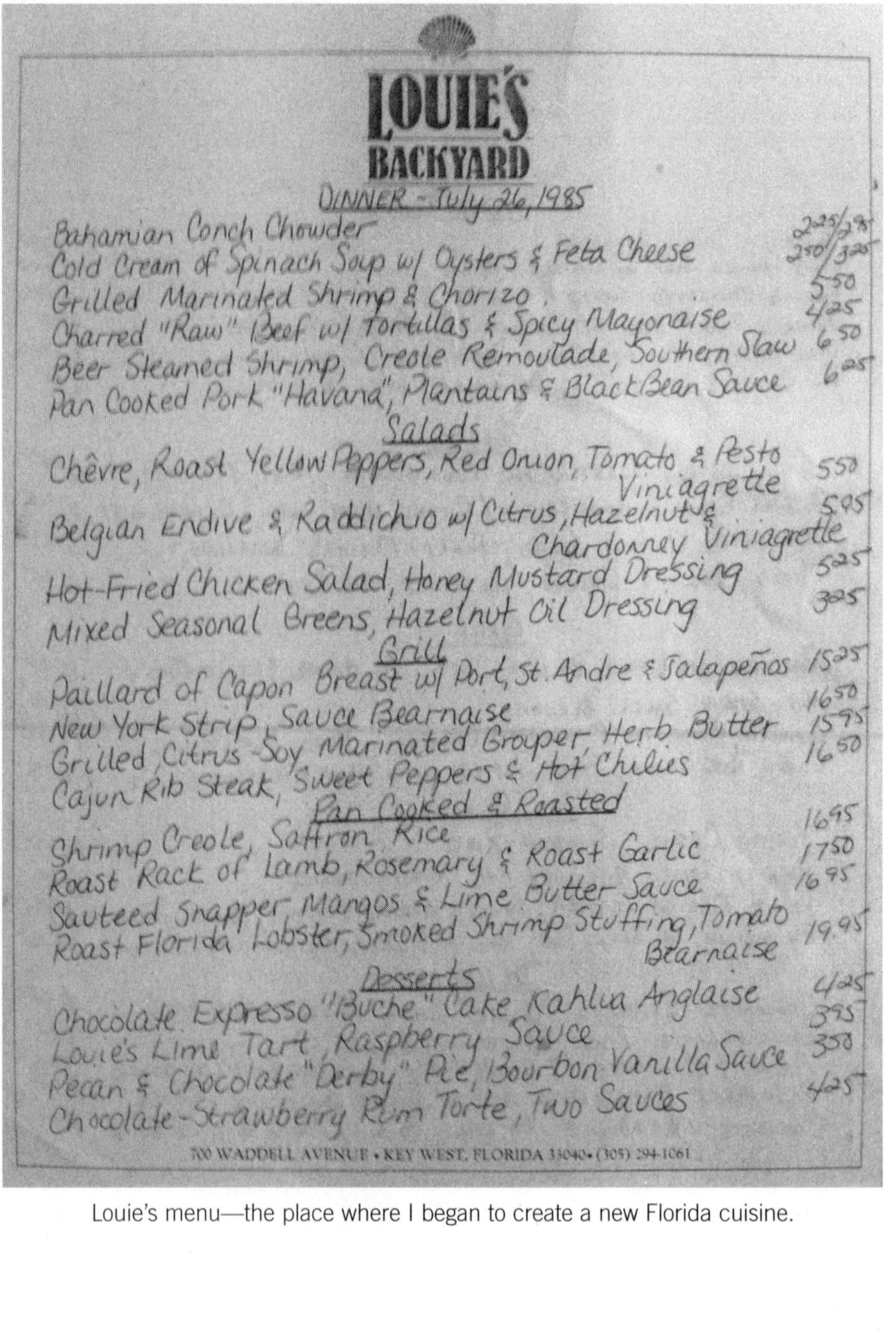

LOUIE'S BACKYARD

DINNER - July 26, 1985

Bahamian Conch Chowder	2.25/2.95
Cold Cream of Spinach Soup w/ Oysters & Feta Cheese	2.50/3.25
Grilled Marinated Shrimp & Chorizo	5.50
Charred "Raw" Beef w/ Tortillas & Spicy Mayonaise	4.25
Beer Steamed Shrimp, Creole Remoulade, Southern Slaw	6.50
Pan Cooked Pork "Havana", Plantains & Black Bean Sauce	6.25

Salads

Chêvre, Roast Yellow Peppers, Red Onion, Tomato & Pesto Viniagrette	5.50
Belgian Endive & Raddichio w/ Citrus, Hazelnut & Chardonney Viniagrette	5.95
Hot-Fried Chicken Salad, Honey Mustard Dressing	5.25
Mixed Seasonal Greens, Hazelnut Oil Dressing	3.25

Grill

Paillard of Capon Breast w/ Port, St. Andre & Jalapeños	15.25
New York Strip, Sauce Bearnaise	16.50
Grilled Citrus-Soy Marinated Grouper, Herb Butter	15.95
Cajun Rib Steak, Sweet Peppers & Hot Chilies	16.50

Pan Cooked & Roasted

Shrimp Creole, Saffron Rice	16.95
Roast Rack of Lamb, Rosemary & Roast Garlic	17.50
Sauteed Snapper, Mangos & Lime Butter Sauce	16.95
Roast Florida Lobster, Smoked Shrimp Stuffing, Tomato Bearnaise	19.95

Desserts

Chocolate Expresso "Buche" Cake, Kahlua Anglaise	4.25
Louie's Lime Tart, Raspberry Sauce	3.95
Pecan & Chocolate "Derby" Pie, Bourbon Vanilla Sauce	3.50
Chocolate-Strawberry Rum Torte, Two Sauces	4.25

700 WADDELL AVENUE • KEY WEST, FLORIDA 33040 • (305) 294-1061

Louie's menu—the place where I began to create a new Florida cuisine.

CHAPTER 17

Louie's Backyard

Key West, 1985–88

MY OLD BUDDY FROM the Pier House, Danny McHugh, called me on the telephone. He caught me right at the perfect time. It was about a year into the whole mind-sucking mess of the Hilton gig when I was going nearly postal and I knew it was me—or them. Danny said, "Nor-Man"—that's how he pronounced it, like two words—"you really ought to come down and talk to the owners of Louie's Backyard." Danny had scored a job there and was the daytime sous chef/butcher, perfect for him and whoever was chef. Danny could knock out a mountain of work in the daytime. By the end of happy hour he became ADD: Adorably Drunken Danny or, just as often, Arguing Drunken Danny.

"What's the deal with the chef there?" I asked from my kitchen office phone in Jupiter.

"Well, besides the fact that we have about ten grand in useless inventory that I think he's getting kickbacks on, he decided to go into the pastry room the other day and lock out the baker so he could bang the nighttime cocktail waitress. And another thing, I don't think she likes guys. Not pretty, Nor-Man. This guy has fucking got to go! He fucking works the hot line in his bare feet!" Danny used to lose it over a guy at the Pier House who wore sandals with a couple of side towels wedged into the tops to cover his toes while working. He made an exception only to Rosie on footwear. "I am not fucking kidding! He's *got* to *go*!"

Hell, I didn't need much convincing. Who knows? Was it time to go back to live in old Cayo Hueso again? We piled up luggage and child in Janet's Toyota Celica and buried the pedal, heading south.

We drove down that string of islands once again and with each passing key I could feel the world and its full weight falling off me and dropping into the scintillating blue around us. By mile marker sixty, Janet was driving and I had my head hanging out the window like a dog. I smiled at the world in a way that a former sinner finds in salvation. We were going to be in Key West. I hadn't lost it in Jupiter! I was okay! I was going home! At least for a visit and maybe for a shot at a new job.

When we got to Key West I could feel my old self come back. I could feel the gentle island town reaching her arms out for me once again. I hoped Danny was right. I hoped the owners of Louie's also felt the chef had to go.

Unfortunately, so did Danny—have to "go," that is. The night before we arrived for my interview it seemed my Irish buddy was "overserved" at the Afterdeck bar at Louie's, got some kind of bug up his ass (trust me, Danny was more than capable!), and decided to express his frustration with the circumstances at work by standing on the top railing overlooking the Gulf of Mexico, dropping his chef pants, and pissing into the water not ten feet from the nearest guest. You could possibly get caught smoking a joint in view of a guest without serious repercussions, but this was, well, pissing in it. Danny had known the manager, John, for years, and John had seen a lot from Danny Boy, but this act of delinquency would not stand.

When Danny showed up for work the next day hoping everyone else had been too drunk to remember the previous evening's antics, John stopped him at the bike rack outside. John's hands shook badly nearly all the time, one of the ravages of being a professional drinker in Key West. But his hands were still that morning and so was his resolve. Danny didn't even bother to speak when he saw John. He didn't even take his cigarette out of his mouth. He backed his scooter up and went out in search of a kindred soul to commiserate with, along with a cold beer. My plan to have Danny there at my side as my right hand and staunch aid had been suddenly—and literally, yes—pissed away.

The day had arrived, though, and it was time to see if we were coming back to Key West to live. I drove over to the corner of Vernon and Waddell and parked in front of the old house that is Louie's. I met the gentleman with whom Danny told me to speak. His name was Proal Perry. He was a good-looking man with a soft-spoken manner. It was a brilliant, shining afternoon.

We sat in the Afterdeck, the name of the Louie's Backyard bar, which sits right on the ocean. Sailboats serenely glided past. It was probably one of the most perfect restaurant locations on earth. We spoke to each other for a solid four hours. I felt a kinship and a bond unlike any other I had with a person I might be working with. Proal was measured, sensible, passionate, soulful, articulate, and thoughtful. What the hell got him into the restaurant business? He was unhappy with the "state of Louie's right now" and clearly very interested in straightening out his restaurant. It was "his" in the sense of the vision he had for it. He had two partners but they were going to accept whatever Proal decided, he told me quite assuredly.

As it turned out he was going to be driving up north to Alabama in the next few days. His children were in school and his wife's mother was coming to visit so the timing was good for him at home. (I was struck by the domesticity—I didn't know a whole lot of married couples with small children in Key West.) He wanted to spend two weeks with an old family friend, also a chef, who was operating a restaurant in Alabama that Proal wanted to "stage" in. The chef's name was Frank Stitt and he was an alumnus of the legendary Chez Panisse I continued to hear about. His restaurant was the Highlands Bar and Grill.

I couldn't believe it; Proal was actually willing to immerse and educate himself more fully in *someone else's* restaurant. This amazed me, and he continued to amaze me with each passing hour that I knew him. He made a plan to stop over for a night in Jupiter and I would cook for him.

Two weeks later, Proal arrived, as scheduled, at Sinclair's American Grill and, for the first time, I fed him. I can remember where he sat, which direction he faced, what he ate, and the supreme smile he had on his face for the entire meal.

Afterward we drove out to a barbeque place where I had a sandwich and we drank some beers. We talked until they shooed us out of there and then we talked in the parking lot until 4 a.m. We reached the conclusion that changed my life. I would become chef of Louie's Backyard in Key West. It was a twelve-year span since Janet and I had celebrated her birthday there. The circle of life was coming around again.

My last day at Sinclair's was June 16. Three days later we pulled out of Jupiter in the early morning; in the late afternoon Janet, Justin, and I pulled into Key West. Justin was back in the town where he had greeted the world four years earlier. It was around four o'clock. By six I was at Louie's and I worked that same night. I cleaned out the tiny chef's office and hauled in my cookbooks. Janet worked on getting our stuff put in storage until we found a house to rent. Proal had an apartment we could stay in. It was owned by one of the managers at Sloppy Joe's, which, I had come to find out, Proal was also part owner of, too.

I was about to meet the Louie's crew and they were about to find out who got their previous chef fired. But, amazingly, Danny had been able to finagle his way back into a job. It turned out that a few days after he was canned he found out that his wife was pregnant. He went back and threw himself on Proal's mercy. "You gotta let me back! Ann's pregnant!" It was one of the first indications of how much of a softie Proal could be. But everyone knew how hard it was to find a worker with Danny's skills. The tourists who were there the night Danny dropped his pants were gone, and the locals couldn't have cared less. One of the town's mottoes is "See the Lower Keys on your hands and knees." Danny could have been elected mayor back then.

The man who could have beaten him (as well as anyone else in town) was a dreamer who came to Key West from Indiana via California. His name was Mel Fisher and his life's mission was to find buried treasure. In 1969 he began to search for the *Nuestra Señora de Atocha*, a shipwreck said to be filled with such unimaginable riches that it propelled him to follow that dream despite the deaths of many, including one of his own sons. The story goes that the *Atocha* was laid to rest somewhere on the ocean floor after sailing out of Havana harbor on September 4, 1622, with twenty-seven other ships in a flotilla bound for Spain. They were overtaken by a hurricane as they entered the Florida Straits, and by September 6, eight of the vessels lay ruined and scattered on the murky ocean floor between the Marquesas and the Dry Tortugas. The man who dreamed of recovering those ships had his passion formed after reading Robert Louis Stevenson's classic tale *Treasure Island* back in his boyhood home of Indiana. He traveled far and wide and accomplished many things in his life, but he set his sights on the *Atocha* like nothing else before it. He toiled alongside his loving wife and family in the pursuit for years. And all during those years in Key West, Mel was heard to say to anyone who would listen, "Today's the day!" It was his mantra. And, of course, almost no one believed him.

It was shortly after we returned to Key West, though, that "today *was* the day!" for Mel. On July 20, his son radioed from below the ocean's vast surface to say, "Put away the charts! We've found the mother lode!" The coconut telegraph crackled with the news. It was like hearing Lindbergh had landed. The bars filled and the streets rang with honking horns and pistol shots. We all took it as a sign that Key West was the place where all of your wildest dreams could come true. What exactly was my dream? I wasn't sure. But I was soon to discover it at Louie's Backyard.

The first time I saw Kelle she had her back to me. I saw a girl with a thin frame. She had no hips. When she turned around to greet me I thought there was something in her arms like a basket of melons. That's when I realized that her arms were at her sides. She wore a cotton T-shirt, standard-issue white chef pants, a bib-style apron, pink sneakers, and a kerchief tying her hair back. She had a pack of cigarettes rolled up biker-style in her sleeve. She wore a shade of lipstick that was in stark contrast to her honey-blonde hair. She eyed me suspiciously. Who could blame her given what the last chef had shown her? But it was hard to focus. I'm sure I was reinforcing her view of chefs, but even women were awestruck by Kelle's breasts; they were not just large, they were almost solemn. How could she stand with only that little body to support . . . them? "What's my job now?" she asked. She sounded like a little kid. When she was unhappy it was clear. She was unhappy with the winds of change.

I asked, "What have you been doing so far, Kelle?"

"Prep." Her voice was as flat as a spatula.

"Well, let's just stay on prep then and see how it goes?"

"Okay." Possibly a hint less flat.

And she very slowly walked toward the back door to the kitchen. She dragged a match along the concrete wall. Her back was to me again. Suddenly the match ignited, and she whirled around to protect it from the breeze blowing gently off the water. She drew the flame to her expressionless face. She pulled on the cigarette. Her lipstick reminded me of my little sister's periwinkle crayon. She looked me straight in the eyes for less than a second, but it stuck. She turned back around, walked out the door, and let the screen door bang shut.

Danny appeared out of nowhere. "Major tits, Nor-Man, but she knows how to work a knife."

Barbara flipped three perfect "flags" of yellowtail snapper all at once in the black steel sauté pan. They arced high in the air over the stove and sailed gracefully backward into the pan she had tipped so perfectly so as not to bruise the fish nor allow the clarified butter to splash up and burn her strong, scarred hands. It was a scene out of Sea World done in miniature. Barbara fought off a smile. She had a good one with the whitest teeth and warmest brown eyes. But something hurt her deep down, and it wasn't just the asshole chef who had just been fired to make way for me. I didn't know what it was but as I came to work with her over the next week, I did know that I wanted to make it go away and have her standing happy with me on one of the most brutal hot lines I'd ever walk.

Danny had told me the story but even he wasn't sure if it was true about the chef before me basically raping the cocktail waitress (Barb's friend) that led to his dismissal. The pastry room had a door that could be locked from the inside because it was also the place some of the priciest ingredients and booze were kept. Shoeless though he might have been, kickbacks from purveyors lined his chef's pants.

Barbara was a hardworking woman of Italian descent. She was as strong as a bull and dedicated. She could outcook most anyone, male or female, I'd ever seen work a line. After meeting and working with her I think he did it to her pal. She was shell-shocked and unsure of what the cooking life was about. They had both had drinks so it was not a clear case. But it was not right.

The world whirred by at a new pace now. I was working like a man possessed. I was getting clearer and clearer on what I was trying to accomplish. By mid-July I had scrapped the entire previous menu. One of the owners became apoplectic when she learned I was taking off the steak salad. It was unthinkable to her. But to keep it was unthinkable to me. She hadn't a clue what I was going to do with this restaurant. None. Hell, I had no idea (not in a conscious way) that I was following an inner guide. I had been through all kinds of cuisines by now. I had moved from my French and Italian phases, through New Orleans and New England. I had dabbled in some Asian things. I had been all over the map. What was next was still terra incognita. I might have wished for one of Mel Fisher's maps.

From the moment I came in at 10 a.m. my work was consumed in preparing for the night service. Louie's was open for lunch but it was quite a simple menu and I had a good crew of two who did almost all of it without me having to work the line. The house was built in 1909, right on the water, by a ship's captain and was a residence for him and his family until Louie Signorelli bought it in the 1960s and operated it with only a handful of tables. The walk-in coolers were down on the ground floor. We were practically below sea level and the moisture made the kitchen drip. We did the receiving down there as well. I worked in that rudimentary, cramped kitchen until we got close to service at night. In the beginning all I had was one decent pot I had gotten from Proal's house. The rest were shit-banged aluminum things I wouldn't touch. I would make one sauce, put it into a bain-marie, clean out the pot, and make the next sauce. I didn't have the pot washer even handle that pot. It was like my own guitar. It was one of my hands.

By late afternoon I would move my precious cargo of sauces upstairs to the main floor and the service kitchen. The hot line could only fit three people. The cold area could fit one. It was summer in Key West and the temperature in that kitchen was criminal. Many nights Danny would hang out after his shift was over and try to make sure I could handle what I had designed. He'd stand at the end by the door with a beer and a cigarette eyeing me nervously. My sauté station looked like Keith Moon's drum kits, like a kid's fort, with milk crates stacked waist-high stuffed with sheet pans and plastic tubs loaded with foil-wrapped mise-en-place—you name it. I prepared for it like a soldier prepares for battle, which it was. Many nights after the last ticket was filled and the last guests given their entrees I'd go down the back steps and toss my cookies. The heat, the pressure, the whole of it was that kind of deal. We would sweat right through our chef coats, our bandanas, our pants, and even the gym shoes we wore.

I was burning on all eight cylinders and some of the folks working with me were getting mighty fed up with me. Camps were forming. One guy I brought down from Jupiter taped an angry note to my scooter one night telling me that everyone was getting toasted from the pace and I needed to "realize I was in Key West and mellow the FUCK OUT!" I ripped off the note and tossed it in the Dumpster.

The next morning, October 11, the *Miami Herald* was on my desk when I got to work. It had never been sitting there before that day. I nearly cast it in the trash when a kind, older guy named Alan, who was from New York and worked salads at lunchtime, said in his distinctly nasal voice, "You might want to read that, Chef." He cackled a bit and sauntered away. I opened the paper and saw the headline in the food section: "Louie's Backyard: New American Dining and Much Much More." Alongside it were four stars! It hadn't been six months since we started our campaign. I was ecstatic and it lifted us all up. We could see that our work had reached all the way to Miami! Maybe even folks in New York would read about us! I felt like Columbus sighting land.

But victory's lap dance was short. It had been almost six months and I still hadn't received the promised partnership agreement. Part of me thought I should have never started the job until the legal paperwork had been completed. But I knew that would have been impractical considering how badly I needed to leave Jupiter.

The next weekend we set the house record for the number of dinners served. At the end of the night (and after a few beers) I angrily told Proal to "skip it. I'll find a partner somewhere else." He told me he understood, but the other two partners stymied him. He finally said, "You know what? We will find another place, another restaurant and you and I will be equal partners in it." My anger melted.

A couple of days later I got a call from my young buddy, Charlie Trotter.

"You need any help down there?" he asked. "I hear you got your four stars right out of the box. Way to go. Listen. I have about three months between things up here in Chicago. I could drive down and maybe you and I could have some fun and kick a little ass? What do you say? Can you use my help?"

"Always, my brother."

"I'm on my way," he said.

Charlie arrived in three days. He was new meat to the nearly all-female line I had ended up with, not that I minded. They were all excellent workers and had an eye for presentation that was fresh. The girls were in quite a tizzy as to who would sweep Charlie off his feet. He got a kick out of Kelle but by then we all had learned that Kelle liked Kate, a woman who waited tables. The other girls tried as best they could to win his time but Charlie was already on his self-engineered missile launch of the "USS *Charlie Trotter*." He seemed to exist with little sleep or food. He only required coffee and the Cuban variety available in Key West was his new passion. They teased him and implied he "must be gay" to ignore them. I only had to remember the buxom girl in Jupiter he was balling near nightly to wise them up: "Quite to the contrary, ladies. Don't be catty. He's got his own mind, that one."

One morning I sat on the deck behind Louie's Backyard. It was beautiful, the humidity was gone, and a light breeze drifted over me. I was studying a stack of cookbooks—French, Middle Eastern, Southwestern, Italian—in pursuit of dishes for my menus, when I looked up to see a sailboat drifting southward. I "drifted" with it for some time, wondering where it might be going and what the passengers would see, touch, and taste when they got there. This thought transfixed me and, just like that, I realized that it was time for me to put away my cookbooks about other people's places. Key West was "my" place now. It was one of those moments of complete clarity: as much as I had drawn from the wisdom and artistry of hundreds of years of European cuisine, it was now time for me to express where and what I was living, and that was Florida.

I thought about how North America's music had evolved, how its literature and architecture and dance were amalgamations of cultures bumping up against one another. Key West was a place where Spanish, African, and Anglo influences converged, yet the foods we were eating (including at my own restaurant) seemed almost frozen in time. No one had yet imagined what kind of fusion cuisine might result if those cultures were expressed in food the way the cuisines of New Orleans, California, and the American Southwest were the gastronomical expressions of those who inhabited these places. A vast range of histories and cultural influences, and an ever-shifting present tense, guides Latin America and the Caribbean culinarily. And the people of this region take great pride in their individuality and diversity. My moment of clarity then became one of resolve. I closed up my books and put away my notes. The sailboat was beyond the horizon now. I could feel Cuba just ninety miles away. The answer had been around me all along. I ate it and drank it almost every day. My new teachers were going to be in the cafés and homes of South Florida, not in the books of France.

In the next weeks and months I went back to some of the same joints I'd eaten in many times since I had first settled in Key West in 1973. I went to the little markets like Fausto's and Five Brothers and studied each item on the shelves to see what magic they could add to my new passion. I went to a restaurant called B's, another called La Lechonera, and another, El Cacique, as well as places that had no names, or at least no signs. I sat on stools at counters and ordered Afro-Cuban-Bahamian fare. I pestered cops and fishermen and housepainters and housewives about what they were eating. Often I asked them if they wouldn't mind translating a menu item for me. I earned the suspicion of many a waitress as I quizzed them, taking notes on a little spiral pad. It got very exciting—I felt like I was cracking a case or solving a puzzle. I envisioned how each meal was cooked and how I could adapt it to my own dishes.

We received word that Prince Rainier and the royal family of Monaco were coming to Key West. His son-in-law, Prince Stefano, was an avid motorboat racer and would be competing in the annual races held in Key West. Even better news was that Princesses Caroline and Stephanie were coming, too! We went into "royal mode."

Purple basil was a novelty at the time, and we ordered an amount that had the distributor calling several states to fill. The slightly soapy aroma still conjures up a near gag reflex in me to this day. But we refused to notice anything negative as the day approached for the royal visit. And then they walked in. It was a beautiful night and they were dressed to the nines. I didn't emerge from the kitchen (I simply didn't do so back in those days). I got plenty of reports, though. The waiters were my contact with them. "They all seemed very polite." "Princess Caroline looks like her mother." "They don't speak much English."

"Enough of the red carpet review," I snapped out of nervous frustration. "What are they ordering?" Whatever they chose, I was determined that the royal meals would be a departure from the standard fare! Perhaps our

Hot Fried Chicken Salad with Honey-Sesame-Sriracha Dressing or maybe Grilled Key West Shrimp with Chorizo Sausage and Blistered Bell Peppers?

Then the order came in: "Five filet mignons *well done*."

My eyes might have fallen out of my head and rolled around on the floor. One of our waiters got me a Heineken unbidden. Well, what the hell. We draped the hammered meat with the purple basil and left it at that. What could we do? They left a stupendous tip the waiters carved up like pirates.

Two days later we got another phone call. The royals were on their way over and wanted an early dinner. We weren't set up for that in any way! But they either spoke little English or preferred to hear what they chose. They arrived and everyone tried to calm me down. I was in my Fernand Point state of mind back then: When a man of position and wealth arrived to the famed chef's legendary La Pyramide restaurant too late for lunch, he told the chef to fix him something even though Point was no longer serving; Point was diplomatic at first, saying his dinner menu was not ready and perhaps the gentleman would join them at dinnertime. The man replied, "It doesn't matter. Just fix me anything." Point replied, "If it doesn't matter then he would not dine chez Point." And turned the man away.

The royals were fuming at having to wait. Minutes passed. Suddenly my kitchen door slammed open and Prince Stefano barged in. He was screaming, "What's the holdup?" He must have learned a little English all of a sudden. But then I saw that he was holding a cigarette. In my kitchen? What? Are you fucking totally insane? I wasted no time. "Get that fucking cigarette and your ass out of my kitchen! I could give a *fuck* who you are. This is *my* kitchen. Get out!" I had entered into a zone in my mind that amazed even me. I was insanely crazy over this effrontery to me and to my ideals as a FREE MAN! It was the prince who was purple now. He was being yelled at by a commoner! I started to come around from behind the line. My all-girl hot line was screaming at the prince, "Get out! Get out! Get out!" That worked. He bolted out the door. Proal was suddenly a man possessed. I couldn't believe my eyes when I saw him, this normally most pacific man, pushing Prince Stefano of Monaco by the shoulder out the front door. I shunned purple basil for about two years.

A letter arrived at our office upstairs at Louie's. A cookbook author by the name of Irena Chalmers wanted to include Louie's in a book called *American Bistro*. The news, unfortunately, was relayed by Proal's female partner, so the full effect of its import was muddled by her uniquely garbled translation of the information. She was the person saddled with paying the bills for the restaurant and she took what solace she could "on the rocks." The actual letter was lost but, to the best of her recollection, a photographer was coming (today? tomorrow? someday?) to take some pictures.

"Of what?" we asked, dimly hopeful we could nudge this nugget of info out of her spinning head.

Lost in translation.

When the photographer arrived the next day we experienced our first fully professional photo shoot at Louie's Backyard. And after the lights were set up and the props were arranged in the middle of our kitchen where the pantry and the hot line intersected, it was verging on the first moments of service. My cooks began to get really upset when the energetic yet portly photographer kept shooting while directing them to move this way as the ticket machine came rattling to life. We knew it was going to be a busy night. But I knew something else. I sensed not only that we were participating in an important American cookbook, we had been included because we were part of a new constellation of culinary stars—I knew we were on the cusp of something quite spectacular.

The two books that Gordon had brought back to me from Spago and Chez Panisse came to mind. We could be joining Puck and Waters in a broad revitalization of American cuisine. We could be reading our names along with the likes of them. My fellow cooks hadn't seen it that way and lacked my willingness to put up with the chaos that was unfolding. They nearly snarled aloud at the cameraman and his assistant. It was getting ugly. Barbara let some hot clarified butter sail out of her pan in what was an obviously intentional salvo. It landed on the photographer's lower leg. Hastily now they got the lights out of the grill area so we could move. The tickets flew out of the ticket box but I was floating on air. People like Jeremiah Tower, Dean Fearing, Anne Rosenzweig, Michael McCarthy, Alfred Portale, Marcel Desaulniers, Nancy Silverton, and Barry Wine; I learned their names and how their sweat and imagination were changing menus all across the map. My contribution to the book was a recipe for Roast Pork Havana and they, in turn, would read about us, and how Key West flavors, Florida flavors, were going to feature in a newly charged American bistro being born.

One night Charlie pulled me outside and said, "It's time, brother. I have to go back up north. It's time for me to do what you are doing. I want to run my own show. I want to open up my own restaurant and my father is willing to help me." I told him I understood. He said, "But I have a favor to ask you. Let me cook a meal for you and Janet. You have never sat out there and eaten dinner on that glorious dining room's outdoor deck and you must very soon or I don't think you will get to for a long time." I surprised myself and said, "Sure." But there was a look in his eye. I have come to know that look better and better over the years, but this was new for him and new for me. My former student was becoming a young master who was ready to head out and make his mark on the culinary world—of "the Grande Cuisine" as he so often called it.

A few nights later Janet and I were seated at a table overlooking the Gulf of Mexico. She looked even more beautiful than the first time we dined at this magical place. What Charlie sent out to us was a succession of dishes that were prepared in our kitchen but created by him and him alone. There was nothing on his menu that was even partially related to what we normally served. He wanted to make each dish a total and original surprise to us. It was hard to fathom how he'd gotten the purchasing and prep done, as well as all the other things involved, without us having noticed it. The last course was a dark chocolate terrine that contained whole poached oranges that were like giant flaming suns set in a jet-black midnight sky. Stunning, like this man I was getting to know better and better with each passing year. In a week he was gone from Key West and on his way in search of the dream he needed to find—or create.

The season was coming on strong and I still hadn't been made a partner. Proal was in the midst of a new relationship that was troubling me, too. I took my own memories of divorce and piled them into the stormy mix. Of course his personal affairs were none of my business but I was being self-righteous to a fault. Proal had fallen in love with a high-energy girl from Washington, D.C., named Connie, who was working at Louie's as a manager. The extramarital affair took my friend and partner on a new whirlwind of emotions—and although I felt for him, I also felt I wasn't being treated fairly.

After service the next night I stormed into the office and demanded from Proal that "Louie's must pay me $100 in cash each week until the legal work is done!" I believed that unless there were actual dollars coming out of their pockets they ("all three of you owners!") would sandbag me forever. He did not like to be put in the same group as his partners and my accusations stung him hard. I could see it in his expressive and soulful eyes.

It was hard for me to stay mad. It was hard for me to be cold. I loved being a chef, and I had things that I envisioned that I wanted to create almost without regard for my financial circumstances.

The following Saturday, Proal took $100 out of his own wallet and gave it to me. Somehow I knew it was simply all going to come together. But I also couldn't help but wonder—when?

Who knows what caused us to drink so much the night before? In Key West, it didn't take a holiday, all it took was the right person to join the bar at the end of a shift and plans could change. I do remember the sauce I created the next day, though how I came to conjure it I could only imagine. Maybe it was the mix of beer and Barbancourt Five-Star Rhum paired with the glowing moonlit waters of the Gulf rocking just a few feet away that inspired me.

When morning came my stomach churned violently. But I had to go into work. I couldn't *not* show up just because I was hungover. I was the fucking chef and I was not going to give my crew the example of calling in sick. I got my scooter key out and drained a cup of espresso. It was raining, dark, and gusty. I pulled a plastic poncho out of the little storage box from under the seat. It had no belt and it flapped noisily in the wind as I cut out of our small lane onto Key West's busy Flagler Street. As I approached a stoplight it suddenly changed to yellow and I skidded to a stop sliding sideways.

The rain started to fall more heavily, and I was getting soaked. I could see drivers eyeing me from inside their cars with a look of mild amusement at my foolish form of transport. I looked down to keep the rain out of my eyes. It was then that I went into an altered state. I was very clearly "seeing" our pastry chef, Sue, making caramel sauce at our piece-of-shit stove in the basement kitchen at Louie's. She had a large, beat-up aluminum pot and was waiting for that magical moment when the caramel is just about to burn and exactly THEN you dump in the heavy cream and whisk like mad. What was nearly going to burn to a bitter waste became lustrous caramel-colored edible ecstasy. I (irrationally) wondered, what if I replaced the water with a combination of vinegar and stock and made a *savory* caramel sauce? The car horns honked at me as the stoplight changed to green. I finally snapped out of my *Kubla Khan* vision. The rain didn't bother me now. I hit the throttle and made a beeline for our kitchen to try this out. My headache was gone. It was moments like this—moments of discovery—that made it all worthwhile. I thought back to my days at the Deerpath Inn and the bleak faces of the men I worked among. This was the other side of that sad valley. This is why we become chefs: to discover worlds of flavors unknown to those before us.

We cooked all through that winter season and our team became better and stronger each week. I was so proud of our menus and what was happening with our reputation. I still had so much I wanted to accomplish for Louie's. I was reading and poring over all the culinary magazines I could read.

Charlie was sending me packets of clipping, and excerpts of stuff he'd come across nearly each week. The plates we had were horrible. Our silverware was a joke. Our equipment was old when it was purchased and the doors hung crookedly on the reach-in coolers so the food was always sweating in the tropical heat. But what was also true was that the guests dined in one of the most beautiful and romantic settings in all of creation and they didn't seem to notice the plates, the cutlery, or the glassware once they tasted our food and breathed in the magical setting of Louie's Backyard.

Danny was quitting. Again. He said, "I've had enough of your shit, Nor-MAN. You want too much! You and your fucking quails flown in from some hick farm in Georgia and the endless trips to the airport and cutting fish whole but having no bones in the middle so we can stuff 'em. Real cute! I'm OUTTA HERE!" and so on. He waved good-bye with a Heineken in hand and slammed the screen door shut.

I was unaware that my mission for four stars by New York standards was grinding down on him and others, but I wasn't about to turn back now. I was, of course, seriously fucked because you don't find a butcher like Danny wandering the streets of Key West. An ad went out. I told my day chef, Doug, to hire anybody who could fillet a fish. I didn't care if they had a bone in their lip and one eye.

About a week later, I came into work at my usual time and there was Leif. He'd put in an application just after having moved into town. I'm not sure if he had a last name or if he'd worked anywhere with a kitchen. But he was standing there in a short-sleeved prep shirt with the snap buttons unbuttoned halfway down his chest and a bright blue bandana tied around a head of hair that a lion would envy. I could not see his face or eyes because he was intently breaking down a forty-pound black grouper at the butcher block. His legs were positioned slightly apart, and his broad shoulders were squared and twitching nearly invisibly with the effort used in breaking off the last bones that connect the spine of the fish to its head. Some scales flew up and speckled his gold and black curls like dazzling ornaments. He freed the pinkish white meat from the dark skin and ivory bones of the grouper, looked up, and smiled triumphantly at me. He had a luxurious black mustache any Harley rider would kill for. A leather choker necklace with a pirate's coin hung around his strong neck. He had no hair on his arms or chest and his skin was toned and perfect as Lucchese cowboy boots.

He turned to the work sink and quickly rinsed his hands, wiped them dry on his apron, and crossed the room in two steps to introduce himself to me. His eyes were large, dark, and an endless bittersweet chocolate brown. "Hi. I'm Leif." I can hardly ever remember meeting a man with such physical beauty and grace. I asked him if he needed anything and he said, "No, just this job." And so, Leif began.

Janet and I accepted Proal and his wife Susan's invitation to come to their nice home just a block or so from Louie's and eat "true Alabama-style barbeque." Janet and I love all things barbeque and we loved being with Susan and Proal. Over the course of the evening we plotted a course to open a place showcasing barbeque. Perhaps this would be a fun way for our families to grow closer?

We went back to Proal and Susan's for another night of barbeque on April 10 and this time Janet cooked her family's Saint Louis–style ribs. April 12 was the Return of Halley's Comet Party and Pig Roast at Louie's, making the barbeque theme seem more and more like the way to go.

Proal and I made an offer on a piece of property on lower Simonton just a short walk from where I'd worked when I was doing barbeque at the Midget more than a dozen years before. It was an artist's gallery called

Aristo's and had some real saltwater character. I was hoping we could close on the deal before an upcoming trip to Miami to cook with a young Californian chef named Michael Chiarello. This would take place at a restaurant called Toby's for what was being called a "James Beard Dinner." I wasn't sure what that was—yet.

I made Conch Lasagna in small tasting portions for an appetizer, followed by Grilled Marinated Tuna with Oriental Vegetables in Garlic-Ginger Vinaigrette for our entree. And "Baker" Sue made her Black Pepper Puff Pastry with Apples, Calvados, and Warm Caramel Sauce for dessert. The next day, on Michael's recommendation, we visited a tropical fruit farm in Homestead and tasted some incredible and vivid-looking fruits, including carambola, *monstera*, *canistel*, atemoya, and sugar apples.

I was down in the basement prepping when Proal came in to tell me that Roddy Brown, who had directed me in *A Streetcar Named Desire* during my Port of Call days, had died suddenly. It seemed like a bad dream. I couldn't imagine that his life force was stilled. I would have guessed that he'd flipped his big black "cigarette" boat and gone out in a spectacular blaze. But it was a heart attack that felled him. He could not have been forty yet!

His memorial service was on May 4, the day before our trip to Miami. It was pure, theatrical Roddy. He, or perhaps his beautiful widow, Rita, had arranged for a full-on New Orleans–style processional band to accompany the mourners to the service at St. Bede's. I decided that there were many things I learned from Roddy Brown during the short time I knew him. "How to have a funeral" could now be added to my list.

On May 8, Proal and I announced to our staff at Louie's that we were moving on to a new joint project. We would still remain at Louie's but we would be dividing our time. Naturally, this was met with the usual array of human responses: envy, distrust, malaise, and outward displays of real happiness for our endeavors. We drank a glass of Champagne in the little bar by the front door, the bar where Janet now worked.

After a protracted negotiation, Proal sold his interests in Sloppy Joe's a few days later. Our new project was funded in ways I'd never imagined and it was time to pursue the goals we'd dreamed of.

Janet and I flew to Illinois with Justin to attend the wedding of one of my cooks from Sinclair's Lake Forest. We had been hearing about a place in Chicago called Café Babareba that was doing authentic Spanish tapas so we went on May 15 to check it out. The chef was a highly respected man named Gabino Sotelino who had been doing classic modern cuisine at Ambria. Babareba was a place as much dedicated to fun as it was to food and it spoke to me about how our rib place should be.

We joined Charlie for dinner on May 17 at the tiny and magnificent restaurant Carlos, along with Mama, Proal, and Susan. Afterward, Proal and I flew to California to have a look at the new restaurants out west we'd been reading about.

When Proal and I arrived in San Francisco we had no real sense of what we might experience. But we had carefully planned to eat lunches and dinners in the places touted as the very best. From the first lunch at Jeremiah Tower's Stars we began to see how exciting New American Cuisine was becoming. In the urban sophistication and electric self-awareness of Stars, we were far from the "Key Westy" porches and ramshackle cottages that stood in for dining rooms. We were light-years beyond the crumbling, spit-and-baling-wire-patched-together kitchens I'd grown up in. At Stars, a wall-less kitchen showcased twenty or more eager young chefs peeling, chopping, grilling, sautéing, mopping, and plating. I imagined piped-in music—maybe "California Dreamin'" wafting around the magnificently coiffed red hair of Jeremiah Tower. We had Fire-Roasted Onions with Ancho Sauce and Braised Rabbit with Pasta and Artichokes.

We drank wine, then espressos, got back to our hotel, cleaned up, changed, and dined at Chez Panisse that night. What can be said? Stars had been joyous, but, as impossible as it was for us to admit, Chez Panisse was even more. Serene? It didn't hurt to have a bottle of 1966 Clos de Vougeot, of course. I sat there with my friend feeling very, very lucky to be alive and sharing the planet with Alice Waters and her restaurant.

The next places were excellent but our standards were now impossible for any other to reach, as good as they were. At Square One, we had a fine salad, Leeks with Mustard and Mimosa Vinaigrette, as well as a perfectly rendered Osso Buco with Risotto and Gremolata.

We drove up to Napa Valley and had lunch at Mustards Grill and enjoyed the campy humor of the menu and the full flavors of the wine country–inspired food. We went to a tiny jewel of a place called Rose et LeFavour with a new friend, Bruce Neyers. Bruce was a winemaker and a marketing director for the legendary Joseph Phelps Winery. (We sold a lot of Phelps wines at Louie's.) We were treated most hospitably by Bruce and his wife, Barbara. They even invited us to an annual bash at their home. In the meantime we had another lunch at Mustards and dinner at Stars.

The Neyerses' party on May 25 brought together wine growers, wine collectors, winemakers, and restaurateurs from all over the Valley. When we arrived Bruce showed Proal and me his garage cellar, a treasure that impressed us both. And it seemed that Bruce intended to open up a good many bottles for this yearly celebration. There were cases and cases of Billecart-Salmon Champagne iced up and ready to go for the arriving guests. Bruce popped a magnum and Proal and I each got a big glass going. It was as if I had never had Champagne before. It was *terroir* all right.

Proal and I were feeling so fine. It was almost like a marijuana kind of fine, the way it was when the weed was easy and lifting. There were folks tending large mesquite grills laden with shoulders of herb-marinated lamb and fat sausages made from locally raised pigs. Grape leaf–wrapped squares of chèvre were being served that had been produced by Laura Chenel, the acknowledged queen of artisan cheese making. Laura herself, Bruce pointed out, was on the other side of the swimming pool having a glass of wine with Alice Waters herself—I was in heaven!

Some members of my generation might have wished for a backstage pass at a Zeppelin concert, but this was just fine with me. We filled up on the simply perfect wine country cuisine and then began a slow march through a thicket of the most sought-after wines that we, being from faraway Florida, had only heard or read about. At Napa Valley parties it was apparently perfectly normal to pull out wine with an enthusiasm that rivals bikers at a tattoo fair. We drank.

Somewhere in the midst of all this Bruce asked me if I wanted to meet Alice. He had heard from Proal that I'd brought my well-worn copy of her very first cookbook. I said, "Sure," trying to sound casual, but I was suddenly, despite the buzz from all the great wine, quite starstruck. I saw her coming through the kitchen screen door. I looked down, almost hoping she'd walk past me and forget the whole thing. But she didn't. Maybe she sensed how nervous I was because I learned later how shy she could be. Maybe her nurturing, maternal instincts took over. She sat down next to me and said, "I hear you want your book signed."

I nodded and handed her my battered copy of *The Chez Panisse Menu Cookbook*. She took it from me, delicately flipping through the pages. *What was she looking for?* I wondered. But then she smiled her angelic smile and said, "From now on these are the only versions of my book I want to sign, the really beat-up, used ones." She placed her childlike signature up front on the half-title page, adding a little heart. I knew I was in heaven now.

The party continued and I even danced with Alice. Proal and I were scheduled to take the red-eye out of San Francisco, more than an hour away. We decided we were fine to head down out of the hills in the rented Mustang. We threw our luggage in the trunk and said our woozy good-byes to our hosts. The party was still in full swing as I backed off the lawn and out onto the highway. Proal was more wasted than I had ever seen him. He had a tremendous capacity for wine and was nearly always "good to go" after a party. I, on the other hand, go down for the count more quickly than anyone else. Yet after connecting with Alice Waters I felt I could drive to Vegas and beat the house!

We were suddenly no longer in the brilliant sunshine of a Napa Valley day but on a pitch-dark, narrow road snaking down a mountain to Highway 29. I couldn't see shit! A series of curves unfurled ahead. I was trying to figure out how to maneuver them when a car came up from behind, its headlights blinding and disorienting me. My seemingly tight grip on sobriety came loose. The car zoomed around us, screeching loudly, hitting the horn. Proal bolted up from his slumber and said, "Are we all right?" I said, "Yeah!" but then I saw the hairpin curve I needed to negotiate and yanked the wheel violently. The Mustang reared and began to buck. We then felt a terrible thud followed by a sickening pitch forward.

Then the engine went dead. We got out and stumbled around the car to see what had happened. We saw that we had simply slid off the road into an unusually steep bank. I got back in the driver's seat and tried to turn the engine over. There was no response. The car was unconscious. We knew we'd miss our flight now. We were probably a mile from the Neyerses' home. We pushed the rental off the road, left our luggage in the trunk, and trudged back. When we got there Barbara pulled us into the house saying how relieved she was we'd "decided not to go." She feared we might have been a little too drunk. "Oh, you boys." We didn't argue as she steered us onto two beds. We fell down the stairs of sleep and when we woke we were as sick and as hungover as two men could be.

It took us hours to come around. Proal handled it better; while I continued to moan, he got on the phone, got us on another flight, and found out from the rental company that when "a car goes through a violent shock it has a cutoff trigger that prevents it from being restarted without a rental agent's assistance." We were lucky fuckups that night.

We retrieved the car, after the rental car guy hit the magic button hidden somewhere in the trunk, and drove on to San Francisco. Again.

On the last day of July, I received a piece of mail that changed everything. It was from a vice president of a major New York publishing house. As I read the letter I seemed to float away, up and out of my body. The office at Louie's appeared as a small tableau below me. A kite of emotion carried me over the house until I was above the trees and saw sparkling water below. I looked down on Pat and Phil, just two little dots and not the huge obstacles I worried they were. The possibilities of life were suddenly much vaster. The New York editor was asking me if I would like to write my first cookbook. She went on to explain that she had recently visited Key West on a short vacation. She stayed at the newly built hotel just across the way from Louie's and had dined with us on a Friday night. She had enjoyed it so much she returned on Saturday for her second meal. She asked if I had saved my recipes over the years. Needless to say, I had not one recipe. I wrote her back the next day and said, "Of course I have all my recipes. What do I do next?" She got back to me and the process began in earnest.

I was still working on sauté and expediting during service, so that left only after service to work on the book. To my amazement there was no tutorial on how I should accomplish this. But she was there for me every step of the way. Her name was Risa Kessler and finally one day she returned to Key West with a few of her colleagues from New York. I can remember walking over to the same hotel where she'd stayed on her previous visit six months earlier. I remember the couch she was sitting on. When I heard her voice talking to her friends I knew which one she was from our many phone conversations. What I hadn't known was what a knockout she was! Risa had style and sass. It was like meeting a rock star. She was excited about *everything.* She was living life on her terms—free and smart and independent. Key West was a funky charm in the bracelet of her cosmos now. And I was the link. I had wanted to find an art form many years ago. Then cooking came along and showed me what I could do. I hoped that writing would be something I could do, too.

On August 9, Charlie wrote me from the Ritz-Carlton in Laguna Niguel. He had dined at Spago for his wife's twenty-fourth birthday two nights earlier and raved about the simple perfection of the place, how well it fit the mood and mode of Southern California. He recited and described each dish the party of seven had ordered. The tone and maturity of his descriptions and the scope of his understanding of the restaurant scene in general were amazing.

In November Charlie sent me one of his trademark "letters" on the back of a chocolate bar wrapper. He told me he was working with his dad on the new restaurant, which Charlie had tentatively named Zeldah. He expressed frustration with delays in construction and permitting but still felt luckier than most. His current reading list included Jeremiah Tower's *Modern American Classics*, which he loved for its insouciance, mentioning phrases like "I developed this dish to cure a massive hangover" and "I discovered the joys of Sauternes and roast beef while sipping Chateau d'Yquem in Richard Olney's home."

Then came another large envelope from Charlie. Inside there were various newspaper and magazine clippings, but there was also a flyer from a place called Georgia Farms in Evanston, Illinois, where Charlie was living. The flyer advertised holiday recipes "presented by Charlie Trotter of the Zeldah Restaurant." There was a recipe for Roasted Quail Stuffed with Wisconsin Brie and another for a Port-Ginger Glaze with credit to Norman Van Aken. The citizens of Illinois would never have known it was one of my recipes, and I would never have seen it. But that was Charlie, always my champion.

He also included a menu with the hopeful opening date of February 5 the following year. (It was on the thinnest paper; it nearly falls apart today as I touch it.) He was hoping for an average tab of $35 a head.

It was in December when Charlie wrote me again, this time from Carefree, Arizona, about his recent dining excursion in New York. Once again

I was struck by his sophistication when it came to judging restaurants, not only in terms of the food but also reputation ("pedigree" would be the word actually), service, and appointments. (I use the word "pedigree" not in the snobbish sense, but rather in the sense of impeccable integrity, which I attribute to his down-to-earth midwestern upbringing by his prosperous but utterly unpretentious parents, Lee and Bob Trotter.)

He had gone to New York to gauge the abilities of Chicago versus New York, no less! It would not be fair to say which of New York's most vaunted restaurants Charlie ripped apart because his motives were neither venal nor personal. Individual evaluation was his process of understanding the size and scope of grande cuisine as it existed then. That being said, his two favorite experiences on that trip were Montrachet, where a young David Bouley was toiling over the stoves, and the Carnegie Deli. He felt neither of the two could be matched in Chicago. Conversely, when he wrote about his experience at Arizona 206 he claimed that the chef was an "intellectually undernourished Jeremiah Tower."

It was so touching to receive these letters and engage in these exchanges. I don't have mine and I know they were not as well written as his. What could I say as to my experiences? They were only of the mind.

Risa came back to Key West during the Christmas break to check on my progress with the book and to show some of her gal pals the little island town she was so smitten with. They came to Louie's for dinner and I came out to have dessert with them after their meal. Risa asked me, "If that was not, indeed, Rita Moreno sitting at the next table and Leonard Bernstein at another?"—she spoke in the most grammatically correct fashion, albeit with a Queens accent ("ever" became "evah"!)—and I said, "Yes." She corrected her espresso to her liking and mused, "I wonder why they are not sitting together." I went over to Ms. Moreno's table. She couldn't have been nicer and seemed genuinely happy to meet me. She loved food! She loved to cook! Emboldened, I asked her the question Risa had posed.

She said, "Oh. Is that him? I never met Lenny before." So I took her hand and introduced them. Risa was uncharacteristically speechless. Key West was like that.

In March of 1987 Charlie continued sending me letters from his apartment on Hinman Avenue in Evanston, addressed to "Monsieur" Van Aken.

But his adoration of all things French was not completely overboard—he opened one letter describing the joys of drinking an Anchor Steam Liberty Pale Ale: "big and full, the way a mixture of barley and hops is meant to be."

In mid-March, another letter arrived from Charlie written on the back of a Hachez Royal Delicate Bittersweet Chocolate bar wrapper. It was a Sunday and he was in the mode of reflection. Another week had now ended and his pursuit of building his dream was progressing. He was already quoting Chef Joël Robuchon, agreeing "that the grande cuisine is 60 percent about service and 40 percent about food," and "who am I to argue with the Master?"

He also was meeting with distributors and considering the length of his wine list. He allowed that he would start with "about 45 bottles: 50 percent American, 30 percent French and 20 percent Italian." He did not want to "go for the jugular from the start."

He had received the first pages of my cookbook *Feast of Sunlight* I had sent him, saying, "Very good these—no *Silver Palate* nonsense about the growing appreciation of fine food. Leave it to you to get right to the crux of the thing, talking about 'shock and seduction' in your intro! The only thing missing," he kidded, "may be some quotes like, 'Give me butter, butter and more butter!' But you can always add them in later, I suppose."

He'd been recently to Monterey, California, working alongside Brad Ogden. He said, "Brad has got to be the most down-to-earth, low-key guy out here. He is psyched to be coming to the opening of the restaurant and with you coming from Florida we will have two 'celeb' chefs."

By mid-May we were in the preopening phase of the Café at Louie's Backyard. Notes in my calendar provide the cadence of our days: waiters' meetings, chit rails installed, purveyors sending samples, and so on.

More and more I was beginning to think of myself as a restaurateur with Louie's and the Café as "my" restaurants. To that end they needed to be quite different so as not to cannibalize one another. Of course they were not mine, but I didn't let that fact stand in my way. I felt responsible to my guests and my sense of mission for the great cause of cuisine! I started my dream sheets with a new header: Dreams for The Café at Louie's. The menu upstairs would feature more Latin/Spanish flavors presented in a style more suited to "grazing" (generous appetizers and "small plates"), and it would be far less pricey than the menu downstairs at Louie's. We opened on June 3, and I was as proud as a new father.

The Café was only open for dinner but I would get in around 9 a.m. and begin the prep alone. My assistant chef was a quiet, no-nonsense woman named Susan Ferry who'd come from the Pier House. She had pale white skin, nearly ivory, and red hair. Her eyes were large and graceful with lashes that could fan a room. She was from Rhode Island and her vocabulary could be as rough as a truck driver's once you got her to speak at all. She was there because she wanted to learn. She was my favorite kind of chef for that very reason. I'd rewrite portions of the menu by noon and we would bend our prep accordingly to accomplish the new additions.

Around 4:30 p.m. I would jump on my bike and roar back home. Sometimes, if she wasn't at work, Janet would fix me a bite to eat, but mostly I needed to shower and get ready for "showtime" at six o'clock. I was working with more chilies than ever before and as I stood at the sink, my fingers would hum as the rushing water stimulated the chilies' capsaicin (the stuff that makes them hot). I'd put on my freshly ironed chef coat and work pants, and roar back to the corner of Vernon and Waddell for a second round in the kitchen, this time with an audience!

To me, it was like being in a Broadway play. Okay, maybe *off*, off-Broadway. Our audiences were but a trickle at first. We knew in our hearts that we had the guns, we had the dynamite, and we could blow up their bridges. But too often when they got up the stairs and realized this part of the restaurant did not overlook the water, they walked back down the stairs, despite the higher prices and more conservative menu. The view and the weather trumped my own inventive notions. I was, in essence, competing with my past. It would not be the last time.

In early June 1987, Richard Manley and Eric De Boer, who owned Key West's best historic restoration business, reached out to Proal with an idea. In appearance and demeanor they were about as alike as Hall and Oates. But their chemistry and various skill sets were a perfect complement to one another. They had purchased the former Q Rooms at the corner of Simonton and Fleming, the very same building where my friend Steve stayed when he first arrived in Key West in 1970 and, by connection, put Key West in my life's path. Steve and Wade were out of jail, and Steve met and became engaged to Janet's angelic sister Pam. If anyone could tame Steve it was Pamela. It was nice to have them in town, getting together with them again, like old times, really.

Manley and De Boer were about to totally restore the large wooden structure and make an elegant high-end guesthouse out of it. There was room in it for a small restaurant. They inquired if Proal and I would like to consider the possibility of doing one in the front corner of the building that would ultimately be named the Marquesa.

I continued to work on my cookbook in the midst of it all. I had no computer to work on. Almost no one did then. I handwrote all the recipes, sidebars, and introductions and I gave them to Louie's office manager, a woman named Donna. Proal had brought Donna over from Sloppy Joe's, where she had fit in with the tattooed, hard-drinking crowd quite well. Donna was as smart as they come and wasn't happy unless she was doing something new. Typing up *Feast* was a bitch of a job but she reveled in the challenge, and I think she took it as a culinary education class with no tuition. Like I say, smart.

On June 12, Janet and I celebrated our eleventh anniversary. I took that day to write the dedication in *Feast.* By the end of June I felt I was ready and sent the manuscript to Risa Kessler at Ballantine Books in New York. What a conflicting rush of feelings! I wasn't sure at all if it was good enough yet but I had to let go of it and see what would come next.

I wouldn't have long to wait as the photography schedule was already in place. We had three days to shoot eight pages of photos. On July 11, Risa returned, this time with a madcap crew the likes of which had not been seen in a Key West restaurant before. In addition to photographer Jeffrey Cardenas and stylist Katy Truax, a couple of Risa's colleagues came, I think, because Risa liked to hang out with them as much as for their editorial skills.

Risa was dazzling with brains, energy, and chutzpah. She dressed for New York at night and for the Hamptons in the daytime. She traveled with a complete stereo system and at least two dozen tapes of her favorite bands. She loved rock and roll and was never happier than when she was whipping somebody's ass in a contest of musical trivia.

We used the Café upstairs as our studio for most of the prep. Three days later we shot the desserts (a layout with six or so dishes), the Lobster

Tortellini in Broth, and the Shellfish Ceviche with Creole Vinaigrette. The next day we shot the Rack of Lamb and the Honey-Glazed Quail. And the following day was scheduled for the Roasted Swordfish with Lardoons and Red Wine Butter, as well as a shot of the Gulf of Mexico as seen from the fabulous vantage point of the Afterdeck, the place I first met Proal.

The plan was to create a food-laden dining table that appeared to float out over the ocean. The table would be jerry-rigged using some plywood and canvas affixed to the top railing of our terrace. Then my sous chef, Susan, and I would simultaneously prepare fifteen camera-ready dishes and get them downstairs and onto the "floating table." We'd have a fantastic cover—we hoped. We all bent to our tasks. Somehow it all came together and when the moment arrived, Jeffrey snapped the Nikon to his satisfaction. It wasn't a moment too soon. A summer rainstorm blew in from nowhere and soaked us all—the food, the wine, and the tablecloth overlooking the horizon. I couldn't have been happier. And Risa couldn't, either: she'd found me and she was taking "me" back to New York to kick a little ass.

In August we began to receive the various legal proposals for the restaurant at the Marquesa. The owners stipulated, among other things, "Twenty percent of the dining room will be reserved for hotel guests at all times." Crazy.

At the end of the month we flew to Chicago to attend the grand opening of the newly christened Charlie Trotter's. (Charlie and his father had rejected the name Zeldah and decided to go with something as straightforward as possible. After calling him Chuck for so many years, I didn't think of him as "Charlie" for quite some time.) He put us up at the Tremont Hotel. Bradley Ogden was his other guest chef and Gordon Sinclair was the third VIP. The dinner was a blur for me. The restaurant was modestly elegant, almost severe, and the kitchen hummed with raw energy. But I couldn't wait to get back home, back to my dream that was finally coming to life.

On September 8, Louie's closed for its annual cleanup and seasonal break. Mid-September is the slowest time of the year in Key West, and it made little sense to pay the staff to stand around. By good fortune it coincided with an event that Proal and I were invited to up in Charleston, South Carolina.

The event was hosted by the Society for Cuisine in America, which would eventually morph into other very successful foodie organizations. In its brief time the organizers created a phenomenon by bringing together the leading lights of the restaurant business for a first-of-its-kind symposium regarding the "white tablecloth" side of the restaurant business. There were all kinds of clinics and demonstrations, and Charleston was suddenly ground zero for the crème de la crème of the industry. People I had read about in magazines were queuing up in the same lines Proal and I were in, waiting for a taste of "low country cuisine" in the evening and at the registration tables for classes the next morning. It was incredibly exciting and validated what we were doing back in Key West.

When I returned home, I received a phone call from Risa. She was so excited. Her publisher had fallen in love with the *Feast* manuscript and they wanted to reshoot the cover. Instead of the floating table, they wanted *me* on the cover! Risa and the photographer would be returning in December for the reshoot.

Meanwhile Proal and I were in the midst of negotiating the lease for the Marquesa project. We'd gotten some of the language changed to be more favorable for us, but in the end they basically were supplying us with an empty "vanilla box." As the preeminent restaurateurs on the island we thought we should have had carte blanche. But Proal was too passive and I was much too naïve. Maybe our lawyer could have been tougher.

Another letter from Charlie arrived, this one written on the back of a menu from the previous night. The menu was divided into four groupings. The first were appetizers and listed Terrine of Wild Mushrooms with Roasted Garlic Vinaigrette; Sausages of Salmon, Shrimp, and Scallop with Crayfish/Tomato Butter; and Sweet Potato Ravioli with Quail, Herbs, and Wild Mushrooms. The most expensive item was the Ravioli at $7; next were three salads, including the Seasonal Greens which went for the princely sum of $3.50; the main courses featured four seafood items, two poultry and two meats. I would have chosen the Seared Tuna with Lemon and Caviar, for $16.50, or the Confit of Duck with Croustade of Sweetbread, Fig, and Apple for $15. Desserts included a study in Pear: Ice Cream, Sorbet, and Hot Tartlet at $5.50.

These were all full portions, no early-bird nonsense. Charlie was not unconscious of the cost of these goods. He felt that he and his father, who was his business partner and mentor, needed to mold not only the public but the Trotter team and if it lost some money in the beginning, that was the price of greatness.

His report was filled with the mixture of joy and exhaustion that comes with opening a restaurant with a three-star standard. He had the great pleasure of feeding two Chicago-based culinary giants: Jean Banchet of Le Français and Gabino Sotelino of Ambria. Banchet called Charlie a few days after the meal to tell him, again, what a fine time they had. Charlie quoted from one of his all-time favorite movies, *Apocalypse Now*, when Dennis Hopper's character says, "'I'm a little man. He's a big man. When he dies, then it dies.' Banchet is the master of this city, as far as I'm concerned, and despite what the critics say, the cuisine of Le Français is superior to that of others. Heavier perhaps but indeed more heavenly and far more delicate with all courses dealing with sea creatures."

He concluded with several postscripts. He had to fire a woman who used to work for me when Charlie worked at Louie's. "These things happen." And he hired two former employees of Sinclair's who worked front of the house with us back in 1984. He said, "This is a small world, this restaurant world, dangerously small."

My last day as chef of Louie's was November 14. There was no celebration. A rift had grown larger than I realized and I was too caught up in my goals and pursuits to recognize that it might have had to do with money. Louie's had turned into a very successful formula with me in the kitchen and now the owners faced an uncertain future. I couldn't be troubled. I had castles to build and windmills to tilt at.

For Thanksgiving we drove up to Sugarloaf Key, twenty miles north of Key West, to the new home of our old friends Rick and Nancy. Rick was another guy I went to high school with who had also ended up in Key West: Nancy was from Maine; we had worked with her at various restaurants and had come to like her a great deal. I brought the turkey. Everyone listened to music and got mellow. Now that there were children in the picture, those who smoked dope went up to the second-floor balcony. When the turkey was done everybody gathered around the table, expecting me to carve. I had a little surprise. I had cooked some tiny quails and packed them into the cavity of the larger bird so that when it came time to pull the "stuffing" out, I "delivered" a litter of five quails. My stoned and buzzed audience went wild.

On December 5, Wade came to visit me at the Café. He looked pretty good. He wanted to see what I was up to. We were a long way from Tom and Jerry's Fireside. He seemed wistful and said, "I should've stuck with this and done what you are doing, old pal." He wasn't sure where he was going to live or what he was going to do. When we were little boys growing up on Diamond Lake, it was Wade who always led the way. But the recent past had clouded his amazing mind.

A few days later Risa arrived for the new cover shoot. It was to be set up on the porch of Louie's Backyard. I was troubled by this decision because I wanted the book to showcase our new restaurant, MIRA. But Risa said, "Not to worry, it just conveys Key West."

Christmas was coming and we let the business fade into the background. No one was going to get much done in Key West during these times. We went to see Justin in a school play and took Proal's two beautiful children with us. Steve and Pam were lovebirds now and we went Christmas shopping on Duval and had dinner together at the Pier House, where Steve had proposed to sister Pam. Life was feeling more "grown up" and it felt good. Pam had worked miracles with Steve and he was so funny and great to be with now, a million miles away from his "Cuban Steve" phase, thank God. I had found the family life that I had missed out on as a kid.

With me no longer working at Louie's every day, I had New Year's Eve off. Proal's wife Susan invited me to be her date for a concert at Jimmy Buffett's new spot on Duval, Margaritaville. To my great joy Jimmy had Stevie Winwood as his musical guest for the end-of-the-year celebration. Janet and Proal had to work, so Susan and I dressed up in our Key West best and went to the packed bar. We had a table in the middle, which was fine, but at some point Susan went to the front to say hello to someone she knew and after a moment I saw her frantically waving me over.

She then introduced me to Jimmy Buffett's parents who said, "Why don't you two sit here?" There were two empty seats that a few cousins had abdicated. Susan and I hugged with gratitude and sat down right in front of Mr. Winwood. He looked fantastic and sounded in top form. We ordered more wine. The evening ended with Stevie joyously belting out a tune he sang with absolute conviction, a tune he first made famous when he was only seventeen and singing with the Spencer Davis Group. I remember singing, no, *screaming* it with my high school buddies on "top down" Saturday nights, proclaiming the ascendancy of our malehood. It wasn't a song. It was an anthem and that night in Margaritaville everyone joined in. It was a New Year's Eve hallelujah! And then as if that weren't enough, when the huge song ended Stevie Winwood stepped off the bandstand, strode into the crowd, and hugged Susan, and then me. Why? I don't know. Was it just pure joy—for the moment, the night, the chance at a new beginning?

Beer-Steamed Shrimp with Mojo Rojo

During the years I was looking for my culinary voice at Louie's Backyard, Janet was working at the other end of the island at the Half Shell Raw Bar off of Margaret Street at Land's End Village. The voices there belonged to Ron Hatfield and sweet Elayne Culpepper of the Big Coppitt Cowboy Band, who rocked that salty joint for special guests like children's author Shel Silverstein. The Half Shell served their shrimp steamed in beer or fried and served with cocktail or tartar sauce—which I loved then, and love still. For the patrons at Louie's, this was one of my riffs on those simple classics.

For the steamed shrimp:

- 1 tablespoon allspice berries
- ½ tablespoon black peppercorns
- ½ tablespoon mustard seed
- 1 teaspoon whole cloves
- 1 teaspoon fennel seeds
- 2 bay leaves, torn
- 4 (12-ounce) bottles of beer
- 1 lemon, cut into quarters
- 1 head garlic, cut in half, crosswise
- 36 large shrimp, still in the shells

Preheat a deep soup pot over medium-high heat. Add the allspice, peppercorns, mustard seed, cloves, fennel seeds, and bay leaves; toast about 30 to 60 seconds. Add the beer. Squeeze the lemon quarters over the pot, toss in the squeezed lemon quarters, and add the garlic halves. When the beer comes to a boil, add the shrimp.

When the liquid returns to a boil, the shrimp should be done. Using a colander, drain the shrimp. Place them in a bowl, cover in plastic wrap, and chill in the refrigerator.

Makes 6 to 8 servings

For the Mojo Rojo:

- 2 red bell peppers
- canola oil
- 6 cloves garlic, minced
- 1 teaspoon habañero chile, seeds and stems removed, minced
- 1 teaspoon cumin powder
- ¾ teaspoon kosher salt
- ¼ teaspoon freshly cracked black pepper, toasted
- 2 tablespoons sherry vinegar
- ½ cup pure olive oil
- ⅔ cup mayonnaise

Preheat the oven to 425 degrees F. Lightly rub the bell peppers with canola oil and place on a baking tray. Place the tray in the preheated oven for about 30 minutes, turning the peppers for even color, until well charred. When the peppers are done roasting, remove to a bowl and cover tightly with plastic wrap. Set aside to steam, about 2 minutes. When the peppers' skins are loose, remove and discard the skin, stems, and seeds, and blot any liquid from the peppers.

While the peppers are roasting, in a bowl combine the remaining ingredients, except for the olive oil and mayonnaise. Add to the roasted peppers and puree in a blender or food processor, adding the oil at the end. Pulse until the mixture is fairly smooth. Season with additional salt and pepper, if desired. Whisk in the mayonnaise. Cover and store in a cool place until needed.

Makes 2 cups

To serve:

Peel and devein the shrimp; place on a plate or in a bowl with a smaller dipping cup of Mojo Rojo for each guest. Serve with fresh lemon wedges and a bottle of Caribbean hot sauce, if you need more heat.

Wednesday, October 13, 1988

*****

Grilled Marinated Key West Shrimp with Chorizo Sausage and Tomato Chutney 8.50

A Mélange of Shiitakes and Golden Chanterelles on Wild Mushroom Toasts with a Vintage Port Infused Cream 10.00

Duck "Ham" with Chervil Pasta, Asparagus Spears and Cracked Black Pepper Brie Cream 8.00

*****

A Mesclun of Lettuces with Roasted Shallots, Diced Mango and Cabecou "Tartines" 7.00

Composed Artichoke à la Russe: Beet Vinaigrette, Sour Cream and Black Caviar 10.00

Pork Taquito Salad with Greens and Guacamole 8.50

*****

Grilled Yellowfin Tuna with Black Olive Purée and Beaujolais Caramelized Red Onions 24.00

Roast Rack of Lamb with Madeira, a Brunoise of Root Vegetables and Tiny Parsnip Pancakes 27.00

Ménage à Trois: Grilled Salmon, Tea and Lemon 24.00

Red Meat with Wine: Seared Rare Filet of Beef with Quail and Foie Gras Ravioli 26.00

"Fish House Fricassée", Lobster, Shrimp, Scallops and Clams Stewed with Vegetables and White Wine 25.00

Chili Spiked Veal Adobo with Pickled Corn Relish, Bean Dip, Tortillas and a Spanish Sherry Wine Vinegar Reduction 25.00

*****

Wines by the Glass

Early Harvest Gewurztraminer, Clos Du Bois, 86 5.00

Chardonnay, Neyers, 85 7.75

Beaujolais Villages, L. Jadot, 87 5.00

The MIRA menu changed daily, driving everyone to new levels—including me.

CHAPTER 18

MIRA

Key West, 1988

FROM THE OUTSIDE LOOKING IN, Proal was on top of the world. He was the co-owner and public face of Louie's Backyard. He was a one-third partner in Sloppy Joe's Saloon. Sloppy's hadn't yet become the national institution it is now but it was a thriving bar and did a considerable business in T-shirt sales. MIRA was to be my first fifty-fifty partnership in a restaurant. I didn't want to run the books. I only wanted to cook! I ceded the business side of our partnership to Proal. How could I not? I had no experience. He had Louie's and Sloppy's.

We were itching to do something new for Key West, and the Café at Louie's was not enough anymore. On our trip to San Francisco we had thoroughly enjoyed the retro charm of Cindy Pawlcyn's Fog City Diner. Diner ideas swirled in our heads. But Proal had spent a lot of his youth in Birmingham, Alabama, and had a long, abiding love affair with barbeque. So did Janet. Initially we had decided to buy, with Proal's money, a former hair salon called the Beauty Box on the corner of Simonton and Angela Streets. It had space for a parking lot, rare in Key West. We decided to call it the Conch City Diner and go super casual with two surefire winning menus—diner food *and* barbeque. It probably would have been a smash. Fate, as it will, intervened one day when we got the call about the old guesthouse that was undergoing a multi-million-dollar restoration. The owners wanted to know if we would be interested in opening a small, elegant restaurant on the property at the corner of Simonton and Fleming. When Proal and I looked at it, we knew in our hearts that we were more smitten with the notion of a French three-star bistro than a no-star American diner/barbeque. The Beauty Box became our office and wine storage and we struck a deal.

The Spanish word *mira* is what we named our restaurant. It means, literally, "look." More often you hear it in a chorus of threes: "*Mira! Mira! Mira!*" said very quickly by someone who is either excited or upset. But Proal, my Ivy League–educated, non-Spanish-speaking friend, came up with the name as a subtle way of imploring guests to "look," spoken very gently, very much like Proal.

I had never been a part of the building of a restaurant when the dirt was where you started. The former rooming house, called the Q Rooms, was being lovingly transformed by two of Key West's finest builders. Clearly this was a harbinger of changing times in Key West. And MIRA was part of that change. Key West was still a charming, even funky place when we watched the workmen lay the imported stone tile floors and paint trompe l'oeil murals on the walls, but change was coming. And we wanted to lead the way. We wanted to show the town—and the world—that French three-star dining had arrived! We were psyched. We were nearly off our rockers with the mission. I got to design the kitchen. It would be, like everything else about MIRA, done in miniature. The whole restaurant with kitchen was about two thousand square feet. We had thirty-eight seats inside and a dozen outside by the pool in the courtyard.

We raced to open and not miss any more of the season than we already had. January is the beginning of high season in Key West, and the month ended with our opening still a few days off. But we set the date for February 11. We decided to have a buffet instead of a seated dinner so more people could attend. We set up by the pool. It was a picture-perfect day and the folks came out in their Key West finery. I was tending Sichuan Barbequed Duck Breasts when a tall, athletic young man came up to me and held out his plate. He seemed more interested in telling me something than in getting some duck meat. I asked, "Hungry?" And he said, "Yes. I'm hungry to be a great chef like you. My name's Todd English. I'm from Boston but I could see doing a place down here like you are." And he cruised on down to Kelle who was slicing Tuna Tatakis.

We opened two days later. I worked sauté and placed my station at the end of the line by a door that let me go into the walk-in cooler through another side door. My worldview was Simonton Street and I could not have been a happier person for it. I hired the dependable Susan, my sous chef from the Café at Louie's. I also brought in Louie's pastry chef, Sue Porter, and Kelle for the prep work. Although the girls wanted to come with me, their departure drove a wedge into the hearts of Louie's other owners. They felt betrayed and they blamed me. This seemed ridiculous to me. I felt they never cared if we served haute cuisine or hot dogs. They had a new chef now who could build a team from the ground up just as I had done. I was blinded by my own needs and desires.

His name was John Henry. He was all by himself and he largely remained that way the entire time he worked with us, but you felt his presence and his power around you all the time. He walked to work and he walked home when all the work was done. I don't know where he stayed but I never wanted him to leave. He worked with a methodical energy that was as determined as any man or woman I ever saw. He washed our pots and dishes, scrubbed the floors and mats, and swept the walks. He broke down the food boxes and washed the windows out on the bright sidewalks in the morning before I'd pull up on my bike. He'd be in a heavy, plaid cotton shirt, a white T-shirt, and navy work pants hitched with a worn leather belt, a mist of sweat gathered on his strong forehead. He was a medium-dark black man with green eyes the color of a wild cat's. When he spoke his sentences were short with an accent that drifted from somewhere out of his Afro-Caribbean past. He seemed to look around you rather than directly at you. His body was trim and he always appeared well groomed, especially for a man who may have lived on the streets. But I didn't know and I knew I wouldn't ever know. The only time I got angry with him was once when my son came to visit me and John Henry had mistakenly left his gun on top of the toilet in the staff washroom—and Justin found it.

My cookbook was done and it was going around New York in galley form. On May 23, I received a letter from Risa. Within it contained a letter written to Risa by the legendary M. F. K. Fisher praising the book. I was blown away. The letter was typed (on a typewriter) with some small errors in spelling, which made it all the more perfect in its authenticity. She said, "This young man has a great future." She had signed her name in ink at the bottom. I called Charlie that night and he clinked a wineglass against the phone to me, to us, and to the Grande Cuisine!

Word was starting to get out already about MIRA, and a *New York Times* reporter came down and did a small piece on us. Chefs Mark Miller and John Sedlar were early guests. In July we did a three-day celebration in honor of Hemingway's birthday and some of Key West's literary lions, led by Jim Harrison, came to see what was going on in the little "salon" on the corner of Simonton and Fleming.

Summer in Key West was always brutal on the tourist industry, and despite our dreams for instant success we hit the summer doldrums just like everyone else. Hemingway Days in July were in the offing and we decided to try and promote and maybe bring more guests in.

I created a three-day menu that ran July 20–22. The first night was themed around Key West and Cuba. We offered Black Bean Soup with Oloroso Sherry, Pork Havana with Caramelized Plantains, Pan-Fried Snapper Pilar, and the Duval Café con Leche Cake. The next night we took Hemingway's Birthday to Spain and did a Zarzuela de Mariscos, Roasted Duck with Red Wine, Chorizo, and a Spanish Potato Tortilla. We finished the three-day fete in Paris with Petit Gris on Pain de Mie with Stone Ground Mustard and Wild Mushrooms, a Warm Confit of Duck in Cabbage Leaves with White Beans and a Garlic Vinaigrette, Tournedos of Venison with which we offered a Hermitage from Jaboulet: La Chapelle, 1985. For dessert we capped the three-day orgy with Maxim's Crêpes, Veuve Joyeuse.

On August 5, the first case of my books arrived at the Beauty Box office. Even though it was morning, Proal cracked open a bottle of Veuve Clicquot and Janet, our dining room manager Sheila, Proal, and I had a giddy toast to *Feast of Sunlight.* This was going to send the guests to our doors in waves! We would snatch victory from the jaws of defeat.

On August 28, we hosted a book-signing dinner at MIRA. I think we wanted to show our investors that we just needed more time (and more money) for our little MIRA to become a world-class restaurant full of discerning patrons. Becoming part of the "new" Key West, we were certain, was finally here.

But it wasn't happening anytime soon. MIRA was running out of money. I looked to Proal, but he had been dealt a huge blow by the IRS and felt too humiliated to tell anyone about it. The money he'd gotten from selling his piece of Sloppy Joe's was being eaten up by Uncle Sam. He didn't have the "mountain of money" anymore. We'd gone to our investors once already, but it looked like we'd need to tap them again or we would go under. This came just as I was preparing to do a national book tour that we both felt (hoped) would be the key to MIRA's promotion and our eventual success.

We decided to close MIRA while Janet and I went on the tour. Somehow Proal would try to find a way to reopen when we got back. On September 11, we met with our investors to ask for a capital call. The next day, with no positive answer, we left for Miami. What might have been one of the most positive and celebratory times of our lives became a hollowed-out reality. We had made such a big mistake. We never should have agreed to pay rent for at least two years. We didn't know that we could have done a deal with a hotel or guesthouse that would have been thrilled just to have us there to drive "heads onto beds," in the parlance of hoteliers. We were paying rent and some nights that summer we had more staff than guests.

One of Proal's old Key West friends, Turk, came to our rescue with the rent. The month of September is brutally slow, so it became an unpaid vacation for the staff, which they neither deserved nor could afford. It was also a chance for me to go out and sell my book knowing that back home the ground was giving way under us. I was a house divided in my own head. But I had to go on! I had to be strong, brave, and dance a little faster! I had no alternatives. You live on a rock the size of Key West you just can't go and get another job in the next town.

Book tours used to be financed by publishers, a perk available to only a handful of cookbook authors today. For an unknown chef like me it was as if I'd won the lotto. I had been almost nowhere but I read the magazines and newspapers and was cognizant of America's culinary leaders beyond the shores of Key West. Charlie sent me clippings, more reliable than any professional clipping service, on all of the developments in the restaurant industry coast to coast. Every month I'd find a heavy manila envelope lying on my desk or cutting board with Charlie's inimitable handwriting flowing over it. Quotes from Miles Davis or Bob Dylan or Johann von Goethe would be written in his small spidery scrawl on the back.

As I surveyed the list of cities scheduled for the *Feast* tour, I began my own list of places where we would, at long last, get to dine.

The two-week book tour started in Miami with a dinner at Mark's Place. It went well enough, but Janet and I were glad to be flying off to Detroit to put some distance between us and the problems back home.

The schedule was hectic but that was good, less time to think. We only had time for lunch in Detroit so we went to the Rattlesnake Club. Jimmy Schmitt was there and I met him after lunch. He was a small man in person with a boyish grin and unruly locks of hair, but he was a giant in my estimation. I gave him a copy of my book, which I planned to do in each restaurant we visited. As I handed it to him, it dawned on me that few other American chefs had authored a cookbook other than the legends like Alice Waters and Wolfgang Puck. Not even Charlie or Emeril. Could my book launch me into another league? New York was next!

Risa was there to meet us and was eager to show us her city. We lunched at Arizona 206 in Manhattan where Brendan Walsh was causing heart murmurs with his bold interpretations of southwestern cuisine. We dined in the diminutive pastoral whimsy of Anne Rosenzweig's Arcadia. It was no larger than MIRA, but people were waiting in line for her famous Lobster Club.

Our time in New York went swiftly, so we bid Risa adieu and caught the shuttle to Boston. We stayed at the Four Seasons right on the Common! We were living in fantasyland all of a sudden; it was like an extreme makeover for us island hippie kids. We felt so fortunate. It was beautiful in Boston and I surprised Janet by getting us a hansom cab, so we clip-clopped along the Common between the morning and afternoon radio shows. Full-page interviews were beginning to appear with my face in some of the country's biggest newspapers. The inevitable Hemingway allusions were there but so were descriptions of my food with comparisons to the paintings of Picasso and Gauguin. I really liked the Gauguin comparison. I liked how he had forsaken cities and moved to the wilds of Tahiti.

The evening of September 18, we made the fateful decision to eat at a place called Hamersley's Bistro. When we entered the small dining room it was early. After the hostess escorted us to our table, Janet pulled her chair in first and as I was getting to mine she said, "Norman! Watch out!" I turned my head to see that I had nearly knocked over a man of very advanced years. Janet's eyes were not staring at the menu (she is one of those people who agonizes over what to order the way a banker scrutinizes a loan application or a scholar pores over an ancient text). Actually, she was trying *not* to stare—at Julia Child. Julia Child was the old man's date! I had not seen his dinner partner as they were seated directly behind me. I had never seen her in person before and marveled at the stature of the woman. My menu decisions were made impossible now as my mind became numb. How to say hello to the great lady? But it was she who broke the ice!

"My! Don't you two young folks have the most marvelous suntans!" she chirped in her famously high voice. Compared to the fair-skinned Bostonians we did come across as pretty copper-toned. I tried to act as cool as I could and said, "We are on a book tour from our home in Key West, Ms. Child." She said, "Call me Julia. What kind of book is it, dear?" It was not like she'd recognize me. I realized that the cookbook I had intended to give to the chef of Hamersley's would be going to her instead. I pulled the copy of *Feast* I'd brought along and gave it to her. She beamed to the entire dining room that had been watching every moment of this and said, "*Feast of Sunlight*! What a lovely title. You must all go out and buy it tomorrow!"

"See! We're on our way now, baby!" Janet smiled and we were in love with Boston, with the whole crazy dream of this restaurant chef's life. We would work it out! Look where we were!

It was a short hop to New York again. The next evening we dined at a small and somewhat quiet restaurant called Rakel. It was a name conjured by conjoining the last names of the money and the chef. I don't remember the investor but the chef was beginning to make waves for his precise and intelligent cooking. His name was Thomas Keller. A movie screen dominated the dining room over the bar, which inexplicably had a video of the traffic of New York City crawling around it. I could not imagine a less fitting image to accompany the courtly French food offered on the menu. Lobster and Red Beet Sauce? I'd have to have that!

The next day was the finale of the East Coast portion of our tour. We had a lunch organized by Lisa Ekus, the phenomenally capable and sweet-hearted cookbook publicity guru who normally took on clients like Paula Wolfort and others of that caliber. Lisa had come to Key West just before the tour and mentored me in the tiny kitchen at MIRA on how to speak to the press. I don't think I got an "A" but she gave it her all. The luncheon was held at the Gotham Bar and Grill and Susan Wyler of *Food and Wine* magazine was there to interview me. The food was grand, and it was true that the chef Alfred Portale was a genius for creating dramatic height to dishes that would have toppled over in the hands of most any other chef, not only in terms of construction but also complexity.

Next we took the red-eye to San Francisco. The miracle of great hotels continued with our lodging at Campton Place. This is where one of the new gods of New American Cuisine, Bradley Ogden, was making big headlines. Charlie had worked for Brad briefly and spoke highly of his commitment to only the finest of American products. We had heard all about his extraordinary breakfasts. But our duties had us up and out the door before first light. We'd stayed at the Campton for a total of five hours, none of which were during a meal service. Brad's food would not be ours.

After a morning television show we did a signing at a bookstore, where I saw my book sitting right next to Jeremiah Tower's book! Amazing! Lunch was at Zuni Café, where I will never forget how delicious the Gnocchi with Brown Butter Vinaigrette tasted, so simple, so divine! I had read how the chef/owner Judy Rodgers had lived with the Troisgros family while she was a high school exchange student (talk about fortunate!) and how it had changed her life.

We went on to Los Angeles where we dined under the spell of "Captain Crunch," also known as Michel Richard. Then it was north to Seattle and a meal at Café Sport with Tom Douglas.

My introduction to these cutting-edge restaurants could never have been afforded in any way other than through the generous coffers of our publisher. We finished our tour in Chicago where I made the biggest impression of all on my family by being on Windy City radio giant Roy Leonard's show. That interview dazzled them more than any *New York Times* piece. They had listened to Roy every morning for twenty years and now here was their son/son-in-law on the freaking *air* with Roy himself. I nearly lost my composure entirely when a call-in listener asked me a leading question, because I knew, but could not say, that the caller was my little sister Bet setting me up.

She said, "Oh, Mr. Leonard [all sweet and innocent], would you ask this great chef where he likes to eat that is not fancy when he comes back home."

The golden-voiced man said, "Great question, Norm." Norm. When I was called "Norm" I knew I was officially back in the Midwest.

I smiled knowing the answer she expected: "Bill's Pub and Pizza in little Diamond Lake, where I was born."

The tour was over and the next day we drove out to Diamond Lake before returning home to Key West. The owner of the pizza place had been told about the show and put my name up on his sign outside on the highway near our home. "Bill's welcomes Norman Van Aken." Wow. Now that was huge to Janet and me.

Proal had managed to get us more investor money. I don't know how he did it but we were able to keep the staff together and reopen on October 1. Proal and I were on very diminished salaries for ourselves.

Each morning I'd leave our home and go to La Farola grocery store near the cemetery. The old Cuban men still played dominoes in the back just as they did the first time I came to Key West and crashed with Steve on Windsor Lane. I would get a large *café con leche* and a Cuban toast and bike down to the Beauty Box where I'd begin to craft my menu for that night. I was still writing my dream sheets, listing names or partial names for dishes that entered my head as I read, showered, drove, shopped, slept, read more, lay next to Janet after making love, or when I was hungry. They were not yet organized into categories but were a free-flowing text of appetizers, desserts, main courses, fish, meat, game, shapes of plates, styles of silverware, kitchen tools I'd like someone to invent. I jotted down words that were not in any dictionary, words I'd conjure to best describe what I wanted to make at MIRA. I sat at my small desk with a few cookbooks and a list of the foodstuffs that either we had on hand or were coming in from purveyors. I'd begin with an 11-by-17 piece of paper and draw a long vertical squiggly line down the left side of the page and a horizontal one about an inch from the top. I'd add the day's date and an inspirational quote that seemed to fit the weather, the events of the day, and the feelings in my heart. As the rich coffee filled my mouth and brain I would weave together three or four first courses, three salads, and six to seven main plates, trying to divide the work evenly among our small crew.

It was the beginning of New World Cuisine and though at times I was still riding with training wheels, I was learning to let go in this free-form university I'd built for myself, a university without walls, without a curriculum, without tuition (a university I could afford), and a university that I loved.

Spanish Queso Soup with Spicy Sour Cream would appear with other choices, like Hot Fried Rabbit Salad with Chipotle-Honey-Mustard Dressing, Torn Greens, and Pickled Vidalia Onions; the Pan-Cooked Fillet of Key West Yellowtail with Citrus Butter also appeared at this time and hasn't left a kitchen I've cooked in since; Gulf Swordfish could still be found, and we served it grilled with Creole Tomato Butter and Black Bean Salsa.

Because the line was in a shoebox shape, as I finished plating a dish (we used beautiful, oversized Villeroy and Boch bone china) at the far end, it would be carried to the window by the cook next to me, just as her plate would be taken to the window upon completion, and so on. Each of us was careful to keep the plates from tipping or toppling the tall, carefully composed hillocks of greens from their regal heights.

When you start your very own restaurant, and you are the chef and co-owner, you have entered a very dangerous world. You become a zealot, a fanatic, an addict. Every other aspect of your life is secondary, at best. You become a ghost to your wife, husband, children, parents, and friends outside the restaurant world. Each moment is about YOUR MENU.

The menu is *who you are.* It is who you are precisely at that moment, that day. Each night is the final attempt to reach some place you have sought in your mind for years. You live and die on the execution of your vision of that menu. You might blow the minds of your cooks, servers, and managers by changing the menu at the latest possible hour (if not later) if you sense something could be better.

Proal became even more consumed in creating a world-class wine list. We pushed and challenged each other. He read as many wine books as I was reading cookbooks: He bought a book on wine. I bought a book on food. He was reading Richard Olney, Jancis Robinson, Alexis Lichine, Anthony

Dias Blue, and a young guy named Robert Parker. I was rolling through Paul Prudhomme, Colman Andrews, Roger Vergé, Marcella Hazan, Ken Hom, and Fredy Girardet. We were hooked. We were on fire with the passion for excellence. Our small wine storage area was soon burgeoning with deep garnet rows of bottles from whichever wine region Proal was mentally and physically in love with at the time. His thirst seemed limitless, a thirst he encouraged in his waiters. They'd never seen such devotion to the grape as Proal Perry was bringing them.

Pre-service at MIRA was a rigorous discourse on food and wine history, the provenance of ingredients, the best pairings of food and wine, the latest of each we'd acquired, who made it, grew it, harvested it, and how it would appear on the plates and in the glasses that very evening! We lived the philosophy "carpe diem!"

One of my most cherished books of all time is A. J. McClane's *Encyclopedia of Fish Cookery.* Everything that has ever wriggled in lake or sea seems to be in this book. From the time of Pliny the Elder, it's all there, and Mr. McClane wrote about it as well as anyone ever has. Better, actually. When he walked into MIRA one night with a party of seven, I was beside myself. After they'd had their main courses and were enjoying dessert, I dashed the few blocks to the office to get my copy of that blue-bound bible. I asked Proal to carry it out to the man I held in such high esteem and ask if he would not mind autographing it. (In those days I never left the kitchen. I always worked the line, so by the end of service I was bathed in sweat, grease, blood, and butter.) Mr. McClane came back to the kitchen and presented me with the signed book. He insisted I come out to the table to meet his guests. I could not refuse him, so I changed into a clean apron and joined them. Proal poured some rare Madeira and that night one of my most valued friendships was born.

I found a book at the Old Island Bookstore on the philosophy of food. It was called *Culture and Cuisine: A Journey through the History of Food* and was written by a Frenchman named Jean-François Revel. It was deep shit for me but I plowed through it, underlining pages and making margin notes. It was helping me to see food in a context I had not known about thus far in my life. As I read and reread Revel's dense ideas—he also wrote about history and literature, politics and religion, with titles like *Without Marx or Jesus*—I began to understand a pattern that had evolved throughout history. From the time of Taillevent, in the 1300s, all the way through to the Nouvelle Cuisine movement of the 1970s, cooking had engaged in a kind of tango between simplicity and complexity.

Revel wrote: "But the difficulty lies in appreciating the difference between silent cuisine and cuisine that talks too much, between the cuisine that exists on the plate and the one that exists only in gastronomical chronicles. Or else, to state the matter in a different way, the difficulty lies in discovering, behind the verbal façade of fancy cuisines, made up of tricks and little secrets that only evolve very slowly, in silence, and that no individual in particular has invented." He also wrote in his introduction, "The gastronomical serial written by the centuries has as its 'plot' the constant battle between the good amateur cook and the thinking chef, a lover's quarrel that, as in all good adventure novels, ends, after many a stormy scene, with a marriage." In the margin I wrote the words, "A Fusion!"

The phone rang at the waiter's station. Baker Sue answered it and said, "Hey, Norman, a man named Michael Batterberry says he's from *New York,* some magazine, and he wants to talk you." Michael Batterberry! Calling me? The same man who, along with his wife Ariane, created *Food and Wine* magazine and were at the time launching a new magazine called *Food Arts.* I took the phone and sat on the floor.

I said, "Hello."

He said, "Hello, Norman?" in his mellifluous baritone that was as distinctive as Julia's famously high register.

"Yes, this is."

"Michael Batterberry here. Tell me more about this style of cooking I keep hearing about. Is it Spanish?"

In late October we flew to San Francisco again. I'd won a cooking contest in Miami and as the winner I was asked to cook one course in a restaurant out there. The Boston winner was Jody Adams and she prepared a rustic, perfectly braised shoulder of lamb. *Feast of Sunlight* was in bookstores across America and I did a book signing before returning to Key West.

I wanted to earn my consulting salary so I organized some "classes" in the upstairs dining room at the Café at Louie's. But it was clear that neither the staff nor the owners wanted me. The looks on their faces, well, they were not the faces of eager learners. These were hardworking people who would rather not have come in an hour early to learn about the etymology of the word "salad."

The one person who would have enjoyed my talks who still worked there was Leif. But, tragically, he had contracted the AIDS virus and died too young.

The season finally arrived in a small spurt with Fantasy Fest at the end of October. It still wasn't the mega-affair it would become in the 1990s, but it was welcome just in time.

In November Gordon came down to visit. After catching up with his old friend David Wolkowsky at a party on David's private island, Gordon moved into the Marquesa for a two-night stay, dining at MIRA both evenings. He was impressed but, typically, worried about the "high tone" of the place in a town like Key West. He doted on me still and offered his opinions on service and public relations. He always loved my food and was supportive even though he worried about the price of it all.

The New Year rolled in and Key West was full of tourists. Our little restaurant filled quickly and provided the illusion that hard times were behind us. But we didn't do the math, and I didn't know how. With only forty seats you can feed seventy guests and think you are minting money. But I was still flying in products from places like Maine and Minnesota to Miami and then, of course, they had to be trucked to Key West. We gave away the bottled mineral water because we thought that's the way they did it in the three stars of France. We had a three-month ball.

When March ended, the ball ended. Our office, the old Beauty Box, had to be sold to meet our mounting debts. It was auctioned on the courthouse steps. The same day I was invited to Hawaii to cook at the Cuisines of the Sun, a culinary showcase at the fabulous Mauna Lani Resort on the Big Island, with chefs Robert Del Grande, Bradley Ogden, and Alan Wong.

The national press knew nothing of our dire straits and continued to call. Baker Sue took the calls from Barbara Fairchild of *Bon Appetit* and Linda Wells of the *New York Times*, and my dear friend Al McClane did a big write up in *Esquire*.

But it was over—on May 28, MIRA had her final night of service. I placed a quote from *The Tempest* on the last menu: "Our revels now are ended."

In June we were invited to the Napa Valley to cook for the Joseph Phelps Winery annual party. Despite MIRA's closing we felt we had to keep hope alive by finding a way to work together in a new venture. For this weekend Proal, Connie, and Janet would be my sous chefs. Connie, we'd come to discover, was great fun and a perfect partner for Proal. She had the best laugh and a never-say-die outlook. Once again we turned our "*no problemo*" faces to the world. We wanted to look like everything was just dandy back at the ranch. Sometimes, if we had the right wine, and enough of it, we fooled ourselves into actually believing it. We certainly had the right wine and volume over that weekend.

We arrived on June 6 and ate at Tra Vigne that night. Michael Chiarello, who'd been the chef we cooked for at our first James Beard Dinner back in Miami, had moved to Napa and presided over a fine meal marked by his simple yet pure passion for a California-meets-modern-Italian sensibility. The next night we dined at the Sonoma Mission Inn with another former Floridian chef, Charles Saunders. The wine country would be a nice place to decamp to, we reasoned.

We had our own dinner to prepare and the next day began early in the garden picking herbs for the meal we would work all day to create. The menu included Antojitos of Black Beans and Chorizo in Grilled Tortillas with Salsa Verde, Sour Cream, and Manchego, Grilled Marinated Shrimp with a Mango Puree and Hot Pepper Paint, Veal Loin Havana with Fire-Roasted Rajas, Pickled Sweet Corn, and a Spanish Sherry Wine Reduction. We finished the meal with Bittersweet Chocolate Brownies, Pineapple, Cuban Bananas, and Coconut Caramel.

The weekend ended on another high note; we were dinner guests at a party at the home of Carl Doumani, proprietor of the famous Stag's Leap Winery. One of the other guests that evening was Jeremiah Tower. He returned my gaze, but I got the sense it was for reasons other than my starstruck gawking.

When we got home and back to our office in Key West, the IRS was waiting for us. At first they were affable, but that lasted about a minute. I retreated to the kitchen. Poor Proal took the heat head-on. The folks back at Louie's were clucking their tongues at the two of us. We had nowhere else to turn. Not in the little town of Key West, for sure. Where would we go? What would we do?

The calendar dictated some specifics that included me doing another dinner at Charlie's in Chicago. (He consoled me and predicted I'd be back in action in no time.) I also attended my high school's twentieth reunion. I was honored as "the most famous grad." "Fame has its price" was all I could think of.

On September 9, Janet and I flew out to Santa Fe, where I was asked to be a guest speaker at a symposium being held by the Society for Cuisine in America.

Santa Fe was beautiful that weekend, and it was jamming with the top names in food, wine, and restaurants. It was the first time I met Emeril. Charlie had predicted that once we met we'd "become lifetime brothers." Charlie was there, too. In fact the panel I was on included Charlie, Emeril, Tom Douglas, and Lydia Shire. Other chefs at the event included Alice Waters, Mark Miller, Dean Fearing, and Robert Del Grande. The night before our panel we met in the lobby of the hotel. Emeril was holding a large cocktail. He pulled up close to me and after only the first moments of meeting him he confessed. "I'm scared. You got a speech ready, Norm? I'm nervous about standing up in front of a crowd of strangers. You doing okay?"

I told him I thought he'd be fine. I thought about making the speech myself and wondered how I'd do.

I had been working on an essay as a spontaneous response to having read *Culture and Cuisine* back at the Beauty Box. It turned into my speech. I titled it "Fusion."

The next morning we all gathered in the large hall. I had made sure I had copies of my piece on "Fusion" for each chair. It was to be my manifesto.

On that morning I joined my colleagues with a sense of mission that was still undeterred. I was proud that Janet and I were included in this group. She sat in the second row so I could keep my nerve up as I read from the lectern. I was shaking a bit, but then I felt her amazing smile and my fears melted.

MIRA Tuna Tartare

Various tuna tartare preparations have taken over the world, but back in 1988 it was still pretty fresh territory to many diners in Key West. It was a huge success for us then and continues to be very popular to this day. We called the restaurant MIRA, which means "look" in Spanish, because we wanted our guests to enjoy not only what they could smell and taste, but also to look at each dish and enjoy what they saw. It was while working at MIRA that I wrote the treatise called "Fusion." This dish was an edible example of the very notion.

½ pound sushi-quality tuna, diced small
2 tablespoons finely diced onion
½ scallion, white part mainly, finely chopped
1 jalapeño pepper, seeds and stems removed, finely minced
1 teaspoon finely minced fresh ginger
1 teaspoon finely minced lemongrass, inner stalks
½ teaspoon sesame oil
1½ teaspoons soy sauce
1 teaspoon mirin
¼ teaspoon rice wine vinegar
¼ teaspoon fish sauce (optional)
1 teaspoon minced orange zest
1 teaspoon lemon zest
kosher salt and freshly cracked black pepper, to taste
Salsa Sriracha, to taste

In a bowl, combine all the ingredients and chill, tightly covered, until you are ready to serve. There are many ways to present a tartare—I like to serve mine using Asian-style spoons or with sesame seed crackers.

Makes 1 fluid cup

CHAPTER 19

Boca, Boca, Boca!

Boca Raton, 1989–90

AFTER MIRA, after the whirlwind national book tour that was about as hollow a victory dance as anyone could ever dance, I returned to Louie's Backyard. I was not wanted. In fact, I was abhorred. The staff had gotten used to the more laid-back, Key West cadence of the chef I'd hired to cook lunch a year and a lifetime earlier. I did what I could to matter to Louie's. Proal was still an owner but after the demise of MIRA he, too, was at a loss and out of the management loop. We were both just emptied out after the death of our little dream of MIRA.

One day I had to fly up to Miami for a meeting. I was standing in the airport waiting for my luggage when a man walked up to me excitedly holding a copy of *Feast of Sunlight*. His name was Bobby, he told me, and he was opening up a world-class restaurant in Boca and "holy shit" if he hadn't been thinking of giving me a call about joining forces with him. He was manic with a Ronald-McDonald-meets-Harpo-Marx-like face. His red hair bobbed as he went on about how "huge" it would be if we joined forces. I hadn't had anyone feeding my sense of ego in such a long time that I closed my eyes and stepped up onto his bandwagon almost immediately. The cops coming on the orders of the IRS, the still-to-be-paid bills to the purveyors, the mocking faces of those who chided us for trying to "fancy up" Key West—all could be gone as quickly as a car could take us up to the sawgrass fantasyland of Boca Raton, Florida.

He offered me a salary that was more than I made at Louie's to start, along with a "piece of the action." He envisioned that we could do $6 million in our first year alone, double what Louie's ever did. It would be a "fantastic kitchen, fantastic dining room, fantastic location," Bobby crooned, "with your fantastic food!"

"Have you ever eaten my food?" I asked Bobby.

"No, no, no. But I can tell, just by reading your book."

I should have known right then to run. But I had no place to go but out of my once safe haven of Key West.

Janet and I drove the six hours to Boca to check out real estate the following week. "Maybe we should join up with this guy and see what happens," we wondered. It was painfully evident that Key West was showing us the door. Bobby offered a solid salary. No more ownership and that meant no IRS worries, if we ever got out of this mess, of course! Bobby asked if we knew of a manager we'd feel comfortable working with on the new venture. We told him about Proal and he said to "have Pearl call." Things could be turning a corner.

In early October I received the first version of the contract to be chef and partner in the new Hoexter's Market. It arrived via fax in the law office of our attorney, Jimmy Hendrick. It was eleven pages in length, which alone set my nerves on edge. Then Jimmy smiled his elfin smile and added, "And they will own your recipes if you ever leave." That was impossible. I, alone, owned what was in my mind! I could not allow that. When Jimmy told Bobby's lawyer that was a deal breaker, Bobby quickly conceded. I realized that this was just another game, another ploy, a chip to be bargained with and that no relationship with anyone except my friend Proal would be based on trust and mutual vision. Bobby wanted to have a piece of me, the piece that was my very core. This time the changes were made and the deal got done. Janet worked her last day as a bartender at the Half Shell Raw Bar on November 9, and we moved to Boca with Mama and Justin six days later.

It was a busy time and I was able to shut out the defeat we'd suffered by throwing myself into the task of getting Hoexter's ready to open. We moved at light speed and I was able to hire some of my most prized teammates to join me. Ed Hale, who'd been with me since Sinclair's in Lake Forest, came, as did Bill Prahl from the Café at Louie's. Even Kelle, my prep angel, came to the shining cement of Boca Raton. By now Kelle had found religion and decided to stop sleeping with girls.

I went into a phase that every chef will recognize and remember: It is the preopening phase of the biggest restaurant of your life. Even a small restaurant can qualify for "the biggest restaurant of your life" because it's based on 99-percent emotion and headspace. Every waking hour of every day and night (and every sleeping hour, too) is all restaurant, restaurant, restaurant. It's the march of the toy soldiers, it's Super Bowl Sunday, it's "Into the valley of death rode the 600," it's *Iron Chef*; but for weeks on end with no end in sight except the ending you dread the most—opening night!

Our date with destiny was leaking away from us: the endless permits needed, countless work stoppages, scary cash crunches; but worst of all was the chronic waffling by the owner of this two-story, $8 million kitsch barn of a restaurant in the far corner of a huge, pretentious shopping mall that had mushroomed out of vacant land not ten years earlier. To design this real estate phenomenon, Bobby had hired the architectural firm Shuster and Associates whose main operative, Louis Shuster, was a constant presence on the site. His (thankless) job was trying to deal with Bobby's wild vacillations, constant kibitzing, and outlandish demands. One minute, Bobby asked that the interior look "more Frank Lloyd Wright" and the next he suggested "maybe more Michael Graves." It was Louis who had the moxie to develop a fully visible "theater kitchen" on the mall side of our space. While many restaurants were showcasing their kitchens to their diners, ours was unusual in that it was also exposed to passersby in the mall. At Hoexter's we would be "performing" not only for our guests but also for the public at large. It was a masterstroke of one-upmanship that had other operators in the mall kicking themselves (and their architects) for being less bold.

For my family the home situation was actually pretty good. Janet and my mom were already longtime buddies, and they set about doing things women are so much better at than men. They set up camp. They made a nest for us. They got Justin squared away for school. He found a friend named Tommy who was from Israel and who lived right next door. The joys of suburban living were new to me, but I welcomed them: waking up to the pleasantly unfamiliar hiss of the automatic sprinkler and coming home to a pool in the backyard were a far cry from waking up in Key West to roosters screeching or coming home to a falling-down drunk kicking over the metal garbage cans. And even though Boca was a relatively short distance from Key West, it was cool enough "up north" to warrant a trip to the mall that Key West would never have and buy a sweater that, in Key West, would never be worn. I guess I was settling in.

I was preparing to become more of an employee, because after what we'd been through, I wanted a reliable paycheck. (We still faced the never-ending pursuit of the IRS.) This was not MIRA and it was not Louie's Backyard. At those places I *was* the menu. I *was* the food. This was a concept restaurant with an owner who had a very strong desire to create a great steak house, but with ties to the Florida "style." He sensed I could help deliver that double whammy. By this time my mind was looking forward to creating different venues. I saw the possibility that in a place like Boca we could do a variety of restaurants (perhaps a bakery?) and fulfill the many different aesthetics in cuisine I admired and wanted to riff on someday. But first things first and that was to open up and get rolling on this huge place called Hoexter's Market.

I woke up, went to work, and I didn't leave until midnight every day for months. I loved it in a weird way. At least I was busy. At least there was a paycheck. At least no cops were coming for me (yet) with papers from the IRS. My mother ironed my chef coats and laundered my chef pants and aprons. My wife made sure there were coffee and bagels and cream cheese waiting for me in the morning. Each morning I would eat, shower, shave, suit up, and motor over to the restaurant feeling pumped, ready, and eager to do it!

Bobby wanted Hoexter's to be "classic New York all the way, but like a hip New York supper club, too." He installed a mezzanine section on the upper deck with tables that surrounded a professional bandstand. He'd bring "top flight" entertainment down from New York. He showed off his state-of-the-art stereo system for anyone and everyone. *The Phantom of the Opera* would boom from scores of speakers at decibels beyond belief at all hours of the day and night. (The appropriateness of this choice of music was lost on me at the time.) Bobby was in love with everything, but mostly with his calculator than almost anything else. For him it was all math and magic with the numbers.

He was incredible. He ran scenarios on customer counts and check averages and estimated how many guests we needed to feed "in season" to reach his number. He decided $6 million was the "break-even" number and we'd have to make 90 percent of that from January through March in order to "cut the nut." The rest would come in by July and then he'd make his profit during the summer. He was relying on me as "the Florida master chef" to make the difference. (He'd show a copy of my cookbook to potential investors for validation.) Bobby had gotten a good deal from the developer on the build-out and the rent structure, but he was still rolling some major dice. And yet, maybe that is what he loved the most—the risk. He was giddy and funny and happy most of the time. He was a backslapper and glad-hander. One afternoon in his office over sandwiches, he read aloud to us from the year-end issue of *Food Arts* magazine and crowed about what the editors of the number one "white tablecloth operator's magazine" had written about me. Here was proof that we were on the path to undeniable victory. I was new to this. I never had worked in New York. Maybe this was how it was done in the big city. Maybe it *was* chaos and gambling and the Andrew Lloyd Webber "Music of the Night" at ninety decibels if you wanted to "score."

"New Yorkers will be flocking into our place. They will remember me from Vanessa's (his old place) and kill to get in here!" Bobby said.

Bobby would be so beside himself that he'd wrap one of his rubbery arms around his body and hug himself as he used the other to bring a cigarette to his lips and drain a third of the pernicious weed into his lungs. He really did love the restaurant and nightclub demimonde. He didn't care about fine dining. He was over the notion of a sophisticated, subdued ambience. He really wanted to recreate a "meat market" like Maxwell Plum's in its prime. He wanted action, babes, drinks, big—no, *monster*—steaks and leviathan lobsters too big to fit in our live tank bubbling away next to the prime rib cooker. He was a freak for the right ingredients and when I met his mother and father I learned why.

His parents had come to Boca before him and taken over a small deli in the mall. They were a sweet old couple who had come up from nothing on the Lower East Side of New York. Lou Shapiro went into the grocery business and did all right. When his golden years approached he left the harsh winters behind and moved with his wife to the growing 'burb of Boca. I had very little experience with "real" deli food, and the elder Shapiros took me in like a lost soul in need of enlightenment and education especially around Jewish food traditions. (They couldn't understand it. How could "a chef no less," never have eaten a brisket sandwich with a Dr. Brown's?) I was a quick study and much happier for it (although I never acquired a taste for matzo ball soup).

After a visit with his parents, Bobby, like so many New Yorkers before him, became hopelessly smitten with the Sunshine State. And, like too many New Yorkers before him, he felt smug about his success in New York and assumed that achieving success in Florida would be like taking candy from a baby. The swelling refrain of "New York, New York" would be one of the few songs that replaced Andrew Lloyd Webber on the CD player that January of 1990.

Set aside the fact that many New Yorkers view themselves as experts on food; it was growing up in the family grocery business that made Bobby (in his mind) a bona fide expert. But, as the saying goes: "A little knowledge is a dangerous thing." I will admit that he had more than a little knowledge but he didn't have discipline, and that was his Achilles heel. We had a decent sized walk-in cooler, but I would come into work and open the door and cases of meat would be stacked to the ceiling, blocking off every other food item in there. This happened whenever Bobby read something or talked to someone about a new cut of meat, a new butcher, or heard about a new country that was exporting the most "killer, show-stopping, balls-to-the-fucking-walls meat known anywhere on earth, I kid you not, you don't know, listen to me, this will make you cream on your topsiders, pal, meat."

The "Dean of New York City butchers," Leon Lobel, was by chance visiting our kitchen one day after Bobby had bought and brought in a full pallet of New Zealand lamb. We'd sampled it the night before and, holding the invoice in one hand and the calculator in the other, Bobby waved his arms in a touchdown motion and pronounced it an "absolute home run." That was Bobby. He wanted it both ways—all the time. He'd look at us to see if we didn't agree, shooting his chocolate-brown eyes at each of us, beseeching us for our approval, counting on the staff to give it. Then he'd pour himself a fat snifter of "Louis Trey" (Louis the XIII), a cognac so expensive it came in its own custom jewel box. But the Manhattan meat guru was in our kitchen the very next day. He said "the New Zealand stuff is, well"—long pause and a hunt around the room for eavesdroppers—"okaaaaaay." He really sawed off and flattened those "a's." And with his thin, sharp, axe-like shoulders, he shrugged that meat inside the shield of a luxurious cashmere sweater. "But there's some stuff we can get, can't tell you where"—his voice rising—"but"—and like the final blow of a cleaver coming through the last joint bone—"it's sooooo much better!" *Thwack.* I could almost see a head dropping into a basket somewhere.

Bobby's face fell in abject pain. Where, he wondered, could he bury this now inferior meat we all had enjoyed so much last night? Where? His face fell upon me. "Come on, Norman. You can make some stuff with this the crowds coming in here will love!"

I said, "Well, maybe, Bobby. But we are going to have to jam it in the freezer 'cause we aren't even open yet." Two days later a shitload of Lobel-stickered meat boxes were piled in a tower in my walk-in. The money was going out in truckloads that must have been nearly as large as the trucks dropping off the new meat.

We opened in January, just after the month or two we should have opened in order to better get ready for the onslaught of winter tourists and second-home Bocans. These part-time locals had plenty of money for a meal and an urgent need to be the first on their block to give a review to every new restaurant in the neighborhood.

Kelle was teaching four Haitian refugees how to prep our food, just as I had taught her in Key West. They were dressed as if for church, a scene made even more surreal by Kelle's leather-bound Bible sitting on her knife bag as she showed them how to arrange perfect rows of vegetables. Their dark faces peered at the young blonde woman in awe and she in turn treated them with the respect of spiritual fellowship.

I was also able to bring back another former coworker, a woman named Lisabet Summa. She had worked at Sinclair's and Sinclair's American Grill, but when I moved to Key West she stayed up in Palm Beach County. She had since become a very gifted pastry chef, who quickly managed to turn Bobby into a believer.

We had the core team assembled, but I still needed a load of line cooks to knock down the numbers Bobby dreamed of. Right next door to

Hoexter's was a restaurant owned and run by one of the most successful restaurateurs of the time in South Florida, Dennis Max. Dennis came out of the most banal restaurant beginnings, but he was in the right place at the right time with one of the shrewdest partners any man ever married—his wife, Patti. Together they had partnered up with a young chef named Mark Militello and wowed the Miami scene of the mid-1980s with a Californian-style restaurant in north Miami. They, too, saw opportunity in Boca Raton and opened up a smallish but always packed Italian/Mediterranean restaurant named Maxaluna. Nothing was more surefire to make a hit in the money department than a "Spago-like" eatery, and they went after it.

But the boys on his hot line were like the boys on many hot lines. If you don't teach them something new every few weeks, or pay them more money, they tend to get bored and move on. That's where we found our line, along with a few others around Boca. They jumped ship and we made ourselves instantly less popular with our neighbors. But the game was an old, established one, and even though I told myself I'd never do that—I did it.

So I got some real musclemen out of that Maxaluna. Tommy Sadler was one of the strongest of them. He became our lead sauté man. His partner at the grill also came from the neighbors. His name was John Penland. He was one of the happiest cooks I ever met. He wanted to beat his personal best by doing more covers on his station than any of the other guys. He would have fought anyone else off his grill. He was like a big basketball player and he roamed around the station, setting a pick, passing, faking, lobbing, and making sure his fish was flipped at just the right moment and with perfect grill lines. Tony, an Italian American kid with tinted glasses, worked the steak broiler.

Meanwhile Tom was the tiger, with his dark green eyes and tautly curled hair. He was built like a wrestler and rarely spoke once service started. When it got really crazy and we began to reach the numbers Bobby loved, Tom would sometimes let out just a little laugh, spoon the sauce over the fourteenth lamb shank, and rearrange the contents of his two ovens to be sure everything was going to come out perfectly. I would have trusted that guy with almost any task. I loved that line. I had three women working on the other side of the kitchen, which was fully exposed to the courtyard that faced the mall's common areas. They were lady tigers and handled all the cold prep and execution. A redhead named Tamara joined us after I saw her cook at Mark's Place in Miami and was impressed with her can-do energy. Another young woman who had just come out of the army worked at Tamara's side. Kelly (we called her "Kelly with a Y") was Irish and a long way from home. She was the life of the party after work, but on the line she and the other two were heads down and all business. When I called for a plate to be "in the window" I could count on it being there. In particular, their salads were marvels of "high *cooking* altitude" assembly. I had developed a dish inspired by *The Art of Vietnamese Cooking* by Nicole Routhier. They took it up to another level entirely. (Had I known then how many we'd sell over the next fifteen years I would probably have never started making the exotic beauties because they were *so* labor intensive.)

We were doing almost five hundred covers a night by the beginning of February. Bobby replaced the two girls who were taking reservations because he felt they were "afraid to take enough reservations at peak times." What Bobby didn't know was that Proal and the other two dining room managers had told them to take *no more than a hundred* in key time slots. (We were a thousand light-years from MIRA now.) So Bobby hired a guy who went by the moniker "Gonzo," a Vietnam vet who wore his U.S. Army jacket to work every day of the year. He didn't work in the office either but preferred to sit in the bar with almost all the lights off, his pens, pencils, an eraser, and the telephone with the big red reservation book in front of him. He would come in with three packs of smokes and by the end of the day two would be gone. He chain-drank Coke. His brown and copper hair hung over his eyes in an uneven row. He was very friendly when he saw anyone from the kitchen back in those early days. Lisabet was a motherly type who couldn't resist showering him with maternal attention in the form of sweets. Every day she pushed a dessert at him. The sugar from the Coke and pastries wired him, and by the end of Gonzo's first week on the job we did almost six hundred covers. Bobby was elated with his new "weapon." When I arrived each day, I always checked the reservation book. It didn't take long before I was telling our man in khaki to "cool it!" But Bobby would come bouncing in, do the math, pat Gonzo on the head, and bound upstairs.

But Gonzo was quickly becoming unhappy. He was shunned by all of us in the kitchen, even Lisabet. She actually started to turn us all out by building a barrier around her pastry shop with speed carts, mixers, and proofing closets, so the only thing she'd have to deal with was making the desserts while her assistant Kevin plated them. She would only speak through Kevin. It got weirder and weirder with her; maybe she was the canary in the coal mine.

Gonzo was living in some apocalyptic phone booth. The ringers never quit. The hold buttons never stopped flashing. The voices on the other end of the lines crackled and shrieked with requests, demands, threats—"We know Bobby!!"—for tables. "We ate at Vanessa's in New York many times!" We were at over 675 reservations by mid-March. When I came to work on March 19, I learned that Bobby had fired Kelle. She had moved to Boca from Key West at my invitation. I was berserk and let him know it. "Too much labor cost," he whined. We were doing unbelievable numbers and he was worried about one gal making less money than any bar back, a woman I had worked with for several years already.

I had to leave town to do the Book and the Cook event up in Philly. It was great exposure for Hoexter's. Even Bobby was happy about it and tried a "let bygones be bygones" approach the night before I left. He had a charm, that I couldn't deny, but I was still dubious and had nightmares. I began to grind my teeth at night. He'd fired Kelle; there'd be more. The doors seemed ready to come off the jet we were flying and I hated leaving even for the weekend. When I got back from Philly Bobby had hired some new "expert" named Michael—another asshole he was willing to pay to sit on his fanny with a calculator and figure out how to slowly decimate my staff. I was moving from being a willing soldier to an enraged combatant, and each day I managed *not* to wring Bobby's (or his new psych-kick's) neck was a good day. But it would not last forever. On the morning of April 26, Gonzo had taken almost eight hundred reservations. When he saw me he grabbed his Coke and retreated behind the bar saying, "Don't kill me! Bobby made me!!"

But I wasn't to kill the haunted man. I wasn't going to kill anyone. I had been awakened that morning by a dream about a dish I wanted to make. A cooking show was on TV that morning. I was hurrying around, as usual. My mom, still in her nightgown, exhaled a long column of cigarette smoke from her chair by the tube. I noted that judging from the concentration, velocity, arc, and distribution of that puff, followed by the subsequent stubbing out of the deadly nail, that, as much as she was not overly opinionated, one regarding this television how-to was upcoming.

"What," she asked me, "is the purpose of all of this tall food chefs are hell-bent on serving these days?"

You know how it is when you feel like you're already behind the clock; this was not a two-word answer. My mind reeled for a short yet satisfying response. Growing up with her I could learn as much by the way she smoked as one might from another's body language or speech. The smoke curled, tightened, and held in the air.

I could see the TV chef had just finished a dish of some, though not staggering, height.

"A lot of it is just for looks, Mom, like the *ravishing* outfit you're wearing right now." She scowled and looked at me through slit green eyes now. "But sometimes it's a great way to give some wonderful textural differences in food."

"What does that mean?" she asked with her match striking out the notion of a too-esoteric excuse or of me getting down the road just yet.

"Well, Ma, you know, it's like a great club sandwich. You bite through the warm, crunchy toast, through the delicate lettuces and juicy tomato, and the crisp bacon, through the meaty pull of smoked turkey and maybe the soft luxuriousness of avocado and mayo, and so on. It works! If you laid out all the components flat on a plate you'd never get that feeling."

"I don't like club sandwiches," she said. "And aren't you late for work?"

She smiled triumphantly and blew me a kiss. Not enough for us. I adored her even when she was busting on me and I went over for a big hug. She stood up and wrapped her arms around me. I loved the smell of her hair and the feeling of her soft yet strong workingwoman's body hugging me back. Everything was going to be fine as long as I could have this with her. She extended her cigarette-free hand and "let" me kiss her fingers as she pirouetted as gracefully as Cyd Charisse and returned to the never-ending pile of laundry. I got my hug and kiss from Janet, too, and hit the street for Hoexter's and another day of war.

But I still had that dream in my head. I didn't even go up to my office to put on my chef coat. I went in the walk-in meat cooler and got out half a dozen ducks. In less than half an hour I had prepped them, as I had dreamed, and slipped them into a rondeau and into the oven behind the main line. The kitchen was as quiet as a library and I loved it at that hour. I set the timer that I would wear around my neck for two hours. I felt good just doing some cooking again for a change. I had duck blood, rice vinegar, orange zest, and dark chicken stock splattered over my T-shirt. The exotic smell of star anise and vanilla from Madagascar scented my palms. I went up the back stairs.

When I got to my office the door was locked and my key wasn't turning it. There was a letter taped to the door. It was signed by Bobby's henchman, Michael—I'd been fired.

I wandered outside into the mall, dazed and confused. My cookbooks and knives were locked behind that office door. I walked past the deli owned by Bobby's folks. They waved at me to come inside, all smiles, clueless. I went to the parking garage and walked a sleepwalker's walk up to the highest floor of Crocker Center and looked at the skyline through the nauseating smell of the cement structure that held me. I looked north and saw nothing. I looked south and wondered what was next. My kitchen timer went off and yanked me back to earth. My ducks! I went to a pay phone by Maxaluna and called Tommy Sadler, my hardworking sauté chef. He knew what had happened and was reeling, asking me what I was going to do, but I said, "Yeah, pussy the way they did it, too. But listen, Tommy, do me a favor."

"Sure, man. You want me to dump your computer files? You want me to throw the switch on the freezer and really fuck these jack-offs up?"

"No, Tommy. I appreciate that sentiment, but do me a bigger favor, will ya? Two, actually. First, find Janet. She's working the bar for lunch and is probably there by now. She doesn't know I've been fired so give her the word."

"Got it. She gonna cry, though?"

"Not likely, Tom. Also, I put a braised duck dish in the oven this morning and it should be nice about now. Please taste it and tell me if it worked. I need to know. Okay?" [Silence.]

"You there, Tom?"

"Uh, yeah Chef, I'm here." [More silence.] "That's it? Taste the dish? You want me to just taste the ducks?"

"Yeah, Tom. I won't miss this fucking town or what these guys did to our team one bit, but if that dish works the way I think it will I want to have it for wherever I end up. So taste it, and let me know."

Latkes with Caviar and Sour Cream

Florida is richly populated with transplanted New Yorkers who came to escape the winters yet held fast to their culinary traditions. My two favorite New Yorkers of all time—my mother and grandmother—taught me to appreciate latkes with caviar. And I appreciate them every chance I get!

- 4 russet potatoes
- 1 sweet onion
- 2 large eggs
- ¼ cup finely ground bread crumbs
- 3½ teaspoons kosher salt
- 2 teaspoons baking powder
- 1 teaspoon freshly cracked black pepper
- 8 scallions, white part mainly, cut crosswise, small rounds
- 3 tablespoons roasted garlic
- canola oil, for cooking

Preheat oven to 375 degrees F. Into a large bowl, coarsely shred the potato and the onion, tossing together so the potato is seasoned with the onion juices. Place the potato-onion mixture onto a sheet of rinsed cheesecloth, gathering up the ends and tying the cloth into a tight bundle. Hang the bundle from the faucet over the kitchen sink for about 15 minutes. Gravity will pull most of the liquid from the potato-onion mixture. Twist the cheesecloth and squeeze the bundle to release any remaining liquid. Carefully unwrap the bundle and place the potato-onion mixture into a bowl, gently fluffing and pulling the fibers.

In a bowl, combine the eggs, bread crumbs, salt, baking powder, black pepper, scallions, and roasted garlic. Pour the egg mixture over the potato-onion mixture and toss to combine and distribute evenly into a batter.

In a heavy sauté pan, add enough oil to come about ⅛ inch up the side of the pan, and heat. When the oil is fairly hot, form a loose cake with the batter and carefully drop the cake into the pan. Sauté until crispy and golden, about 1½ to 2 minutes per side. Remove, and place on absorbent toweling. Repeat with the remaining batter.

When you're ready to serve, place the latkes on a baking sheet in the preheated oven for about 2 to 3 minutes, just to heat through. Serve with a dollop of sour cream on each latke, and top with the best caviar the budget will allow.

Makes 16 to 18 latkes

CHAPTER 20

a Mano

Miami Beach, 1990–93

JIMMY HELD WHAT APPEARED to be a copy of the night's reservation sheets. He clutched the papers under his arm and waved joyously to the ancient front-desk woman with the alabaster face makeup and the Mikado-black hair. She waved dementedly back, shaking her hooped jewelry and Hawaiian muumuu-clad body. They spoke no common language but she positively loved Jimmy. Almost everybody did. He entered softly through the heavy door with the carved wooden hand signifying the name, "a Mano" (by hand). The hotel owner sat there at one o'clock in the afternoon having his very first cup of coffee, reading *El Nuevo Herald,* not even looking at Jimmy at that hour. Jimmy placed the papers on the maître d' stand underneath one of the oversized wine lists, leaving them there for the relatively new assistant manager who would, no doubt, see them when he came in at two o'clock to do the table assignments for the waiters.

Jimmy, you see, had been there a half hour before and disapproved of the number of reservations said assistant manager had accepted for the seven o'clock and eight o'clock time slots. The manager would soon discern, on the sheet of paper covering the reservations page, a replication of the area of a man's physiology that went from the tip of the phallus to the circular Leonardo-da-Vinci-meets-Robert-Mapplethorpe-like detailed illustration of an anus. (James Breen's, which replication Jimmy had produced by having hoisted himself, sans pants, on the delicate glass of the office copy machine, carefully keeping the majority of his weight balanced on the frame of the device, while cleverly using his apron as a photographer would use a blanket to cut out the light.) Béla Károlyi would have beamed over this gymnastic maneuver.

Leaving "Boca, Boca, Boca" was the only option. I have never understood the attraction of that man-made "mallburb." It is the spiritual and physical opposite of Diamond Lake, where I grew up, and Key West, where I was happiest. But every journey is part of the life we live, and so it was now time for quite another.

I had been out of work only a short time but we had no savings. I was still being hassled by the IRS from MIRA days. The same guy who sold the kitchen equipment to us at Hoexter's, Kenny Cohen, was making fresh scores with the slowly waking Miami Beach. He called me one day and told me to call the guy who had bought the Betsy Ross Hotel, a Cuban named Novel. So I called. He invited me to meet him, which I told Kenny about. He offered a very helpful bit of advice: "Take cash."

I started work at 1440 Ocean Drive at the beginning of July. My family was still in Boca and I drove the hour or so commute each way that summer. No big deal. It gave me a chance to regroup.

Janet started looking for a new place for us, something less expensive and closer to our new employer. It meant Justin would have to switch schools once again.

Going to Miami Beach around 1990 was like arriving at Sutter's Mill when they first discovered gold. The beach was giddy, delirious, particularly the Deco District of Ocean Drive.

Before that time Miami Beach had been in a long and seemingly endless decline. It was an anomaly in the history of urban living. The waterfront candy-colored hotels were filled with retirees largely in the final years of life. They sat on rockers facing the ocean, struggling to keep warm in their thin sweaters and blankets while the tropical sun blazed down on arthritic limbs and weathered faces. They hobbled to drugstores and counted their coins out of plaid penny purses to aging cashiers. The beach was locked in a time capsule, and it seemed that once its residents finally passed on, the Art Deco hotels would shelter only ghosts and tropical tumbleweed would roll over the terrazzo-tiled lobbies.

But then some European photographers, perhaps undeterred by the shabbiness, beheld the magical light that descends from heaven to this little section of earth. And like night follows day, along came the fashion models—impossibly beautiful girls for whom this pastel-hued ruin with the dazzling light and limitless horizon became a stage they would exploit in relative languor for the next two or three years. But when you have girls you get boys. And when you have boys, in a place like this, you get, well, more boys. Many, *many* more boys! And the median age of Miami Beach began to sink like ice cream down the chin of a child in the endless sun and fun.

Ocean Drive was like a life-sized Monopoly game board, as were Collins and Washington (between Fifth and Tenth Streets) and, slowly, Lincoln Road Mall. Shock became the order of the day in real estate: places that once went for $10 per square foot doubled, tripled, quadrupled, and more with each passing month. The young and eternally young in mind and libido moved into the neighborhood and the "gray flight" began as landlords raised rents. At first all it took was a fractional raise and the elderly residents had no choice but to book north. Living on a fixed income creates a very finite awareness of one's realities.

But the young and reality were not on speaking terms. Miami Beach was a celebration of skin, and the economic dynamics that supported it were cafés, clubs, gyms, roller-skating shops, tattoo parlors, bars, coffee shops, and the restored hotels that housed the ever-more-youthful visitors coming from New York to get a look, a feel, a taste, and often a new lease on a new life.

It was with a mixture of attraction and uncertainty that I took the job of directing the concepts for the restaurants at the Betsy. The first one in the small colonial-style hotel at 1440 Ocean Drive was about ready for business. It was a near-comical, amateurishly designed space. The kitchen was down a steep flight of stairs. Whoever worked down there was going to feel like they had been conscripted on a U-boat. The dining room was dominated by hard, stark, whiter-than-white spaces. If you dropped a plate on the floor you would have heard the crash well into the next week. A single hair or bread crumb stood out like a rebuke against the whiteness. I couldn't begin to think about a menu that might fit this polar dining space. Then there was the other dining room, the one with the faux eighteenth-century interior. But once I went outside and smelled the ocean across the short expanse of park and felt the warmth of the sun gentled by the steady breezes of Ocean Drive, I began to relax and see a way.

I also began to learn who my new employer was. He was like Al Pacino's character in *Scarface*, a man who also "loved the American Dream with a vengeance."

Novel (he pronounced it "No-Vell" with the accent on the "Vell") grew up in the Oriente area of Cuba. He had a strong face with high cheekbones. There was some scarring there from acne long ago, and it added more "tough handsome" to his look. His eyes caught everything and gave only what he wanted to give, which was usually a cagey construction of his desires, aspirations, lies, delusions, and machinations. But still, he was charming. He was built like a middleweight boxer or a baseball player. He didn't have big muscles but he was agile and when he was standing and talking to you, it became more of a dance than a conversation. He was almost always just a few moments away from extreme emotion, whether it was joy, anger, fury, need, humor, or seduction. When he got excited a soft hail of saliva would sometimes hit your face. He wouldn't blink or excuse himself in a way that conveyed real dismay, but he'd laugh through his slit green crescent eyes and literally pull at my forearms to draw me into his world, his force. Sometimes he'd butt me with his chest and then circle around me. He'd pull me to the bar and we'd drink and talk and drink some more. And it was mesmerizing to me at first. I had never known anyone quite like him before; I had known aspects of him in other people, but never the whole composite of what made Novel uniquely himself. He was fiercely, proudly, and staunchly right wing. He may have bought the Betsy Ross equally for the flags and name as for the real estate.

In the beginning, before we opened a Mano and all of my hours were consumed with it, Novel took me all over Miami Beach and Little Havana to show me "his America."

One of the first places he took me to in his well-worn white Cadillac was La Esquina de Tejas, where Ronald Reagan famously ate when he visited Little Havana in 1983. When the valet stepped up to take the car he saw Novel put a gun in the glove box, slamming it shut but not locking it, and said nothing. It was not easy to question Novel. The food at La Esquina was tired and underseasoned fare, but Novel was proud to show me off as "his chef." We went to the always-packed Cuban mainstay called Versailles, which also served conventional, unexciting food.

The café's *cortadito* (a very strong espresso, from the Spanish word *corter*; it is "cut" with milk) and guava *pasteles* were the saving graces of the place. I returned to Versailles from time to time just to order them. Next we went to the more Spanish Casa Juancho. Novel schooled me in some of the Latin dishes I hadn't seen before and dramatically improved my "menu Spanish." He got a kick out of teaching me about his culture, his past. He was proud. We went to little cigar factories and for a while I became a cigar smoker.

Novel also took me to a place I will always regard as one of my favorite small markets anywhere—*Palacio de Los Jugos*—the Palace of Juices! Here I wandered the aisles with him, gasping at the perfect exotic fruits like guanabana, mamey, sapote, sapodilla, canistel, as well as excellent Jamaican papayas, Florida avocados, and bowling-ball-heavy pineapples just bursting with perfumed juice! In addition to the whole fruits you could get a mad array of freshly juiced beverages made right there on the spot. (Hence the name.) It is compelling to watch sugarcane get crushed, its plank-hard fibers rendering milky clear nectar that bees would swarm to. But the tamarind *jugo* was my favorite, with its tart notes following the first wave of tropical sweetness. It had that one-two punch I looked for in many of my sauces.

At Palacio you were not confined to only fruit. No. This was a freewheeling Latin American *mercado* (market) where you could get a killer pork sandwich, rocket-fuel Cuban espressos, addictive plantain or *malanga* chips fried to order, mojo-marinated roast chicken, black beans, red beans, *Moros y Cristianos* (a plate of black beans—the Moors—and white rice—the Christians), guava and cream cheese, *chicharrones* (big wafers of fried pork rind sprinkled with salt), a Novel favorite. And should you need some western wear you could get cowboy hats, cowboy boots, and cowboy belts. His tours were an unforgettable illustration of how Miami had become home to so many cultures from so many countries. And as soon as they arrived, they began to integrate into the matrix of the city. The swell of new immigrants did not bother Novel. He believed in the American Dream. And what did Novel's American Dream mean to me? It meant new flavors. I was earning another "culinary degree" from a worldly professor.

Novel was passionate about food. He did not confine himself to his Cuban roots. He loved Italian food, Jewish delis, and French cuisine. New York was Novel's favorite city in the world. It's where he had gotten his start in America. He had come over, like so many others, in 1960 or 1961. Initially processed at Miami's Freedom Tower, he spent a few days there before he went to Manhattan to make his fortune, the classic immigrant story. He started with nothing. He didn't even speak English yet. He hustled like a man possessed, selling shoes and cologne out of his car, where he slept as well. He bathed in the sinks of public restrooms, but he always wore a starched white shirt and polished shoes on his sales calls. As we flew over Manhattan on our way to a three-day James Beard event, Novel reached across the back of my seat, grabbed my head, and physically turned my face toward the window. He was so excited to see New York again, and he wanted me to share his excitement as the city rose beneath us.

He was so proud, and his pride was fierce and undiluted. He taught me about capitalism, how it began. He taught me more about street-level economics than any other man except my own father. In the beginning I almost think I came to love the man. But something in me knew to hold back, despite his charm and the charms of South Beach, as we opened the Stars and Stripes Café, and later a Mano, at the Betsy Ross Hotel on fabulous Ocean Drive.

It had been just over two months between jobs, a long time to make no money. Though he hadn't come up with a contract Novel paid me $500 a week to get the ball rolling, five one-hundred dollar bills under the table. This was not going to work in the long term, but I had to get some money for the family. Maybe I'd have to find a second job.

Just before getting fired at Hoexter's, I had been invited by the Fetzer Winery in Mendocino, California, for a big weekend event celebrating their spectacular new organic garden. The Fetzers were mildly chagrined when they learned I'd been fired, but the ads had already gone out and so they were sort of stuck with me. Janet and I left for San Francisco on July 12. The day before I had coaxed my sous chef, Bill Prahl, from Hoexter's to join me at the Betsy. He did, so we left him in charge. We dined at Jeremiah Tower's new place, 690, and Wolfgang Puck's Postrio, before driving up to Mendocino. It was blisteringly hot in the wine country that summer.

The Fetzers had invited quite a lineup of chefs not only to cook but to discuss the craft of cooking. Once again I was immersed with a group of talented chefs who could not only prepare brilliant food but were also knowledgeable about its place and value within our culture. I had not had this discourse in my Key West days and it fed me in a whole new way. Chefs included Stephan Pyles of Dallas, Anne Rosenzweig of New York, John Folse of New Orleans, and John Ash of California. Julia Child was the big draw, and Stephan and I participated in an early-morning radio show hosted by San Francisco restaurateur Narsai David. It was highlighted by us drinking Gewürztraminer out of coffee cups with Ms. Child at eight o'clock in the morning in the fragrant, perfect, and expansive gardens that the Fetzer family had created.

When the weekend ended, Janet and I got back in our rental car and drove to the Lark Creek Inn for an early dinner with one of California's brightest star chefs, Bradley Ogden, before catching the red-eye home. We hadn't realized that the Lark Creek Inn wasn't exactly an inn, so we had to change from our shorts and T-shirts into dinner clothes in an upstairs office that Brad's staff courteously vacated for us.

Back at the Betsy I was becoming more than the chef. It was August and the beach outside was quiet, but there was a vortex swirling within the walls at 1440. I was doing the wine list, the liquor inventory, dealing with front-of-the-house employees and managers, setting up offices for them, arranging storage, making design decisions, overseeing public relations, training staff, as well as dealing with the craziness of living mostly without my family.

The wine sales reps came calling, engaging in a kind of courtship that seemed too good to be true. The three big companies all wanted to dominate our wine list. The biggest by far was called Southern Wine and Spirits. Southern didn't want merely to dominate the list, they wanted to own it all. And they sent in a saleswoman to get the job done. She was committed and more than capable of getting my attention. Samples were flooding my cramped office and my brain. "Taste the Steltzner Cab, Chef Norman. Like it?" She had small, perfectly white teeth and perfectly applied red lipstick. "I'll leave the bottle." And she blew me a kiss as she backed out the door with the heavy valises of wine she had to drag from account to account. She had steely strength in a ballerina's body.

The machinations and subplots of who was doing what behind the many closed doors of a hotel were getting more interesting each day. One night it got an extra layer of weird.

(Scene: A dark hotel room.)

It's late and I'd been out with Novel. As I fumble with my key and enter the room I smell musky cologne. I stop in my tracks and notice a feminine shape in my bed.

"Janet?"

A voice returns: "*Que?*" There's confusion in the tone but a girlish giddiness, too.

I ask, "Kay?"

The voice: "*Novel?*"

Me: "Uhh, no."

Voice: "*Quien?*"

"Ken?"

"*Quien es?*"

"Ken S.?"

She bleats out, "Wheeeeeere's NoVEL?" And I see her now pulling my sheets up around her naked bosom.

"Hey, I don't know, but he'd better not be in here or on his way! This is my room! Now I'll step into the bathroom while you get your things and get out of here!"

It wasn't more than fifteen minutes later I could hear her voice again coming from down the hall, screaming now, "Oh Papi, oh Papi, oh Papi!"

It was so disturbing at first, I opened my door to try and understand it. So had a few other guests of the Betsy Ross. A guy who looked a lot like Mickey Rourke was just across the hall, saw me, yanked his head in the direction of the woman's wailing, and gave me a smile and a thumbs-up. A male grunting noise was heard and the banging of a headboard. She was no longer in the wrong room—or maybe she was.

It didn't take long to figure out that Novel probably had a coke habit and that the hotel's interior designer was also his supplier. I never saw them do the blow. She looked normal enough when she entered the hotel lobby. But when she came out of Novel's office she was a kaleidoscope of facial contortions and nasal gulping. He would be bouncing up and down on the balls of his feet, smiling, eyes slit into his flirt mask, going nowhere but believing he was going to the top of the American Dream. My instincts to stay back a little were now making a bit more sense.

We needed a second car, so Janet stayed overnight with me at the hotel then flew back to Illinois with Mama. Once again, they drove back together, this time in Mama's car. We started lunch service on August 10 and Novel slipped me another $500 in cash.

At the Betsy our "dining room" was out on the sidewalk; every day we set up tables, chairs, and umbrellas and every night we put them away. That was how Miami Beach worked. The Deco hotels had scant interior space so the newly widened sidewalk on Ocean Drive became the prime money-making real estate to the restaurateurs up and down the increasingly crowded street.

As fall approached we actually began to get stronger and stronger with our food at the Stars and Stripes Café. I had some great cooks/chefs joining me in the cramped little kitchen. Ed Hale from back in Sinclair's days, Bill Prahl from Louie's Backyard and Hoexter's, and a young man named Randy Zweiban joined us; he had just moved down from New York City after finally giving up the dream of being a drummer. He had a strong, lithe rocker's body and brown hair that was getting quite thin despite his youth. Eddie was the old man on the line, and he was smart enough to use his experience and let Bill and Randy do the heavy lifting. I was moving forward with the million details of creating a fine-dining restaurant across the lobby while still overseeing the Café. Throughout the construction process, we were constantly surprised by who dropped in—increasingly, the world was coming to South Beach and checking out the scene, chefs, and winemakers from all over America.

In October of 1990, Janet and I flew up to New York after Charlie engineered a weekend with Emeril and wives. The six of us stayed in an awful hotel called the St. Moritz on Central Park. It was even worse than the rooms in the Betsy, far worse actually. But we weren't in the rooms for much more than four or five hours each night. For the rest of the time we were "doing New York." Emeril was still with his second wife, Tari, and

Charlie was with his second wife, Lynn. We went out the first night to a jazz club and at some point in the evening a manager came over and told Tari to put out her cigarette. He was unnecessarily rude about it. That ticked me off and I showed my disgust with the management by eating an unlit one, a tremendously bad move.

Charlie had lined up lunch at Le Bernardin and dinner at Bouley, two of the most rarefied restaurants to be found in New York at the time, with Bouley being the most sought-after reservation in the city.

I woke up feeling absolutely horrible from the raw tobacco in my gut. But when Charlie sets up one of these culinary tours you have to get on board the "Charlie Train."

We dressed in our finest and I seemed to rally. Janet was radiant and so we joined our friends in the lobby, got into taxis, and went to the famous Le Bernardin. The brother-and-sister team of Gilbert and Maguey Le Coze had hired Chef Eberhard Müller as *chef-de-cuisine*. Müller was a picture of Gallic pride. His physique was trim and tall, and he watched us from the kitchen door as we swept through nine courses of seafood, the foundation of their menu. Raw fish came first. Then fish that had been barely cooked arrived and were consumed. We went on to grilled fish and sautéed seafood, in ascending modes of richness. We drank at least a bottle of wine per person despite the night Charlie had planned still ahead of us. The combination of excess food and wine awoke the torpedo of nicotine that had lain dormant in my intestines.

Just before the dessert menus were handed out I had to bolt to the restroom. I was, in an instant, in the grip of a seemingly near-fatal fever, sweating and dizzy. I wanted Janet to come save me but I was alone in a men's bathroom and it was my own stupid fault. I reeled in pain and psychic dismay. Then, a miracle occurred: all the food that had ever been in me rushed out into the toilet bowl. It was salvation! I cleaned myself up and rejoined our party feeling as if I could, at last, go on.

When I returned, Emeril looked up from the desserts that had been scattered in every direction on the table and said, "You okay, brother?" I was ushered back to my chair by a maître d' and said, "I am no longer the Marlboro Man." Em smiled broadly at me and then yanked his head toward the far side of the room, changed his face to a concerned one, and said, "Brother Chahlie's been havin' a word with the chef over there for a while now."

I looked and saw Charlie with his arms crossed over his chest and a look of more than mild annoyance, or at least subdued exasperation. He walked back to our table and sat down. He said, "We are done." We all looked at each other and realized that Charlie wanted us to leave. So we did. Once outside he explained.

Tari and Lynn both lit up cigarettes and I moved as far away as I could. Charlie began. "So I went over there to thank Chef Eberhard and it's going along fine. He asked me what was going on with Charlie Trotter's, so I told him that we had just introduced an all-vegetable tasting menu."

We knew this, of course, and we thought it was pure Charlie to do an all-veg menu and so we loved it.

Charlie went on. "This guy, who's just served us like nine courses of fish in a row, looks at me and says, 'All vegetables? That's eeeeeet?' And so I said, 'Yes. Up until desserts, of course.' And then he looks me in the eye and says, 'That's bullshit.'

"Mind you I just paid the abysmal cocksucker for our meal and he's telling me an 'all-veg menu is boooool-sheeeit.'" (Charlie doing a drop-dead haughty French impression now.) Emeril and I started to walk back to the dining room to have a word, but Charlie ran past us both, turned around, and put up his hands to stop us.

So we went back to the hotel with barely enough time to shower again and change into new clothes.

Our reservation was set for nine o'clock but Emeril had disappeared. We waited in the bar at the hotel. We had no way of knowing where he'd gone for almost an hour. Reservations at Bouley back then were the toughest in Manhattan. It didn't matter that we were chefs or that Charlie was with us. Charlie was the bigger dog then. Em hadn't scored his fame yet. We finally got a call from Emeril. He and his wife had had another fight and they almost didn't make it at all. So we were an hour late at the door and we were given a frosty reception. That didn't help the situation. Charlie was almost always giddy at times like these—the more "on the edge" the better. He loved a good dustup. We weren't hungry after the epic lunch at Le Bernardin. In all honesty, I hated to admit or face that I was still not fully recovered from my cigarette ingestion idiocy.

We were led to a round table near the middle of the room. Emeril perked up when he saw that during the time we were waiting for him Charlie had gone ahead and ordered the evening's wine lineup. These bottles were rare gems, and the idea of missing out on them due to the lateness of the hour or condition of our guts was not an option.

This was at the absolute apotheosis of an establishment that had declared itself to be the "it" restaurant and was having its moment of near deification in the greatest city on the planet. Nothing was hotter in New York at that time. And given some real electricity, the night might have gone in a different direction. But the servers had drunk the Kool-Aid, too. The menus were massive recitations of the self-abasing, tortured retrieval of the celestial provenance of each ingredient and how it had been so cleverly wrought into genius bits of barely recognizable goodness. At least that is the way Emeril and I were seeing it. The evening was like some doomed parody of a Catholic mass as channeled by characters in a play by Mamet or Shepard. Every forty-five minutes (or more) the service team would appear to finally bring on the next couplet in the epic Bouley poem. They would lower the saucer-sized, nearly empty plates in unison, beaming, transfixed as they genuflected in front of the food, speaking in some unknown or dead language at a whispery decibel, allude to what was on each dish, and then back away, retreating several steps in reverse, heads bowed.

After two or three of these grim, lethargic episodes we realized that no amount of wine would disguise the outcome: we were the unhappy victims of a very slow car crash. Emeril was growing less willing to go along with each grinding minute. He sat at the table with his elbows on his knees by this time. His chin was barely an inch off the hundreds-of-dollars-a-yard tablecloth. His eyes sunk like a basset hound's. He would pull down a glass of wine, eye it like a long-lost friend at an Irish wake, take a swallow, smile the ironic smile of a man who has just lost something near and dear, and say, "I'm dying here." And he'd say it with that tone and accent that comes from a European dockworker's most earnest plaint. The word "here" was "heah." The word "dying" was "dyyyyyyyin'." The sentence ended with a thud, a hammer blow, a threat of imminent endings. "I'm dyin', Chaaaaaarlie." "Dyin' heah, Noam" (me). "Dyin', Jan" (Janet). "Dyiiiiiiin', Ms. T." (Tari). His protestations moved Charlie to a level of amusement I had not seen before. I think Charlie was hoping one of us (Em or me) would repeat the scene that had occurred not so long before when we tossed some chairs around a very expensive bar in Aventura, Florida.

But Emeril's turmoil was seemingly of no import to the acolytes at the Mission of Duane Street. As the black-garbed waiters arrived after another near-hour of absence, stroking the rich thread count of the Frette tablecloth, invoking another moment of bliss was at hand yet again for us fortunate souls, Emeril would do a Jekyll-and-Hyde snap-up in rapt attention, beaming as if he'd just received celestial enlightenment from the Buddha himself, and say something like, "This is just fantastic, fellas, just really, *really* fantastic." The waiters were way ahead of him on this assessment and when they'd returned to their pews near the kitchen Emeril would turn around and mutter, "Fantastically fucked up" or "Fantastic my ass" and then he started with, "I'm gonna order a pizza Char." "Gonna order a freaking fuckin' pizza right heah as sure as I'm born." "Cuz ya know why? Cuz I'm staaaaaavin."

Janet and Mama had looked everywhere for a new place for us. One Sunday, after another crushing week of work, we all took a ride to the village of Perrine, about as far south as you can get in Miami before you are in the keys, to show me the house they had rented. Maybe it was a sign. Maybe they wanted to go back to the gentler world. I tried to make it work, but a few weeks of commuting to the beach and back to Perrine every night proved nearly deadly. After working a sixteen-hour day it was too much. I moved into the hotel six days and nights a week, going home on Sunday mornings and returning to room number 234 on Monday afternoons. I don't recommend it as a way of keeping a family together and oneself sane. But after the failure of MIRA and the nightmare of Boca I had to make whatever sacrifices were necessary and this seemed to be one of them.

The New Year of 1991 began and it was as if God just jammed his foot on the accelerator. The days and daze of both Key West and Boca were left swirling in the past now. It was all about Miami Beach. My luck was to be there right at the beginning of it all. It seemed like everyone wanted to take a juicy bite. On January 4, the *Miami Herald* gave our little Stars and Stripes Café three stars! Twelve days later we were asked to shoot the cover of *South Florida Journal* on top of the Betsy Ross with me presenting my Down Island French Toast. We had hired a really talented chef out of Tampa named Scott Howard solely to create the amuse-bouche program and he would do a flight of them for some seriously foodie tables, much like tapas would come to be known in later years. One of the typically elaborate was a tiny "box" of potatoes, hardly bigger than a stamp. Each "wall" of which was made of paper-thin crispy potato wafers filled with ultracreamy mashed potato and topped with caviar. It took hours to make enough for a single night of service.

By now, our team was as hardcore as they come. One woman who worked the garde-manger station was so intent on making it she pissed in her pants one night rather than leave the rush. We were shocked but she refused to quit. The hours we worked didn't matter. With us it wasn't a worry about burnout—it was sex, plain, pure, and powerful. We wanted to see the smiles—the look of a guest in rapture, the look that said they understood what we were doing—multiple times.

In February, *Food Arts* did a photo shoot in the dining room. Marion Burros dined with Nancy Harmon Jenkins at a Mano in March. The *New York Times* ran a photo of me holding one of my dishes on the blazing sands of Miami Beach in April. The *Miami Herald* gave a Mano an "Exceptional" rating in May. Meanwhile my calendar that notes these dates is also a prep list: "pull bones for duck stock," "make 24 spring rolls," "finish the Ancho-Guava jam." In July, *Time* magazine ran a photo and the James Beard Foundation called and invited us to do our first James Beard Dinner at his historic home in Greenwich Village.

The energy was so positive and wonderful and supportive! It seemed like we would never go back to the rough times. Novel was impressed and delighted with the invitation to do the Beard Dinner. He brought his lovely wife, Alicia, into a Mano to show off "his" restaurant. She loved our take on the foods she grew up with and how we twisted them in new and different directions. The Cubano community at large loved a Mano and came in celebrating, which made Novel even happier.

Novel decided he and Alicia wanted to go to New York with us, so on August 3 we all flew north. Janet and I sat in front of Alicia and Novel, and when the New York skyline came into view we all felt such a rush of life's possibilities. Novel booked us a table at the famed Le Cirque. He had been there some years past and knew the name of Le Cirque's owner, Sirio Maccioni. I was impressed he cared, but I was more curious about the young chef about whom I had been hearing, Daniel Boulud. We had an amazing meal but now I felt that for all the press attention being piled on us back on the beach, and walking up and down these streets, being in a place like Le Cirque, and tasting Daniel's food all reinspired me to want to do the very best we could at the Beard House.

My young chef from the Betsy, who was coming on the strongest, not as a cook so much but as an "all around," was the former New Yorker, Randy Zweiban. When he came to the realization that he could not make it as a punk rock drummer he fled to the kitchen. All the energy he used to punish the skins was now poured into making the food happen. He didn't weigh more than a buck thirty then but he was pure heart. He took the responsibility of transporting the food and traveling with two more of our crew. Together we cooked the night of August 5 at the home of the late James Beard. Risa came to the dinner and she was her stunning, funny, witty self. She even managed to handle Novel, but in truth, I wasn't surprised as she could handle just about anyone.

When we got back home the *Time* magazine article came out the following week naming a Mano the best of Miami. Not only the beach but all of Miami!

Then one of Miami's own came back from Hollywood. Mickey Rourke decided to return to boxing under the alias of "Marielito." He trained at the Fifth Street Gym where Muhammad Ali had trained when he was still known as Cassius Clay and, later, the Great One, and had made the place famous. I'm not sure how Novel and Mickey met but they were made for each other, and it wasn't long before Mickey was staying at the Betsy Ross with his girlfriend Carrie Otis. (Girls who looked as good as Carrie are often referred to as "knockouts." She may have earned the sobriquet the hard way with the pugilistic actor, but I don't know.) Our lead bartender Mario, who'd been around the South Beach scene for years, came to me first and told me the actor was in the dining room and wanted to meet me. I was instantly excited as I thought of him then as a near-Brando figure who'd never gotten to realize his potential due to bad breaks, not a lack of talent.

When the door swung open to my hot line, a man who looked like a street bum stood there. He had a knit skullcap on and black bib overalls. He hadn't shaved in a week. Yet his eyes shone with a feral intensity and he seemed coiled with an energy that lay just inside a hazy front. He said something like, "Novel thinks you're great." I said something back about that being nice and went on to compliment his work. He gave me a twisted smile and said maybe he'd come back soon for dinner.

Charlie came down in September with his wife, Lynn. It was their first time away from their baby, Dylan Thomas Trotter, who had been born back in May. Janet sat on one of the three semicircular banquettes that were the most coveted seats in the dining room. Lynn was overwhelmed from the traveling; after a few glasses of white Burgundy on an empty stomach followed by my Down Island French Toast, she fell sound asleep. Charlie and Janet were solid dining partners and Charlie simply carried on, ordering some great wine, and the two of them talked old times. As it came time for desserts Lynn awoke from her nap. Charlie, bemused as he often is when conventions are bucked, sweetly asked her if she'd like some dessert. She surveyed the scene, then declared, "Yes. I would like some dessert. I'll have another order of the yummy Down Island Toast thing." I joined them at the table after that and Charlie and I got another bottle going. They were staying at the hotel, so one thing led to another and by two o'clock in the morning Charlie and I were in the Betsy Ross swimming pool in our underwear challenging each other to race after race until we both nearly drowned.

Despite all the craziness my love of reading had not fallen completely by the wayside. Somehow a book came into my hands called *Why We Eat What We Eat* by a chap named Raymond Sokolov. Although the work was short, it was packed with information that swarmed my mind. I thought about why I cooked the way I cooked and how I could cook with greater meaning and intention. I thought about where I was working and about the places I had worked during my cooking career. I felt even more fired up to continue to blaze new trails in menu composition and during this time my menus were filled with items like:

Bone-In Cracked Conch Chowder, served with a club sandwich of cracked conch, held together with fish bones we'd gleaned and cleaned from grouper frames for toothpicks; Foie Gras Stuffed and Roasted with First of the Season Wild Morels in a Port Wine Reduction, Golden Gooseberries, and a Confit of Shallots; Lobster, Scallop, and Tiny Shrimp Quesadilla with Avocado, Organic Plum Tomatoes, Red Onions, Ribbons of Greens, and Aged Sherry Dressing; Vietnamese Soft Spring Rolls with

Somen Noodles, Tuna Maki Roll, Paw Paw Goi Du Du and Ponzu-Peanut Dipping Sauces; Grilled Lapsang Souchong Tea Stuffed Salmon Spiral with Wild Mushrooms, Spiked Leeks, Red Wine Essence, and Salmon Potato Wafers; Bajan-Spiced Grilled Red Snapper with a Sweet Potato-Sweet Corn Hash and a Jicama-Green Onion and Oranges Slaw; Key Lime Natilla en Tortilla with Cilantro Sirop and a Hot Hot Honey.

I went for a run down the sands of Miami Beach one day and it hit me that since I was constantly being compared to three or four other of my chef colleagues in the greater Miami area, we should join forces and coauthor a cookbook together. Evenly splitting the profits four ways and dividing the work equally among us appealed to me. My reasoning was simple: if we didn't, someone else would approach us possibly offering dramatically less money, if any at all. The fact that we were all scheduled to do a Meals on Wheels event very soon at Turnberry, the site of so many fundraisers during that time, gave me the opportunity to suggest the idea while the notion was still an optimistic one.

On October 12, 1991, a thousand people made their way to the giant ballrooms where I would join the potential author group I had in mind: Mark Militello, Allen Susser, Douglas Rodriguez, and Robbin Haas. Robbin was the executive chef of Turnberry, a dynamic personality who could bring his southwestern influences; Mark could call on his Mediterranean flavors; Allen could bring his French flair; and Douglas his clearly Cuban style. I would do what I would do. I was the only one of the group who had already been published and, in an effort to make the idea more palatable, I decided I would play a very neutral role.

As the prep mounted furiously that afternoon I called a meeting in Robbin's office. Mark, Allen, and Doug each grabbed a chair. Robbin was dealing with details in the dining room and was delayed so I spilled the idea to the other three. They all agreed so fast my head almost spun. Then Mark added, "But just the four of us, not Robbin." Since Mark was at that point a very strong draw, and Robbin was new to the South Florida scene, we acceded to his point. When Robbin came back into his office he wasn't any the wiser. I felt a little bad but it was always hard to get more than two chefs to agree about anything. In my neutrality I asked if anyone had a relationship with an agent. Mark said he did. It was the same person who had coauthored his wildly successful books, John Harrison. That was accepted. Of lesser importance but still in the spirit of fairness, we agreed to use Allen's accountant and Doug's lawyer. I would go solo in the mix.

The plan moved swiftly forward and by December we had a proposed contract from John to act as our agent. He flew in from Santa Fe and worked diligently to provide a template for a cookbook on the emerging new cuisine of South Florida, with a quartet of chefs/authors attached. He was positive that not only could we get a publisher but that it would sell a massive number of books. This was going to be child's play. All we had to do was come up with about twenty-five recipes apiece! The market for chef-authored cookbooks was still not yet flooded back then, and we felt quite sure that we could get a publisher to give us a budget for full color photography throughout. It was a rare moment with a feeling of camaraderie that was not so normal between some of us. Now we could applaud each other's successes as opposed to feeling the deadly pall of envy. The more press the other guys got could only mean we'd each sell more books! Simple, right?

We went through the legal motions to incorporate. John helped us schedule meetings with each other to push the project along. On December 19, we met at Doug's lawyer's office and he asked us what the name would be for our corporate entity. We looked at each other. This was kind of fun. Doug said, "Mango Mafia!" He almost giggled at how much he loved his own idea. I loved the big guy and it was fine with me. The lawyer was adamant, though: "No references to Mafia, fellas!" So someone suggested "Gang." Another offered "The Mango Gang, Inc." And so it went. We wrote personal checks, rolling the dice that soon enough John would have an advance for us to divvy up and cover all the start-up expenses. Mark made the first meeting, held one morning at his restaurant, but missed the second at Yuca where Doug was working, and then the third at Chef Allen's in Aventura.

We should have known that Mark would drop out. He just wasn't the kind of guy to hang in a group. But it was the fact that he had his lawyer call Allen and deliver the news, and did not tell us himself that really ended what was a frail, at best, attempt to band together. John Harrison was flabbergasted as he had "four if not five New York publishers competing for the project." The Mango Gang was a bust, except in the memory of the press where it lives on and on, and like a mango fallen from a once-green tree onto a black section of asphalt, oozing on.

Throughout the months of October and November a Mano kept rolling on. In early December of 1991, I was approached by a man who had worked for NBC for many years with a proposal for a project he'd been thinking about. He believed that chefs ("lots of 'em!") on television were going to become a really big thing. He was an affable guy named Richard, and his wife, Candace, also worked in television, for the BBC no less. He seemed to be legit but I wasn't so sure he was right about his vision. Nonetheless it all added up to a way to maybe sell more cookbooks and it could be fun to tool around South Florida and have this guy videotape me shopping and cooking with my kitchen crew. His idea was to get NBC to air the show twice. Then he would get Florida's two largest retailers, Publix grocery stores and Burdines department stores, to stock and sell videocassettes of the show. He banged out some numbers on the bar at the Stars and Stripes one afternoon over a bottle of wine and it became clear that this could be big. Another manifestation of the wild and crazy days on South Beach was under way.

The year ended on some high notes. Luminaries continued to come to a Mano to see what was going on, including Tom Margittai of the Four Seasons, Marvin Shanken of the *Wine Spectator*, dessert maven Barbara Kafka (one of my new staunchest supporters), Maida Heatter, who brought in Random House giant Jason Epstein, and Patricia Wells came from Paris.

Another person who started to come in with increasing regularity was Marsha Sayet (a "Miami Beach grad," she beamed), who helped cofound the local chapter of the American Institute of Wine and Food (AIFW) at the Betsy Ross a few months earlier. She was pretty, very animated, seemed to have a very keen interest in what I was doing, and visited often that winter.

In early March we taught at the La Varenne cooking school located at the Greenbrier Resort in White Sulphur Springs, West Virginia. It was like going back into the pre–Civil War era! The other chefs who were part of the same program that year were Marcel Desaulniers from Williamsburg's The Trellis, Dean Fearing out of Dallas, Jasper White from Boston, Michael

Romano from New York's Union Square Café, Tom Douglas from Seattle, Alfred Portale from Gotham Bar and Grill, and Jean-Louis Palladin of Jean-Louis at the Watergate. He was a Michelin-starred chef and the only one among us who could say that. The only way to make a mark in a situation like this is to do what you do—and no one else does! So I brought a celebration of Latin flavors to the whitest place I'd ever been.

Things were going well, but the fact remained it wasn't my place. Novel was a loose cannon. He was getting the "restaurant disease." This is when a person who has no experience whatsoever begins to think he is suddenly ready to take over the role of manager. Novel began to think he could be my new Proal. I had to remind him nearly nightly to go upstairs and change out of his bathing suit and ratty T-shirt if he wanted to hang out at the bar and hit on girls.

In June, Janet and I accepted an invitation to do another Book and the Cook event in Connecticut. We stopped in New York on the way back and accepted an invite for lunch from the chef of the 21 Club, Michael Lomonaco. I wish Nana and Mama could have been there with us that afternoon. They would have enjoyed being treated as royally as we were.

When we returned a new guy came into a Mano. He was chubby with blondish hair and, apparently, a stack of cash. For a while he seemed intent on buying out a Mano from Novel and renting the space. It would have offered us some respite (or so it seemed) from having to deal with Novel's bad behavior in the dining room, but Proal and I wondered if we weren't going to trade in one set of problems for another. Maybe life's lessons were beginning to make inroads. (Sales of *Feast of Sunlight* had not burned off the advance yet, so we were still living on my Betsy salary.) So when he came to my tiny office with legal agreements outlining our role as "his employees" we showed him the door.

On August 14, 1992, a tropical wave began its life off the west African coast under a ridge of high pressure to the north. Over the next two days it grew, moved, and developed an area of convection, which is one of the major modes of heat transfer within fluids, with the heat itself often causing the fluids around it to move. It became a tropical depression and it moved south of the Cape Verde Islands. These islands sit in a swirl off the west coast of Africa where, for nearly three hundred years, they served as the last landfall for slave ships en route to the Caribbean. On this day the little wave would have not raised an eyebrow among the Portuguese and African islanders.

But on the morning of August 22, that little wave had become one of the top three hurricanes of all time as it screamed across the Atlantic. In the predawn hours of August 24, Hurricane Andrew slammed into South Florida as a category five storm with winds gusting over 165 miles per hour, throwing off cyclones like cherry bombs on a hellish Independence Day. It left a quarter of a million of our neighbors homeless, destroyed over eighty thousand businesses, and caused a hundred thousand residents to pack up over the following weeks and leave Dade County for good. The financial damage was tallied to be over $26 billion. On the evening preceding the storm Novel was on the roof of the Betsy Ross on a lawn chair with a shotgun, a flashlight, and a radio. He had left a hand-scrawled sign on the door of the hotel: "Looters will be shot."

We were in our home in Miami Shores when the storm arrived. We retreated further and further into the house until we were finally squeezed into the bedroom closet with a mattress pulled over our heads. Just before the power went out we'd spoken to Steve and Pam, who were back in the keys. They said they were going to stay put and ride it out. It was lucky for them they did. Attempting to drive off the island might have been disastrous.

The sound of such a storm is awful. It's a screaming, groaning, wailing wall of complaint, misery, torture, and Judgment Day. It's as if all the souls of Africa that were ever chained to a ship had ridden with that storm to descend on the shores of America for a final payback. It is a nightmare that ends briefly when you pass out from the stress and then becomes real again when you wake up and see the world shaken loose from its anchors which seemed so permanent just a day ago.

With the dawn we could see we'd survived and, except for the large tree that once gave beautiful shade to our home and was now leaning uprooted on our roof, we were okay. The sky shook with rain spasms as long bands of the storm continued to pelt us like cans strung to a car rattling behind it. There was, in between, a silence that is normally only found deep underwater or way out on a prairie on a windless day. The sound was that of a world before gas, steam, and electricity. The breezes shook the trees that still stood and stirred the fallen branches lying on the wet streets and trashed yards. I took a camera, pulled on a poncho, and walked out in our neighborhood. A gray vapor hung on every image. Wetness and the smell of freshly ripped tree bark filled my senses. I heard sirens wailing on the highway half a mile away. I wondered how bad it had been for our family in Key West.

We were stuck for several days. The police had closed Miami Beach to all nonresidents. There was no electricity and even if you had gas in your car there was nowhere to go. We played cards and Monopoly and listened to the radio, trying to find the rhythm of a normal day—a day before Andrew.

A week passed when we finally got the okay to head back to a Mano. When we did we threw ourselves into cooking for the impromptu shelters. It was good to have work again. In less than a month we fed two thousand people in the first Hurricane Andrew Benefit at Turnberry. Bobby Flay, Julian Serrano, John Sedlar, Don Pintabonna, George Marrone, Debra Ponzcek, and even a few Hawaiian chefs who had just suffered a major storm back home—Jean-Marie Josselin and Mark Ellman—were there. They all came to a Mano for dinner the next night.

On September 18, we did another charity event for about five hundred called Miami's for Me at the Venetian Pool. The servers dressed in Asian-styled costumes to serve the Asian-inspired dish I'd created. It had been raining and my guys carried me on their shoulders past the shocked faces of the other South Florida chefs, who were all dressed in standard whites. These events were becoming more like theater of the absurd or a festival of freaks. The food wasn't enough—we wanted to create a spectacle and blow some minds.

When we got back to the Betsy real chaos erupted. Novel had fired Proal. It was some typical stupid shit with Novel just being drunk. The next morning he'd forgotten all about it, or so it seemed.

Just a few days later I received a fax from two *Gourmet Magazine* writers out of London. They wanted to include a Mano in an article, and the recipes they sought included my Vietnamese Soft Spring Rolls with Oriental Noodles, a Sesame Crusted Soft-Shell Crab, Green Apple Slaw, and Ponzu-Peanut Dipping Sauce. They also wanted the Rhum and Pepper Painted Fish with Mango Habañero Mojo and a dessert, Caramel-Stuffed Éclair with Rhum Flamed Nino Bananas and Mamey Sapote Ice Cream. It was electrifying to think that my dishes would be read about in Great Britain.

Another piece of good news also came along. Dick Akin had gotten Julia Child to consent to appear on *Holiday Feast.* It was all set for November 13.

Mickey Rourke was back from the gym. He saw the video cameras as the techs lugged them through the front door of a Mano. Every morning I'd see him come back from a workout, and it kind of impressed me to see him straightening out. He bobbed and weaved his way over to where I was setting up for the demo portion of *Holiday Feast.*

MR: So is this your restaurant, man?

NV (me): Uh, no, not exactly, I mean, I created it.

MR: But you don't own it?

NV: No. Novel owns it. I'm the chef.

MR: So Novel is your boss?

NV: He leaves me alone . . . pretty much.

MR: That's some bullshit cuz until you own it you ain't gonna be free. Sorry. Way it is.

NV: Workin' on it. I had a little restaurant in Key West with my friend.

MR: What happened?

NV: It was a little too arty for the town.

MR: It's a delicate balance. I can hang with that. But you chefs don't go fuckin' turnin' into pansy-ass muthafuckas like actors in fuckin' Tinseltown. Don't go fuckin' Hollywood or you are gonna be fucked up and plastic. Keep it real. Stay away from the agents and the money trap. You might not be rich but you could be happy and able to sleep at night.

And then he left. Under a hooded sweatshirt, his fists tucked into the pockets of his sweatpants. He shuffled out of the kitchen, head down, avoiding everyone, like he was hiding his identity and his soul. I didn't have the time to tell him, "Rich? Rich, Mick? I'm just looking for even. I'd just like to get the IRS finally off my ass."

We shot a few dishes being prepared and that was pretty easy. The next scene Richard was setting up would be one with me tooling down Ocean Drive in a hot red Thunderbird convertible owned by a buddy of his. The idea was that this would be the opening. I had a loud tropical shirt on and a long fish earring dangling from the side of my face. Aviator Ray-Bans completed the look. The weather was perfect and the street was jamming with folks up and down the boulevard of blatant lust. Folks rubbernecked to see the cameraman risking his life as he craned out the window of the rented white Toyota in front of me. Richard nearly lay down on the backseat, peering up as needed to direct the action, but he had to be sure he didn't pop into frame. We did the take about five times before he was happy. The whole shoot was timed around the fact that Julia Child was coming in that evening and had agreed to appear in the video. I couldn't believe our luck on that. Dinner was scheduled for seven and the script called for us to do an interview in the lobby of the hotel just before she'd dine with members of the AIWF's Miami chapter. Ms. Julia had cofounded the gastronomic society some years before with Robert Mondavi. I was glad that we were taping at that time because even though all of this was going on I still had a kitchen to run.

After we wrapped up the convertible scene and my "Welcome to a Mano, I'm Norman Van Aken" spot I was free to go back to my office, write the menu for the night, change into whites, and start prepping.

Richard took a break to watch the earlier taping. It was agreed we'd meet back in the lobby at six o'clock sharp to set up the shoot in anticipation of Julia's arrival.

She was on time and already in makeup when she strode into the Betsy Ross. Things were looking good. She seemed perfectly delighted and right at home. Then she announced that she preferred to have dinner first and shoot after, "If that's all right." What could Richard or I say? "Sorry, lady. We got a budget and a schedule"? She could tell us to run out and get our asses tattooed with "I love Julia" and we'd probably be on our way to do it. Okay! Plan B!

So I jumped back on the hot line and we rolled into service. The crowd was abuzz with the recognition that culinary royalty was in the little L-shaped dining room. She was ensconced in the so-called power booth with a few adoring AIWF acolytes around her. It had been a busy day and a long one already. I got pounded on sauté and my nerves were getting a real workout between the newness of doing television and the fact that Julia Child was in the house. I steadied myself with a large glass of Chardonnay.

Julia dined with nine others. All of them had tasting menus but she had oysters, a salad, and snapper.

Around 10:30 she was ready to go out into the lobby and shoot our scene. Julia was amazing. She'd probably been up since dawn and had already had a full day of "being" Julia. She'd just finished a three-hour meal with wines amid a dining room packed with fans and friends. She was no spring chicken anymore, but when the cameras started flashing she took to it like a hit of nitrous oxide. I, on the other hand, was beat, frazzled, and losing my grip on consciousness as we sat there in the straight-backed, faux-colonial chairs while Dick and the camera crew struggled to get the best light, sound, and action out of the scene. Dick's wife sat in for Julia after she'd finished her part and bid us "Adieu!" "Bon appetit!" and so on. Now we could do the interminable shots where it looks like I'm speaking and listening to Julia but actually it's Dick's wife posing as Julia. She made great sport of my exhaustion and giggled at me as I finally tottered off to my room on the second floor.

On November 28, the *Miami Herald* TV guide listed *Holiday Feast* in the Best Bets column along with Christmas specials from Bob Hope and another with Neil Diamond. Even better, our tax attorney, Ed Guttenmacher, called to tell Janet and me that the IRS had decided to drop our case and we were free! I thought of one of my first screen idols: "Top of the world, Ma!"

But as 1993 opened I was still going through a lot of anger, worries, and frustration that the whole world of a Mano was at the mercy and whim of Novel. I was still financially strapped. The legal bills from the IRS didn't disappear with the release. I had been treated for TMJ about a year earlier and I astonished my doctor by continuing to break the night braces because I was grinding them so hard. I was looking for an out. How could I take my team somewhere safe? I was beginning to meet more often with Marsha Sayet, who was married to a successful doctor. Maybe they could start up an investment group? Charlie had talked to me about how Wolfgang had put together a group of investors for one of his restaurants. Chinois?

Charlie and Emeril were pushing for Janet and me to join them on their first magnificent journey to "Mother" France. "It will be great! The Triangle will take on the Frogs!" Larry Stone, the wine genius, was also going. It would have been so cool. But I was increasingly afraid to leave a Mano for more than a day or three. Who knows what havoc would occur without someone (me) to watch over my crazy Cuban patriarch? And on top of the TMJ, I was beginning to make Janet wonder if I had inherited my mom's narcolepsy. I was falling asleep in midsentence.

We flew to D.C. in March to cook for an AIWF dinner. It was the launch event for the South Florida chapter, and cofounders Marsha Sayet and Carole Kotkin were going along to celebrate and help orchestrate the weekend.

We began with a dinner at Galileo. The big teddy bear chef Roberto Donna was in his element that evening as a gent named Bill Clinton was dining at one of the prized tables. Washington was a town I could see cooking in for a living! We had a fantastic lunch the next day at Michel Richard's restaurant Citronelle and afterward we got a private tour of the White House by one of Marsha's "Beach High" buddies. The kitchen reminded me of being back at the Greenbrier. Washington was dripping with history. Miami Beach dripped with neon. We were on a roll and dined at the Jefferson Hotel, then being run by the intense and unstoppable Patrick Clark. I have memories of cooking with him at Charlie's and watching two volunteers peel six hundred grapes for a garnish on a rabbit dish he made.

There were panel discussions that we took part in. Allen Susser, Robbin Haas, and Douglas Rodriguez were my cochefs, and it was kind of perfect to be extolling the wisdom of "New World Cuisine" in the O.A.S. building.

Flags from so many countries hung from the massive columns. We felt proud that "our" South Florida cuisine clearly embraced a multitude of nations and peoples from many disparate lands.

We dined at the newly opened Red Sage that evening. We'd eaten at Mark Miller's Coyote Café in Santa Fe not too long before. This place was on steroids compared to the New Mexico version. I liked the former much more. This was a restaurant built with a Disney mindset. The ceiling changed colors. We left Washington and Janet and I flew on to New York. Jason Epstein had invited us to dinner and I wasn't going to say no, even if it meant selling some blood to afford the flight.

Jason Epstein had just finished a piece he'd written for the *New Yorker* on Chinese restaurants in Manhattan. It was "over ten thousand words," he told me. He was a man of inestimable talent, curiosity, and opinion and, for some, ego. To me he was a great new teacher and a champion of my work. He was publishing my new cookbook, he told me, and he was also publishing "the New York great chef, Daniel Boulud" at the same time. Janet and I were invited to the home he'd created with his wife, Judy, on Broome Street. She was a reporter for the *New York Times*. As we drank wine and they had martinis, she shared memories of her life growing up, in part, in Miami. She was pretty and, I was not surprised to learn after having watched her move, a former dancer. She'd lived an amazing life already. It was easy to see why Jason was in love with her.

We walked through some light snow to the first of four restaurants Jason was taking us to. We were joined by the billionaire publishers of Condé Nast Publications, Si and Don Newhouse. "Please call me Si. Please call me Don." Don's wife was also along and she and Judy and Janet hit if off immediately. Life was getting better by the (won) ton.

The next night we had a date with Chef Michael Lomonaco of 21 Club and his wife Diane. Being a couple in the restaurant business was not the most typical thing. And even couples who survive the biz often find that chefs spend more time going out with their crew than their wives or husbands. So we were delighted to accept Michael's invitation to this night on the town. We had a pretheater dinner at Jean-Georges Vongerichten's new restaurant Vong. Jean-Georges was making big waves with his "fusion" cuisine. Perhaps the only other chef who was breaking down the barriers of French cuisine in this way was the Swiss-born Gray Kunz over at Lespinasse.

We had a very good meal, and I was inspired by the way Jean-Georges had loosened up the definition of "fine dining" at Vong. We hopped in a cab and rode through a downpour to the Michael Beck Theater and watched a very entertaining production of *Guys and Dolls.*

We had tied the trip to Washington with an invite to do another Book and the Cook event in Philly. The city was flooded with chefs. We had a plan to meet John Harrison, our would-have-been-agent/coauthor of the ill-fated Mango Gang book, at the opening party, which was held at a restaurant owned by Chef Jack McDavid. Jack was an instant media success dressed, as he always was, in a chef jacket under "OshKosh B'Gosh" denim bib overalls. His cornpone persona was no act. Bobby Flay was the cohost. Jack had built a still and he was passing out moonshine. Everyone was getting a taste of the "likker." We found John at the back of the bar, alone, quietly taking in the whole raucous and merry scene. John was from Sherwood Forest, England, and through crazy happenstance ended up working with the peripatetic Mark Miller organizing his extremely successful career. I was hoping for some of that magic to come my way.

John lit up when he saw the two of us.

"Congratulations!" he yelled over the din.

"For what?" I yelled back. He reached into his satchel and pulled out a fax so we would not have to carry on trying to hear each other. I took the paper and read it. I looked back at John. He didn't know we didn't know. I'd been nominated for a James Beard Award! Best Chef of the South East Chef Norman Van Aken of a Mano!

The last time I felt like that was when I got Risa's letter of invitation to write *Feast of Sunlight.* The world grew smaller below me again and all the people in the bar were my soul mates. I willed Janet up into this heavenly feeling, we hugged each other, then glided back down to earth and hugged John. Then we had some moonshine.

The next day, the wake-up call to get the prep started for our dinner at the Adams Mark Hotel was rough, but as I splashed my face in the sink I looked up in the mirror and gazed at a guy who was on the road back now, baby.

The phone rang in the room. It was a woman named Karen Page. She and her partner were about to finish a book called *On Becoming a Chef*. They wanted to be sure to include me as "the next new great chef." We met at the White Dog Café for a lunch interview with Karen and her mate, Andrew Dornenburg. They were excited about their project and shared some of their insights after having learned so much about the personal sides of some of America's reigning chefs and restaurateurs. It was such an important feeling to me to know I was going to be able to take care of my family doing the thing that I had come to love.

We returned to Miami, and I rode to work on my big red scooter from Key West days. It was a bit dangerous to ride it on the much busier and meaner streets of Miami. But I loved being out in the wind and we didn't have another car anyway. I came up Ocean Drive to the parking lot just off Fifteenth Street and parked.

When I got to the Betsy Ross I bounded up the steps with a feeling of great joy. I was about to share the Beard news with my team.

"Where's Proal?" I asked Scott Howard, who was uncharacteristically sitting on a stack of milk crates in the kitchen reading a newspaper.

"Fucking crazy-ass Novel fired him last night. Says he's gonna work the door and you are gonna work the kitchen from now on."

"Where is Proal?"

"No clue."

"Where's Scarface?"

"He's sittin' over in the Stars and Stripes side with his buddy Mickey." I walked across the terrazzo floor and into the small café. Novel was with Mickey Rourke. They looked like they'd been up all night again.

"Novel, did you actually think you could fire Proal and that I would stay at a Mano?"

Mickey leaned way back in his chair and eyed me with a cocky grin.

Novel jumped up to his full height, puffed out his chest, and shot back, "But a Mano made you famous! You will never leave!"

Something deep came up from inside of me, something that would have been immediate and familiar to my father. I said, "Tell you what, Novel. I will fight you over whether Proal stays or goes. Outside!"

Mickey Rourke jumped up and said, "On the beach! I'll ref!"

The momentum was born and had hit an unstoppable pace. A few of the cooks and servers who'd come in, unknowing, tagged after the three of us as we climbed the dunes toward the waves. Mickey said. "First guy on his back loses!"

Novel's face was pure 'hood but his body was in no shape. He'd been beating it senseless for the last year and a half with alcohol and worse. He tried to kick some sand at me and that only infuriated me to a place where fear doesn't live. I charged him and threw my arms around his chest and lifted him up in a big bear hug, turned him 180 degrees, and dropped him on the sand with me on top. He let out a whoosh of vodka-laced breath and then threw up as I let him go. His hair hung down over half his face. His skin was slicked with sweat, puke, and sand and his eyes showed a feline sorrow.

I let the hate drain out of me. I felt bad for the old guy. He may have sensed it, even knew how to extract it from me. He smiled and pulled himself up. Mickey helped steady him. Novel brushed him off. Then the actor grabbed my right hand and held it up in victory.

Novel sprung back to life again. His tolerance for destruction, resilience, and fortitude were freakish. Then he said, "Proal is still fired. I never agreed to nothing!"

I looked at him and then I knew it was over. This was the last of it. No more. But not Roberto Duran's "*No Mas*" in that legendary boxing match. This "*no mas*" was mine, however, and I said something to Novel that I knew would make him hate me for leaving.

I came up close to him and made sure he was seeing my eyes. When he stared back in defiance still I uttered a phrase to him: "*No pasa nada.*" It was a phrase from a story he told about his father, a phrase his father had taught him to say to an adversary, that the adversary "didn't even exist anymore."

"*NO PASA NADA!*" And I left. Novel and Mickey stood with the ocean behind them, squinting as I walked toward the colonial, flagged, and bannered Betsy Ross Hotel.

Janet drove in and we wordlessly loaded up my cookbooks, saved menus, and knives. We got in the car and, now that we were alone, I told her what had happened. She got out of the car, closed the door, and walked around to my side. She said, “Come on.” She took me by the hand. I got out and she hugged me with her strong arms. We walked to the shore and along the sands of the Atlantic Ocean, just like we did when she was seventeen and a maid in Fort Lauderdale, and I was a cook heading to Key West to see what I could see. Hand in hand, we walked, heading south, listening to the ocean, once more.

Vietnamese Soft Spring Rolls

This was a recipe I began making a few years before the birth of a Mano, but I think it reached its zenith in the small kitchen on Ocean Drive, as far as my versions of it. A chef I really loved having on the team named Maria figured out how to write the word "delicious" in Japanese—with wasabi. Of course almost no one got it but when a person literate in the Japanese language did understand it we felt a kind of kinship with humanity that bordered on the cosmic.

For the marinade and dipping sauce:

- 2 tablespoons plum sauce
- 5 tablespoons hoisin
- ¼ teaspoon ground cloves
- 3 tablespoons ketchup
- 2 tablespoons rice wine vinegar
- 1 tablespoon fresh lime juice
- 2 tablespoons minced fresh ginger
- 5 tablespoons sesame oil
- 3 tablespoons cilantro leaves
- 1 tablespoon mirin
- 2 cloves garlic, minced
- 3 tablespoons chile oil
- 1 tablespoon sugar
- ½ cup red wine vinegar
- 2 tablespoons soy sauce
- 1 tablespoon cracked black pepper

In a bowl, mix all the ingredients together. Reserve.

For the noodles:

- 1 sleeve (2¼ ounces dry weight) uncooked somen noodles

In a large pot, cook the noodles in rapidly boiling salted water for about 30 to 45 seconds. Rinse quickly under cold running water, and drain well. Toss the noodles with enough marinade to evenly coat. Reserve the remaining marinade for dipping sauce.

For the filling:

4 (8½-inch) round rice paper wrappers
1½ cups cooked duck or chicken or pork
3 cups shiitake (or other) cooked mushroom caps, sliced
kosher salt and cracked black pepper, to taste

Season the protein with the salt and pepper. Fill a wide, shallow bowl half-way up with warm water. Working one by one, dampen the wrappers in the water until they are pliant. (This usually takes 1 to 2 minutes per wrapper and should be done immediately prior to stuffing.) Remove and pat dry.

To fill each roll, place some of the marinated noodles about a third of the way down the wrapper. Fold in the bottom and each side of the wrapper burrito-style, then add some of the meat and some of the mushrooms, and continue rolling, keeping a little pressure on the bundle as you roll.

Reserve the filled spring rolls between layers of slightly moist toweling in the refrigerator until ready to serve. (*Note*: Spring Rolls may be made up to 4 hours before serving.) Trim off the ends (you can eat or discard them). Slice the rolls into bite-sized sections. Serve with the reserved remaining marinade in small dipping cups for each guest.

Makes 2½ cups

THE "FEAST OF FRIENDSHIP" DINNER

Sunday, January 7th, 1996

Perrier-Jouët, "Flower Bottle" en Magnums

****

Various Canapés and Tapas

Raji: Crostini of Aubergine with Curry Leaf Emulsion in Olive Oil
Emeril: Smoked Chicken and Homemade Andouille Sausage Strudel
with Emeril's Homemade Worcestershire Sauce
Charlie: Sonoma Foie Gras Bread Pudding with Quince Preserve
Norman: Yuca Stuffed & Crisped Key West Shrimp with
Very Black Bean "Jus" and a Hot Bonnet Whip

~

Raji: First Plate

Rougail of Lobster in Petite Purses with Red Pepper and Mango Coulis

*

Etude Pinot Blanc, 1994

*

Charlie: Second Plate

*

Indiana Bobwhite Quail with Collard Greens, Rice Beans,
Lambs Tongue and Wild Mushroom Sauce

*

Etude Pinot Noir, 1993

*

Norman: Salad Plate

*

Twice-Baked & Truffled Tiny Potatoes with
a Petite Salad, Pulled Pork *Havana* & a Mojo-Pork Essence Drizzle

*

Etude Pinot Noir Rosé, 1994

*

Emeril: Entree Plate

Pecan-Crusted Millbrook Venison Chop with
Bourbon Mashed Sweet Potatoes, Port Wine Glazed Root Vegetables and
a Caramelized Apple Reduction

*

Etude Cabernet Sauvignon, 1989 en Magnum
Etude Cabernet Sauvignon, 1992

Desserts

****

Raji's: Blue Cheese Crème Brûlée with Rose Water and Jaggery
Emeril's: Hawaiian Vintage Chocolate Pecan Pie with Spiced Cream & Spiced Pecans
Charlie: Bosc Pear, Chestnut and Maple Custard Napoleon with Persimmon
Norman's: Baby *Buñuelos* with Guavaberry Sirop and Mamey Sapote Ice Cream

~

Topaz, Late Harvest Semillon-Sauvignon Blanc, 1989

"FEAST OF FRIENDSHIP" SPONSORS

AMERICAN AIRLINES THE BILTMORE HOTEL CARNIVAL CRUISE LINES
ETUDE WINES FLAGLER GREYHOUND TRACK NATIONSBANK PRIVATE CLIENT GROUP
DOROTHY AND HENRY NORTON SOUTHERN WINES AND SPIRITS

Feast of Friendship menu

Epilogue

The Triangle Comes Full Circle

TWENTY YEARS PASS in the blink of an eye. Your child grows up and your bones grow old. The shit that used to scare you makes you smile at who you used to be. The desperately needed recognition from "colleagues" is much less needed than a barbeque with your family and friends.

You may wonder why I didn't keep writing about the years after the day I left Novel at the Betsy Ross Hotel. I came into the culinary world I write of here with "no experience." The ad in the newspaper I answered was the door I entered first. Who knows? Maybe another book lies in me yet and it will be all about the years that followed. Or maybe I'll just leave it here.

I will tell you, albeit briefly, what you may already know, and what you may not, about the people who enriched my life and enlivened these pages.

The white sands of South Beach still lie impassively, brilliantly as when I was a child coming to this very edge of water and sky. The waves roll and recede in an aural pattern that hypnotized me so long ago it is more instinct than memory. I can't help but smile in Miami Beach. But then the smile fades. Miami Beach is always looking for another lover.

Yet friends keep it all alive and real. No one friend has flown higher and still kept me just as close as has Charlie. And that is what brought me back to South Beach on February 25, 2012, to the South Beach Wine and Food Festival Tribute to Charlie Trotter Dinner.

A bond that started out with a very young man earnestly looking for a place in my kitchen turned into thirty years of a kind of admiration that transcends a shared profession or shared interests. It is brotherly love. And with Emeril on hand it is elevated once again. It is "triangular," if you know what I mean.

So, with a crowd of seven hundred diners expected, plans were made in dizzying detail and size. Some of the plans were made a full year ago when Charlie first learned he had been chosen for the honor and distinction. The question that many should have wondered was this: Will Charlie even fucking show up? Hah! How little do they know about my brother and how crazy he can be. It would be exactly like him to quote a book title he loves, and then act on the urging of that title.

The book was written in 1929 by Robert Graves and titled *Goodbye to All That*. Charlie has spoken to me about it many times and one day he will say "good-bye to all that" at a function of massive proportions. For this is not to be the last farewell for Charlie Trotter. As I write these words (and by the time you read them it will have happened) his path has led him to close down his venerated namesake restaurant after twenty-five years of brilliance. It will take at least as many years to account for how amazing it was. I can guarantee that, short of death itself, he will be back. And his return, however it manifests, will be both new—and right.

Tony Bourdain, Martha Stewart, Italian winemaker Angelo Gaja, South Beach's Festival impresario Lee Brian Schrager, and seven hundred other people who paid more than $500 a ticket, all moved in a nearly predestined, highly orchestrated rendezvous with the final onstage moment when Charlie accepted his trophy at the end of the meal cooked by Emeril, Wylie Dufresne, Michelle Gayer, and me. We would not be breaking chairs at the end of *this* evening, but we will always have *that* evening long ago in Aventura.

So where are they now?

Charlie is retiring to go to college. Or so it seems.

Emeril is in business with Martha Stewart as well as doing his own thing seemingly everywhere but now happier than ever, living in a quiet town with his sweet wife Alden and the children.

Tony is writing, doing television, traveling the world, and being as funny and smart as any person to have ever (once upon a time) strapped on an apron.

Novel is dead but some say his ghost hovers over the Betsy Ross.

Bicycle Sammy, Toké, Danny McHugh, Black Betty, Butchie, Bud Man, and Wade still drink with me at the Green Parrot in Key West, though I'm the only one who can see them. I can see Risa, Chipp, Jeff, Proal, Cayce, and Steve, too, and that is a comfort. Especially when John or Chicken is pouring.

Justin married beautiful Lourdes in 2012 and now their baby (our first grandchild), Audrey Quinn Van Aken, has lit up all our lives!

Justin and I wrote our first cookbook together, titled *My Key West Kitchen*. It is out all over the country and showing the love and flavors we found on the mesmerizing island she has been . . . and remains.

Janet and I are still holding strong, cruising back and forth up and down the keys. Still cooking. Still walking the beach. Still listening to Derek and the Dominoes . . .

Fusion

Paella Moderna

•

Stacer Ropa Vieja

•

Tuna or Sword Fajitas

•

Pineapple & Banana Chili Rice

•

Salmon Salsa w/ Stacking

•

Rustic

Roquefort Soufflé w/ Hot Apple Sauce

•

Roast Garlic Scrambled

Leg of Lamb w/ Smoky White Beans & Herbed Tomatoes

•

Pork Sausage in Caul en Cocotte w/ Warm Potato Salad

•

Vermicelli Torta Forestiere

•

Mise

Ocean Salad

•

5 Spice Or

•

Hot n' Na

•

Gar Small

Copper Pots

•

Tangine

•

Fork Broc

•

Rosemary Th

•

Pastrichee M

•

Caviar in presentat

•

A Service of Olive Oils & Vinegar

•

Make a Cream Lobster Stew & into tiny saucer cool. Top w/ a Lobster soufflé & Bake (se w/ a crêpe)

•

Shrimp Split the shell

Fish Market

Brisque w/ Roast Be Restaurant